Immigrant Women Workers
in the Neoliberal Age

Immigrant Women Workers in the Neoliberal Age

EDITED BY NILDA FLORES-GONZÁLEZ,
ANNA ROMINA GUEVARRA,
MAURA TORO-MORN,
AND GRACE CHANG

UNIVERSITY OF ILLINOIS PRESS
Urbana, Chicago, and Springfield

Library of Congress Control Number: 2013939073

This book is dedicated to the memory of Leonila Vega

Contents

Foreword

MARY ROMERO

The poems spoke about the alienating, hurtful and
disorienting experiences of working in people's homes,
of taking charge of that most personal space and of their
employers' most precious possessions—the children—and yet
being treated as second class citizens or as if they are invisible.

"They don't care about us," said one of the panelists, while
another said, "They are deceiving people. They only pretend
to be your friend. I say to them, I am the employee, you are
my employer. I am not your family."

Allison Julien prefers to keep her personal life separate
from work. "The more people know about you, they use it
against you," she said. "At work, I'm a nanny. After work, I'm
an activist, writer, social organizer!"

*"'There's so much to say . . .': Writings
from the Domestic Workers United Workshop"*

Reading *Immigrant Women Workers in the Neoliberal Age*, I reflected on the description from a PEN World Voices Festival 2012 panel, "There's so much to say
. . . ," by members from Domestic Workers United. Writing, reading, and sharing
their experiences through poetry, these immigrant domestic workers expressed
the frustration, anger, loneliness, and humiliation of working in private homes,
toiling long hours without breaks, being denied health care and social security
benefits, receiving low wages, and being treated as unskilled labor. There is an
irony that only these women experience because they are given the responsibility to care for "employers' most precious possessions—the children"[1] while being
subjected to verbal abuse and disrespect. Allison Julien's quote captures many of
the women's experiences sharing their thoughts with other immigrant domestic
workers. They are low-wage immigrant women from Mexico, Latin America,
the Caribbean, Africa, and Asia. They toil in an economy that is unregulated,
invisible, and mostly shielded from public view in private homes. They are nannies, housekeepers, cooks, elder-care workers, and dog walkers. However, their
work lives do not define them. Simultaneously, they are mothers, grandmothers, and daughters caring for their own parents. These women have dreams for

their children and for making their own lives better. Women, including Allison Julien, Christine Lewis, and Joyce Campbell, are also activists and organizers for Domestic Workers United; they work closely with the National Domestic Workers Alliance (NDWA), conducting a major campaign to pass a Workers Bill of Rights in every state. Since many of the women are caring for the elderly, NDWA has trained workers with skills to provide quality care. Their campaign, Caring Across Generations, has brought numerous organizations and community groups together "to bring dignity and value to the contributions of our nation's aging population and the workforce who cares for them."[2] In response to the growing number of immigrant families being separated by the draconian immigration policies and law enforcement, NDWA is also actively involved with other advocacy groups in We Belong Together Campaign. This volume is an important contribution because the research presented captures the complexities of immigrant working women in the United States.

Nilda Flores-González, Anna Guevarra, Maura Toro-Morn, and Grace Chang have edited an important anthology of scholar-activists who are writing and researching immigrant women workers at a time of growing nativist-racist sentiment, increasing income inequality, and economic recession. Contextualizing the era of neoliberalism, the reader is grounded with an understanding of the political, economic and social structural conditions at the global and national levels producing massive international immigration and the challenges migrants face. While past immigrants have found refuge in ethnic enclaves and informal economies, the conditions immigrant women workers face today are not the same. There have always been debates over the amount of social mobility in ethnic enclaves, although they did provide employment and resources that were otherwise unavailable to immigrant workers. Unfortunately, the recession hit ethnic businesses with a powerful blow and fewer opportunities are found. Working conditions in the informal economies have also worsened. Entrepreneurial enterprises are limited to the shadows, outside the view of law enforcement. Employers hiring nannies and housekeepers are cutting back hours and pay is less secure. Yet, as these scholar-activists demonstrate, immigrant women workers are navigating the precarious economy and raising families and many are actively engaged in local and transnational organizing.

Central to the analysis in each of the studies included in the volume is an intersectional approach. Recognizing that gender differs by racialization processes and is class based, the immigrant women workers are positioned in different margins of the formal and informal labor sector and have different obstacles to navigate depending on their immigration status. Nationality and class background partly determines immigrant women's ability to standardize their resident status or develop options to become naturalized citizens. Single mothers, transnational mothers, and mothers of children of mixed citizenship status all face unique challenges under current immigration policies that prohibit access to public services, make entry into the United States extremely costly and dangerous, and provoke fear of deportation as a constant determinant in their everyday movements and activities. The 287 (g) agreements and Secure Communities have resulted in hundreds of families being separated. In 2010 alone, 226,000 immigrants were arrested, one-third of which were women with children or partners who are U.S. citizens.[3] These women encounter family obligations and restrictions that are also structurally determined by their age and gender. Working immigrant mothers may also find themselves supporting elderly parents by sending remittances to their home countries. Young adolescent girls working as domestics, nannies, or street vendors may find patriarchal rules that limit their activity and may find themselves constrained by rules and obligations their brothers do not have. Immigrant women find themselves ethnically stereotyped in ways that may enhance their employability but restrict them in specific occupations or limit their advancement in the formal sector.

Researchers and community organizers have both noted the significant role that low-wage immigrant workers, many of them women, from Mexico, Latin America, Africa, and Asia have in rebuilding organized labor in the United States. As the editors note in their critique of the neoliberal state, the structural changes in 1980s and '90s created the circumstances for an emerging immigrant labor movement in the United States. In the mid-1980s and into the 1990s, immigrant workers in Los Angeles, Houston, and Miami participated in the Janitors for Justice movement. In September and October of 2003, immigrant activists boarded buses to Washington, D.C., in a symbolic Freedom Ride for immigrant workers' rights. The fight for legalization and the right to work with justice and dignity has continued. The immigration reform protests that took place in March through May in 2006 were among the largest in the country's recent history. After six years of organizing workers, the National Domestic Workers Alliance celebrated the passing of the New York Bill of Rights in 2010. This legislation gained workers the following rights: eight-hour day, an overtime rate established for both live-in and day workers, a day off every week, entitlement to three paid days off a year after a year of employment, and protection against discrimination and sexual harassment. They plan to move state by state until domestic workers' rights are recognized. In the following year, NDWA joined their international sister organizations and campaigned for recognition at the 2011 International Labour Conference in Geneva. The First Convention and Recommendation on Decent Work for Domestic Workers was passed, which affirmed the rights of immigrant domestic workers in the global economy. Immigrant organizing efforts have successfully brought together various organizations and communities to fight for social change and justice.

The National Coalition for Immigrant Women's Rights issued a list of concerns for constructing an "equitable immigration policy" that defends and promotes equality for immigrant women and their families in the United States.[4] This list supports the findings and recommendations made by the scholar-activists who contributed to *Immigrant Women Workers in the Neoliberal Age*. On top of the list is a call for immigration options for undocumented men, women, and children that does not put them at risk from traffickers, smugglers, intimate partners, or family members. Among these options must be a path to citizenship that allows immigrant families to stay together, to work freely in safe environments with equal rights and without fear of arrest, to travel across borders, and to have access to educational opportunities.

The editors and authors of *Immigrant Women Workers in the Neoliberal Age* produced this volume with input from community activists, and their research questions were generated from their own activism working with immigrant women workers. I thank the editors for inviting me to give a keynote address at their public conference at the Chicago campus of the University of Illinois in 2010. Being part of this dynamic exchange of research findings and among community activists highlighted the significance of keeping social justice issues at the forefront of our academic endeavors. Each of the authors contributing to this volume has approached her or his study with the commitment to present the voices of the women who shared their experiences. In doing so, the reader is offered a rare opportunity to comprehend work, family, and immigrant issues as immigrant women workers do. Accentuating their subjective understandings offers new ways of conceptualizing personal and social agency, while recognizing the structural constraints of everyday life. This volume stands as a model for scholar-activists engaged in building collaborative relations with immigrants and advocacy organizations in a struggle to gain human and civil rights for all workers.

Notes

1. "'There's so much to say . . .': Writings from the Domestic Workers United Workshop," Pen Live! Pen American Center, May 14, 2012, available at http://penlive.tumblr.com/post/23059235125/theres-so-much-to-say-writings-from-the-domestic (accessed November 24, 2012).

2. National Domestic Workers Alliance, Caring Across Generations Campaign, available at http://www.caringacrossgenerations.org/ (accessed November 24, 2012).

3. National Coalition for Immigrant Women's Rights, End, don't mend, broken enforcement program; Women, 287 (g) and Secure Communities (S-Comm), citing Julia Preston, "Latinos Said to Bear Weight of a Deportation Program," *New York Times*, October 18, 2011, available at http://www.nytimes.com/2011/10/19/us/latinos-said-to-bear-weight-of-deportation-program.html (accessed November 24, 2012).

4. See the National Coalition for Immigrant Women's Rights website, available at http://nciwr.wordpress.com (accessed November 24, 2012).

Acknowledgments

This project was possible through generous funding from the Ford Foundation. We want to thank Laine Romero-Alston, Helen Neuborne, and Pablo Farias from the Assets Program at the Ford Foundation for their support for this project. We are especially grateful to former Ford program officer Dr. Héctor Cordero-Guzmán for his commitment to our project. His vision to develop collaborations and partnerships between academics and community organizations is at the core of this project. In addition to his vision and support, Dr. Cordero-Guzmán has been an inspiration for his commitment to social justice.

We also appreciate the support given by the University of Illinois at Chicago, especially the Office for Social Science Research, the Department of Sociology, the Latin American and Latino Studies Program, the Asian American Studies Program, Hull House, and the Rafael Cintrón-Ortiz Latino Cultural Center. Thanks to Dr. Francesca Gaiba and Tracy Sikorsky for skillfully managing our project, Lisa Lee for opening the doors of the Hull House for our conferences, and Marta Ayala and Candace Hoover for assisting us with registration and logistics during the conferences. We want to recognize the support from Barbara Risman, head of the Department of Sociology and Maria de Los Angeles (Nena) Torres, Director of the Latin American and Latino Studies Program. Finally, we were blessed with the assistance of Dr. Pallavi Banerjee, who served as our graduate assistant for two years.

This project began in 2008, when a group of scholars, practitioners, and community activists gathered for two days at the Ford Foundation to talk about labor, gender, and migration. From this dialogue emerged our project, which grew into a four-year collective effort that has resulted in this book. Through gatherings in 2009 and 2010 at the University of Illinois at Chicago, we continued our conversations and shared our academic and activist work. The coeditors thank the contributors of this volume for their work, dedication, and commitment to the project. Contributors also deserve praise for role modeling to us how to do research that is attentive to not only the social conditions facing communities of color but also building friendships and political alliances that connect academics and activists. We are also grateful to the many practitioners and activists who participated in our gatherings and were fundamental in the development of our ideas. We also want to thank the immigrant women and activists who shared their stories of struggle with us. Their untiring battle for justice, dignity, and respect for immigrant workers is an example of what is possible through collective action. We were particularly touched by Leonila Vega, who fiercely advocated for the rights of home care workers, and who passed as we wrapped up this project. We dedicate this book to the memory of Leonila Vega.

We appreciate the commitment, support and guidance offered by Larin McLaughlin and Dawn Durante at the University of Illinois Press. We also want to thank UI Press's design, marketing, and production staff, especially Dustin Hubbart, Joe Peeples, Jennifer Reichlin, and Roberta Sparenberg. We are grateful to the two anonymous reviewers who provided invaluable feedback on the manuscript.

On a more personal note, we collectively appreciate the unwavering support provided by our colleagues. We are most thankful to our families who provided encouragement, support, and unending love along the way.

Nilda Flores-González . . . Anna Guevarra . . .
Maura Toro-Morn . . . Grace Chang . . .

Immigrant Women Workers
in the Neoliberal Age

Introduction

Immigrant Women and Labor Disruptions

MAURA TORO-MORN,

ANNA ROMINA GUEVARRA,

AND NILDA FLORES-GONZÁLEZ

In the middle of the first decade of the twenty-first century, a casual observer living anywhere in the United States would have concluded, without hesitation, that immigrant labor was indispensable to this country's economy. Mexican film-maker Sergio Arau capitalized on this observation, showing audiences what would happen if a sudden fog simply wiped out the Mexican population in the state of California. In *A Day without a Mexican* (2004), Arau humorously shows that in the absence of gardeners, nannies, painters, cooks, service workers, mechanics, and other low-wage workers, chaos ensues and the state is paralyzed. The film underscores the point that is at the center of this edited volume: low-wage immigrant workers—many of them women from Latin America, Africa, and Asia—play a vital role in the postindustrial neoliberal U.S. economy.

Demographic data makes this point clearer: in 2010 the U.S. Census reported that approximately 12.2 percent of the total U.S. population was foreign-born, and an estimated 6.1 percent were foreign-born women (Grieco et al. 2012). According to the Pew Hispanic Center, undocumented immigrants make up 3.7 percent of the nation's population and 5.2 percent of its labor force, and of the 11.2 million undocumented immigrants, about 71 percent (8 million) are members of the labor force (Passel and Cohn 2011). Foreign-born women constitute approximately 51 percent of the immigrant workforce and earn less than native-born women (Bureau of Labor Statistics 2011). Immigrant women are vital to the economy as they concentrate in low-wage industries with increasing labor needs in the domestic, service, production, transportation, and material moving occupations (Bureau of Labor Statistics 2011). In these industries, they face language barriers, limited access to government workforce programs, discriminatory employment practices, and risks of workforce injuries and illness (Gammage 2002).

This book focuses on the labor experiences of low-wage immigrant women workers, primarily Asians and Latinas, in the era of neoliberal globalization. It brings together the work of a diverse group of scholars and activists who share a commitment to global social justice. Drawing from original research, this collection of essays developed through two conferences sponsored by the Ford Foundation and hosted by the University of Illinois at Chicago, and in conversations sustained over a period of four years. The essays explore the ways in which neoliberal globalization has impacted the economic, political, and social lives of immigrant women both at home and abroad, and the ways in which immigrant women respond to neoliberal forces impinging on their lives. We use the term *labor disruptions* to refer to interruptions in immigrant women's labor patterns due to the social and political processes resulting from neoliberal globalization. Our conceptualization of labor disruptions encompasses both "for-pay" labor and gendered labor within the family. Together, the essays address three main questions: How do neoliberal globalization and the neoliberal state disrupt the lives of Asian and Latina immigrant women? What strategies do immigrant women deploy to deal with these disruptions? How do immigrant women, with the assistance of community-based organizations, organize and mobilize against these disruptions?

Labor Disruptions and Neoliberal Globalization

The mantras of the neoliberal era such as the "global market place," "free trade," "private ownership" and "flexibility" alongside the tropes of living in the "digital age" with an infinite capacity for instant exchanges and free flow of information promise a world of peace, prosperity, equality for women, and democracy for all. Under the auspices of neoliberal globalization, a new ethos of life has emerged, characterized by material acquisition, commercialization, and consumption, particularly in the global North. Feminist writer Alison Jaggar (2001) argues that we have come to view neoliberal globalization as an inevitable consequence of progress and modernization. Broadly, the essays collected in this volume aim to show how neoliberal globalization—understood as market-driven processes that fundamentally aim to create the conditions for the flexible accumulation of capital in both the global North and global South—hides a reality that is complex, contradictory, and disruptive of labor and family processes.

In theory, neoliberalism refers to a vast body of political economic theories that put primacy on the principles of capitalist economic competitiveness and individual responsibility under the guise of freedom and choice (Harvey 2005). Neoliberal policies advocate for free markets, free trade, and the privatization and deregulation of industry (Cowie 2001). The linchpin of this capital accumulation strategy has been the global assembly line, better known as maquiladoras. More than three decades of research on the global assembly line have exposed the oppressive conditions that its largely female workforce face (Chang 2000; Fernandez-Kelly 1983; Leacock and Safa 1986; Ong 1987; Tiano 1994). Feminist scholars have shown the global assembly line as a deeply gendered, racialized, and classed structure with contradictory outcomes for men, women, and their families (Bonacich and Appelbaum 2000; Chin 2005; Cobble 2007; Freeman, 2000; Mohanty 2003; Salzinger 2003). Today, new scholarship deploying inter-sectionality theory across a transnational space show how shop-floor politics continue to be shaped by gender and gender politics (Bank-Muñoz 2008).

Migrations—whether internal, regional, or international—have become a survival strategy and a way to resolve the structural inequalities and labor disruptions created by neoliberalism (Toro-Morn and Alicea 2004). Feminist scholars in the field of international migration have produced a rich body of work documenting the growing feminization of migration (Castles and Miller 2009; Ehrenreich and Hochschild 2002; George 2005). Detailed and rich ethnographies have deepened our understanding of migration as a gendered process by beginning with the recognition that gender entailed social practices that shape the outcomes of migration while also shaping the process itself (Hondagneu-Sotelo 1994; Pessar and Mahler 2003; Segura and Zavella 2007; Toro-Morn 2008). While we understand the role of networks in the migration experience, we now know more about the different ways in which these networks work for men and women (Menjivar 2000). Just as work has the potential to reconfigure gender relations within the family, migration has the potential to (re)construct the gender division of labor for immigrant families across transnational fields (Hirsch 2003; Hondagneu-Sotelo 1994, 2003; Kibria 1993). Even more significantly, scholars have tempered the exuberance and excitement of the scholarly work that claimed migration as a way to free women from the patriarchal gender knot. Rather than liberating women, migration often replaces some forms of oppression with others. The women at the center of this collection offer evidence of how neoliberal globalization engendered their migration: some were uprooted from their native lands and turned into laborers for multinational corporations in their own countries (see chapters 2 and 9); others became nannies and care workers for middle class white families and co-ethnic immigrant families in the United States (see chapters 4, 5, 6, and 9); while others became part of the reserve army of labor for the service, beauty, and care-work industry (see chapters 7, 8, 9, and 14).

The twin forces of neoliberal globalization and the neoliberal state create labor disruptions with profound consequences at the workplace and at home. Neoliberal economic and political policies drive women to migrate to the global North, lock them into low-wage labor, deny them and their families of legal protections, criminalize their undocumented status, and threaten or follow through with deportation and family separation. As Toro-Morn argues in chapter 2, Elvira Arellano's life story embodies the labor disruptions that this volume seeks to make relevant to studies of neoliberal globalization. In Mexico, Arellano became unemployed due to economic policies implemented by a Mexican neoliberal state bent on making the North American Free Trade Agreement (NAFTA) work. She migrated to Tijuana where she worked in the maquiladoras, but work conditions were oppressive and wages meager. Like other immigrants, she crossed the U.S./ Mexico border without documentation. In the United States, she became a working mother and faced the predicament of providing for herself, her son, and her family in Chicago while working two jobs but still making meager wages. For many women like Elvira, there was the added problem of working and living in the shadows, without documentation. In the aftermath of 9/11, deportation and criminalization became the policies of a neoliberal state that could not (would not) distinguish between "terrorist" and "low-wage laborers." Eventually, the "mano dura" of the neoliberal state, as Toro-Morn called it, deported Elvira, while her son, a U.S. citizen by birth, remained temporarily in the United States. Arellano's story exemplifies the conditions that push many women like her to take to the streets and protest on behalf of themselves and their families. Her life story is connected to Flor Crisóstomo (see chapter 14), also a working mother and activist who challenged the neoliberal state to recognize how globalization has uprooted indigenous communities across the Americas.

Neoliberal globalization has been accompanied by the marketization of the state (Ong 2006; Rose 1999) in both the global North and South. This process materializes in practices enforced by a neoliberal state governing its citizenry through the familiar tropes of individual freedom and by claiming to produce entrepreneurial and self-governing subjects who will thrive with minimal support or protection from the state. In the global South, neoliberal globalization has undermined the sovereignty of nation-states, increased consolidation of power in the hands of wealthy and affluent elites, and destabilized notions of citizenship (Mohanty 2003). Guevarra (2010) has documented how in the Philippines, the state has entered into the labor-brokering process by turning citizens—potential immigrants—into commodities. Through a regulated network of employment agencies and the development of gendered and racialized ideologies that capitalize on the construction of Filipino women's pride and national duty, this neoliberal state has managed to ensure its survival by securing a place in the global economy as a provider of care workers, domestic workers, and nurses. The Philippine state has marketed a particular gendered and racialized form of Filipina docility, transforming them into the most desirable workers in the global economy. Guevarra and Lledo (see chapter 13) show

how, once abroad, internalized ideologies about the low value of their work renders Filipino workers vulnerable to workplace abuse.

As a neoliberal state, the United States is also deeply invested in the creation of gendered and racialized ideologies about immigrants that labels them as "good" (deserving) or "bad" (undeserving) immigrants. In chapter 3, feminist scholar Grace Chang exposes how the anti–sex trafficking agenda of the United States as a neoliberal state results in the criminalization of sex workers and diverts attention from other forms of low-wage labor trafficking. In other words, this regime downplays or ignores the fact that migration, whether forced or not, is a consequence of societies that have been destroyed by neoliberal globalization. Further, this regime promotes a limited definition of human trafficking as an issue that involves only sexual violence against women, without recognizing racial, economic, and imperialist violence. Indeed, Chang argues that these state-sponsored antitrafficking and rescue activities are "less about combating trafficking than about rationalizing and promoting state-sponsored human trafficking" in the form of cheap labor. The actions of the neoliberal state mask the forms of violence perpetrated by its agents—whether they are policymakers advocating on behalf of trafficked women, or ICE immigration agents deporting women, splitting families, and creating the conditions that make low-wage workers even more vulnerable.

In the United States, neoliberal globalization has also increased social class inequality. Neoliberal globalization has led to declining employment opportunities for white working-class men, while driving white working-class women out of the home and into the labor force. Many of these women joined the expanding service sector, taking jobs as cashiers and shop-floor workers in megastores such as Walmart (Sernau 2011). Among blacks, these processes further fracture already fragile working-class families, consolidating the role of black women as primary providers, expanding the number of working poor, and leaving many men and women outside of labor processes altogether (Savas 2010). At the other end of the social class spectrum, for white upper- and middle-class professionals (and, some might add, a growing transnational elite social class), these changes translated into expanding job opportunities, massive consumerism, and a reprieve from tedious, dreadful, and consuming housework such as cooking, cleaning, and child care (Glenn 2002). Because of the low cost of immigrant labor, middle-class families can afford to eat out frequently and hire the services of nannies, gardeners, and cooks—luxuries previously reserved for affluent and elite families (Boris and Parreñas 2010; Hondagneu-Sotelo 2001). As we show in this volume, this low-wage work was and continues to be done primarily by immigrant women from the global South. Here we add the voices and experiences of Nepali and South Asian immigrant women who come to the United States to work in the homes of affluent Indian families and the small businesses of co-ethnics (see chapters 4 and 5).

Neoliberal globalization has consolidated the restructuring of formal and informal economies and the distribution of social resources that affect the accessibility to these economies and the livelihoods that depend on them. These labor disruptions are certainly gendered and racialized and have a disproportionate impact on communities of color. They are disruptions created and maintained by a neoliberal state in coordination with supranational organizations like the International Monetary Fund and the World Bank and corporate entities like Walmart or Hewlett Packard—which, in concert, have significantly altered both the livelihood and working conditions of workers. As we describe below, they are disruptions that have had deleterious effects on ethnic enclaves as they transform them into spaces that can no longer provide viable employment. They have also altered the composition of informal economies and contributed to the emergence of new demands for particular types of work in highly unregulated spaces such as in the domains of care work, a topic that we also elaborate on in this book. However, this book also highlights the ways in which the very subjects of these disruptions have identified and countered the effects of these disruptions as they organize and cultivate spaces of resistance and re-imagine alternative futures.

Labor Disruptions in Ethnic Enclaves and Informal Economies

In *The World Is Flat*, *New York Times* columnist Thomas Friedman (2005) proclaimed the "flattening" effect of neoliberal globalization to denote the emergence of a leveled playing field across the globe. However, the massive economic changes spurred by neoliberalism have resulted in greater socioeconomic disparities. While the socioeconomic status of some, particularly the professional white middle class, has increased, many have experienced downward mobility. That is, rather than leveling the field so that everyone can compete fairly, neoliberalism has exacerbated inequality around the globe and resulted in deep social-class cleavages, unresolved racial and gender fault lines, and unequal access to the economy. This inequality is more pronounced among immigrants who are excluded from legitimate avenues for economic progress and steered toward the informal economy.

The informal economy, once considered an anomaly of advanced capitalist societies (Sassen 1998, 2008), is an expanding labor sector, and often the only employment alternative of choice for displaced workers. The informal economy has traditionally been constituted as work that is situated outside of legally regulated enterprises, without the security of contracts, benefits, or social protection. Although we know much about men's involvement in the informal economy, women's involvement and its impact on gendered work is missing from scholarly accounts and remains poorly understood. Several essays in this book take us back to a familiar landscape—the streets of Los Angeles and the ethnic enclaves of New York, Chicago, and Boston—to show how low-wage immigrant women are stretching the boundaries between home and work through their involvement in the informal economy. Adding to the small but growing body of studies on women in the informal economy, such as Bao (2001), Dallalfar (1994), Kang (2003), Parreñas (2001, 2005), Smith (2006), Westwood and Bachu (1988), these essays shows how the informal economy not only blurs the traditional—yet unstable—boundaries between home and work, but also creates new spaces where this waged work gets carried out in creative ways. In other words, the informal economy blends work and family life in ways that are not possible in the formal economy.

Within the informal economy, street vending offers the greatest flexibility and continuity between work and family life as women can care for their children while vending. The Latina street vendors that Lorena Muñoz (see chapter 7) talked to in Los Angeles preferred street vending to other jobs because of this flexibility. Child care has always presented a problem for immigrant women who lack resources to pay for it or have insufficient family networks for assistance. Street vending then provides immigrant working mothers the flexibility to be able to care for their children while earning a living. Unlike stereotypical perceptions of street vending in Latin America, street vending in Los Angeles is highly organized and stratified. Muñoz found that in keeping with established gendered norms that define the street as a space for men, women create culturally acceptable feminine spaces in street vending by limiting their activities to food vending. However, it takes a great deal of knowledge and skill to navigate these highly unregulated and at times dangerous spaces for women and their children.

If the streets are not safe for street-vending women, they are even more dangerous for the children and teenagers who participate in street vending. In chapter 8, Emir Estrada and Pierrette Hondagneu-Sotelo show how street vending extends to, and involves the whole family. Although child labor is illegal, street vending relies on the participation of family members, children and adults alike. Estrada and Hondagneu-Sotelo found that girls are an asset to the family business because they are perceived by customers to be cleaner in the preparation of food, friendlier and less threatening than boys. As a result, girls are afforded more freedom and independence from their parents. But street vending takes a toll on teenage girls, as many faced what Estrada and Hondagneu-Sotelo call the "third shift" of work and had difficulty handling home, work, and school responsibilities. Yet, for teenage girls, the benefits of street vending outweigh the perils. They perceive street vending as grueling work that rewards them with economic independence, tangible business skills, and valuable lessons on economic survival.

Another dimension of the informal economy where immigrant women find work opportunities is in the expanding care-work industry. As Eileen Boris and Rhacel Salazar Parreñas (2010, 1) point out, "one of the most striking features of contemporary global capitalism is the heightened commodification of intimacy." Asian and Latina immigrant women have become part of the growing number of workers in the informal, highly personal, physically and emotionally draining work of elder care. In chapter 9, Lucy Fisher and Miliann Kang capture how certified nursing assistants (CNAs) working in long-term elder-care facilities manage the stigma attached to doing the "dirty" work of caring for patients, many of whom are bedridden. The Asian and Latina immigrants who worked as CNAs faced a specific predicament as their precarious immigration status, in combination with their devalued occupation, stigmatize them. As a strategy, they engage in boundary work to reinvent and reinterpret "dirty" work as worthy. Fisher and Kang found that CNAs engaged in building "boundaries of moral worth" by focusing on the nursing skills and caring attitudes needed to perform their jobs. Immigrant women providing care for the elderly in private homes have different attitudes toward their job. In chapter 10, María de la Luz Ibarra shows how more personal and "fictive kinship" relationships develop between caregivers and their elderly wards. Unlike CNAs who are responsible for several patients, caregivers working in private homes care for one elderly ward. The physical and emotional intensity of caring for someone in the last years of life, and often providing hospice care as death nears, leads to the development of strong bonds between caregiver and ward. Ibarra argues that caregivers and wards become "part of each other's family" as caregivers become permanent fixtures around the household, and the caregivers' relatives assist to provide around-the-clock care when needed.

The ethnic enclave provides employment opportunities for immigrant women often through informal labor arrangements. Although sociologists have made significant and indelible contributions to the study of the ethnic enclave (Alberts, 2005; Portes and Jensen 1989; Portes and Rumbaut 1996; Wilson and Portes, 1980), a gendered view of the ethnic enclave remains elusive. Some of the essays in this volume point to the highly stratified nature of the ethnic enclave where gender dynamics disadvantage immigrant women workers. In chapter 5, Pallavi Banerjee) shows how these gender dynamics play out in small businesses where Southeast Asian women work. Although these women achieve some economic independence and self-actualization through work, and enjoy working in a familiar environment, working for co-ethnics makes them vulnerable to exploitation and abuse. They often labor long hours in work environments where there are few, if any, personal boundaries. Banerjee found that co-ethnic employers refer to them as "part of the family," a trope that Mary Romero (1992, 2011) found to be at the center of employer's exploitation and abuse for Latina domestic workers. Similarly, in chapter 4, Shobha Hamal Gurung and Bandana Purkayastha found that Nepali immigrant women are recruited to domestic work in wealthy East Indian households. Despite their high levels of education, Nepali immigrant women found themselves employed as nannies and housekeepers because they lack legal status or the English language skills needed to work in the occupations they were trained for. Yet many felt that the exploitation and drudgery that accompanied their work are outweighed by the remittances they are able to send home to support their families, as well as community projects.

The importance of ethnic enclaves and networks for immigrant women seeking employment cannot be underestimated. In chapter 6, Margaret Chin shows how gender dynamics in the ethnic enclave deem women more vulnerable and more susceptible to changes in the economy. Focusing on the drastic economic changes that besieged New York City in the aftermath of 9/11, Chin examines how the garment industry, once the backbone of the Chinese ethnic enclave, suffered a devastating blow as the city practically shut down and the economy went into recession. Among displaced Chinese workers, women in particular experienced more difficulty in finding alternative employment. While the Chinatown enclave provided women with employment, it also limited their social networks and the development of skills that could help them find jobs outside of the enclave. Men, on the other hand, had access to social networks outside of the enclave, leading to employment opportunities in the health and hotel industries. According to Chin, Chinese immigrant workers survived the economic crisis not thanks to the ethnic enclave but to the community organizations that provided training and prospects for other job opportunities, a topic we turn to next.

Labor Disruptions and Immigrant Women Grassroots Organizing

It is befitting that our project began in the midst of the immigrant rights movement and comes to a close as the Occupy movement unfolds. Both movements denounce the devastating effects of neoliberal globalization that results in increasing class, gender, and racial disparities. The experiences of immigrant working women are interconnected to these struggles. Indeed, immigrant communities, and low-wage immigrant workers in particular, have been at the forefront of organizing against the devastating effects of neoliberal globalization (Cordero-Guzmán et al. 2008). Community organizations are at the forefront of this struggle as they address the day-to-day injustices faced by low-wage immigrant workers. As various scholars have highlighted (Fine 2006; Meléndez, Theodore, and Valenzuela

2009; Milkman, Bloom, and Narro 2010; Sullivan and Lee 2008), labor unions and worker centers have helped champion the demands of low-wage workers for living wages and humane working conditions.

Some of the essays in this volume illustrate how community organizations not only help resolve day-to-day problems, but are also critical spaces for the cultivation of grassroots leaders and activists. In chapter 11, Jennifer Chun, George Lipsitz, and Young Shin highlight how the organization Asian Immigrant Women Advocates (AIWA) has developed a grassroots approach to community organizing and empowerment that places immigrant women workers at the center of social change and prioritizes their leadership development over concerns about organizational efficiency. This grassroots model of leadership development recognizes the ways in which workplace and labor market inequalities are interconnected, and to a large extent worsened, by relations of power in the family and community. This intersectional approach interweaves race, class, gender, and other axes of power and inequality that deeply affect the lives of immigrant women. With this approach, AIWA created a space that transforms immigrant women into leaders.

Along the U.S./Mexico border, labor unions and worker centers have been organizing workers in the maquiladoras. In chapter 12, Michelle Téllez discusses the organizing work of La Colectiva Feminista Binacional on the Tijuana/San Diego border. Téllez illustrates the ways in which this organization promotes workers' rights through the development of a gendered consciousness. By creating a politicized *transfronteriza* identity, La Colectiva Feminista Binacional promotes cross-border solidarity rooted in a feminist politics that places women's rights at the center of the fight against oppression. By cultivating connections across the border, holding workshops to support workers, establishing income-generating ventures, and supporting cross-border actions against the maquiladora industry, La Colectiva Feminista Binacional creates a unique binational community in which women emerge as leaders transformed by their awareness of the intersection of gender, race, and social class in their lives.

Consciousness raising is at the center of the Pilipino Workers Center (PWC) described by Guevarra and Lledo in chapter 13. This organization serves Filipino immigrants who provide elder and end-of-life care in private homes. Most Filipino caregivers are highly educated and have advanced degrees but had no previous caregiver experience. Experiencing downward mobility, many feel devalued by their notions that caregiving does not require skills or training, a problem that also surfaced in Fisher and Kang's work, described in chapter 9. Also, the unregulated context of home care work renders them more vulnerable to abusive practices. PWC helps them develop human capital by providing a community of support where workers can systematically share knowledge and caregiving techniques, as well as learn about their rights as workers. Furthermore, PWC helps workers develop leadership skills and provides a means for advocating collectively for their rights.

Clearly, community organizations have emerged as not only problem solving institutions, but more importantly training grounds for leaders and activists. The struggle for work, immigration, and human rights in the neoliberal era requires new leaders, innovative strategies, and community allies. In New York, the work of a community organization, Esperanza del Barrio, represents yet another effort to address the needs of immigrant women workers. Drawing on ethnographic data, in chapter 1 Victoria Quiroz-Becerra shows how street vendors in New York City frame their campaigns and articulate their demands by drawing on the connections among neoliberalism, gender work, and alternative notions of citizenship. Vendors and activists have strategically organized against both police harassment and restrictive policies on vending licenses. As Quiroz-Becerra argues, neoliberalism is a double-edged sword: on one hand the neoliberal city renders immigrant women vulnerable to selective law enforcement and few formal outlets for protection, and on the other hand "neoliberal discourses seem to provide a common ground from which to negotiate." As she observes, Esperanza del Barrio activists employ and subvert the very neoliberal discourses at the root of their oppression, thereby turning them into a tool for resistance.

Organizing locally but thinking globally is at the center of social action against neoliberal globalization. In this respect, two essays in this collection show clearly how day-to-day struggles are connected to larger struggles for global equity. The stories of two women, Elvira Arellano and Flor Crisóstomo, bring to the forefront the predicaments faced by working mothers, thereby making this new wave of social activism responsive to the needs of women. What Pallares and Flores-González (2010) call the "public square" has been transformed by the subjective experiences of these immigrant women activists. While their stories show the ways in which neoliberal globalizing forces have created oppressive working conditions for low-wage immigrant women, they also point to the resilience and creativity with which these women are responding to and challenging these forces and emerging as social agents of change. As discussed earlier, in chapter 2 Maura Toro-Morn traces the struggles that propelled Elvira Arellano to become a leading voice in the struggle against deportation and family separation locally, and transnationally upon her deportation. In portraying the devastating effects of neoliberal economic and immigration policies on a family, in chapter 14 Flores-González and Gomberg-Muñoz show how for immigrant women the personal sphere of home and work is deeply political. In the midst of a broken and punitive immigration system and a global neoliberal economic order, Crisóstomo and other immigrant women transform the narratives that define their lives. Their essay follows the transformation of Crisóstomo from an indigenous Mexican single transnational mother into an indigenous immigrant and family rights activist. Crisóstomo's transformation comes from her realization that neoliberal globalization is at the center of her plight as a transnational working mother. Her politicization through the immigrant rights movement, her eventual defiance of a deportation order, and her binational indigenous activism provide not only a sharp critique of neoliberal globalization, but also show how a global social justice framework transforms women, their families, and the meaning of parenting in a transnational and neoliberal era.

Reflections on Research for Social Change

The terrain that has emerged in this book is vast, complex, and ambitious. We offer a view of the intimate spaces of care work done in the privacy of homes; the relentless and oppressive conditions of work in service industries; the insecurities of garment workers pushed from protective ethnic enclaves; and the dangers, difficulties, and dreams of Latina mothers and daughters who work as street vendors. We also offer a window into the uncertainties faced by displaced and deported working mothers who continue to struggle to provide for their families. We show how service workers engage a neoliberal ideology and how grassroots movements have made some promising inroads in organizing workers to address the various forms of disruptions that this neoliberal economy brings. This anthology takes up these issues using an interdisciplinary lens that includes anthropology, Asian American studies, Latina/o studies, feminist studies, geography, sociology, and nursing. In keeping with our collective feminist research values, in the last pages of this introduction, we offer our reflections about the challenges facing future scholars of labor and migration processes.

This volume brings together a group of scholar-activists who share a commitment to social justice that goes beyond research. Many of these authors have devoted a significant part of their personal lives and academic careers to social justice issues and to collaborating with community organizations that advocate on behalf of the human and civil rights of immigrant women and workers. At this critical juncture, we offer this book not only as new empirical research but as a model for building collaborations among immigrants, community groups, and scholar-activists based on a new ethic of trust, justice, and community building.

This book is grounded in the knowledge that as neoliberal globalization continues to alter the political and economic landscape of communities in the global North and global South, our methods, approaches, and conceptual language for studying these labor disruptions need to be sharpened and infused with new sensibilities. We hope that the essays included here encourage current and future researchers to deploy innovative approaches for doing research among members of poor and disadvantaged and immigrant communities. Scholarly efforts have failed to examine the subjective experiences of those in the low-wage labor market and have excluded the voices of the subjects that are at the center of these struggles. This volume employs a diverse range of intensive qualitative methodologies, including in-depth interviews, oral histories, and ethnographies, to expand our knowledge and understanding of immigrant women as they respond pragmatically and creatively to these labor disruptions.

Giving a space for immigrants to voice their struggles is of utmost importance today as they face increased vilification as criminals through local, state, and federal policies, through public media campaigns, and through nativist attacks. The recent passing of state immigrant control legislation in Arizona, Alabama, and North Carolina, along with other states considering similar legislation, further federal efforts to curb immigration through border enforcement and deportation campaigns. The implementation of punitive immigration policies at the local, state, and national level has led to fear, distrust, and apprehension among immigrants. It has also rendered them more vulnerable to abuse and exploitation. We hope that students, academics, and activists continue to work together to produce knowledge that is attentive to these issues and that empowers us all to become agents of change.

References

Alberts, Heike. 2005. "Changes in Ethnic Solidarity in Cuban Miami." *Geographical Review* 95(2): 231–48.

Arau, Sergio. 2004. *A Day without a Mexican*. Mexico City: Televisa Cine.

Bank-Muñoz, Carolina. 2008. *Transnational Tortillas: Race, Gender, and Shop-Floor Politics in Mexico and the United States*. Ithaca: Cornell University Press.

Bao, Xiaolan. 2001. *Holding Up More than Half of the Sky: Chinese Women Garment Workers in New York City 1948–1992*. Urbana: University of Illinois Press.

Bonacich, Edna, and Richard Appelbaum. 2000. *Behind the Label: Inequality in the Los Angeles Apparel Industry*. Berkeley: University of California Press.

Boris, Eileen, and Rhacel Salazar Parreñas, eds. 2010. *Intimate Labors: Cultures, Technologies, and the Politics of Care*. Stanford: Stanford University Press.

Bureau of Labor Statistics. 2011. *Foreign-Born Workers: Labor Force Characteristics—2010*. U.S. Department of Labor (USDL-11-0763). http://www.bls.gov/news.release/pdf/forbrn.pdf.

Castles, Stephen, and Mark J. Miller. 2009. *The Age of Migration: International Population Movements in the Modern World*. 4th ed. New York: Guildford Press.

Chang, Grace. 2000. *Disposable Domestics: Immigrant Women in the Global Economy*. Cambridge, Mass.: South End Press.

Chin, Margaret. 2005. *Sewing Women: Immigrants and the New York City Garment Industry*. New York: Columbia University Press.

Cobble, Sue, ed. 2007. *The Sex of Class: Women Transforming American Labor*. Ithaca: Cornell University Press.

Cordero-Guzmán, Héctor, Nina Martin, Victoria Quiroz-Becerra, and Nik Theodore. 2008. "Voting with their Feet: Nonprofit Organizations and Immigrant Mobilization." *American Behavioral Scientist* 52(4): 598–617.

Cowie, Jefferson. 2001. *Capital Moves: RCA's 70-year Quest for Cheap Labor.* New York: New Press.

Dallalfar, Arlene. 1994. "Iranian Women as Immigrant Entrepreneurs." *Gender and Society* 8(4): 541–61.

Ehrenreich, Barbara, and Arlie Hochschild, eds. 2002. *Global Woman: Nannies, Maids, and Sex Workers in the New Economy.* New York: Metropolitan Books.

Fernandez-Kelly, Maria Patricia. 1983. *For We Are Sold, I and My People: Women and Industry in Mexico's Mexican Border Industrialization, Female Labor Force Participation, and Migration Frontier.* Albany: State University New York Press.

Fine, Janice. 2006. *Worker Centers: Organizing Communities at the Edge of the Dream.* Ithaca, N.Y.: ILR Press.

Freeman, Carla. 2000. *High Tech and High Heels in the Global Economy: Women, Work, and Pink-Collar Identities in the Caribbean.* Durham: Duke University Press.

Friedman, Thomas. 2005. *The World Is Flat: A Brief History of the Twenty-First Century.* New York: Farrar, Straus, and Giroux.

Gammage, Sarah. (2002). "Women Immigrants in the U.S. Labor Market: Second Rate Jobs in the First World." In *Women Immigrants in the United States: Proceedings of a conference sponsored by the Woodrow Wilson International Center for Scholars and the Migration Policy Institute,* ed. Philippa Strum and Danielle Tarantalo, 75–95. Washington, D.C.: Woodrow Wilson International Center for Scholars. http://stage-wilson.p2technology.com/sites/default/files/womenimm_rpt.pdf. Accessed December 27, 2012.

George, Sheba. 2005. *When Women Come First: Gender and Class in Transnational Migration.* Berkeley: University of California Press.

Glenn, Evelyn Nakano. 2002. *Unequal Freedom: How Race and Gender Shaped American Citizenship and Labor.* Cambridge, Mass.: Harvard University Press.

Grieco, Elizabeth M., Yesenia D. Acosta, G. Patricia de la Cruz, Christine Gambino, Thomas Gryn, Luke J. Larsen, Edward N. Trevelyan, and Nathan P. Walters. 2012. "The Foreign-Born Population in the United States: 2010." *American Community Survey Reports.* http://www.census.gov/prod/2012pubs/acs-19.pdf. Accessed May 13, 2012.

Guevarra, Anna Romina. 2010. *Marketing Dreams, Manufacturing Heroes: The Transnational Labor Brokering of Filipino Workers.* New Brunswick, N.J.: Rutgers University Press.

Harvey. David. 2005. *A Brief History of Neoliberalism.* Oxford: Oxford University Press.

Hirsch, Jennifer. 2003. *A Courtship after Marriage: Sexuality and Love in Mexican Transnational Families.* Berkeley: University of California Press.

Hondagneu-Sotelo, Pierrette. 1994. *Gendered Transitions: Mexican Experiences of Immigration.* Berkeley: University of California Press.

———. 2001. *Doméstica: Immigrant Workers Cleaning and Caring in the Shadows of Affluence.* Berkeley: University of California Press.

———. 2003. *Gender and U.S. Immigration: Contemporary Trends.* Berkeley: University of California Press.

Jaggar, Alison M. 2001. "Is Globalization Good for Women." *Comparative Literature* 53(4): 298–314.

Kang, Miliann. 2003. "The Managed Hand: The Commercialization of Bodies and Emotions in Korean Immigrant-Owned Nail Salons." *Gender and Society* 17(6): 820–39.

Kibria, Nazli. 1993. *Family Tightrope: The Changing Lives of Vietnamese Americans*. Princeton: Princeton University Press.

Leacock, Eleanor, and Helen Safa, eds. 1986. *Women's Work: Development and the Division of Labor by Gender*. South Hadley, Mass.: Bergin and Garvey.

Meléndez, Edgardo, Nik Theodore, and Abel Valenzuela. 2009. "Day Laborers in New York's Informal Economy." In *The Informal Economy in the Developed World*, ed. E. Marcelli, C. Williams, and P. Joussart-Marcelli, 133–50. London: Routledge.

Menjivar, Cecilia. 2000. *Fragmented Ties: Salvadoran Immigrant Networks in America*. Berkeley: University of California Press.

Milkman, Ruth, Joshua Bloom, and Victor Narro, eds. 2010. *Working for Justice: The L.A. Model of Organizing and Advocacy*. Ithaca, N.Y.: ILR Press.

Mohanty, Chandra Talpade. 2003. *Feminism without Borders: Decolonizing Theory, Practicing Solidarity*. Durham: Duke University Press.

Ong, Aihwa. 1987. *Spirits of Resistance and Capitalist Discipline: Factory Women in Malaysia*. Albany: State University of New York Press.

———. 2006. *Neoliberalism as Exception: Mutations in Citizenship and Sovereignty*. Durham: Duke University Press.

Pallares, Amalia, and Nilda Flores-González, eds. 2010. *¡Marcha! Latino Chicago and the Immigrant Rights Movement*. Urbana: University of Illinois Press.

Parreñas, Rhacel Salazar. 2001. *Servants of Globalization: Women, Migration, and Domestic Work*. Stanford: Stanford University Press.

———. 2005. *Children of Global Migration: Transnational Families and Gendered Woes*. Stanford: Stanford University Press.

Passel, Jeffrey S., and D'Vera Cohn. 2011. *Unauthorized Immigrant Population: National and State Trends, 2010*. Washington, D.C.: Pew Hispanic Center.

Pessar, Patricia, and Sarah J. Mahler. 2003. "Transnational Migration: Bringing Gender In." *International Migration Review* 37(3): 812–46.

Portes, Alejandro, and Leif Jensen. 1989. "The Enclave and the Entrants: Patterns of Ethnic Enterprise in Miami before and after Mariel." *American Sociological Review* 54(6): 929–49.

Portes, Alejandro, and Rubén Rumbaut. 1996. *Immigrant America: A Portrait*. 2nd ed. Berkeley: University of California Press.

Romero, Mary. 1992. *Maid in the U.S.A.* New York: Routledge.

———. 2011. *The Maid's Daughter: Living Inside and Outside the American Dream*. New York: New York University Press.

Rose, Nikolas. 1999. *Powers of Freedom: Reframing Political Thought*. Cambridge: Cambridge University Press.

Salzinger, Leslie. 2003. *Genders in Production: Making Workers in Mexico's Global Factories*. Berkeley: University of California Press.

Sassen, Saskia. 1998. *Globalization and Its Discontents: Essays on the New Mobility of People and Money*. New York: New Press.

———. 2008. "Two Stops in Today's New Global Geographies: Shaping Novel Labor Supplies and Employment Regimes." *American Behavioral Scientist* 52(3): 457–96.

Savas, Gokhan. 2010. "Social Inequality at Low-wage Work in Neo-liberal Economy: The Case of Women of Color Domestic Workers in the United States." *Race, Gender, and Class* 17(3/4): 314–26.

Segura, Denise and Patricia Zavella. 2007. *Women and Migration in the U.S.–Mexico Borderlands: A Reader*. Durham: Duke University Press.

Sernau, Scott. 2009. *Global Problems: The Search for Equity, Peace, and Sustainability*. 3rd ed. Boston: Pearson/Allyn and Bacon.

Smith, Andrea E. 2006. *Women Entrepreneurs across Racial Lines: Issues of Human Capital, Financial Capital and Network*. Northampton, Mass.: Edward Elgar Publishing, Inc.

Sullivan, Richard, and Kimi Lee. 2008. "Organizing Immigrant Women in America's Sweatshops: Lessons from the Los Angeles Garment Worker Center." *SIGNS: Journal of Women in Culture and Society* 33(3): 527–32.

Tiano, Susan. 1994. *Patriarchy on the Line: Labor, Gender, and Ideology in the Mexican Maquila Industry*. Philadelphia: Temple University Press.

Toro-Morn, Maura. 2008. "Beyond Gender Dichotomies: Toward a New Century of Gendered Scholarship in the Latina/o Experience." In *Latinas/os in the United States: Changing the Face of America*, edited by R. Rodriguez, R. Saenz, and C. Menjivar, 277–93. New York: Springer.

Toro-Morn, Maura, and Marixsa Alicea. 2004. *Migration and Immigration: A Global View*. Westport, Conn.: Greenwood Press.

Westwood, Sallie, and Parminder Bachu, eds. 1988. *Enterprising Women: Ethnicity, Economy, and Gender Relations*. London: Routledge.

Wilson, Kenneth, and Alejandro Portes. 1980. "Immigrant Enclaves: An Analysis of the Labor Market Experiences of Cubans in Miami." *American Journal of Sociology* 86: 305–19.

PART 1

Critique of the Neoliberal State

1

Street Vendors Claiming
Respect and Dignity
in the Neoliberal City

M. VICTORIA QUIROZ-BECERRA

On a cold and windy morning in February 2009, I traveled to downtown Brooklyn to attend a march in support of street vendors called by Esperanza del Barrio, an organization working with Latina street vendors in East Harlem. The objective of the march was to protest the existing caps on food cart permits and general merchandise licenses that New York City imposed two and a half decades earlier. According to the organization's press release, "The City profits from hard working vendors by enforcing these antiquated and unjust regulations. Interactions between officials and vendors have also become increasingly aggressive. The unacceptable policy adopted by the Department of Health to pour bleach on the food of street vendors has added to tensions. It is time for a change. The City must put an end to the unequal and improper regulation of the vendors and instead, create laws that will encourage economic and cultural growth" (Esperanza del Barrio 2009).

At around 9:00 A.M., we started to line up in rows of three to make sure that we would not obstruct pedestrian traffic as we walked across the Brooklyn Bridge toward City Hall in Manhattan. Placards were distributed among the approximately fifty people who had arrived. As we made our way across the bridge, we shouted slogans while passersby read our signs and smiled approvingly. A driver shouted encouragingly and raised his fist in support. Tourists took pictures, trying to capture, I imagine, a "true" New York moment. As we reached Manhattan, we started to shout louder, "¡Aquí y allá! ¡El trabajo es dignidad! [Here and there! Work is dignity!]" "¡Consejales escuchar! ¡Trabajar no es ilegal! [Council members listen! Working is not illegal]." We made our way to City Hall, where metal barriers were already lined up, flanked by a dozen police officers. We moved diligently to our designated protest space. Despite the relatively low turnout, a handful of mainly Latina immigrant vendors appropriated that small patch of public space near City Hall to voice their demands for recognition of their livelihood and respect of their persons. This was not the first time that these women street vendors appeared on New York's public scene. They had been organizing for over six years, creating coalitions across ethnic lines and engaging City Council members to support their demands.

We stood there until noon, shouting our slogans. Alternating between Spanish and English, we shouted, "¿Qué queremos? ¡Permisos y licencias!" "What do we want? Justice!" In Spanish, vendors were asking for permits and licenses; in English we were demanding justice. This (mis)translation did not result from "limited language abilities" or vendors' arbitrariness but rather symbolized the various discourses on which grassroots activists draw to articulate their demands as well as the various social and political spaces and contexts where these discourses are articulated. Social movement scholars (McAdam, McCarthy, and Zald 1996; Tarrow 1998) talk about processes of framing to refer to the shaping of grievances into claims that resonate with broader audiences. In framing demands, activists draw on existing cultural understandings to appeal to a broad set of actors in various contexts. Demands must resonate not only with the people whom activists seek to mobilize but also with policy makers, politicians, and potential allies. How do street-vending grassroots activists frame their demands? On what discourses and cultural understandings do they draw to frame their demands? How are these demands then translated into policies and laws?

In this essay, I analyze grassroots organizing around street vending in New York City since 2003, paying particular attention to the debates surrounding vending in the city and the ways activists and government officials alike have framed the issue. Street vendor organizers have framed their campaigns and articulated their demands by drawing on neoliberal discourses as well as gendered constructs and alternative notions of citizenship. Grassroots activists and their supporters have framed the demands of street vendors by appealing to ideas of free enterprise and individualism. These frames resonate with prevailing discourses of neoliberal forms of urban governance that emphasize individual entrepreneurship and targeted state intervention in the market. Simultaneously, activists base their demands on notions of recognition and respect as humans, independent of legal status. Gendered notions of family and women's roles within it are also central to the framing of street vendor demands. Although I focus mainly on one organization, Esperanza del Barrio, I also draw on other actors to get a better understanding of how issues surrounding street vending are framed.

Neoliberalism and Urban Governance

Since 2003, New York City has seen a reemergence on grassroots organizing efforts among street vendors. These efforts have generated renewed interest and debates about the use of public space and the state's role in regulating that space.

Historically, questions about street vending have reflected different ideas of the city, its inhabitants, who can use public space, and for what purposes (Bluestone 1991). During the Progressive Era (1890s–1920s) ideas of order, cleanliness, beauty, and efficiency guided urban planning. Streets were conceived as spaces where traffic could freely circulate. Shopping was transferred indoors in the form of retail arcades and department stores that conveyed images of order and control and bourgeois consumption. Consequently, street vending was seen as in opposition to ideas of modern urban commerce and middle-class mores, and as contributing to street congestion and neighborhood deterioration. The creation of formal zoning statues and street vendor regulations in New York City reflected these ideas. Vendors were moved out of the streets and confined to less visible and more controlled spaces (for example, street markets underneath the bridges connecting Manhattan to the outer boroughs). Thus, although central to the economies of many neighborhoods, particularly those where new immigrants settled, street vendors were relegated to public spaces away from those that symbolized modern city life (Bluestone 1991).

Ideas of the city and its inhabitants have subsequently changed. Prevailing neoliberal discourses in the United States have shaped how we think of urban areas. Neoliberalism is an ideology as well as a form of governance and a driver of urban change (Hackworth 2007; Ong 2006; Sites 2006). As an ideology, neoliberalism refers to the "belief that open, competitive, and unregulated markets, liberated from all forms of state interference, represent the optimal mechanism for economic development" (Brenner and Theodore 2002, 350). This ideology has shaped economic restructuring projects and has been expressed with greater intensity in urban settings. Neoliberalism as an economic model requires particular technologies of governance. As a form of governance, neoliberalism guides and regulates the political, following market-driven "truths" and calculations (Ong 2006). Leitner and her colleagues (2006, 4) note that neoliberal governmentality takes particular forms within urban areas: "The neoliberal city is conceptualized first as an entrepreneurial city, directing all its energies to achieving economic success in competition with other cities for investments, innovations, and 'creative classes.'" Within this context, municipal bureaucracies are professionalized agencies promoting economic development, privatizing urban services, and creating competition among public agencies. Public policy decisions are based on cost–benefit calculations. In New York City, the neoliberal project began in the mid-1970s as a response to fiscal crisis. During its initial phase, the neoliberal agenda included policies geared to market stimulus and austerity programs. In its second phase, policies targeted state intervention (Sites 2003).

Neoliberalism requires particular subjects that differ from the ideal of citizen, a subject endowed with rights claims to the state. Under neoliberalism, a person ought to be "a self-enterprising citizen-subject who is obligated to become an 'entrepreneur of himself or herself'" (Ong 2006, 14). Workfare programs are one example of the adoption of this notion of neoliberal subject. Neoliberal subjects, however, are not neutral. On the contrary, gender is central to realizing neoliberal projects.

Gender constructs and their associated hierarchies are often used to recruit labor and discipline workers (Mills 2003). The case of assembly shops is a case in point. Ong's (1987) analysis of assembly shops in Malaysia shows how women are specifically recruited because they are perceived as more adept at performing assembly work and conforming to the disciplines that this work entails. Thus, gendered ideas that view women as delicate and easily domesticated are articulated with neoliberal forms of production. Domestic work, care work, and other service industries so central to neoliberal economic development rely on gendered constructs. Gender constructs shape how certain jobs are construed as women's work and rendered less valued or unimportant and therefore are amenable to neoliberal projects in search for cheap, docile, and flexible labor. Street vending, however, although a service industry, stands outside in some ways from other forms of low-wage labor women enter. Women's entrepreneurial activities in the informal sector have often been seen as contributing to destabilize gender hierarchies.[1] What is important, then, is understanding how gender constructs are interwoven within particular neoliberal projects. As Mills (2003, 47) notes, "Gendered hierarchies help to produce a segmented and flexible global labor force. However, the ways in which hegemonic gender meanings structure the lived experiences of actual women and men vary widely."

Thus, neoliberal projects do not constitute a coherent set of policies that can be realized independently of local particularities. Neoliberalism takes different forms depending on the scale and space where they actually take place, resulting in "destructive" and "creative" moments (Brenner and Theodore 2002) and areas of "exception" (Ong 2006). Neoliberalism is a contingent process that takes different forms across space and along other processes of urbanization. The institutional manifestations of neoliberalism are uneven, incomplete, and varied. These disjunctions create room for contestation and redefinition of neoliberal projects (Hackworth 2007). Leitner and her coauthors (2006) argue that contestations to neoliberalism may take advantage of the technologies born out of neoliberalism. Within the context of neoliberal forms of urban governance and their contestation, I look at the claims of street vendors, asking how they work within and contest neoliberal forms of governance.

Vending in the City

Street vending in New York has often been an occupation taken by newly arrived immigrants. In the early twentieth century, Irish, Italian, Greek, and Jewish immigrants walked the city's streets, selling all sorts of foods and merchandise, mainly in poor neighborhoods, such as the Lower East Side, where immigrant communities concentrated. Street vending was often seen as a way for immigrants to enter the economy, a path that might eventually lead to upward economic mobility. In practice, however, the "rags to riches" narrative was rarely realized, and many people spent between ten and fifteen years peddling in the streets before moving to different trades (Bluestone 1991). For many vendors, street vending ensured low overhead costs; for consumers, it was a means of purchasing merchandise at lower prices. Today, street vending continues to be a trade taken up mainly by immigrants, although vendors' places of origin have changed as the city's demographic outlook has shifted. Scholars see the growth of the informal economy, including street vending in immigrant neighborhoods, as the result of structural factors present in postindustrial economies as well as a way for immigrants to supplement wages in the formal economy and as alternatives to low-wage employment (Zlolniski 2006).

To date, no comprehensive surveys provide an overall picture of the characteristics, working conditions, levels of income, or challenges that New York's street vendors face. A small-sample survey conducted by the Street Vendor Project of the Urban Justice Center (SVP) found that New York City had between twelve and thirteen thousand street vendors (SVP 2006).[2] According to this survey, most vendors (83 percent) are foreign born, with the top countries of origin (at least among vendors in Lower Manhattan) Bangladesh, China, and Afghanistan. Most of the members of Esperanza del Barrio are from Latin America, primarily Mexico and Ecuador. For many in the survey, vending is a last resort after facing barriers to employment in the formal economy.

Street vendors, unlike workers in other low-wage labor markets, are not usually viewed as "workers" in the traditional sense of the word. They are often considered entrepreneurs who own their own businesses, even though these enterprises often yield low and moderate incomes and entail long hours and harsh working conditions. According to the SVP survey (2006), 83 percent of vendors reported working independently. Unlike other low-wage workers, vendors have relative autonomy in their workplaces in the sense that they can set their own schedules and work rhythms, though such freedom is often illusory. More than a quarter of the vendors in the survey noted that they valued the flexibility associated with street vending. One woman street vendor preferred her occupation "because here no one bosses me around, no one shouts at me, no one scolds me" (Moda 2008b [translated by author]). Before becoming a vendor, this woman had spent twelve years working in the garment industry.[3]

Vending also has a gendered dimension. Women often take up this type of job to "supplement" their household income—even when the income generated represents a substantial part of the household total—while tending to household responsibilities and child care. One of the founders of Esperanza del Barrio noted, "I started vending because I had my three kids in school, and I never liked my sons or daughters to be hanging out in the streets. . . . If I were to go to work in a factory, I would be leaving at seven in the morning and arriving home at seven at night, and my kids would be completely alone all day long. So I chose to sell tamales. I would bring my kids to school, then I would go to sell, and then I would return and would start cooking for them and later my children arrived" home from school (Moda 2008a [translated by author]).

In many cases, street vending allows women to tend to non-income-generating reproductive responsibilities while earning money. As with other forms of low-wage work that women enter (for example, domestic work and care work), the division between productive and reproductive activities is blurry. Vendors often sell food prepared in their own kitchens, transforming their homes into workplaces. Similarly, vendors sometimes bring their children to work, transforming the workplace into a space in which reproductive tasks are performed. Thus, street vending alters traditional gendered spatial segregation of labor, although this process does not necessarily imply the empowerment of women.

Despite—or maybe because of—the informality of street vending, local governments historically have attempted to control it by regulating public space and codifying vending activities. The New York City Administrative Code (1985) defines a general vendor as "a person who hawks, peddles, sells, leases or offers to sell or lease, at retail, goods or services, including newspapers, periodicals, books, pamphlets or other written matter in a public space." Various city agencies, state laws, and constitutional law regulate street vending. The city classifies vendors in three main categories, depending on the type of merchandise sold: general merchandise, food, and printed material. Each category of vending has its own set of rules and regulations. For example, unlike vendors of general merchandise, booksellers and artists do not require licenses, since their activities are considered free speech and thus protected under the First Amendment. In addition to vending licenses, food vendors must obtain permits for their pushcarts, which must conform to specific sanitary standards. The rules regarding where vendors can set up shop vary depending on which category of merchandise they sell.

Vendors in New York City face two main issues, one related to enforcement, the other related to licensing. Enforcement of street-vending rules and regulations currently falls under the purview of various agencies, including the Department of Consumer Affairs, the Department of Health, the Department of Transportation, the Fire Department, and the Police Department (NYPD). Vendors found in violation of regulations receive summonses that are handled by the Environmental Control Board or the Criminal Court, depending on whether the violation was considered a civil or a criminal matter. Given the complexity of vending regulations and rules, only 26 percent of the vendors surveyed by the SVP (2006) adequately understand all regulations. The result has been the creation of a system of decentralized enforcement: NYPD officers who are in direct contact with vendors have considerable latitude in interpreting and enforcing regulations. NYPD officers are supposed to be trained in vending rules, and members of the department's specialized Street Peddling Task Force receive additional training (Liu 2007). Given the complex systems of rules and regulations and types of vendors, NYPD officers' enforcement of the law and issuing of summonses seem arbitrary to most vendors.

The other issue facing vendors is that related to licensing and permits. In 1979 the city limited the number of general vending licenses to 853; four years later, a cap of 3,000 food cart permits was established (New York Committee on Consumer Affairs 2005b). In 2008, the city passed a new law allowing an additional 1,000 fruit vending cart permits to be used in specific neighborhoods (New York Committee on Consumer Affairs 2008). The cap on license and cart permits has meant that only a handful of vendors are licensed or have permits. According to SVP codirector Michael Wells, two-thirds of these permits are not used by their original owners; instead, they have been sold on the black market for between eight and twelve thousand dollars.

Dealing with Law Enforcement

The current system of regulation and decentralized enforcement has created much confusion among vendors and given ample latitude to law enforcement. This tactic of enforcement is in accordance with neoliberal forms of governance geared toward creating a stable political infrastructure and targeted government intervention. That is, rather than addressing the issue, the city has opted for targeted enforcement that is activated when a crisis arises and remains dormant at other times (Devlin 2006). In this way, the role of the state is not to protect citizens' rights or to regulate the economy but to manage crises in a decentralized and flexible fashion. In everyday practice, this approach means that vendors have to endure harassment from various city agents (police, health department inspectors) and face (seemingly) arbitrary enforcement of rules. For activists, this situation meant mobilizing vendors to target specific actors (for example, particular police precincts) rather than seeking an overall change in enforcement policy.

In 2006, I met three of the founders of Esperanza del Barrio at a leadership development workshop organized by the Mexican consulate and Baruch College. Regular police harassment had motivated the founders to organize. In some cases, police had confiscated merchandise because the vendors lacked licenses.

The affected vendors unsuccessfully sought help from a well-known Mexican organization. Then they continued meeting regularly to attempt to solve some of the problems they were facing. In 2003 this informal gathering of women vendors became a nonprofit organization whose initial goals included the removal of the cap on pushcart permits, the removal of the requirement that vendor licenses would be granted only to those who could prove their legal immigration status, the creation of business-development workshops, the improvement of relations with the police, and the strengthening of the community of vendors (Jones 2008). Some of Esperanza del Barrio's first public actions were related to the issue of law enforcement, one of the most pressing challenges the women faced on an everyday basis.

Indeed, dealing with the police has been reported as one of the main challenges faced by both licensed and unlicensed street vendors. The SVP (2006) found that 23 percent of vendors described police harassment as a particular problem. Contact with the police can entail getting a ticket for violating one of the myriad vending regulations, getting arrested for operating without a license, and having merchandise confiscated. Some women vendors have reported being fondled during police searches. In addition, vendors reported that the police commonly engage in racial discrimination.[4] The criminalization of vendors is often combined with racialization of vendors and xenophobia. According to one woman street vendor, "September 11 brought many tragedies, and one of them was the closing of factories. We were left without work, and as a consequence Latinos are the most affected. We are discriminated against because we do not speak English. The police intimidate us, they mistreat us when we are arrested. We ask the Police Department to protect us because we are more afraid of the police than of delinquents. We want [the police] to stop confiscating our merchandise. Enough of so much harassment! We are workers trying to survive and support our families" (El Proyecto de los Trabajadores Latinoamericanos 2003 [translated by author]).

This was the situation that Esperanza del Barrio members encountered in the early 2000s. Street vendors in East Harlem are mainly Latina women and seem to be specifically targeted by the police. They started meeting with officials in the Twenty-third and Twenty-fifth Precincts in East Harlem. Three women from Esperanza del Barrio recalled for me their dealings with the police department. At first, officials at police precincts in El Barrio did not want to deal with the women. Time and much public pressure in the form of direct action were required before they were able to have a dialogue with precinct officials. Ideas of respect and recognition stood at the center of these women vendors' organizing campaign and demands.

Vendors organized numerous rallies in the neighborhood, demanding an end to police abuse. In one such event in August 2003, women vendors, their children, and supporters rallied in the streets of El Barrio to denounce police abuse. Vendors argued that the police were targeting area vendors, most of whom where Latina immigrants, using excessive force, searching them without cause, and even using racial slurs. Pedro Prado Ocegueda, the pastor of a Baptist church who supported the vendors, noted, "They are human beings that are doing as much as they can to survive and we ask you [the police] in the name of the Lord to be respectful and have respect for the women as human beings" (D'Ambrosi 2003). Challenging police abuse of street vendors was framed as involving recognition, or the right to have rights—that is, the right to be recognized as a full human being and a member of the political community. Vendors were denouncing not just police brutality but also the denial of their personhood by the use of force. Flor Bermúdez, director of Esperanza del Barrio at the time, noted, "We are not asking the police to stop enforcing the law but to enforce it in a respectful manner" (D'Ambrosi 2003). Vendors' demands here went beyond issues of legality/illegality, because the notion of respect is not inscribed in legal codes but emanates from a particular notion of personhood. The view that women were engaged in this kind of work to support their families was also common. In relying on traditional gender constructs of women's role as reproducers, women were challenging police abuse.[5]

The NYPD responded to the women's argument with a written statement: "The Police Department is addressing complaints from legitimate business owners and community leaders regarding street-vending violations. The law is being enforced as it exists" (D'Ambrosi 2003). In using such language, the police placed the demands of some citizens within the realm of the legal while denying the same status to the vendors' claims, which do not fit neatly within notions of legality. Rather, their claims are closely related to what Rosaldo and Flores (1997) have termed cultural citizenship. According to these authors, claiming *respeto* represents "an effort to claim space within a public sphere" (70). In demanding respect for their persons and their work, street vendors were claiming a space within the political community. Simultaneously, vendors were drawing on notions of free enterprise and gender to demand that the police let them earn a living and fulfill their roles as protectors of their families.

Esperanza del Barrio continued engaging with the chiefs of police at the Twenty-third and Twenty-fifth Precincts through what organizers termed accountability meetings to ensure fair treatment for vendors (Jones 2008). Although these meetings eventually led to declines in police harassment and in the number of tickets vendors received, these gains were not easily achieved. The women vendors believed that over time, they gained recognition and respect from police at these precincts. In addition, participation in a coalition, New York Street Vendors United (NYSVU), enabled members of Esperanza to continue pressing for an end to police abuse. NYSVU formed a subcommittee to address the issue of police harassment. In one of its first actions, the group planned a March 24, 2004, meeting with police officials to be held at the Our Lady of Pompeii Church (SVP 2004). The public hearing with NYPD officials brought 150 vendors of multiple ethnicities to testify regarding police abuse. NYPD officials consequently agreed to meet regularly with coalition members to improve police-vendor relations (Jones 2008).

Reform Efforts

In the media, organizations and politicians continue to construe street vending as immigrants' entrance into New York's economy and a step toward reaching the "American Dream." According to one report, "Wave after wave of new arrivals have used the New York City streets as their entry into the American marketplace. Today's peddler is tomorrow's Macy's or Sears" (Task Force on General Vendors 1991, 4). This view of street vendors conforms to a prevalent narrative of the nation where hard work and determination can bring anyone from rags to riches, the Horatio Alger story all over again. In advocating for street vendors, this narrative, however, is articulated through dominant neoliberal ideologies that emphasize entrepreneurship as the basis of citizenship. Advocates of street vendors have found in neoliberal notions of self-sufficiency and limited state intervention a common ground from which to articulate their demands and gain support of policy makers and politicians.

Since the number of licenses was capped in 1979, it has become virtually impossible to obtain a license.[6] Thus, thousands of vendors work without proper licenses or permits. One woman member of Esperanza del Barrio's board of directors noted that "our primary struggle is to obtain permits for [food] carts, because currently we have our personal licenses,[7] and sometimes the police take it into consideration that we already have the personal license, but sometimes they don't. So the Department of Health, they give us tickets, and they are very expensive. . . . We adapt a supermarket cart to sell . . . we cannot have adequate carts according to the [Department of Health] because we don't have the [cart permits]" (Moda 2008a [translated by author]).

Thus, vendors currently can meet certain requirements but not others. Vending can at times be considered a legal activity (because she has a personal license) and at other times can be considered illegal (because she lacks the proper cart permit). Vendors are situated in a space where notions of legality and illegality are rather fluid and subject to interpretation by different authorities. What this means for the everyday experience of vendors is a sense of arbitrary enforcement, but, this environment, however, corresponds to the city's neoliberal agenda of targeted and flexible enforcement (Devlin 2006). From its beginnings, Esperanza del Barrio has focused on increasing the number of street vendor licenses and permits. Group members realized that in addition to direct action, they had to create a broad-based alliance of vendors and work directly with city council members, whose support Esperanza sought (Jones 2008).

On May 1, April 7, and October 9, 2003, the city's Committee on Consumer Affairs held hearings on the issue of vending, with testimony from employees of the Department of Consumer Affairs and the Criminal Justice Coordinator's office as well as members of vendor advocacy organizations, including Esperanza del Barrio, and business organizations. Vendors also testified. Consumer affairs commissioner Gretchen Dykstra handed onions to council members, explaining that "the city's vending laws are like an onion. It has many layers, and after a while, one can't help but cry" (New York City Council 2003). Everyone seemed to agree that something had to be done. The question was, what?

At one of these hearings, the SVP and Food Vendors' Union Local 169 presented a document, "Ten Ways to Improve Street Vending in New York" (Food Vendors Union and Street Vendor Project 2003). The document presents street vending as a hallmark of New York City, providing jobs for members of marginalized communities (for example, immigrants, people of color, and disabled veterans) and a service to those who live and work there. The document portrays vendors as "entrepreneurs who ask for nothing more than the opportunity to earn a decent living on the street." Its first recommendation is increasing the number of general licenses and food cart permits on that grounds that "removing the cap on licenses and permits . . . could create thousands of jobs during a time of rising unemployment and government cutbacks. By bringing vendors into the system, the city will also collect millions in additional tax revenue."[8] Although the document did not represent the views of all organizations, many actors soon adopted its language. First, the document acknowledges the retrenchment of the state in the provision of unemployment and social services. Rather than challenging the government's reduced role, however, the document calls for limited state involvement in regulating the market by removing caps on licenses and permits. Removing the state from regulating the market will create jobs. The document relies on the image of the self-reliant, self-sufficient individual entrepreneur who only needs an "opportunity" to pursue her/his goals. The state is expected to be a regulator of individuals (not the market) by bringing vendors into the system. This way of framing vending appeals to a neoliberal subject but leaves unquestioned both the retrenchment of the state and the regulation of individuals.

At an October 9, 2003, City Council hearing, vendors announced the formation of the NYSVU. The original members of the coalition included the SVP, the Coalition against Anti-Asian Violence, Organizing Communities, the Latin American Workers Project, Esperanza del Barrio, the Bangladeshi Vendors Association, and the New York Immigration Coalition. The NYSVU's three main objectives were greater access to licenses and permits, freedom from police harassment, and more space for vending (SVP 2003). On November 18, about three hundred street vendors of different nationalities met at Judson Memorial Church in Washington Square for the first Street Vendors Convention (Errol 2003).

After the convention, NYSVU members met every week to discuss their strategy. Two subcommittees were created to address issues related to changing vending laws and to address police harassment. The legislative subcommittee of the NYSVU established a five-point proposal that would guide its work and included removing the licensing cap, modifying the twenty-foot rule for setting up shop to ten feet,[9] opening all streets to vending, leaving six feet between vendors, reducing fines by the Environmental Control Board from a maximum of $1,000 to $150, and training police officers regarding street-vending laws (SVP 2004).

INTRO 621

On April 12, 2005, City Council members Philip Reed, John Liu, and Miguel Martinez presented Introductory Bill 621 (Intro 621), "A Local Law to Amend the Administrative Code of the City of New York, in Relation to Vendors." Intro 621 sought a comprehensive reform to the administrative code that regulates street vending.[10] According to Intro 621, one of the problems with the system at that time was the categorization of vendors and the application of different rules and regulations to each category, which made it difficult for both vendors and law enforcement to understand such rules. Intro 621 proposed establishing regulations that would apply to all categories of vendors, increasing uniformity of restrictions, enforcement, and penalties.

Intro 621 also proposed opening all streets to vending except those surrounding the World Trade Center site, but limited the number of vendors per block face to three, with those spots distributed according to vendor category. The measure further proposed raising the number of general vendor licenses from 853 to 2,000 by 2007, in accordance with one of the vendor advocates' central demands. A numbering scheme would determine vendors' priority to any spot in dispute, always giving disabled veterans priority over all other vendors. The bill introduced a fingerprinting requirement to obtain general and food vendor licenses.[11] First Amendment vendors would be licensed, although no restrictions would be imposed on the number of such licenses in keeping with a 1996 court ruling (*Bery et al. v. City of New York*), and these vendors would be subject to the same rules and regulations as general vendors.

Intro 621's various provisions generated opposition among artists, small business organizations, street vendors, and their supporters. At the first hearing, protests took place outside City Hall. Artists claimed that the bill would infringe on their First Amendment rights. Small business organizations feared that members would be hurt by the increase in the number of vendors. Vendor advocates were concerned about the proposed fingerprinting requirements for licensing (Kludt 2005). A representative of the New York Civil Liberties Union (2005) testified at the second hearing that the group was "concerned that the proposed regulatory scheme would unduly burden protected First Amendment activity. The bill also raises privacy and due process concerns." Intro 621 ultimately did not become law.

INTRO 491-A

During the second hearing on Intro 621, council member Charles Barron and others introduced Intro 491, which proposed amending the requirement that non–U.S. citizens applying for vendor licenses show proof of authorization to work in the country. On June 9, 2005, the Committee on Consumer Affairs heard testimony on Intro 491-A (an amended version of Intro 491), which proposed that "no City employee ask about the immigration or citizenship status of any person applying for a general or food vending license. Additionally, the language of the local law would make it clear that information about an applicant's immigration status would have no effect on the application or renewal of a vendor's license" (New York Committee on Consumer Affairs 2005a). Vendor advocates supported the bill since estimates showed that the number of vendors not authorized to work in the United States was as high as six thousand (Sanchis 2005).

According to the document, Intro 491-A was "designed to assist vendors to successfully integrate into the City's business community and encourage equality and entrepreneurship." The committee passed the bill that same day, with Barron noting, "This piece of legislation speaks to the importance and value of immigrants, who work so hard to participate equally in the business sector of New York City, thereby increasing their chances of upward social mobility" (New York City Council 2005). According to Barron, the measure would help "to cease the harassment of vendors who contribute so much to our City's economy" (New York City Council 2005). Two weeks later, the City Council voted 42–8 in favor of Intro 491-A, and on July 11, Mayor Michael Bloomberg signed the bill into Local Law 66 (New York City Office of the City Clerk 2005).

In analyzing the text of Local Law 66, it is possible to see its articulation through various discourses. In framing the argument, the text refers to New York's history as an entrance for immigrants and their contributions to the city's cultural and economic vibrancy. This narrative is intertwined with neoliberal discourses. "The City's interests in community health and safety, administrative efficiency and justice are best served by a system where immigrants can more fully participate in the City's economy and services. . . . Allowing access to the City's services will help vendors successfully integrate into the City's small business system and cooperate with City agencies. Vendors will provide more revenue to the City through licensing fees and taxation. . . . More residents will be able to support their families. . . . By providing greater access to vending licenses, the City will encourage equality and entrepreneurship" (New York City Office of the City Clerk 2005).

In immigrants' participation as economic subjects and integration into the business sector, the state finds immigration status irrelevant. As Leitner and her colleagues (2006) have noted, one of the features of neoliberal governmentality is in its unidirectional character. That is, institutions and individuals ought make their activities visible to the state for calculation. The government services to which the law refers are not those associated with what T. H. Marshall (1950) called social rights, which were meant to guarantee full exercise of citizenship in the face of structural inequality. Rather, state services take the form of regulatory and monitoring technologies—in this case, licenses and permits. The integration of immigrants called for by the text is integration into the state's economy and regulatory system, not into the city's civic and political life. In this context, equality does not refer to a structural equality or equality before the law; it is equality to enter and participate in the market.

The language of Local Law 66 contrasts with the director of Esperanza del Barrio's view of the triumph. She told a reporter that the measure represented "a great step to eliminate discrimination and to achieve greater equality in the street vendor industry. The current laws are anti-immigrant and discriminatory" (Bonilla 2005 [translated by author]). Her comment refers to structural inequality inscribed within the law. Contrasting the law's language with the director's comment demonstrates how organizers often articulate their advocacy efforts through various discursive terrains and illustrates how organizers' demands can be translated into policies and laws.

Conclusion

After several years of direct action, coalition building, and negotiation, street vendor advocates such as Esperanza del Barrio had gained some limited ground. A dialogue with law enforcement had been initiated, constituting the first step toward ending harassment. This opening represented a form of recognition on the part of law enforcement of the existence of a group of individuals who for the most part worked without state sanction. In this way, law enforcement was forced to deal with the presence of nonlicensed vendors and to decide on the treatment of these individuals. Vendors had made harassment a public issue, and although no citywide policy was pursued to address this matter, it nonetheless drew public attention.

The passage of Local Law 66 represented another accomplishment for Esperanza del Barrio. Regardless of their immigration status, vendors could file for licenses. The caps on licenses and permits, however, limited the practical effects of this gain. Vendors continue to work under a convoluted set of regulations and remain subject to potential harassment by authorities. The Department of Health recently adopted a policy of pouring bleach on the food of street vendors who have allegedly violated health codes. It is not difficult to see the symbolic nature of this act. At one level, bleaching the food prepared by vendors is a direct commentary on the perceived unsanitary nature of the food sold in the streets. At another level, this act can be seen as a state disciplinary technology intended to sanitize the streets of its less-than-desirable elements. In light of the fact that the majority of vendors, at least in El Barrio, are Latina women, the practice acquires gendered and racialized dimensions. Vendors have resisted this practice. At the February 2009 march, one slogan we chanted as we crossed the Brooklyn Bridge was, "¡Cloro, no! ¡Permisos, sí! [Bleach, no! Permits, yes!]."

After the defeat of Intro 621, Esperanza del Barrio has continued to work with City Council members, particularly Barron. On May 10, 2006, a new proposal to address the issue of licensing and permits was introduced.[12] Intro 324 proposed increasing the number of general licenses to 15,000 and the number of food cart permits to 25,000; once these limits were reached, further increases would take place in increments of 5 percent per year. Esperanza del Barrio fully backed the new initiative, but it has proceeded slowly. The Committee on Consumer Affairs and the Committee on Immigration did not hold hearings on the bill until 2008, more than two years after the measure was introduced, and no final action has yet been taken. Like earlier efforts at reform, Intro 324 relies on neoliberal understandings of vendors, the role of the government, and the market and appeals to constructions of a neoliberal subject—self-sufficient and self-reliant—as well as conventional narratives of the nation.

According to Intro 324, "street vendors are an indelible part of New York City's cultural landscape," and vending has been a way for immigrants to enter and contribute to the city's economy, offering people "the opportunity to be self-sufficient, work legitimately, and support their families." Vending is a way for many to realize the American Dream through hard work. Street vending is a permanent part of New York City's public space, part of the city's uniqueness and by extension its competitive advantage. The measure also points out that "the currently excessively low caps also artificially prevent the free market from functioning efficiently, and allow some to capture unfair economic windfalls by monopolizing the limited number of licenses." Here the state is viewed as obstructing the workings of the market. In this view, the intervention of the state in regulating free enterprise creates distortions (that is, monopolies). By referring to the state's intervention as "artificial," the bill naturalizes the market. Thus, removing licensing caps—that is, the state intervention—is the only way to restore the market's "natural" order. Thus discursively, the imposition of caps on licensing and permits was challenged using one of the tenets of neoliberalism: minimum state intervention in regulating the market.

Esperanza del Barrio continues to use ideas of respect, dignity, and rights to frame its work. The organization has restarted its direct-action strategies to push forward the initiative. The coalition spearheaded by this organization, which worked to highlight street vending in the city years ago, is weaker now, however. Internal disagreements have arisen about how to frame the issue. To appeal to a larger public, particularly elected officials, activists often rely on neoliberal discourses, which seem to provide a common ground from which to negotiate. By adopting neoliberal ideas of self-sufficiency and limited government intervention, activists have challenged local government policies and achieved some of their objectives (Changfoot 2007). But what is lost in the translation?

As I stood in the cold, shouting along with street vendors in front of City Hall, I started to become more and more aware of every utterance. "¡Consejales escuchar! ¡Trabajar no es ilegal! [Council Members, listen! Working is not illegal!]." "¡Aquí y allá! ¡El trabajo es dignidad! [Here and there! Work is dignity!]." I pondered how the ideas of dignity and respect so central to grassroots organizing would be translated into laws, how these claims will be articulated through prevalent neoliberal discourse, shaping and being shaped by its meaning.

Notes

1. For example, the microfinance movement emphasizes lending to women so that they can achieve economic self-sufficiency, independence, and empowerment by developing small enterprises.

2. Two main limitations of this survey are the small sample size (one hundred persons surveyed), and the geographic concentration of the survey to Lower Manhattan.

3. In many cases, vendors sublet or rent food carts or work for people or companies who have licenses or permits. Anecdotal evidence indicates that this practice is often a family or co-ethnic affair, but I have not found a study documenting this practice.

4. Regulating the use of public spaces in particular neighborhoods has often been inscribed within existing racializations of those same neighborhoods. The Giuliani administration's displacement of street vendors in Harlem in the mid-1990s is an instance in which authorities targeted a particular area where the majority of vendors are African American or African (Austin 1994; Hicks 1994a, b).

5. There is a long history in Latin America of women's use of traditional gender constructs to challenge the state. See Radcliffe and Westwood 1993.

6. Some estimates are that it would take about twenty-five years for a person to obtain a license through official channels.

7. There are no limits on the number of food vendor licenses, but food vendors also must obtain cart permits.

8. The other nine recommendations included ending forfeitures, abolishing the review panel (a panel in charge of determining which streets are closed to vending), reforming enforcement, streamlining the bureaucracy, writing a manual with vending rules and regulations, legalizing craft vending, improving adjudication, abolishing bidding for vending spots in city parks, and providing small business assistance.

9. Vendors are not allowed to set their stands within twenty feet of any doorway.

10. The Committee on Consumer Affairs held hearings on Intro 621 on April 18, and May 4, 2005.

11. Other provisions of Intro 621 included changes to the existing penalty scheme, renewal of food vendor licenses if all violations were remedied, and notification of the location of goods confiscated by the police.

12. Intro 324 was presented by Barron and supported by council members Letitia James, Melissa Mark-Viverito, Rosie Mendez, Diana Reyna, Larry B. Seabrook, Kendall Stewart, Darlene Miguel Martinez, Darlene Mealy, Sara M. Gonzales, and Maria del Carmen Arroyo.

References

Austin, Regina. 1994. "'An Honest Living': Street Vendors, Municipal Regulation, and the Black Public Sphere." *Yale Law Journal* 103:2119–31.

Bluestone, Daniel M. 1991. "'The Pushcart Evil': Peddlers, Merchants, and New York City's Streets, 1890–1940." *Journal of Urban History* 18:68–92.

Bonilla, Santiago. 2005. "Indocumentados con licencia." *Diario Hoy,* June 24. Available at http://www.telemundo47.com/noticias/4649411/detail.html. Accessed December 2008.

Brenner, Neil, and Nik Theodore. 2002. "Cities and the Geographies of 'Actually Existing Neoliberalism.'" *Antipode* 34:349–79.

Changfoot, Nadine. 2007. "Local Activism and Neoliberalism: Performing Neoliberal Citizenship as Resistance." *Studies in Political Economy* 80:129–49.

D'Ambrosi, Ronald. 2003. "Protesters Urge Respect for Vendors." *New York Sun,* August 27.

Devlin, Ryan. 2006. *Illegibility, Uncertainty, and the Management of Street Vending in New York City.* Breslauer Symposium, University of California International and Area Studies. Working Paper 16.

El Proyecto de los Trabajadores Latinoamericanos. 2003. "Vendedores ambulantes preparan actividad por el día del trabajo." Press Release. April 30.

Errol, Louis. 2003. "Cry of the Vendors." *New York Sun,* November 18.

Esperanza del Barrio. 2009. "Esperanza del Barrio to March for Vendor Rights." Press Release.

Food Vendors Union and Street Vendor Project. 2003. *Street Vendors Unite! Recommendations for Improving the Regulations on Street Vending in New York City.* New York: Food Vendors Union and Street Vendor Project.

Hackworth, Jason. 2007. *The Neoliberal City: Governance, Ideology, and Development in American Urbanism*. Ithaca: Cornell University Press.

Hicks, Jonathan P. 1994a. "Police Move Street Vendors in Harlem." *New York Times*, October 18.

———. 1994b. "Vendors' Ouster and Boycott Divide." *New York Times*, October 23.

Jones, Jessica M. 2008. "'Pa'lante, Pa'lante, Vendedores Ambulantes': Post-Citizenship Politics, Neoliberal Exceptions, and the Political Mobilization of Undocumented Immigrants." Bachelor of Arts thesis, Wesleyan University.

Kludt, Amanda. 2005. "Street Artists and Vendors Aren't Sold on New Bill." *Villager*, April 20–26.

Leitner, Helga, Eric S. Sheppard, Kristin Sziarto, and Anant Maringanti. 2006. "Contesting Urban Futures: Decentering Neoliberalism." In *Contesting Neoliberalism: Urban Frontiers*, ed. H. Leitner, J. Peck, and E. S. Sheppard. New York: Guilford.

Liu, Ya-Ting. 2007. *A Right to Vend: New Policy Framework for Fostering Street Based Entrepreneurs in New York City*. Cambridge: MIT Department of Urban Studies and Planning.

Marshall, Thomas H. 1950. *Citizenship and Social Class, and Other Essays*. Cambridge: Cambridge University Press.

McAdam, Doug, John D. McCarthy, and Mayer N. Zald. 1996. *Comparative Perspectives on Social Movements: Political Opportunities, Mobilizing Structures, and Cultural Framings*. New York: Cambridge University Press.

Mills, Mary Beth. 2003. "Gender and Inequality in the Global Labor Force." *Annual Review of Anthropology* 32:41–62.

Moda, Luiseño. 2008a. *Esperanza del Barrio: Grassroots Organizing*. Video recording by Luiseño Moda. Available at http://www.vimeo.com/3392068.

———. 2008b. *Esperanza del Barrio: Saliendo Adelante*. Available at www.vimeo.com/2846861.

New York City Administrative Code. 1985. *Title 20: Consumer Affairs, § 20–452(b)*. Available at http://24.97.137.100/nyc/AdCode/entered.htm.

New York City Council. 2003. "Committee Hears Testimony from City, Vendors at Oversight Hearing on Vendor Licensing and Regulations." Press Release. April 7.

———. 2005. "Committee Votes to Protect Immigrant Vendors." Press Release. June 9.

New York City Office of the City Clerk. 2005. *Local Laws of the City of New York for the Year 2005: No. 66.*

New York Civil Liberties Union. 2005. "Testimony of Irum Taqi on Behalf of the New York Civil Liberties Union before the New York City Council Committee on Consumer Affairs Regarding Int. 621, In Relation to the Regulation of Street Vendors." Available at www.nyclu.org/node/753.

New York Committee on Consumer Affairs. 2003. "General Vendor Licensing and Regulation." Briefing Paper. April 7.

———. 2005a. "Introductory Bill No. 491-A: A Local Law to Amend the Administrative Code of the City of New York, in Relation to the License Application Requirements for General and Food Street Vendors." June 9.

———. 2005b. "Introductory Bill No. 621: A Local Law to Amend the Administrative Code of the City of New York, in Relation to Vendors." May 4.

———. 2008. Introductory Bill No. 665: A Local Law to Amend the Administrative Code of the City of New York, in Relation to Green Carts. February 26.

New York Committee on Consumer Affairs and Committee on Immigration. 2008. "Hearing on Intro. 324-A, Intro. 419, Intro. 828, Intro. 830, Intro. 834, Intro. 846." November 14.

Ong, Aihwa. 1987. *Spirits of Resistance and Capitalist Discipline: Factory Women in Malaysia.* Albany: State University of New York Press.

———. 2006. *Neoliberalism as Exception: Mutations in Citizenship and Sovereignty.* Durham: Duke University Press.

Radcliffe, S. A., and S. Westwood. 1993. *"Viva": Women and Popular Protest in Latin America.* London: Routledge.

Rosaldo, Renato, and William V. Flores. 1997. "Identity, Conflict, and Evolving Latino Communities: Cultural Citizenship in San Jose, California." In *Latino Cultural Citizenship: Claiming Identity, Space, and Rights,* ed. W. V. Flores and R. Benmayor, 57–96. Boston: Beacon.

Sanchis, Eva. 2005. "Reconocen a los ambulantes inmigrantes." *El Diario,* June 24.

Sites, William. 2003. *Remaking New York: Primitive Globalization and the Politics of Urban Community.* Minneapolis: University of Minnesota Press.

———. 2006. "Contesting the Neoliberal City? Theories of Neoliberalism and Urban Strategies of Contention." In *Contesting Neoliberalism: Urban Frontiers,* ed. H. Leitner, J. Peck, and E. S. Sheppard, 116–38. New York: Guilford.

Street Vendor Project of the Urban Justice Center. 2003. "Vendors, Groups Announce New Coalition." *Vendor Newsletter,* Fall, 2.

———. 2004. "Update from Street Vendors United." *Vendor Newsletter,* Winter, 2.

———. 2006. *Peddling Uphill: A Report on the Conditions of Street Vendors in New York City.* New York: Street Vendor Project of the Urban Justice Center.

Tarrow, Sidney G. 1998. *Power in Movement: Social Movements and Contentious Politics.* New York: Cambridge University Press.

Task Force on General Vendors. 1991. *Balancing Safety and Sales on City Streets: A Report on Street Vending to Mayor David N. Dinkins.* New York: Department of Consumer Affairs.

Zlolniski, Christian. 2006. *Janitors, Street Vendors, and Activists: The Lives of Mexican Immigrants in Silicon Valley.* Berkeley: University of California Press.

2

Elvira Arellano and the Struggles of Low-Wage Undocumented Latina Immigrant Women

MAURA TORO-MORN

For more than a year, Elvira Arellano, a Mexican immigrant, took sanctuary from deportation at the Adalberto United Methodist Church in the heart of Chicago's Puerto Rican community. Before leaving for Los Angeles she issued the following statement: "My decision to enter sanctuary was a decision based on my faith, my love and responsibility for my son Saúl and my commitment to my people and the 4 million other U.S. citizen children like Saúl. [We] must take action in September to stop the raids, deportations and separations of families that are destroying millions of lives across this country. . . . We cannot just sit by and watch our families be torn to pieces for the next three years. I cannot."

On August 15, 2007, she traveled to Los Angeles to attend an immigration rally; four days later, she was apprehended by U.S. Immigration and Customs Enforcement (ICE) and deported to Tijuana, Mexico, where her son, Saúl, then eight years old and a U.S. citizen by birth, eventually reunited with her. Her story represents a significant chapter in the era of ICE apprehensions, deportations, and abuses. In January 2009 the Department of Homeland Security admitted that since the turn of the twenty-first century, the agency had deported more than one hundred thousand parents of children who were U.S. citizens by birth. The criminalization of undocumented immigrants has led to a dramatic increase in the number of Latinos sentenced to prison terms in U.S. federal courts. According to Mark Hugo Lopez and Michael T. Light (2009, 1), researchers with the Pew Hispanic Center, in 2007 "Latinos accounted for 40% of all sentenced federal offenders—more than triple their share (13%) of the total U.S. adult population." Moreover, "immigration offenses represented nearly one-quarter (24%) of all federal convictions, up from just 7% in 1991. Among those sentenced for immigration offenses in 2007, 80% were Hispanic."

Seventy-five percent of those sentenced for immigration crimes were convicted of entering the United States unlawfully or of residing in the country without authorization. But Elvira Arellano's story is more than just statistics.

This chapter examines how neoliberal globalization processes—in both Mexico and the United States—have shaped Elvira Arellano's life choices, her agency, and politicization as an undocumented immigrant woman. In Mexico neoliberal reforms resulted in the end of her employment by a small firm. Internal migration has become a strategy used by Mexican men and women—and many other Latinas/os across the hemisphere—to deal with unemployment, job displacement, and expanding family responsibilities engendered by globalization and neoliberal policies. She migrated to Tijuana, an important point of entry to the United States for both documented and undocumented immigrants through the 1990s. Arellano, like other working daughters and mothers in Mexico, supported herself and her parents through *maquila* work, but such employment proved unreliable. After one unsuccessful attempt, she crossed the Tijuana–San Diego border without documentation in 1997.

In the United States, Arellano followed the migrant trail of low-wage work, which took her to the state of Washington. She eventually moved to Chicago, where she had friends who could help her secure more reliable work. Historically, immigrant women have played an important role as a source of cheap labor in a range of unskilled low-wage occupations in the U.S. labor market (Chang 2000; Glenn 1992). Arellano became part of this labor force when she was recruited to work as part of a cleaning crew at O'Hare Airport. In Chicago she lived under the radar, a term anthropologist Ruth Gomberg-Muñoz (2010) found popular among undocumented workers in the city. From Chicago, Arellano supported herself, her son, and her family in Mexico by working two jobs in the low-wage service industry. For an immigrant woman such as Arellano, working and living without documentation meant living with the fear of being apprehended, deported, and separated from her son.

In the aftermath of the September 11, 2001, attacks on the World Trade Center and the Pentagon, the U.S. neoliberal state reorganized and (re)consolidated a border-control-enforcement bureaucracy accompanied by sweeping immigration and law enforcement policies that resulted in the widespread persecution, criminalization, and deportation of low-wage undocumented workers like Arellano. The social and political consequences of these changes can be seen in the number of work raids, criminal prosecution of immigrants and their families through new anti-immigrant legislation at the state level, vilification of undocumented immigrants in the popular media, and an increase in hate crimes committed against Latinos. Arellano was arrested for working with a false Social Security number and asked to report for deportation in 2006. She defied her deportation order and immigration authorities by seeking refuge at the Adalberto United Methodist Church. This act placed her at the center of the ensuing controversy about immigration reform and the status of undocumented immigrants whose children are U.S. citizens, a controversy that continues today and that has escalated to significant proportions. Defying ICE authorities by seeking refuge in a church became a strategy to avoid deportation and a public challenge to a neoliberal state that perceived her as a "criminal." This chapter is based on an interview I conducted with Elvira Arellano during her time in sanctuary and on written materials I subsequently collected. The interview took place in Spanish, and unless otherwise noted, I provided all translations of key quotes.

This work builds on the theoretical and empirical insights generated by such prominent feminist scholars as Bonnie Thornton Dill, Patricia Hill Collins, Evelyn Nakano Glenn, Grace Chang, Mary Romero, and Chandra Mohanty. Collectively, this body of work has analyzed the historical conditions of women workers across several nationality groups and in different historical locations. Together, they offer a powerful narrative that recognizes the vulnerabilities that women of various racial groups and in various historical locations face as workers and mothers. This chapter builds on these authors' work by drawing on the theoretical constructs they have proposed and by using the historical insights they have generated to produce a new narrative that now includes the vulnerabilities of recent Latina immigrant women workers.

Elvira Arellano: Worker, Mother, Immigrant, Activist

Arellano's life story must be viewed in the larger context of the history of Mexican labor migration to the United States and the changing labor needs of the U.S. economy. Gomberg-Muñoz (2010, 27) writes that "there is a common misconception that labor migration from Mexico to the United States is fueled by a lack of economic development in Mexico." She adds, "the movement of labor and goods across the U.S.-Mexico border is and has been an essential component of the economic development of both nations." Arellano's migration was connected to the monetary crisis that hit Mexico in the aftermath of the enactment of the North American Free Trade Agreement (NAFTA), "a program that was supposed to relieve Mexico's debts and allow the economy to modernize and prosper" (Gomberg-Muñoz 2010, 33). In the 1990s, like millions of Mexican men and women, Arellano was drawn to the border region in search of work to support her family, and when choices there became limited, she made yet another move, across the United States–Mexico border. In so doing, she became one of the estimated 4.9 million Mexicans in the 1990s who crossed the United States–Mexico border without documentation (Nevins 2002, 6). As a working mother in Chicago, she struggled to provide for herself and her family by working two jobs in the low-wage service industry. The challenges of securing child care and the dangers of working without documentation added a great deal of stress and difficulty to her life. As a religious woman, she turned to her faith and church for support. In addition, her transnational family networks—in particular, her frequent phone conversations with her mother—also provided her with another form of support. By December 2002, ICE work raids had become commonplace in Chicago and throughout Illinois. Her arrest and eventual court-ordered deportation led to a series of events that would catapult her to the center of the most significant national and international social issues of the decade: the plight of the estimated 12 million undocumented men and women in the United States and their families. Arellano embodies the plight of immigrant working mothers with United States–born children who work and contribute to their communities and families but lack state legitimacy to live productively and with their families intact. Her son, Saúl Arellano, became her advocate and the voice of yet another significant collectivity: United States–born and –raised children of undocumented parents. Elvira Arellano was deported in 2007, but she was not silenced. She continues to fight for immigrant rights from Michoacán, Mexico, where she resides with her son, thereby adding a transnational dimension to this new wave of the immigrant rights movement.

From Working Daughter to Working Mother

Elvira Arellano talked about how turmoil in the Mexican economy affected her employer:

> Between 1995 and 1996, the Mexican peso was devaluated, and that is when our beloved country faced a huge economic crisis. Then, I worked as a secretary in a store that was more like a supermarket. The front of the store was the supermarket, at the other side there was a pharmacy, and behind there was a hotel. I wrote checks for the delivery trucks, those that delivered merchandise to the store. I also deposited money in the bank and was in charge of keeping the books. There were four owners—four brothers. I had more contact with the oldest of the four brothers. I saw the situation that they faced up close. I saw how they counted the money to cover the store's expenses and the money was not enough. I saw how they had to borrow from their cousins and other family members to cover basic necessities. . . . It was a very difficult situation. I went to the bank with my boss, and at the bank they did not want to accept one of the checks he had deposited. It was all very sad to see my boss crying. He was walking in front of me, visibly upset and aware that soon the bank would be coming after his properties. Eventually, they lost it all.

The crisis Elvira's employer faced was rooted in the contradictions of Mexico's "economic miracle," the popular name of Mexico's economic restructuring program. A full analysis of this particular period of Mexican economic history is beyond the scope of this chapter, but the larger outlines of this crisis are relevant to understanding what happened to Elvira and to millions of other working-class Mexicans during the economic crisis. It is also even more significant that this economic crisis took place in the aftermath of NAFTA's passage, which consolidated deregulation of investment flows and the reduction of transaction costs for investors (Morales 1997).

According to political scientist Remonda Bensabat Kleinberg (1999, 80), the manipulation of the Mexican peso was an important strategy used by President Carlos Salinas Gortiari (1988–94) to benefit international capital and create the perception of "Mexico as a stable investment environment" to ensure NAFTA's passage. But the administration of Salinas's successor, Ernesto Zedillo (1994–2000), could not sustain the peso's value, and its devaluation had profound effects for Mexicans across social classes. In Kleinberg's (1999, 81) words, the Mexican "economy literally shrank by 7 percent; . . . unemployment rose to 40 percent and inflation surpassed 12 percent . . . [I]nterest rates reached 80–105 percent, tripling payment loans, and mortgages. . . . [D]omestic sales of products fell by 70 percent." For ___ss Mexicans the peso's devaluation meant increasing hardship because ___ummeted (Kopinak 1995). According to Kathryn Kopinak (1995, 36): ___ buying power of the minimum wage was a third of what it had been ___, the Zedillo administration continued to promote neoliberal policies by bringing the private sector into the recovery process.

Arellano's actions exemplify one way Mexicans dealt with the crisis and labor disruptions engendered by neoliberal globalization in Mexico. Faced with unemployment, she moved to Tijuana, along the United States–Mexico border, where she thought her employment prospects might be better. This impression resulted from what is known as "the NAFTA effect" (Morales 1997), whereby expectations rose amid popular promises by speculators and popular commentators in Mexico and the United States about the social and economic gains facilitated by the treaty. Indeed, Arellano moved to Tijuana naively expecting to find work as a secretary, but doing so proved difficult because she didn't have the required skills for such a job in that area of the country. Aware of her deficiencies, Arellano instead turned to work on an assembly line, a choice made by many women who must provide for themselves and their families:

> It was hard looking for work as a secretary. To work as a secretary in Tijuana, you must know computer skills and English, since it is so close to the U.S.-Mexico border. I also had to have a visa in the event that my job demanded crossing the

U.S.-Mexico border and running errands in the U.S. I didn't have those skills and was not eligible for those kinds of jobs. It took me about a month to find work, and that was when I decided to apply for work in one of the factories. I can't remember the name of the first factory where I worked, but they made electronics.

After eight months there, she moved to another factory, where she inspected car stereos. Eventually, however, work in the *maquila* industry proved too unstable and difficult.

Feminists have studied the gendered organization and inequalities found in the *maquila* industry (Fernandez-Kelly 1983; Kopinak 1995; Muñoz 2008; Salzinger 2003; Tiano 1994). Arellano's experiences are very much in keeping with the collective experiences of Mexican women workers in the *maquila* industry. Maria P. Fernández-Kelly's classic ethnographic work, *For We Are Sold, I and My People: Women and Industry in Mexico's Frontier* (1983) first exposed the deplorable and oppressive conditions Mexican women faced in the *maquilas*. Women still constitute the majority of *maquila* workers and are still hired to fill "the least skilled and poorest paying jobs" (Kopinak 1995, 31). Further, recent scholarly work offers greater insight into the gender segmentation women have faced on the shop floor and how these labor practices shape women's wages (Muñoz 2008; Salzinger 2003). More recently, Leslie Salinger's critically acclaimed sociological study, *Genders in Production: Making Workers in Mexico's Global Factories* (2003), challenges the prevailing notion of women workers as "docile daughters," proposing instead that docility is very much produced and contested on the shop floor through managerial rhetorical practices, and that women engaged in some of these practices as a way to cope.

Crossing the Tijuana/San Diego Border

In the 1990s, the Tijuana–San Diego transborder urban zone became a paradoxical site. On one hand, NAFTA brought an increasing integration of markets and commerce; on the other hand, the area became what Joseph Nevins (2002, 144) described as a "landscape of control and fear over immigration." The Tijuana–San Diego border area became and remains among the most trafficked by cars and people in the world. For example, in 1999, more than 2 million commercial trucks passed through the three commercial ports of Calexico, Otay Mesa, and San Ysidro. On any given day, more than forty thousand people crossed the Tijuana–San Diego border, some to work in San Diego, others to work in the maquiladoras on the Mexican side of the border (Nevins 2002, 6). This economic and social integration took place alongside the increase in the number of people crossing the border without proper documentation. In the 1990s, the boundary fence between Tijuana and San Diego had gaping holes, and casual observers could watch as migrants and smugglers gathered each afternoon. At night, unauthorized immigrants could be seen engaging in "Banzai runs" along the highway (Nevins 2002, 3). Nevins (53) observes that "the scale of unauthorized immigration across the boundary in the San Diego area increased at a far greater rate than the capacity of U.S. authorities . . . to police the boundary." The state response to the perception that the border was out of control came in the form of Operation Gatekeeper, President Bill Clinton's legislative effort to strengthen border control and presumably stop the perceived flood of undocumented immigrants.

The larger context for understanding the development of Operation Gatekeeper and the events following 9/11 can be found in the contradictions of neoliberal globalization for the nation-state. Nevins (2002, 176) points out that "globalization often leads to an increase in demands upon the state to protect the nation." In this case, Operation Gatekeeper "helped to create the category 'illegal' through the construction of the boundary and the expansion of the INS's enforcement capacity" (11). This became a new way of seeing the nation, its sovereignty in the global era, and its citizens in relation to immigrants, many of whom were now perceived as undesirable because of their illegality" but remained desirable as a source of cheap labor. Arellano's initial border-crossing experience took place in this context.

More than ten years after Operation Gatekeeper, the Tijuana–San Diego area has become one of the most heavily policed borders in the world. One unfortunate consequence of Operation Gatekeeper and the post-9/11 militarization of the border has been the creation of alternative crossing routes through the California and Arizona deserts, which have one of the most dangerous crossings in the world because of the high incidence of immigrant deaths as a consequence of dehydration, famine, and violence. The American Civil Liberties Union has described the situation as an "international humanitarian crisis" (Gomberg-Muñoz 2010, 52). More than five thousand migrants are estimated to have died along the United States–Mexico border (Gomberg-Muñoz 2010, 52).

Arellano was aware that because she was a single female, crossing the border entailed serious risks, and she feared for her safety. The business of migrant crossing using coyotes was and remains a male-dominated space. Women traveling alone have been assaulted, robbed, and raped. She attempted to cross the border using fraudulent documents but was arrested, detained, and sent back. In the context of Operation Gatekeeper, her actions constituted a federal felony and became part of her permanent record. With the help of a coyote, she crossed the border on foot with three other women. A friend picked her up in California and flew her to the state of Washington, where other friends were waiting to take her to work the following day.

Immigrant communities and networks are important for the survival and adaptation of newer immigrants (Menjivar 2000). Immigrant networks provide initial help with finding a job, an apartment, clothing, and all the necessities that soften the initial cultural shock and ease the incorporation processes. For example, Gomberg-Muñoz (2010, 53) reports that in Chicago, undocumented immigrant men help one another with expenses, including sponsoring the passage of at least one of their friends or family members. In other words, a relative or friend in the United States would send money to pay a coyote to smuggle a friend or relative into the country, adding an economic dimension to familial bonds.

Immigration is a "gender transformative odyssey" (Hondagneu-Sotelo and Avila 1997, 552), and immigrant communities are places where men's and women's lives are transformed. Within months of her arrival, Arellano became involved with a man: "I arrived in September and by October I was involved with Saúl's father. We started going out, and a relationship developed, after a while our relationship was not what I expected, but I was pregnant by then. I was three months pregnant when the relationship ended. I assumed complete responsibility for our baby. I decided to have the baby by myself without his help."

Scholars have begun to document the impact of migration on the sexual lives of immigrant men and women, but little is known about what happens to immigrant women such as Arellano who become involved with immigrant men and become single mothers in the aftermath of their migration. Jennifer S. Hirsh's ethnography, *A Courtship after Marriage: Sexuality and Love in Mexican Transnational Families* (2003), describes how cultural practices relating to marriage and sexuality are redefined in the context of migration. Growing evidence also indicates that immigrant men become involved with women in the United States while simultaneously married and supporting a family in Mexico (Hondagneu-Sotelo 1994).

Arellano subsequently left Washington for Chicago, where she had more support and where her son's godparents lived, but it is not clear to what extent the situation with Saúl's father contributed to her decision. Arellano had no idea what to expect until she came to the city: "I thought it was a small place, but when I got here, I saw how big it was."

Balancing Work and Family in Chicago

Life in Chicago was not easy for a working mother. Some of the problems Arellano encountered stemmed from her undocumented status, her limited knowledge of the language, and her lack of resources. Other problems she faced stemmed from the difficulties of work in the service industry, where there is no job security, the pay is low, and the hours interfere with mothering responsibilities. According to

Arellano, "It was very hard! First I tried searching for work through temporary employment agencies. Sometimes they had work, [but] other times there was nothing, and I needed something more reliable. It was hard because I had to pay rent, buy food, and other things. I also had to pay for Saúl's care and the car payment. I had to buy a car. It cost me about eight hundred dollars, but it was always breaking down. Every month I had to pay so much to get it fixed. It was so hard! I started selling cosmetics, but sometimes people would not pay me."

She found steady work on an evening cleaning crew at O'Hare Airport. She worked with three other women and earned the minimum wage, $6.50 per hour, forty hours per week. Her $900 pretax monthly salary qualified her as a member of the ever-growing working poor population. One frequently cited misconception about undocumented workers is that they do not pay income taxes. The reality is that many undocumented immigrants pay income taxes; moreover, those who work using fraudulent Social Security numbers, as Arellano did, contribute to the system but will not benefit from it. To make ends meet, she supplemented her O'Hare cleaning work by cleaning private homes during the day.

Sociologist Evelyn Nakano Glenn (1992, 20) has coined the term "institutional service work" to describe the "heavy, dirty, back-room chores of cooking and serving food in restaurants and cafeterias, cleaning rooms in hotels and office buildings, and caring for the elderly and ill in hospitals and nursing homes." Arellano performed what Glenn described as lower-level public reproductive work. Although some labor laws have been introduced to protect workers in a variety of occupations, including the service industry, undocumented women remain vulnerable because of their status. Gomberg-Muñoz (2010) has identified a paradox underlying the lives of Mexican undocumented workers in the United States. On one hand, Arellano and others in this category have become the iconic image of illegality. In the media, this image is accompanied by tropes that stigmatize these immigrants as stealing citizen jobs, taking and abusing state resources, being uneducated, and threatening communities around the nation. In the case of immigrant women, the trope of using children as "anchor babies" has become more pronounced. Yet on the other hand, undocumented Mexicans are also perceived as desirable and hardworking low-wage workers. Lost in the paradox is the reality of their lives—how working-class Latinos/as have lived productive lives at the bottom of the labor market.

As a working woman, one of the most significant problems Arellano and other mothers face is securing child care (Toro-Morn 2008). It is paradoxical that most Latinas today are employed as nannies, domestics, and live-in maids yet cannot find care for their own children. In fact, many working mothers leave their children behind in their countries of origin. Feminist scholars Pierrette Hondagneu-Sotelo and Ernestine Ávila (1997) argue that transnational mothering practices represent one way to resolve the contradictions of economic restructuring for working mothers. At first, Arellano's cousins watched her son, "but once they told me that they could not care for him precisely at the moment that I was leaving for work. I could not afford to miss work. On that particular day I found myself so frustrated, I went to the street to ask my neighbors if they knew of anyone who could care for Saúl. I could not think clearly. Eventually, I asked another cousin who lived nearby with his son. I asked [the cousin] to care for [Saúl] for me as a favor because I was off the following day and I was going to look for more reliable care."

Arellano eventually moved in with her cousin, who was able to provide both more reliable care for Saúl and affordable housing, and her life became more settled. Nevertheless, Arellano still found the situation difficult and dealt with her problems in part through prayer and regular church attendance—in her words, putting herself in "the hands of God." Arellano also frequently sought her mother's help and advice over the telephone. A few days before her arrest, she told her mother that she was thinking about returning to Mexico: "The situation I was facing was very difficult, and I said to myself, 'I am barely making it here. . . . I cannot save; I have so many expenses.' I wanted to save to buy a better car, but the money was not enough. But my mom reminded me that one of the reasons I had decided to stay is because I wanted Saúl to have a chance in life, a good education." Like Arellano, women have historically sought the advice and support of other women in their families and communities. Moreover, the transnational literature maintains that the burden of emotional and financial support for the family falls on Latina immigrant women.

The Criminalization of Low-Wage Undocumented Workers in the Aftermath of 9/11

Historically, U.S. border patrol and enforcement was conducted by the Immigration and Naturalization Service (INS), a branch of the Department of Justice (Nevins 2002), popularly known among Latino immigrant communities as La Migra. Feminist scholar Grace Chang (2000, 110) argues that the INS and the border patrol have functioned "to regulate the flow of immigration to ensure a reserve army of labor." In other words, the INS sought not to stop immigrants from crossing the border but simply to regulate the flow in order to make sure that whenever there were labor shortages in certain industries, labor needs were met (Hu-DeHart 2007, 93). Evidence of this tacit understanding can be seen in that immigration and boundary enforcement were not national political issues in elections until recently. Peter Andreas (2009, 9) points out that during the 1990s, policing the border went from "one of the most neglected areas of federal law enforcement to one of the most politically popular." The "escalation of immigration control," a term Andreas coined to describe this particular period of border enforcement, coincides with the implementation of Operation Gatekeeper and the (re)construction of undocumented immigrants as "illegals." Before 9/11, "illegal aliens" were perceived as a threat to the social fabric of the nation (Andreas 2009; Nevins 2002). After 9/11, "illegal aliens" were perceived to be a threat to nation-states around the world (De Genova and Peutz 2010).

The attacks on the World Trade Center and Pentagon radically altered the administration of border enforcement. After 9/11 the INS was removed from the Department of Justice and placed in the newly created Department of Homeland Security as ICE. Further, the neoliberal state intensified the rhetoric already apparent as part of Operation Gatekeeper. Now, not only were immigrants undesirable because of their "illegality," which made them an affront to the nation-state, but working without documentation became one of the new tropes of the fight against terrorism. A national narrative regarding immigrants, their children, and their families became absurdly vicious, as evidenced by the rants of public figures such as Lou Dobbs and Bill O'Reilly. The 1990s "landscape of control and fear" reached an unprecedented climax in the first decade of the twenty-first century. Work raids became common practice, resulting in record numbers of deportations of men and women whose only "crime" had been working and living in the United States without proper documentation.

The morning of September 11, 2001, Arellano saw the news and called her employer, wondering whether she should report to work. She was told that most flights had been canceled and that she did not have to come to O'Hare. After flights had resumed, she was called back to work. By December 2002, airports had been identified as a primary site that needed added security measures, and ICE launched Operation Tarmac, a sweeping program that investigated anyone who worked at transportation facilities and for companies that provided support services to the transportation industry. Arellano was caught because she was using a fraudulent Social Security number. Not only was doing so a federal felony, but because she worked at a major airport, in the aftermath of 9/11 it was a particularly serious offense.

Her recollection of her arrest and detention illustrates Arellano's fortitude and resiliency as a working mother facing a government bureaucracy that perceived her as a criminal. She faced the *mano dura* (strong hand) of the neoliberal state yet spoke truth to power, in particular with regard to the care of her son:

> The federals arrived on the morning of December 16, 2002, around eight o'clock. I was asleep when they knocked on the door. They knocked on the door and said, "It is the police." Honestly, I thought that they were the local police because earlier in the summer someone had been killed in the neighborhood. My cousin said that the police had come around asking questions. I thought it was them again.

When I opened the door, they showed me their IDs. They asked me, "Are you Elvira Arellano?" I replied, "Yes." They asked me if I had firearms in the house and who else lived here with me. I replied, "No, I live here alone with my son, who is asleep." . . . "Do you have an ID?" they asked. I said "Yes, but I have it in the car." They asked me to get it. That's when they came inside . . . and I noticed that they had a big folder with all my documents. That's when I realized what was happening!

They asked me if I had anyone who could care for my son because I had to go with them. I told them that I was alone. They asked about my cousin, what time did he arrive.

I knew that my cousins did not have any papers, so I got worried about them, too. I did not want them getting caught in the middle of this. To myself, I prayed to God that [the cousins] would not show up. It must have been God's hand, because they usually worked through the night and tended to come home in the mornings, but they had been laid off for a week and were not home that morning. It must have been God's hand at work.

ICE officials asked me if my cousin could care for my son when he got home. I told them that I did not want to leave him behind because sometimes my cousin does not come home after work. They asked, "Where does he work?" I replied, "A construction site, but I don't know where it is." I had to lie because I did not want them to get caught up, too.

I asked them if [Saúl] could come with me. They replied, "No, he cannot go with you." I asked them, "Who is going to care for my son, Saúl?" They replied, "The state will take care of him." I told them the state does not support my son. I am his sole supporter. I work to provide for his care and for all his needs. Neither the state nor the government supports my son!

Arellano was clearly uncomfortable, but her son's well-being remained important to her, and she stated forcefully to ICE officials that she alone had provided for him.

She then woke up Saúl and explained to him what was happening. She was concerned about the impact on him and tried to soften his impression by telling him that the officials were from her work and that she had to go with them to answer some questions about work. But Saúl understood what was happening and became visibly upset: "He saw all the men in the room, and he started to cry, 'Who are they, Mami? What are they doing here?' I hugged him and told him, 'Don't ask me any more questions, please. We have to go. They are people from work. I will have to go to work with them. When I get back I will get your favorite treat from McDonalds.' I was trying to calm him down and reassure him that I was coming back." One of her neighbors realized what was happening and offered to help with Saúl, but Arellano declined to leave him with a stranger and instead arranged to have ICE officials stop at the home of her babysitter, who agreed to take care of the child.

After Arellano dropped off Saúl, ICE officials attempted to restrain her, but she resisted. They insisted it was official procedure. Suddenly, she realized the severity of her problems. She told the officials, "I am not a delinquent! I had not robbed or killed anyone and that I was going of my own accord, that I was not going to run away." They replied that it was "standard procedure." They added, "'We did not do it before because your son was with you.'" Elvira added, "When they reminded me about my son, I felt the magnitude of what was happening to me, and I started to cry. I was worried about Saulito, us, and our future. What would happen to us? But then I realized, 'I am not going to let them see me cry; I am not a criminal!'"

She was taken to a detention center with other women. There, she said, "It was a sea of tears." She asked some of her fellow detainees to pray with her, saying, "God is great, and he is going to help us. We have to face what's ahead knowing that God is with us. We must be grateful because that we are alive, we are healthy, and very soon we are going to reunite with our families." She was eventually released with a deportation order and subsequently sought help from Pueblo sin Fronteras, a Chicago community organization that offers assistance to immigrants.

Chicago had already become a major space for political protests and massive marches calling attention to the plight of undocumented immigrant families and communities and challenging the punitive anti-immigrant legislation that had been considered in Congress (Pallares and Flores-González 2010). According to sociologist Amalia Pallares (2010), Arellano participated in these marches. Further, Mayor Richard Daley declared Chicago a sanctuary city. When Arellano became the first immigrant woman to seek refuge in a local church, she reenergized the sanctuary movement across the United States. Pallares writes that Arellano "invoked not only an ancient tradition of churches harboring those seeking a safe haven but the more recent U.S. political experience of churches providing sanctuary to Central American refugees fleeing persecution during the 1980s" (221). Overnight, Elvira became an immigrant rights activist, and her son became the face and voice of a significant population in the Latino community: U.S. citizens with undocumented mothers. Her case received coverage from both Spanish- and English-language media outlets.

Sanctuary, Mobilization, and Deportation: Becoming the Voice of a Community

Elvira declared: "My decision to enter sanctuary was a decision based on my faith; my love and responsibility for my son, Saúl; and my commitment to my people and the 4 million other U.S. citizen children like Saúl." Arellano's analysis of her situation thus included not only an awareness of her individual predicament as a working mother but also her growing awareness that she was not alone, that she was part of a larger community facing very similar problems. She and Saúl lived for more than a year on the second floor of the Adalberto United Methodist Church. Sanctuary represented both an individual and collective strategy to work within the political establishment to stop Arellano's imminent deportation and to help other families in a similar predicament.

Arellano became the symbol of inter-Latino political solidarity (De Genova 2010, 6). Chicago's Annual Puerto Rican People's Parade nominated Arellano and her son as honorary grand marshals in 2007. The parade traveled down Division Street, the heart of Chicago's Puerto Rican community, and when the marchers passed the church, Arellano waved a Puerto Rican flag.

While in sanctuary, Arellano and her son became celebrities. Both were interviewed and photographed for English-language newspapers (including the *Chicago Tribune* and *New York Times*) and local and national TV stations. Spanish-language newspapers (*Hoy* and *La Raza*) and television stations (Univision and Telemundo) also capitalized on her story. Her story was covered throughout the Americas, appearing in newspapers in Argentina, Puerto Rico, and Brazil. She appeared frequently on Univision's *Primer Impacto* and other news shows. She was also the subject of numerous letters to the editor and editorials that appeared in newspapers around the nation. At the same time, she received hate mail, and anti-immigration-rights activists picketed the church.

In the summer of 2007, she left sanctuary to attend an immigrants' rights rally in Los Angeles. On August 19, 2007, after she spoke at a rally at Our Lady Queen of Angels, a Roman Catholic church, ICE agents stopped her car and arrested her. She was eventually deported to Tijuana, Mexico. Her decision to leave sanctuary was based on the realization that much had changed in terms of the political landscape that promised immigration reform. As she put it, "I could not sit here, arms crossed, observing while other working mothers like myself and millions of children like Saúl faced the destruction of their families. I had to do what I could to tell the Democratic Party that immigration must not die, because we are not dead. I had to force this country to see what they did not want to see."

Her decision to leave sanctuary can be interpreted in many ways. After immigration reform had failed, a political amnesty or the passage of a new immigration bill would not occur until after the November 2009 national elections, if then. Leaving sanctuary could also be seen as a test of ICE's seriousness about her deportation given her newfound celebrity status. At another level, Arellano's civil case was pending in the U.S. courts, and the deportation of Saúl, a U.S. citizen, would complicate the case. In the end, leaving sanctuary must have been a bittersweet moment for Arellano.

Since his 2008 election as U.S. president, Barack Obama's promise to push for immigration reform has so far proved hollow, and Congress has recently failed to pass a measure that would have provided a path to citizenship for undocu mented immigrants. But Arellano's deportation has extended the political space of the immigration rights movement transnationally. In Mexico, she remains an activist for deported Mexicans and their families, many of whom are, like Saúl, U.S. citizens by birth. She travels around the country and speaks publicly about immigration issues. She has appealed to the Mexican congress several times on behalf of immigrants and immigration policy. She has found her return to Mexico difficult, because even her modest standard of living in the United States was easier on her and her son. She sees Saúl as part of a larger struggle that has not ended with their deportation, and in the summer of 2010, he traveled to Washington, D.C., to speak about his plight and that of his mother. The forced relocation of a U.S. citizen raises many questions about the legal protections accorded by citizenship rights.

Discussion and Concluding Thoughts

Elvira Arellano's story embodies—in the fullest extent of this word—the labor disruptions that are a central organizing theme of this volume. Her name, face, and body become a historical instance—a biographical moment—of how economic restructuring in Mexico, accompanied by neoliberal reforms, resulted in her internal displacement and eventual border-crossing experience. As neoliberal globalization policies deepened in Mexico, women from a variety of social classes and indigenous groups have become immigrants (see Flores-González and Gomberg-Muñoz, this volume). When cast against the backdrop of women's experiences in the hemisphere, Arellano's story deepens our knowledge of how single women integrated into the migration process become agents of change in their families and communities.

Latina women across the hemisphere have borne the brunt of colonization, the transition from agriculture to industrial capitalism, and now globalization. Theoretically, we know that the gendered construction of reproductive labor lies at the center of women's oppression (Glenn 1992). We also know that the racial division of reproductive labor is central to understanding the experiences of women of color—whether in their home countries or abroad—and is the source of hierarchy and interdependence among women. The thread that connects the experiences of women like Arellano to her sisters in Latin America and the Caribbean is the role that they have played and continue to play in the racial and gender construction of reproductive labor. The indigenous woman who migrates to Lima, Peru, to do domestic work has much in common with Arellano, an undocumented immigrant woman in the global North. Historically, these working daughters eventually become working mothers as they form families of their own and become more permanent workers in the economy. As working mothers, whether in their countries of origin or host communities, women face a range of problems and difficulties that stem from deeply patriarchal and racialized ideologies about women's role and worth.

The liberal and neoliberal states have not been kind to working daughters and working mothers throughout the hemisphere. The liberal state engendered by the American Revolution and the ideals of democracy institutionalized a legal and social system based on patriarchal authority. Sociologist Bonnie Thornton Dill (1998, 428) points out that early in U.S. history, "white women had few legal rights as women, [but] they were protected through public forms of patriarchy that acknowledged and supported their family roles of wives, mothers, and daughters because they were vital instruments for building American society." By contrast, racial and ethnic women experienced the oppressions of a patriarchal state and were "denied the protections and buffering of a patriarchal family." African American, Mexican American, and Asian American women were not protected by the cult of domesticity and became part of America's reproductive labor force. As a collectivity, racial and ethnic women were "treated primarily as individual units of labor rather than as members of family groups." Such women "labored to maintain, sustain, stabilize, and reproduce their families while working in both the public (productive) and private (reproductive) spheres." As is still the case today, the state did not protect them either as workers or as mothers.

The historical continuities in the labor disruptions faced by black women, Latinas, and other immigrant women under the current neoliberal regime are striking. Today, Mexican women workers such as Arellano continue to be seen as individual units of labor under the auspices of globalization. They continue to be left out of protective policies as laborers and as mothers. As racialized and gendered units of labor, women find themselves in a host of occupations that are underpaid, undervalued, and exploitative. This segment of the Latino community continues to be vilified as lawbreakers, as workers who steal jobs from Americans, and as criminals because of their undocumented status.

Arellano's story is also significant because of the power of her voice and the organized collective action that she has sparked. Her courage to speak on behalf of working mothers who are facing deportation or have been deported connects her to the role that women have played as agents of change throughout Latin America and the Caribbean. She has gained a place in the annals of Latino history alongside women such as Comandanta Ester of the Zapatista Army of National Liberation in Chiapas; Rigoberta Menchú, the Guatemalan human rights activist who won the Nobel Peace Prize in 1992; and Puerto Rican nationalist Lolita Lebrón.

References

Andreas, Peter. 2009. *Border Games: Policing the U.S.-Mexico Divide.* 2nd ed. Ithaca: Cornell University Press.

Chang, Grace. 2000. *Disposable Domestics: Immigrant Women Workers in the Global Economy.* Boston: South End.

De Genova, Nicholas. 2010. "The Deportation Regime: Sovereignty, Space, and the Freedom of Movement." In *The Deportation Regime: Sovereignty, Space, and the Freedom of Movement,* ed. N. De Genova and N. Peutz, 33–67. Durham: Duke University Press.

De Genova, Nicholas, and Nathalie Peutz, eds. 2010. *The Deportation Regime: Sovereignty, Space, and the Freedom of Movement.* Durham: Duke University Press.

Dill, Bonnie Thornton. 1988. "Our Mother's Grief: Racial Ethnic Women and the Maintenance of Families." *Journal of Family History* 13:415–31.

Fernández-Kelly, María Patricia. 1983. *For We Are Sold, I and My People: Women and Industry in Mexico's Frontier.* Albany: State University of New York Press.

Glenn, Evelyn Nakano. 1992. "From Servitude to Service Work: Historical Continuities in the Racial Division of Paid Reproductive Labor." *Signs* 18:1–43.

Gomberg-Muñoz, Ruth. 2010. *Labor and Legality: An Ethnography of a Mexican Immigrant Network.* New York: Oxford University Press.

Hirsh, Jennifer S. 2003. *A Courtship after Marriage: Sexuality and Love in Mexican Transnational Families.* Berkeley: University of California Press.

Hondagneu-Sotelo, Pierrette, and Ernestine Avila. 1997. "'I'm Here, but I'm There': The Meanings of Latina Transnational Motherhood." *Gender and Society* 11:548–71.

Hu-DeHart, Evelyn. 2007. "Surviving Globalization: Immigrant Women Workers in Late Capitalist America." In *Women's Labor in the Global Economy: Speaking in Multiple Voices,* ed. Sharon Harley, 85–102. New Brunswick, N.J.: Rutgers University Press.

Kleinberg, Remonda Bensabat. 1999. "Strategic Alliances: State–Business Relations in Mexico under Neo-Liberalism and Crisis." *Bulletin of Latin American Research* 18:71–87.

Kopinak, Kathryn. 1995. "Gender as a Vehicle for the Subordination of Women Maquiladora Workers in Mexico." *Latin American Perspectives* 22:30–48.

Lopez, Mark Hugo, and Michael T. Light. 2009. *A Rising Share: Hispanics and Federal Crime.* Washington, D.C.: Pew Hispanic Center.

Menjívar, Cecilia. 2000. *Fragmented Ties: Salvadoran Immigrant Networks in America.* Berkeley: University of California Press.

Morales, Isidro. 1997. "The Mexican Crisis and the Weakness of the NAFTA Consensus." *Annals of the American Academy of Political and Social Science* 550:130–52.

Muñoz, Carolina Bank. 2008. *Transnational Tortillas: Race, Gender, and Shop-Floor Politics in Mexico and the United States.* Ithaca: Cornell University Press.

Nevins, Joseph. 2002. *Operation Gatekeeper: The Rise of the "Illegal Alien" and the Making of the U.S.-Mexico Boundary.* New York: Routledge.

Pallares, Amalia. 2010. "Representing 'La Familia': Family Separation and Immigrant Activism." In *¡Marcha! Latino Chicago and the Immigrant Rights Movement,* ed. A. Pallares and N. Flores-González, 215–36. Urbana: University of Illinois Press.

Pallares, Amalia, and Nilda Flores-González, eds. 2010. ¡Marcha! Latino Chicago and the Immigrant Rights Movement. Urbana: University of Illinois Press.

Salzinger, Leslie. 2003. Genders in Production: Making Workers in Mexico's Global Factories. Berkeley: University of California Press.

Tiano, S. 1994. Patriarchy on the Line: Labor, Gender, and Ideology in the Mexican Maquila Industry. Philadelphia: Temple University Press.

Toro-Morn, Maura. 2008. "Beyond Gender Dichotomies: Toward a New Century of Gendered Scholarship in the Latina/o Experience." In Latinas/os in the United States: Changing the Face of America, ed. R. Rodriguez, R. Saenz, and C. Menjivar, 277–93. New York: Springer.

3

This Is What Trafficking Looks Like

GRACE CHANG

In the twelve years since the passage of the landmark Trafficking Victims Protection Act (TVPA) of 2000,[1] U.S. journalists, policymakers, heads of state, and celebrities have been greatly preoccupied with the issue identified in both popular and policy discourses as "sex trafficking." This phenomenon is defined under U.S. federal law as "migration achieved through force or deception for the purpose of coerced prostitution or sex slavery" (TVPA 2000). Addressing the United Nations General Assembly in September 2003, U.S. president George W. Bush identified sex trafficking as "a special evil" and declared that "those who create these victims and profit from their suffering must be severely punished." He went on to say that "those who patronize this industry debase themselves and deepen the misery of others. And governments that tolerate this trade are tolerating a form of slavery" (Allen 2003).

Similarly, one U.S. columnist, Nicholas Kristof, virtually made his career for years out of his journalistic exploits with two Cambodian girls working in brothels, beginning his *New York Times* series with an article called "Girls for Sale" (2004a). Kristof bought time with two girls to interview them on film. He paid off their debts to the brothel owners and returned the girls to their families, giving each of them one hundred U.S. dollars to start small businesses. He then did follow-up visits and stories on each of the girls the following year.[2] One, Srey Neth, had "successfully" reintegrated into her village and become a hairstylist through training provided by a foreign nongovernmental organization (NGO). Kristof (2004c) lamented that the other girl he "freed," Srey Mom, had returned to the brothel from which he had helped her escape.

Throughout the series, Kristof portrayed the plight of the girls as stemming from defects of Cambodian culture and the low valuation of girls within it rather than as having systemic roots in the global economy that led to the girls' vulnerability to trafficking or exploitative labor in the first place. In one column (2004b), he observed, "It is precisely this low status of peasant girls in so many countries that makes the trafficking possible. For trafficking to be wiped out, the low status of girls needs to be addressed through literacy and job programs and other efforts." When Kristof was flooded with letters from American do-gooders asking if he could "free one for me too" if they were to send him one hundred dollars, he admonished readers that this is not the solution (2004d). Instead, he praised the Bush administration for "leading the way" on trafficking and proposed that trafficking could only be eradicated when the low social value and self-esteem of girls in Cambodian society is changed through literacy and job programs.

Students and others who have responded to my critiques of Kristof have suggested that he at least saved these two girls from this terrible plight. Yet this rescue ideology is precisely the problem with Kristof's and the U.S. government's approach to the issue, framing trafficking as a problem stemming from Third World people's backward cultures and need for U.S. influence, instruction, and intervention. The dominant framework conveniently and commonly propagated by media, government, and celebrities casts the United States and figures such as Kristof as saviors and Third World girls and women as helpless, ignorant, and sometimes ungrateful victims saved by these U.S. heroes.[3]

These rescue narratives completely obscure the real roots of human trafficking as a direct result of the forces of globalization. Analyses of trafficking as a consequence of the deliberate underdevelopment of Third World nations and the destruction of their subsistence economies and social service structures through neoliberal policies imposed by First World institutions are largely lost in these oversimplified, sensationalized, and sexualized accounts.[4] Thus, in U.S. media and public policy discourses alike, the term *human trafficking* has become synonymous with *sex trafficking*, which in turn has been equated with *sexual slavery* and *prostitution*.[5] Human trafficking, while primarily an issue of coerced labor— and only sometimes involving coerced movement—is rarely seen as a labor issue and instead has been framed almost exclusively as an issue of "violence against women" or "sexual violence." Yet in human trafficking cases, the labor involved is not predominantly sexual labor, nor does the violence encompassed in trafficking always involve sexual violence. The many forms of violence enacted in human trafficking can include racial and sexual violence (and in these instances, not just against women) as well as economic and imperialist violence.

The Anti–Sex Trafficking Agenda

It is not surprising that the American public has missed these dimensions of human trafficking when we consider the kinds of stories that have dominated our media. Furthermore, the federal government has focused its efforts almost exclusively on prosecution within the sex industry, even though the TVPA (2000) defines "severe forms of trafficking" as (1) sex trafficking in which a commercial sex act is induced by force, fraud, or coercion or in which the person induced to perform such an act is under eighteen; or (2) the recruitment, harboring, transportation, provision, or obtaining of a person for labor or services through the use of force, fraud, or coercion, and for the purpose of subjecting that person to involuntary servitude, peonage, debt bondage, or slavery.

In my research in the United States, I observe that the second clause of the TVPA could be applied to every sector where immigrant workers are present or prevalent and where their immigration status and lack of worker rights makes them vulnerable to extreme labor exploitation. The federal government, however, has focused almost exclusively on the first clause, concentrating its efforts on prosecution within the sex industry, so that "sex trafficking" has come to be equated with commercial sex. Specific language in the law emphasizes that "whether or not an activity falls under the definition of trafficking depends not only on the type of work victims are made to do, but also on the use of force, fraud, or coercion to obtain or maintain that work" (U.S. Department of Labor 2002). Yet while the law defines trafficking as including labor exploitation in many sectors other than commercial sex, the state agenda has been strictly imposed to focus almost exclusively on so-called "sex trafficking."

While the focus on sex trafficking is not codified in the letter of the law, it is very much cemented in practice. The focus on sex trafficking is enforced globally through restrictions that require any foreign NGOs receiving U.S. federal funding to take the "anti-prostitution pledge," attesting in a grant application, a grant agreement, or both that they "do not promote, support or advocate the legalization or practice of prostitution" (22 U.S.C. § 7110 [g] [1] [2006]). This approach, of course, reinforces the criminalization of prostitution and implies the criminalization of any activity in support of or serving sex workers. Even though two court rulings have struck down the "anti-prostitution pledge" for U.S. NGOs, U.S. advocates report that groups that do not comply with the anti–sex trafficking agenda are rapidly defunded, just as they are internationally (Chang and Kim 2007, 322). Instead, new groups, often church-based organizations with little or no experience in antitrafficking work or providing services to survivors of trafficking, are being funded. Internationally, the requirement has forced some NGOs to forego U.S. funding in order to continue to provide essential services to sex workers or has led others to discontinue these services in favor of continued funding (Chang and Kim 2007). Furthermore, it has made many U.S. organizations fighting for sex worker rights, domestic worker rights, and migrant labor rights generally reluctant to associate with one another, let alone collaborate.

The natural alliances between, for example, migrant sex workers and domestic workers struggling for their rights have been made risky.

In an effort to address this issue, I organized a conference held at the University of California–Santa Barbara in October 2009, called "This Is What Trafficking Looks Like." Participants included trafficking victims/survivors; scholars; attorneys; organizers from the immigrant rights movement across the industries of domestic work, farm work and sex work; and antitrafficking advocates and service providers. The gathering focused on three questions: (1) What is the true agenda behind the emphasis on sex trafficking in the U.S. government antitrafficking regime? (2) What are the actual functions and impacts of antitrafficking policy and practice? (3) How do we develop a response that truly serves the needs and rights of trafficking survivors and immigrant workers in general, across labor sectors?

Participants noted that we shared a common frustration, spanning the various approaches in our work to combat trafficking: a great focus in the U.S. public, media, and policy on the issue of "sex trafficking" and virtually no awareness or concern for other dimensions of human trafficking. Antitrafficking advocates from across sectors and across the country consistently report that in the United States, people are most commonly trafficked in and into domestic work, not sex work. For example, one of the foremost antitrafficking organizations in the country, the Coalition to Abolish Slavery and Trafficking (CAST), has reported that among the trafficking survivors they have served in the Los Angeles region, 40 percent were in domestic work, 17 percent in factory work, 17 percent in sex work, 13 percent in restaurant work, and 13 percent in servile marriage (McMahon and CAST 2002).[6] The antitrafficking and immigrant worker rights advocates I have interviewed over the past decade have consistently corroborated this pattern, noting the predominance of trafficking in the domestic work sector and the neglect of this sector in U.S. government antitrafficking responses (see Chang and Kim 2007, 325).

Moreover, many advocates have observed that the U.S. government itself has produced two documents questioning the effectiveness of antitrafficking policy and practice here and abroad in the past decade. The U.S. General Accounting Office (GAO) issued a 2006 report that stated, "More than 5 years after the passage of the landmark antitrafficking law, the U.S. government has not developed a coordinated strategy to combat trafficking in persons abroad . . . or evaluated its programs to determine whether projects are achieving the desired outcomes." Furthermore, the GAO study noted, "There is also a considerable discrepancy between the numbers of observed and estimated victims of human trafficking." Similarly, in the same year, the U.S. Department of State (2006, 53) observed that within the United States, since the passage of the TVPA, between 2000 and

2005, only 616 people benefited from the TVPA through receipt of a T-visa.[7] This number contrasts starkly with the estimates of 50,000 people per year trafficked within and into the United States, reported by the State Department in 2002 and since bandied about in the media and policy circles (Miko and Park 2002; see also Jahic and Finckenauer 2005).

Advocates say that the huge gap can easily be accounted for by including people who are trafficked in industries other than the sex industry but who are not recognized or treated as trafficking victims under the law or in public sentiment. Innumerable cases of immigrant domestic workers suffering gross labor abuses fit the legal definition of severe trafficking yet are not acknowledged or addressed as trafficking cases. Immigrant rights, domestic worker, and sex worker rights advocates and antitrafficking advocates point to the many real victims of trafficking who are not protected or served under the current policy.[8]

This Is What Trafficking Looks Like

The testimony of members and organizers from two groups at the 2009 forum on trafficking revealed the challenges of working and organizing for labor rights under the current antitrafficking regime, so narrowly focused on the sex industry. Cita Brodsky (2009), member and gender rights community organizer for the DAMAYAN Migrant Workers Association, a group of Filipina migrant domestic workers organizing for better conditions in this sector in New York, shared her story as a survivor of trafficking:

> I was brought here in 1997 by my diplomat employer. As a domestic worker of a diplomat, I started [working] pretty early and ended very late at night—that's roughly from fifteen to seventeen hours a day. I was paid per month $430 dollars. You can just imagine, you can do the math, but roughly it's seventy cents an hour.

Brodsky added that many members of the community of domestic workers in New York City and the New Jersey area face abuse because their work is not covered by many labor protections, and thus they are "really isolated and very vulnerable to dehumanization and abuse from employers."

Brodsky (2009) also offered an analysis of the large-scale migration and exploitation of women like herself, largely educated and skilled, leaving the Philippines to join the ranks of migrant Filipina domestic workers worldwide: "There are 4,300 immigrants every day, and 70 percent of them are women, and they end up as domestic workers. In our analysis, it's modern-day slavery, and it's also the [effect of] globalization on the poor countries and people [migrating] usually to fill the low-wage [jobs] around the world, [providing] the cheap labor of the imperialist nations, like the U.S." Brodsky called for holding the Philippine government accountable, particularly for its practice of maintaining and fueling official labor export programs. These generate remittances that enable the Philippine government to make the interest payments on the foreign debt to countries such as the United States; according to Brodsky, "every day there are 4,300 Filipino people that go to 196 countries to migrate. And this forced migration of the people is supporting the Philippine economy. . . . Based on our research, if the migrant workers all stop sending money, the Philippine government will collapse.[9] That's how we understand trafficking."[10]

DAMAYAN has recently completed a report, based on a six-year community-based participatory action research project providing data and analyses to illuminate how globalization and imperialism create the conditions that facilitate this human trafficking. The report lays out in detail how both sending governments such as the Philippines and receiving "host" countries such as the United States are the primary beneficiaries of the active export and exploitation of Filipina migrant women laborers. DAMAYAN found that half of the domestic workers sent between 26 and 75 percent of their average weekly incomes of $400–600 in remittances to their families. The total came to $17.3 billion in 2009, boosting the Philippines economy tremendously, while the women lived on the remainder of their meager earnings in one of the most expensive metropolitan areas in the United States (DAMAYAN et al. 2010, forthcoming). Massive revenues averaging $3,000 per person accrue to the Philippine and U.S. government agencies administering the immigration papers for the migrant women, as well as to immigration attorneys (forthcoming, 52). Finally, private household employers benefit from the cheap labor of their employees, capturing huge savings on the backs of Filipina workers (forthcoming, 22–42).

The report features women's testimony that lays out in no uncertain terms the women's recognition that all of these benefits come at their expense. They know all too well that they are expected to serve as sacrifices for the benefit of their families and their home country, that they are compelled to, in their words, "mortgage their lives" for the lives of their families (DAMAYAN et al. 2010, forthcoming). In an incisive critique, they observe further that the Philippine government shamelessly promotes the rhetoric of "sacrifice" in an effort to keep women acquiescent and to rationalize the government's unwillingness and inability to provide any protection for these overseas workers. But while much of the testimony reflects how women indeed choose to make sacrifices for their families back home, it also shows that they do not subscribe to the state rhetoric. Nor does it render them passive victims or martyrs, but instead strengthens their resolve as leaders in resistance against these exploitative forces.

At the 2009 trafficking forum, Ana Liza Caballes, coordinator of DAMAYAN, discussed and showed media coverage of an ongoing trafficking case then being fought by DAMAYAN member Marichu Baoanan. When Baoanan, a paramedical college graduate with a nursing degree, was recruited in Cavite, an hour outside of Manila, she thought she was going to be working as a nurse in the United States. She paid the equivalent of about five thousand U.S. dollars to arrange papers to migrate, having mortgaged the title to the lot on which her house sits. Upon her arrival, she was instead forced to work as a domestic worker for an ambassador to the Philippines, Sir Lauro, stationed in New York. She worked sixteen hours a day for three months and was paid one hundred dollars over that time, the equivalent of about six cents a day. When she arrived, her employer seized her passport and insisted that she would need to work to pay off the cost for bringing her to the United States. Baoanan cooked, cleaned the large town house where the ambassador's family constantly entertained large groups of guests, and cared for the ambassador's five-year-old grandson until late at night. She was fed poorly, was hit with a broom by the grandchild, was not allowed to use the phone, and was not provided with proper clothes or shoes for the winter, despite her requests for these basic provisions.

In 2008, Baoanan filed a civil lawsuit against her employers, *Baoanan v. Baja et al.*, alleging fifteen counts, including trafficking, forced labor, peonage, and slavery. Caballes emphasized that the suit as well as the campaign simultaneously launched for justice for Baoanan began with fighting against the diplomatic immunity that her employers and others have used to abuse their employees with impunity. The campaign also focused on confronting the Philippine government to recognize the benefits and profits it receives directly from the exploitation of Filipina migrant workers such as Baoanan. At the July 9, 2008, press conference in New York to launch the campaign, Baoanan spoke to the importance of trafficking victims bringing to light the conditions they face: "What I want to say to people like me who were oppressed or will be oppressed: Don't be afraid to speak out or to come out in the open. Let us fight for our rights. We are not alone. We need to face people who abuse us and our weaknesses, because if we do not speak up, they will continue to abuse us" (DAMAYAN et al. 2010, forthcoming).[11] Baoanan's legal case culminated in a settlement "to the satisfaction of both parties" that included a provision restricting Baoanan from disclosing the details of the settlement.[12] Nevertheless, the case can be celebrated as the furthest such a case involving a challenge to diplomatic immunity has ever gone in U.S. legal precedent. Moreover, despite the "gag" on the settlement terms, Caballes observed that the groundbreaking campaign for justice for Baoanan has served to educate DAMAYAN members and organizers and encourage other victims of trafficking in the domestic work sector to escape their situations, come forth, and often file suit against their traffickers.

Victims Made Criminals

Elizabeth Sy (2009b), another participant at the 2009 trafficking forum, discussed the unique challenges she faced working with Southeast Asian women and girls, mostly Mien, Lao, Vietnamese, Thai, and Cambodian, in the underground sex trade in Oakland, California. Federal antitrafficking policy defines as trafficking victims all individuals under the age of eighteen engaged in commercial sex, regardless of how they may self-identify as participating in the trade. In the context of this policy, Sy said: "[There is] this sort of dual identity that these young women have, which is both criminal and victim. . . . Everybody knows they're victims of exploitation, but they're still being processed as criminals. They're still being arrested. They're still being detained. They're still looked at the same. And they're still getting slapped with these five-hundred-dollar restitution fees when they get out of juvenile hall."

In 2003 Sy co-founded Banteay Srei (an organization named for a Cambodian women's temple) to create a space for these women and girls, most of whom were born in the United States, to get the tools to empower themselves and their communities. According to Sy (2009a), the founders noticed that there were many Southeast Asian girls recruited into street-based sex work encountering criminalization, juvenile detention, and no services. Banteay Srei's founders wanted to find more effective responses to serve these girls' needs. The program has a number of components, including peer-based learning, early prevention, and cascading leadership models, so that girls can return to their communities as leaders, recruit more members, and rotate leadership.

Banteay Srei's programs include a photodocumentary program to educate both laypeople and policymakers, women's health education, and SAUCE, a traditional cooking program that meets once a month to bring in elders and community members to teach cooking and to share their stories of survival in the immigration experience. The girls' stories reflect the trauma of their families surviving genocide in their home countries as well as the process of being Americanized. Sy (2009a) observed that the girls have these and many other vulnerabilities, which is why they are so easily recruited into underground sex work: "If we can strengthen their support networks and deliver family-oriented resources to them while they are still living with their families, it will enable them to transition out of sex work if and when they're ready for it—so we try to give them leadership and employment opportunities."

Sy's intensive work as a case manager initially involved going to meet the girls at juvenile hall, accompanying them to court, working with probation officers to help deliver transition services, and working with their families. Sy (2009b) explained, "We do a lot of family services[,] . . . talking about what's happening with the girls' lives and . . . work with preventive health agencies, and get [the girls] reenrolled in school." She also worked as a training coordinator with Asian Health Services staff in Oakland, helping trainees to recognize signs and symptoms of sexual exploitation and to develop an agency-wide protocol as a model to be used by community-based health clinics where clients might go to get tested for sexually transmitted diseases and pregnancy. Sy noted that the goal was to build rapport between patients and health providers so that girls would bring their peers.

Sy (2009a) highlighted the values of this approach over the criminal justice system, where most of the girls have primarily experienced trauma:

> If we can reach them with health services before they are incarcerated or hit the criminal justice system, it is less traumatic and less costly than the criminal justice approach. Success, as we define it, is when we connect them to resources and they are accessing them without us, no matter where they are in their lives, not just if they are transitioning out [of sex work]. It's not always in our power to have someone transition out, because they are dealing with such levels of oppression, no one agency can fix it. They may have been recruited by someone who is oppressing them and been exploited, etc., but once you get into it and you're making fifteen hundred dollars a day in sex work, it's hard to transition.

Sy (2009a) added that multiple factors contribute to Banteay Srei members and those identified as commercially sexually exploited children (CSEC) entering and staying in the sex industry: "The other reality is that they come from unstable environments with no economic or educational opportunities and grew up in a society that objectifies and exoticizes them and tells them that they can't achieve in any other way."

Sy (2009a) cautioned that there is no simple fix, and solutions will involve the work and collaboration of multiple community-based organizations (CBOs) on a macro level: "When we look at the large-scale [view] of how someone is recruited and why they stay in this work, no agency—and not the criminal justice system—can fix this. We have to recognize intervention is needed at all levels of the spectrum and the whole journey. . . . What can CBOs do to create culturally relevant responses? My job is to convince other CBOs and health clinics to come on board with this, and I do the trainings for that."

Between 2006 and 2009, Sy worked with Oakland's Sexually Abused Commercially Exploited Youth Safe Place Alternative, a collaboration between public health workers, the probation department, and local law enforcement to try to develop a model to help local organizations that serve sexually exploited minors to work together. Sy (2009a) observed, "We're working within [the] collaborative network . . . to help inform the influence of policies so that we can ask for more funds to go toward diversion programs that will *not* force girls to be policed within juvenile hall in order to get those services but to give them access before that point of arrest happens."

Finally, Sy (2009a) commented on the challenges of funding, particularly the dilemma posed by the antiprostitution pledge in the U.S. federal funding requirements for Banteay Srei: "We don't get any federal funding, but we looked at the funding [requirements] and the [antiprostitution] pledge requirement. It is different when you are working with youth, and many [other organizations] were okay with signing, but our approach is nonjudgmental and working against the criminalization of the work and of the youth . . . so we are not willing to engage with people debating on the legalization [of prostitution] issue, etc. We see no benefit to it." Thus, Sy's organization has chosen to stand true to its sex worker rights principles and does not receive U.S. federal funding, even though it is arguably serving victims of trafficking as defined by the law. Moreover, Banteay Srei is doing some of the most effective work in the country with young immigrant women and girls in the sex trade, providing members with comprehensive, culturally sensitive services on multiple levels as well as training many other agencies and organizations in the complex work of serving these communities. Banteay Srei thus exemplifies how the U.S. federal antitrafficking regime does not benefit many of the people it might claim to serve under the law, but instead hinders effective service provision to these communities.

The testimony from the members and leaders of DAMAYAN and Banteay Srei reveals the irony that immigrant women in the domestic work industry face abuses that are largely neglected within the antitrafficking regime even when their situations are extremely coercive and exploitative, encompassing all of the features of trafficking as defined by the law. Meanwhile young immigrant women and girls working in the commercial sex industry are not served but are instead criminalized and victimized by the "enforcement" measures taken ostensibly to protect them under these same policies.

Prosecution, not Protection or Prevention

Kathleen Kim, former director of the Human Trafficking Project and staff attorney at San Francisco's Lawyers' Committee for Civil Rights and currently a professor at Loyola Law School, has noted the same patterns in her observations from work in the field of antitrafficking for over a decade. Kim has served countless survivors of trafficking and advocated for the rights of many others who have not been identified as such within the legal framework promoted by the federal government.[13] Kim (2006) sees the greatest challenge in doing antitrafficking work within the current U.S. regime as "an ideological struggle," explaining: "From my perspective as a human rights lawyer wanting to provide protection to the broadest category of migrants possible under the law, I find that that comes into direct conflict with what law officials want, which is a narrow application of the law to enforce prosecution of crimes and keep out criminals." The focus on enforcement and prosecution and the explicit and exclusive criminalization of prostitution frustrates Kim and many others working for the rights of survivors of trafficking within a broader immigrant and labor rights framework.[14] Kim (2004) says: "When I do get a sex trafficking case, the government eats it up, saying that they will provide all of these benefits, while they are not interested in what I believe are the more egregious labor trafficking cases. I'll get, 'Maybe the Labor Department will be interested in that.'" Yet in Kim's and other trafficking victims advocates' experiences, the Labor Department is not interested in cases involving violations outside of the commercial sex industry either.

Operation Gilded Cage (U.S. Department of Justice 2005), identified by the government and media as the largest sex trafficking case ever in the United States, illustrates well the challenges advocates face in this work. In 2005 law enforcement agents identified ten massage parlors in San Francisco where they believed trafficking was occurring and "recovered" more than 120 women through a typical "raid and rescue" operation. The women were brought to a California military base, where they were detained, and agents attempted to screen them to determine who was a victim before calling in service providers twenty-four hours later. Kim (2006) reports: "We went to help them after their preliminary screenings, but when we got there, many women were already on a bus set for detention and potentially deportation because it had been decided that they were not trafficking victims. Then there were the remaining women, and it became a mad race for the attorneys and advocates to interview the women and get their stories in order to identify them as victims or not." While the advocates generally convinced the government to interpret the law as they recommended, Kim (2006) says, "it was a real struggle," as the law enforcement agents involved, including the Federal Bureau of Investigation, Immigration and Customs Enforcement (ICE), and the San Francisco Police Department, did not share the advocates' conceptions of "victims."

Yet the case was framed quite differently in the mainstream media, where the television and print news outlets reported stories of Korean migrant women being rescued from sexual exploitation and slavery. The media did not report that most of the women were voluntary sex workers who were not trafficked or that the labor exploitation they did experience resulted from their vulnerable immigration status and their exclusion from labor protections as sex workers. In the United States and around the world, migrant women voluntarily engaged in sex work in massage parlors and brothels have often faced untold abuses by law enforcement agents and deportation or "rescue and restoration" against their wills (Chang and Kim 2007).

As Carol Leigh (2005), longtime sex worker rights organizer and current director of the Bay Area Sex Workers Advocacy Network, wrote in an editorial shortly after the raids on the massage parlors:

> The premise of separating the "innocent victims" from the "sex ring volunteers" ... ignores the realities of their situation. Some may have originally "participated voluntarily," but may still be victimized through abusive working conditions and when payments are not applied fairly to the worker's debt. Plus, although the government claims to offer special visas to protect these women, in order to qualify for these visas, federal law states that she remain only as long as she assists with the investigation and prosecution of the traffickers. This cooperation and ultimate deportation could result in extreme jeopardy for the migrant and her family.

Leigh (2005) points out the real dangers faced by trafficking victims and migrant workers alike without labor or immigration protections and under strong coercion to assist in the criminal prosecution of traffickers or employers, who may continue to threaten the migrants and their families. Leigh suggests that trafficking victims might be better served by policies that recognize "the complexities of sex work, migration and trafficking" as well as the real vulnerabilities of all migrant workers under current law: "Until we can begin to support rights for migrant workers and craft policies to support their needs to work, we are stuck in a quagmire that attracts, then rescues 'innocent victims.'"

Leigh's analysis reflects a critique of antitrafficking policy and practice shared by many immigrant worker rights advocates in sectors other than commercial sex. These activists also report that the focus on sex trafficking and the prosecutorial approach obstructs their work in damaging and divisive ways. For example, Ai-jen Poo (2006), formerly of Domestic Workers United and founder and director of National Domestic Workers Alliance in New York, observes:

> We see this as a metaphor for the whole issue: the government is saying that trafficking victims are real, legitimate victims only because they were at the mercy of criminal traffickers, but the root causes of trafficking are the same root causes of exploitation of migrant labor in general, which is happening in every workplace and industry in the United States. . . . The trafficking framework is being used as a tool to try to polarize an issue that really is very deeply connected, to create poles within an arena of struggle. The government has really taken on only the trafficking that it wants to address, with a heavy focus on criminal penalties for traffickers and so little relief for so-called victims of trafficking.

Poo (2006) points out that the government's anti–sex trafficking agenda offers very little to those few who manage to qualify as legally defined "victims of trafficking" while leaving too many people suffering the same conditions without legal recourse or resources: "People on the ground doing work to try to serve these communities see a fine line between those who've been trafficked and [those] who haven't, in legal terms. We deal with people every day who have suffered labor exploitation and coercion experiences that are just as severe as trafficked people. . . . That the government is trying to give so many resources to [what it calls] trafficking creates conflicts for serving others and prevents seeing the issues clearly." Poo suggests that the approach to trafficking be reframed without "trying to criminalize one aspect of migration." While she recognizes the need to penalize traffickers, she argues that the focus should be on why there is not enough relief and support for survivors of trafficking and why the relief that exists is so difficult for survivors to access.

Poo's concerns are echoed among workers and advocates across several movements. All of these activists agree that the government's antitrafficking agenda fails to benefit anyone in their membership or broader communities.[15] I argue further that the U.S. government's true goal in the intensive focus on so-called sex trafficking is not to serve victims of trafficking but instead to serve its own agenda of criminalizing sex workers and diverting attention from forms of trafficking that could be identified as sponsored by the U.S. government. Such forms include instances of labor trafficking that are tolerated by the government or, worse, directly orchestrated through U.S. policy and practice. For example, guest worker programs such as the Bracero program date back to World War II, when primarily Mexican men were imported and exploited as temporary low-wage farm workers to fill wartime labor shortages. Perhaps more insidious are situations of labor exploitation of migrant workers in which the U.S. government not only did not protect the victims but also often aided abusive employers in disciplining and disappearing immigrant workers.

"Good" Immigrants or Bad Models?

On a larger scale, I argue that the hidden agenda behind U.S. antitrafficking policy and practice is to create a dichotomy between "good" and "bad" immigrants in public sentiment, thereby helping to support and rationalize otherwise untenable public policy. In this schema, the "good" immigrants are the "legal" guest workers—those who are superexploitable, manageable, and easily disposable within the legal framework. They share these desirable traits with trafficking victims, who are also exploitable yet ultimately not as manageable or disposable and thus remain in a gray area as victims who are sometimes categorized as good, innocent and helpless, and sometimes not. The unequivocally "bad" immigrants, then, are the undocumented even though they too are most likely victims of neoliberal policies that forced them to leave their home countries and made them vulnerable to being trafficked without either immigration or labor protections.[16] Yet they are, in the eyes of the state, the least manageable of immigrant groups and thus the least desirable.

The ability to create these categories of "good" and "bad" immigrants allows the U.S. government and its citizenry to have their cake and eat it too. The government can keep expanding the guest-worker and neoliberal policies that create these categories of importable and disposable workers, and still claim to be keeping the country safe from "dangerous, criminal immigrants" and to be keeping jobs, benefits, and rights safe for "real Americans" through increasingly violent immigration enforcement laws and practices. The Obama administration initially promised that its immigration enforcement efforts would be targeted at deporting only those immigrants with violent criminal records and at prosecuting "bad-actor employers," but the focus has shifted away from those with criminal records to those with simple immigration violations and minor infractions. The shift is explained quite simply by the government's introduction of higher deportation quotas, with a goal of four hundred thousand persons a year,[17] and the expedient tactics employed to fulfill them. Immigration officials have admitted off the record that it is much easier to meet that goal by focusing on deporting noncriminal immigrants guilty of minor infractions such as traffic violations (which may take only hours to process) than to deport people with serious criminal records (which take an average of forty-five days to process) (Hsu and Becker 2010; *Los Angeles Times* 2010).

Against this backdrop of official policy and unofficial practice in the immigration enforcement arena, I now turn to a case of extreme labor abuse, tantamount to trafficking, of immigrant workers in the United States in the meatpacking industry in Postville, Iowa. The federal government knew of the abuses at the site but did not protect the victims. Instead, it actively facilitated the punishment and removal of the immigrant workers as "criminals" in what was intended to be a "model" of U.S. immigration law enforcement.

In May 2008, following a raid at the Agriprocessors kosher meatpacking plant in Postville, 389 workers were arrested, were detained at a cattle exhibit hall, and suffered multiple abuses at the hands of U.S. government agents. About 30 of the mostly Guatemalan migrants were women, while 18 were children between the ages of fourteen and seventeen. Many of the women had young children who were with babysitters or in school at the time of the raid. Recalling the incident, one woman said, "Many women were terrorized, and they were saying, 'What about my children? What about my children?'" (Argueta and Rivas 2010). Victims and witnesses said that ICE agents were verbally abusive, insulting and threatening the workers. In one instance, officials pulled a man's hair and threw him to the ground and hit him. When one woman tried to run away, a female agent screamed, "Stop, whore! Stop, bitch! You have no place to run!" (Argueta and Rivas 2010).

Many of the women ultimately were released to house arrest, forced to wear monitoring bracelets around their ankles. Now unable to work, many could not provide food for their families. Some older children who were workers were arrested and detained with the adults. One young boy whose mother was detained said that she pretended she had no children because she was afraid they would seize her children also. Officials refused to release her even after learning of her children's existence. Many of the detainees served five months in prison, while some of the plant managers (potentially responsible for 9,311 counts of child labor violations) fled the country shortly after the raid. According to federal labor law, children under the age of eighteen are expressly prohibited from "operating power-driven meat-processing machines, and slaughtering, meat packing or processing, and rendering" (Fair Labor Standards Act, 1938). It was alleged that Agriprocessors commonly hired underage workers to fill the incessant demand for manpower, and that the company knowingly overlooked the age of its minor workers.

Despite the company's gross violations of labor laws and child labor laws, the migrant workers arrested at the plant were treated as criminals rather than victims and targeted to be made examples of by the U.S. government. They were charged with aggravated identity theft, with a minimum sentence of two years in prison. Many subsequently accepted a lesser charge of Social Security fraud, the penalty for which was five months in jail before ultimate deportation. Erik Camayd-Freixas (2008), a professor of Hispanic studies at Florida International University and a certified federal interpreter, has argued that the government offered this "deal" to the workers with full knowledge that most would plead guilty to the lesser charges, thus providing ample numbers of people who could readily be identified—indeed, demonized—as immigrant "criminals" (see also Preston 2008). According to Camayd-Freixas, even though interpretation was provided to the workers when they were charged, many were not native Spanish speakers or were not literate in Spanish, instead speaking indigenous Guatemalan languages. More importantly, in most cases, the plant managers had provided workers with the false identification numbers or documents, and the workers did not know that these might belong to someone else (Argueta and Rivas 2010).

In May 2009, almost a year after the Postville raids, the U.S. Supreme Court ruled in *Flores-Figueroa v. United States* that the charge of aggravated identity theft cannot be applied unless a person knowingly uses the identity of a real person. But this ruling came too late for Postville's migrant workers, victimized first as workers at Agriprocessors then as examples to scare other migrant workers. Ironically, the decision centered around the placement of the word *knowingly* and the technical question of which terms the word modified in the federal statute prohibiting aggravated identity theft.[18] The emphasis in this case on the concept of "knowingly" committing a crime begs the question of whether we can hold the U.S. government accountable for *knowingly* facilitating the abuse and exploitation of the workers in question here. Indeed, it could be argued that the U.S. government actively orchestrated the criminalization and prosecution of the Postville workers to serve as examples of "bad" criminal immigrants. As the narrator of the documentary on Agriprocessors suggests: "Postville was an experiment designed to instill fear among the country's immigration population. It was supposed to be a pilot operation to serve as a model for future raids" (Argueta and Rivas 2010).

The Postville case involved labor exploitation of workers certainly fitting the legal definition of severe forms of trafficking. Yet even though teenage minors were employed in the slaughter of animals with power machinery, they were not initially identified as trafficking victims in the media. Nor were the even younger children who were separated from their parents when they were arrested, detained, and deported from Postville. Indeed, the media barely picked up these stories, perhaps because they did not involve sensationalized tales of women or children in the sex industry. Instead, we are bombarded with stories of child sexual exploitation every day and told that it is the central story, the "face" of human trafficking. While U.S. media distract viewers with these tales, the U.S. government plays more than an incidental role in the criminalization and terrorization of innocent men, women, and children who well could be identified as trafficking victims. As David Wolfe Leopold of the American Immigration Lawyers Association said in testimony following the Postville raids, "ICE should direct its enforcement resources towards investigations of high level threats to security and employers that deliberately violate the law, not workers who are merely trying to feed their families and contribute to the U.S. economy and social fabric" (Argueta and Rivas 2010).

The Postville workers were targeted to be showcased as dangerous criminals and "bad" immigrants, but the case highlights how the real crimes were perpetrated and condoned by agents of the U.S. government at every level under the guise of "enforcement." Sex worker rights advocates know this phenomenon all too well, and their voices in the debate surrounding trafficking must be heeded. They do not view sex work as inherently coercive or exploitative but instead see sex workers face state violence every day, often with abuses at the hands of enforcement agents. Advocates also understand clearly how sex workers are used alternately as criminals and victims in the federal focus on "sex trafficking," which only impedes their struggles for labor rights and freedom from state violence. Sex worker rights organizers observe that the U.S. government's purported antitrafficking activities and policies do not protect any workers' rights and instead regularly violate them. Melissa Ditmore and the Sex Workers Project of the Urban Justice Center have presented research from interviews with forty-six people, including migrant sex workers and trafficked persons, social service providers (among them caseworkers and attorneys for trafficked people), and law enforcement personnel (among them federal and immigration agents). Ditmore (2009) reports:

> Social-service providers we interviewed identified problems that arise because the criminal justice approach to trafficking is not based on victims' needs and rights but instead on finding people to prosecute. For the people targeted, raids are chaotic events difficult to comprehend while they are in progress. Service providers and attorneys both cited trauma and detention as commonplace consequences of raids, and how people are treated after being rounded up in raids bears directly on their later willingness to speak frankly about their experiences of victimization.

Ditmore (2009) concludes that many of the interviewees who self-identified as being trafficked were able to help themselves, that the service providers who reported such cases did not learn of them as a result of raids, and that people familiar with sex work and those who have experienced trafficking situations themselves are better able to identify victims of trafficking. She emphasizes that police and the criminal justice system have not been effective in either identifying or helping victims of trafficking, noting that in a number of cases "trafficked sex workers have been arrested multiple times without ever being identified as victims of trafficking." Thus, she recommends that antitrafficking efforts should focus on building public awareness within sex worker and immigrant communities about resources available to "people in coercive situations," instead of the current prevalent practice of raids (Ditmore 2009).

Similarly, Sex Workers across Borders (SWAB), a grassroots group of sex workers and their allies, has taken as its mission exposing and critiquing the effects of U.S. trafficking laws and practices:

> We are concerned that rather than protecting sex workers from violence and abuse, anti-trafficking measures are sometimes used to police and punish female, male, and transgender migrants and sex workers, and to restrict their freedom of movement. For example, the U.S. TVPA and TVPRA are ineffective and harmful in dealing with the diverse instances of forced labor . . . and conflate forced labor/slavery with prostitution. Yet, prostitution is not the only industry in which trafficking occurs, and refusing to differentiate between consensual and forced prostitution does nothing to help people who really are victims of forced labor. (SWAB 2007)

SWAB was formed to advocate for "more ethical, humane policies to combat forced labor, slavery and servitude in all industries." In one conference call discussion, a SWAB member questioned why all other work, including agriculture and manufacturing, is automatically seen as consensual but sex work is not. She asked, "So people want to work at Wal-Mart and go to work every day because they love their jobs?" (SWAB 2007).[19]

This bold observation leads to the question of what other forms of exploitation and labor violations are being committed without generating an ounce of moral outrage or global policing by the U.S. government. This, I argue, is the real function of the U.S. federal focus on sex trafficking: It enables the U.S. government to decriminalize what I would call U.S. state-sponsored trafficking programs, like the "guest worker" programs in place and perennially proposed for expansion. It also distracts attention from the fact that U.S. economic violence through neoliberal policy impoverishes people so that they are vulnerable to being trafficked in any country, in any industry, in the first place. Transnationally, these neoliberal policies facilitate the push of migrant workers out of the Third World, while guest worker and other immigration policies support the pull by exploitative employers into the United States and other First World host countries. At the same time, the focus on "sex trafficking" criminalizes not only sex work and sex workers but also neglects immigrant workers in many sectors, rendering all of these workers more vulnerable to abuses by employers and by state and law enforcement agents of all kinds.

These are the real dangers and pitfalls of the U.S. federal antitrafficking agenda and its equation of human trafficking with "sex trafficking," "prostitution" and "sexual violence." The federal antitrafficking regime and the focus on sex trafficking are smoke and mirrors, hiding many other egregious forms of violence on every level, too often perpetrated by agents of the state. These agents, our policymakers and enforcers, knowingly orchestrate these systems of exploitation and, at worst, aid abusive employers or, at best, look the other way. More importantly, they try to dupe us into doing the same.

In stark contrast to the many dubious antitrafficking and "rescue" operations orchestrated by the federal government, workers and advocates are creating and articulating feminist, immigrant, and sex worker rights responses to trafficking that serve the needs of all migrant workers, including sex workers and survivors of trafficking broadly defined. My interviews with members of these organizations and the participant comments at the 2009 trafficking forum reveal a broad consensus that many of the responses to the issue of human trafficking by U.S. feminist scholars and policymakers alike have been inadequate and problematic. Some observers suggest that a U.S. antitrafficking regime has emerged from an unholy alliance among Christian Right groups, feminists, and policymakers determined to use the trafficking issue for their own interests (Chang and Kim 2007). I argue that the complex of antitrafficking and "rescue" activities conducted by the U.S. government and U.S.-based or international NGOs indeed serve a specific function that is less about combating trafficking than about rationalizing and promoting state-sponsored human trafficking.

Notes

This chapter is drawn in part from a conference, This Is What Trafficking Looks Like, held at the University of California, Santa Barbara, in October 2009. The conference was made possible by generous support and sponsorship from Héctor R. Cordero-Guzmán, program officer, Economic Development, Ford Foundation; Nilda Flores-González and Anna Guevarra, Sociology Department and the Low Wage Work, Migration, and Gender Project, University of Illinois at Chicago; and numerous departments and individuals at the University of California at Santa Barbara, including Chancellor Henry Yang; Dean David Marshall, College of Letters and Sciences; Dean Melvin Oliver, Division of Social Sciences; Eileen Boris, professor and Hull Chair, Feminist Studies, the Interdisciplinary Humanities Center; and Ricardo A. Alcaíno, director, Office of Equal Opportunity.

1. The TVPA was reauthorized and supplemented by the Trafficking Victims Protection Reauthorization Acts [TVPRA] of 2003 and 2005.

2. See http://www.nytimes.com/kristof for the complete series.

3. I have presented this critique of Kristof's approach at a variety of academic and service provider conferences, including Con/vergences: Critical Interventions in the Politics of Race and Gender, University of California Berkeley, February 6, 2004; Freedom Network Conference, Chicago Kent College of Law, Chicago, Illinois, March 15, 2006; Sex Work Matters: beyond Divides, CUNY Graduate Center, New York, New York, March 30, 2006; and Intimate Labors: An Interdisciplinary Conference, University of California Santa Barbara, October 5, 2007; as well as various keynote addresses and in undergraduate classes with very mixed responses from audiences.

4. See Chang 2000 for a more comprehensive discussion of neoliberal policy and coerced migration.

5. I use the term sex work to recognize the labor of commercial sex and to counter the abolitionist or antiprostitution position advanced by some self-identified feminist individuals and groups who argue that prostitution is inherently exploitative and violent toward the women engaged in it. This position also proposes that women cannot engage in commercial sex or prostitution of their own volition under any circumstances, regardless of how the women may self-identify or describe their work. See Barry 1979; Hughes 2000; Hughes, Raymond, and Gomez 2001.

6. Servile marriage can be seen as encompassing both sex work and domestic work. If we were to redistribute the numbers across these two categories, domestic work remains the industry in which most trafficking victims are found. If we were to attribute this group entirely to sex work, we would still have 40 percent in sex work, equal to the number in the domestic work category.

7. The T-visa provides a number of benefits to qualified trafficking victims, including cash assistance and federal public benefits, temporary work authorization, and the opportunity to apply for permanent residence.

8. There is greater public awareness of trafficking in the manufacturing sector than in the domestic service, agriculture, and hotel and restaurant sectors. See, for example, Julie Su's (1997) documentation of the Thai sweatshop case in El Monte, California.

9. According to Yolanda Stern, President of the Philippine-American Chamber of commerce, "If overseas migrant workers would stop remitting money for merely three days, the Philippine economy would immediately collapse" (DAMAYAN 2010, forthcoming).

10. For a discussion of how both the Philippine government and employment agencies actively encourage the labor export and brokering of Filipina migrant women as nurses and domestic workers transnationally, see Guevarra 2009 and Chang 2000.

11. Video recording available on YouTube, "Justice for Marichu Baoanan! Campaign Short," uploaded August 6, 2008, by DAMAYANmigrantworker, http://www.youtube.com/watch?v=5VF_ZVIa-Lo (accessed December 3, 2012).

12. The phrase "to the satisfaction of both parties" is standard language for legal settlements of this nature, according to Ana Liza Caballes (2012), coordinator of DAMAYAN.

13. Kathleen Kim and Nancy Harris served as co-counsel for Alice B., a Kenyan woman trafficked in 2002 to the United States and forced to work under abusive and exploitative conditions as a domestic for a prominent Kenyan journalist studying on a fellowship at Stanford University. See Yeung 2004.

14. According to the U.S. Department of State (2011), "The '3P paradigm—prevention, protection and prosecution—continues to serve as the fundamental framework used by governments around the world to combat human trafficking."

15. Poo (2006) said that legislators explicitly told her group to remove the language about trafficking from the early drafts of the Domestic Worker Bill of Rights (passed in August 2010) because this was "not their issue."

16. For example, structural adjustment policies imposed on indebted nations as preconditions for loans from the World Bank/International Monetary Fund destroy subsistence economies in many poor countries, compelling mass migration that is subsequently facilitated and capitalized on by both sending and receiving countries' governments. See Chang 2000.

17. In 2011, 397,000 people were deported from the United States, a higher number than in any recent administration. See Applied Research Center 2011.

18. 18 U.S.C. 1028A(a)(1). In the final decision, Justice Stephen Breyer wrote, "[The law] requires the Government to show that the defendant knew that the means of identification at issue belonged to another person. As a matter of ordinary English grammar, 'knowingly' is naturally read as applying to all the subsequently listed elements of the crime. . . . Finally, the Government's arguments based on the statute's purpose and on the practical problems of enforcing it are not sufficient to overcome the ordinary meaning, in English . . . of Congress' words" (Syllabus, *Flores-Figueroa v. United States*, Certiorari to the U.S. Court of Appeals for the Eighth Circuit, No. 8-108, argued February 24, 2009, decided May 4, 2009).

19. SWAB was created after the Revisioning Prostitution Policy conference in Las Vegas, Nevada, July 9–12, 2006.

References

Allen, Mike. 2003. "Bush Warns U.N. Assembly about Dangers of Trade in Sex Slaves." *Washington Post*, September 24.

Applied Research Center. 2011. *Shattered Families: The Perilous Intersection of Immigration Enforcement and the Child Welfare System*. Executive Summary. November 2011: 3.

Argueta, Luis, and Vivian Rivas. 2010. *abUSed: The Postville Raid*. Film. Maya Media. http://www.abusedthepostvilleraid.com/. Accessed December 5, 2012.

Barry, Kathleen. 1979. *Female Sexual Slavery*. Englewood Cliffs, N.J.: Prentice-Hall.

Brodsky, Cita. 2009. Testimony at This Is What Trafficking Looks Like forum, University of California, Santa Barbara, October 23.

Caballes, Ana Liza. 2012. Interview May 14.

Camayd-Freixas, Erik. 2008. "Interpreting after the Largest ICE Raid in U.S. History: A Personal Account." Manuscript. June 13. http://graphics8.nytimes.com/images/2008/07/14/opinion/14ed-camayd.pdf. Accessed January 8, 2013.

Chang, Grace. 2000. *Disposable Domestics: Immigrant Women Workers in the Global Economy*. Boston: South End.

Chang, Grace, and Kathleen Kim. 2007. "Reconceptualizing Approaches to Human Trafficking: New Directions and Perspectives from the Field(s)." *Stanford Journal of Civil Rights and Civil Liberties* 3:318–44.

DAMAYAN Migrant Workers Association and the Urban Justice Center Community Development Project, with writing assistance of Ninotchka Rosca. 2010. "Doing the Work That Makes All Work Possible: Research Narrative of Filipino Domestic Workers in the Tri-state Area." Executive summary. October 23. Urban Justice Center, New York.

DAMAYAN Migrant Workers Association and the Urban Justice Center Community Development Project, with writing assistance of Ninotchka Rosca. Forthcoming. "Doing the Work That Makes All Work Possible: Research Narrative of Filipino Domestic Workers in the Tri-state Area." Full Report. Urban Justice Center, New York.

Ditmore, Melissa. 2009. "Kicking Down the Door: The Effects of Anti-Trafficking Raids in the USA." *Research for Sex Work* 11:10–13. http://www.nswp.org/sites/nswp.org/files/research-for-sex-work-11-english-francais.pdf. Accessed January 8, 2013.

Ditmore, Melissa, and Sex Workers Project. 2009. "The Use of Raids to Fight Trafficking in Persons." http://www.sexworkersproject.org/publications/reports/raids-and-trafficking. Accessed September 6, 2011.

Fair Labor Standards Act. 1938. As amended 29 U.S.C. 201, et seq.

Guevarra, Anna Romina. 2009. *Marketing Dreams, Manufacturing Heroes*. New Brunswick, N.J.: Rutgers University Press.

Hsu, Spencer, and Andrew Baker. "ICE Officials Set Quotas to Deport More Illegal Immigrants." *Washington Post*, March 27, 2010.

Hughes, Donna. 2000. "The 'Natasha' Trade: Transnational Sex Trafficking." *National Institute of Justice Journal* (January): 1–9.

Hughes, Donna, Janice Raymond, and Carol J. Gomez. 2001. "Sex Trafficking of Women in the United States." Report. Coalition against Trafficking in Women.

Jahic, Galma, and James O. Finckenauer. 2005. "Representations and Misrepresentations of Human Trafficking." *Trends in Organized Crime* 8:25–40.

Kim, Kathleen. 2004. Interview. March 8.

———. 2006. Interview. October 7.

Kristof, Nicholas. 2004a. "Girls for Sale." *New York Times*, January 17.

———. 2004b. "Going Home, with Hope." *New York Times*, January 24.

———. 2004c. "Loss of Innocence." *New York Times*, January 28.

———. 2004d. "Stopping the Traffickers." *New York Times*, January 31.

Leigh, Carol. 2005. "Behind the Moral Panic, an Opportunity to Work." *San Francisco Chronicle*, July 22.

Los Angeles Times. 2010. "Border Laws Intensified." April 22.

McMahon, Kathryn, and Coalition to Abolish Slavery and Trafficking. 2002. "Speaking Out: Three Narratives of Women Trafficked to the United States." Report. Los Angeles.

Miko, Francis T., and Grace (Jea-Hyun) Park. 2002. *Trafficking in Women and Children: The U.S. and International Response*. http://fpc.state.gov/documents/organization/9107.pdf. Accessed January 8, 2013.

Poo, Ai-jen. 2006. Interview. August 30.

Preston, Julia. 2008. "An Interpreter Speaking Up for Migrants." *New York Times*, July 11.

———. 2010. "Suit Points to Guest Worker Flaws." *New York Times*, February 1.

Sex Workers across Borders. 2007. Mission Statement. August 10. Available at Prostitutes' Education Network: Trafficking Policy Research Project. http://bayswan.org/traffik/swabmission.doc. Accessed December 5, 2012.

Su, Julie. 1997. "El Monte Thai Garment Workers: Slave Sweatshops." In *No Sweat: Fashion, Free Trade and the Rights of Garment Workers*, ed. Andrew Ross, 143–49. New York: Verso.

Sy, Elizabeth. 2009a. Interview. September 18.

———. 2009b. Testimony at This Is What Trafficking Looks Like forum. University of California, Santa Barbara, October 23.

Trafficking Victims Protection Act. 2000. Public Law 106-386.

Trafficking Victims Protection Reauthorization Act. 2003. Public Law 108-193.

———. 2005. Public Law 109-164.

U.S. Department of Justice. 2005. "29 Charged in Connection with Alien Harboring Conspiracy." Press release. July 1.

U.S. Department of Labor. 2002. "Trafficking in Persons: A Guide to Non-Governmental Organizations." http://www.dol.gov/wb/media/reports/trafficking.htm. Accessed May 16, 2011.

U.S. Department of State. 2006. *Trafficking in Persons Report*. http://www.state.gov/g/tip/rls/tiprpt/2006/. Accessed September 6, 2011.

———. 2011. Office to Monitor and Combat Trafficking in Persons. *The 3Ps: Prevention, Protection, Prosecution Fact Sheet*. www.state.gov/documents/organization/167334.pdf. Accessed July 6, 2012.

U.S. General Accounting Office. 2006. *Better Data, Strategy, and Reporting Needed to Enhance U.S. Antitrafficking Efforts Abroad*. http://www.gao.gov/cgi-bin/getrpt?GAO-06-825. Accessed August 8, 2007.

Yeung, Bernice. 2004. "Enslaved in Palo Alto." *S.F. Weekly*, Feb. 18.

PART 2

Ethnic Enclaves

4

Gendered Labor

Experiences of Nepali Women within Pan-Ethnic Informal Labor Markets in Boston and New York

SHOBHA HAMAL GURUNG

AND BANDANA PURKAYASTHA

A mother who works as a nanny in New York City to provide a good life for her children reports, "I haven't seen my children for five years. They were very young when I left. They were ten, eleven years old. Now, when I see their photographs, I can't even recognize them. They've changed so much. They've grown so much." This lament has become more familiar as a growing body of literature has begun to document the experiences of female migrants who work in the informal economy in wealthy countries while attempting to maintain transnational families. The literature on contemporary female migrants has begun to track their experiences, their methods and reasons for migrating, and their subsequent work experiences (Ehrenreich and Hochschild 2002; Hondagneu-Sotelo 2001; Hondagneu-Sotelo and Avila 1997; Kofman 2000; Louie 2001; Pessar 1999; Sassen 2006; Ward 1990; Wichterich 2000). This chapter focuses on a little-studied group of women, Nepali migrants who work in the informal economy in the United States providing care work for wealthier families. We draw on their experiences to confirm some of the trends identified by work on Latinas and Southeast Asian women. We also examine two issues that have not received much attention. The Nepali women's experience shows the beginning of a segmentation of the informal labor market for care work, where wealthier co-ethnics seek female labor based on cultural similarities. Their experiences also show that while they send remittances back to their home countries, some of this money is sent to nonfamily members.

The data for this chapter are drawn from a study we conducted in Boston, New York, and Los Angeles, though we focus here on Boston and New York. After a brief discussion of the existing theoretical framework, we provide an introduction to Nepali migrants. Then we present the data on the women's experiences in the labor market. We conclude by discussing two insights from this study. We emphasize that within-ethnic-group social location—Nepali Americans' social location in relation to wealthier Indian Americans (and their religious and linguistic similarity to this group)—shapes the economic opportunities available to these women. We also show that some Nepali women, especially those who worked in the formal sector in Nepal, have begun to "bank" their social capital in their home countries. These findings further extend a field that has previously been based mostly on Latinas' home and mothering experiences.

Transnational Gendered Migration and Labor

Scholars now recognize the labor shifts that have occurred with recent global restructuring: feminization of jobs and increased segmentation of opportunities for women from the global North and South have been driven by large-scale female migration. Thus, as more women in the global North gain education and avail themselves of opportunities in the formal economy, the task of care work shifts to women from the global South. While reproductive labor has been seen, at least symbolically, as nonpaid work performed within homes by women, for middle-class and affluent women, the actual tasks have often been shifted onto poorly paid women or men or slaves. In addition, it is also clear that contemporary globalization has created a polarized international racialized gendered division of labor; reproductive labor has become a productive paid-work arena for immigrant/migrant women (Hondagneu-Sotelo 2001; Hondagneu-Sotelo and Ávila 1997; Romero 1992). Parreñas (2001) uses the term "global care chains" to describe the ongoing process of wealthy mothers seeking work in the paid workforce and hiring desperate women from poor countries to care for family and household needs.

Romero's (1992) and Hondagneu-Sotelo's (2001) seminal studies on Chicana/Mexican workers document the raced/classed/gendered nature of these care jobs. Even though these women's work is crucial for the functioning of the formal economy, these workers in the informal economy remain vulnerable and susceptible to different forms of oppression and exploitation. As Romero (1992, 159–60) reports, "The daily rituals and practices of domestic service reproduce the systems of gender, class, and race domination. Even though domestics are paid workers, they do not escape the sexism attached to housework but rather carry the burden for their middle-class women employers."

Studies in the United States and Europe of women who work in care jobs (e.g., Hondagneu-Sotelo 2001; Kofman 2000; Louie 2001; Romero 1992; Parreñas 2001) have documented the feminized nature of these jobs. Such care work remains unregulated, invisible within the domestic sphere. The care workers—for example, nannies and housekeepers—are poorly paid, rarely get any benefits, work very long hours, and remain vulnerable to employer whims. Faced with a labor market segment where there is no opportunity for advancement (and few opportunities to organize against exploitation), these informal women workers experience deskilling and brain waste, and downward occupational mobility takes place (Kofman 2000; Parreñas 2001). Equally important, these jobs in the informal economy offer no avenues to claim permanent political status—that is, citizenship—based on their records of working in these jobs.[1]

Examining the impact of these women's earnings, scholars have pointed out that these female migrants send money back home to support their families. While this pattern of women migrants sending money back home is not a new phenomenon—for example, Irish women in late nineteenth-century America did the exact same thing—in earlier periods, the remittances have been studied through the lens of transnationalism (Diner 1983). Thus, scholars look at "the processes by which immigrants forge and sustain multi-stranded social relations that link together their societies of origin and settlement" (Schiller, Basch, and Blanc-Szanton 1992, 7). A series of studies has documented how migrants and their children build and maintain lives in the countries of residence and countries of origin (e.g., Ignacio 2005; Levitt 2001; Portes 1997; Purkayastha 2005; Waters and Levitt 2002).

Examining poorer female migrants' transnational ties with their home countries and families, scholars have shown that many women struggle with providing emotional labor (and material resources) to their distant family members (Parrenas 2001). On the one hand, the money they send back to provide a better life for their families becomes a part of the understanding of a good mother's role. On the other hand, if a woman is married and has children back home, then her physical separation causes additional emotional pain and suffering. Hondagneu-Sotelo and Ávila (1997) report that 40 percent of migrant Latina mothers are separated from their children. Although these mothers cross national borders as a consequence of economic necessity and to improve their children's lives, they experience guilt and criticism. Our study shows similar patterns and provides more data to support the women's struggles as mothers who attempt to balance these numerous and contradictory expectations of gendered female roles. However, we find that the focus on how women fulfill their gendered role in families and communities leaves out another aspect of these remittances. Some women have begun to send money back to nonfamily entities, sometimes with the explicit intention of creating social capital at home.

In sum, we expect that the racialized feminized exploitative nature of care work and the struggles with providing emotional labor to families at a distance are typical of this sector of informal economy workers. However, we seek to answer two additional questions. First, does an ethnic group's relative visibility affect the kind of opportunities a woman from the group can access? Since recruitment into these jobs is partially based on the employers' ability to see a group as potential labor for these care tasks, what do the experiences of groups such as Nepalis tell us about the nature of labor markets? Second, does it make a difference if the women are relatively well educated? In other words, do women retreat primarily to their mother roles when they use their earnings from these marginalized jobs? Since Nepalis are subsumed within the category of South Asian Americans, a group that is widely regarded as well educated and relatively affluent, does their social location facilitate their access to the informal job market? We find that they end up in a narrow niche segment of this market—that is, the majority of these women initially work primarily for Indian families based on their apparent similarities in culture. Moreover, since many of the Nepali women are educated, do we find their resources concentrated on their family's welfare? We find that the women build social capital by putting aside part of their money to build community resources such as schools, women's organizations, and the like. They thus invest in extra family social status.

Method

The research draws on an analysis of thirty-five Nepali women workers whose ages ranged between sixteen and sixty-five.[2] Their work experience in informal economic sectors was the primary criteria for inclusion. By using snowball sampling, research participants were approached and selected through personal contacts and social networks. To ensure that their voices come through clearly, the information was gathered through semistructured and in-depth interviews. We interviewed the participants mostly in Nepali and Hindi and conducted two waves of interviews.[3] After asking a few structured questions to get a consistent base of demographic information, we asked questions about the women's process of migration, how they found their jobs, the nature of their jobs, and their lives in general in the United States and, if applicable, in Nepal. We mostly allowed women to follow their line of thought, though we prompted them about themes in which we were interested. Because Hamal Gurung is Nepali and Purkayastha is Indian, and we both are immigrant women living in the United States who are active in South Asian community-based service work, the women felt comfortable sharing their personal lived experiences. Hamal Gurung translated all interviews from Nepali or Hindi into English.

Since we are relying on a snowball sample, we cannot generalize these data to the entire Nepali American population. Given the extreme difficulty in reaching this population and in gaining the trust of the group, we use this small number of cases to comment on some of the less visible processes in low-wage work among immigrant women. We expect that further studies will validate these findings.

Female International Labor Migration: Nepal Context

The migration of Nepali men, especially Gurkha soldiers, has received both scholarly and general recognition.[4] In recent years, however, Nepali female international migration has also attracted increasing national and international journalistic attention. In particular, such attention has focused on female victims of trafficking and the sex trade, as well as women in domestic service who are physically, mentally, and sexually abused.[5] Nepali female migration first garnered notice in the early 1990s. Women previously migrated as wives, but now women are initiating labor migration as they seek work in other countries, particularly in the Gulf, Southeast Asia, and the United States. Our participants' migration trajectories reflect this trend.

Our research participants indicated intersecting economic, political, social, and personal reasons for migrating. Economic reasons included supporting their families, repaying family debts, investing in their children's education, and building homes. Political reasons mainly included safety and security issues in politically unstable Nepal. At the time of our survey, Nepal was experiencing major political turmoil, and many women indicated that they could not return there because of the unsettled conditions. Overlapping social and personal reasons included family conflict, unhappy conjugal life, single motherhood, and the desire to join family members in the United States. In most cases, the women migrated for a combination of reasons. The social, economic, and personal reasons for these women's international migrations resembled those found in Hamal Gurung's (2003) earlier work on migrant and local Nepali women in carpet production in Nepal, indicating that women migrate both within and across national boundaries for somewhat similar reasons.

Demographic and Socioeconomic Backgrounds

The immigrant women in our study who work in the informal economic sector come from a variety of backgrounds, representing different castes/ethnicities, marital statuses, religious affiliations, and educational backgrounds. The majority of the participants were in their forties. The common assumption about those who work in the informal economic and service sectors is that they are people from lower socioeconomic backgrounds in their countries of origin and possess little or no education. However, the majority of the research participants had four years of college education (table 4.1). Our informal impression of the Nepali community (no formal data were collected on this group) indicates that this profile is consistent with the larger population of Nepali female migrants.[6]

Table 4.1. Demographic and Socioeconomic Backgrounds

Age	Caste / Ethnicity	Marital Status	Education	Religion
42	Chettri	Widow	M.A.	Hindu
47	Newar	Married	Nursing	Hindu
40	Brahmin	Married	B.A.	Hindu
40	Tamang	Married	B.A.	Hindu-Buddhist
46	Gurung	Separated	High School	Buddhist
28	Tamang	Married	MBA	Buddhist
42	Thakuri	Married	B.A.	Hindu
43	Thakali	Married	B.A.	Buddhist
38	Gurung	Unmarried	High School	Buddhist
39	Chettri	Unmarried	High School	Hindu
42	Brahmin	Married	B.A.	Hindu
41	Chettri	Married	M.A.	Hindu
54	Newar	Married	B.A.	Hindu
46	Brahmin	Married	High School	Hindu
41	Chettri	Separated	B.A.	Hindu
43	Chettri	Married	B.A.	Hindu
52	Chettri	Married	Two Years College	Hindu
43	Gurung	Separated	B.A.	Buddhist
38	Brahmin	Married	B.A.	Hindu
50	Chettri	Married	Two Years College	Hindu
50	Chettri	Married	Two Years College	Hindu
41	Thakali	Widow	Two Years College	Buddhist-Hindu
48	Newar	Unmarried	Two Years College	Buddhist-Hindu
39	Chettri	Married	B.A.	Hindu
51	Newar	Married	B.A.	Hindu
57	Brahmin	Married	M.A.	Hindu
50	Chettri	Married	High School	Hindu
40	Chettri	Married	M.A.	Hindu
50	Gurung	Married	Non	Buddhist-Hindu
47	Chettri	Married	High School	Hindu
40	Hindu	Married	B.A.	Hindu
44	Chettri	Widow	Two Years College	Hindu
46	Chettri	Married	Two Years College	Hindu
47	Chettri	Widow	Two Years College	Hindu
35	Brahmin	Married	B.A.	Hindu

Informal Labor Market Work

DRUDGERY, ISOLATION, AND EMOTIONAL
AND SOCIAL COSTS OF CARE WORK

Given their educational backgrounds, which gave them an elite status in Nepal, where education rates among women are low and the female literacy rate is just 34.9 percent (Central Bureau of Statistics 2001), the women experienced significant downward mobility after arriving in the United States. A majority of our participants worked as nannies or housekeepers, while a few worked in restaurants or retail stores, and some combined child care with restaurant or retail shop work. The highly educated women, especially those who had worked in professional fields in Nepal, said that they had experienced a devaluing of their education, skills, and knowledge in the United States. They were not happy with their current work but had been drawn to these jobs for a variety of reasons: some women lacked the proper legal documents to work in formal sectors, some found that their credentials and skills did not transfer to the United States, and some lacked English proficiency.[7] The easy availability of such jobs through word of mouth was an important factor.

Forty-six-year-old Abha, for example, had worked for a nongovernmental organization (NGO) and was involved in political and community-based social work in Nepal but had become a babysitter in the United States. In her words,

> There is definitely a huge difference between working in an NGO and working as a babysitter. Even though there is a difference between these two jobs I've held, I have to endure it because of my problems. When I worked in the NGO, I used to sit in meetings with my friends, and we talked about the social issues and problems of our community and village and the ways to solve them. I served my community and village in Nepal while working in the NGO, whereas in America, I'm serving just one family. And I am basically like a domestic servant here. There is an immense difference between these two jobs. It's like the difference between day and night. No matter how big the difference, though, I am compelled to do this job in order to pay my debts.

Similarly, forty-year-old Sarina had worked for an NGO in Nepal, but in the United States she had found weekend employment in a restaurant while babysitting on weekdays. Her babysitting job was socially alienating and monotonous, and the restaurant work was physically exhausting. She said, "I have become a wage worker here; there is no possibility for upward mobility. I worked in an NGO in Nepal, and my job was respectable. I used to travel a lot. My education and skills are useless here. It would be nice to have a good job, but I don't have a work permit, so I am stuck in such jobs."

Binta, a forty-two-year-old babysitter, resented the lack of recognition of her academic credentials and skills in the United States and expressed her experiences with being deskilled:

> I worked in Nepal as a teacher and as a social worker, but the money I earned wasn't enough for my kids to go to a good school. All of my friends told me to stay here and think about my children. In the beginning, I wasn't sure what kind of job I would get. When I heard about babysitting, I was startled because it's sort of like a housekeeping job, and I had never even taken care of my own house when I was in Nepal. I found that my professional skills and the degree that I have from Nepal are totally worthless here, so I started to look for other jobs. And I ended up babysitting.

The jobs feature isolation, a lack of structure with regard to responsibilities and hours, low pay, and no benefits, all of which are similar to the conditions that Latina immigrants to the United States experience in domestic service (Hondagneu-Sotelo 2001; Hondagneu-Sotelo and Ávila 1997). After one woman's employer took a weeklong vacation, she was told to make up the time by working weekends. And as Hondagneu-Sotelo and Ávila (1997) found for Latinas, leaving behind their children takes an emotional and psychological toll on Nepali mothers.

Tara, a forty-one-year-old babysitter, had been a high school teacher and social worker in Nepal. After she had been teaching illiterate adult women for five years, her husband married another woman and moved away, leaving Tara with sole responsibility for her children. She lamented,

> I used to cry all the time because I wanted to go back to Nepal. I used to have nightmares about my children. I missed them so much that whenever I heard a kid talk, I would think that they were my kids and they were saying "Mommy." But I ended up staying here in the States. My relatives and family reminded me that I have a tremendous responsibility upon my shoulders to take care of my children, and since I'm in the Land of Opportunity, I should make use of that. The fact that my husband has two wives doesn't help either. I call [my children] almost every day, sometimes twice a day. They tell me not to spend so much money on phone cards. I tell them that if I don't hear their voices, then I will go crazy. I called them this morning to wake them up because they have their exams going on right now. I'm constantly worrying for them. I question if they've eaten or if they're warm. I am physically here, but I am mentally with my kids all the time.

THE VALUE OF CULTURE IN SEGMENTED INFORMAL LABOR MARKETS

Women's networks and transnational connections are the crucial and determining factors for accessing work. Friends and acquaintances of the research participants who were already working in care work played an influential role in getting them jobs. Almost all of our research participants got their jobs through their friends and through word of mouth. Social networks helped these women find sponsors and invitations to come to the United States, and then jobs and places to live after they arrived.

Social and cultural capital were assets for both women and employers. The women's ethnicity, education, previous work experience, and cultural backgrounds attracted employers. In New York, the majority of our research participants worked for Indian families, particularly as nannies. Indian families seek out and value Nepali women for their mothering role, shared culture, and language. The same factors make Nepali women prefer to work in Indian households. Particularly in the initial stages of their work lives, and especially if they are older (in their late forties and fifties), Nepali immigrant women feel comfortable working with Indian families. In such a way, South Asian connections and relationships are carried over into transatlantic cities. Abha's employers are Indian, and she and they have bonded through their culture and common religious orientation. As Abha said, "When I was in Nepal, I had wished to make a temple for Goddess Durga. I didn't have enough money, so I borrowed from the NGO that I worked in and hired construction workers to build a temple. I will also place a statue of Goddess Durga in the temple. I'm a true devotee of the goddess. My employers are also devotees of Goddess Durga. When I heard that, I felt like it was God's decision to bring me to their house."

Shared culture and language provide a sense of comfort and security for both employers and employees. These factors, however, do not eliminate unequal power relations. In the long run, gradually increasing workloads can lead to different forms of oppression and exploitation, though that subject is not addressed in this essay. As for Latinas, Nepali women's experiences mirror duality—on the one hand, they are considered part of the family; on the other hand, they are frequently asked to perform tasks that fall outside the original job description. Such dualities are evident in the following statements: "Today, when I was about to come here, they had bought me a handbag as a gift for Mother's Day. They are very good to me. My employers own a clinic. They're both doctors. One of them is a brain doctor. The other one is a pediatrician. They have given me training in the clinic as well. When the clinic is very hectic, I help them by taking temperatures and recording them." Women's ability to get jobs also depends on how particular employers view these women's roles in relation to their socioeconomic and cultural backgrounds. Meena, a fifty-four-year-old babysitter, returned to Nepal after watching a child for two years. Her employer subsequently traveled to Nepal to ask her to come back and look after his child. Before her first stay in the United States, Meena had taught high school, and her employer particularly valued her ability to teach his child as well as her knowledge of both English and Hindi and her ability to cook vegetarian food. According to Meena,

> I've tried teaching the two-year-old different languages, and that's why the parents are very impressed. I also teach different dances to the kid. Even the kid is very pleased with me. He ignores his mother and asks for me. If the kid wasn't so attached to me, then babysitting would have been very difficult for me. Older kids don't like the idea of a babysitter. They become very difficult and cry for their mother. But this kid isn't problematic. I knew how to deal with this kid. I observed what makes him happy and what makes him sad. I learned that he loves to dance. They have different kinds of music, and when I play the music and pretend to dance, he becomes very happy. When he cries, and if I dance, then he becomes

very curious and stops crying. Thinking back on my own life, I wasn't even as involved with my own child. When he was four years old, I sent him to a private boarding school in Darjeeling, India.

Meena's case suggests that employers are selective in hiring nannies, valuing special qualities and particular backgrounds. Although care work is viewed as and labeled an unskilled job, in reality, it is not. Employers are drawn to experienced and educated workers (particularly teachers) who can perform multiple tasks.

Transnational Remittances

BUILDING SOCIAL CAPITAL AND SOCIAL ASSETS

When we examined the types of networks these women maintained with people in their home countries, we found that transnational ties were maintained through remittances. Most of the previous literature has focused on women's contributions to the family unit—that is, women send money for their children and spouses or elderly parents, to build or extend family homes, and generally to contribute to family resources. We found that the remittances existed on a continuum. Although many of our participants sent money to their families, others sent money to community organizations, such as religious institutions, or to nonreligious NGOs. In sum, these women were building family and community resources, a trend identified by Levitt (2001). However, mainstream literature on transnational community building does not often note women's role in this process.

Sending money home to family members, especially children or elderly parents, is a well-recognized phenomenon, and our participants frequently mentioned doing so. But we often found that the Nepali women's remittance patterns combined family obligations with community/cultural obligations. The remittance patterns also indicated the continuity of women's established relationships, where the boundaries between family and community are blurred.

Rita, a forty-seven-year-old child-care provider and house cleaner explained,

> Women send their income back home for family and for social causes. I see this person who always wears the same clothes every day. She says that she gives all of her income away to a temple and family back home. She has two children back home who she financially supports. I take inspiration from her. She sacrifices personal pleasure for the greater good of the community back home. . . . I send money back home to my family members, especially to my mother. She then gives some to temples. . . . When things are good, I send back a lot, and sometimes when I don't have too much money, I send a little less. So it isn't always fixed. I send it through friends who are going back to Nepal and through money transfer agencies. And most of the women do the same. So it's hard to tell exactly when and how much.

Other interviewees confirmed Rita's statement that it is hard to specify how much money they send and how often they do so. Equally important, they all recognized that some of the money would be given to temples or for *pujas* (rituals in praying to and worshiping various gods and goddesses). This giving is not organized as money given by congregations to churches. Our participants were Hindus whose religious lives are not based on congregational membership (see Hamal Gurung 2009; Ranjeet 2009). Money given for religious purposes is simply part of a family's obligation, a part of everyday living. In some ways, we can characterize this giving as continuing a culturally recognized way of contributing money.

NGOs, SOCIAL WELFARE ORGANIZATIONS, SCHOOLS, AND CHILDREN

Other participants give money to NGOs and social organizations to sponsor and support orphan children and to educate underprivileged children. Ten of our participants indicated that they send money for nonfamily/community entities, thus building and maintaining status and social capital at a distance as well as demonstrating a philanthropic humanitarianism despite the ongoing challenges and hardships they contend with on a daily basis in the United States. Before Abha came to the United States in 2003, she was politically and socially active in her community. She was the chair of her municipality, defeating nine men to win election to that position. She subsequently became a board member of a Nepali NGO, the Women's Federation for World Peace, and she is now a life member of the organization. Although she lives and works in New York, she maintains her connections to the Nepali organization: "I keep in touch with them. Some of my friends who are here wanted to work in the NGO here, so I noted their names and sent their names back to my head office in Nepal. The head office in Nepal contacted the office here, and my friends could work in the NGO as well." Binta, too, maintains her connections with her communities and organizations back home:

> I was very proud of the status that I had in Nepal as a teacher and as a social worker. But after coming here, I feel guilty that I am a babysitter. However, I also send money back to the organization that I used to work with, and I feel like I have given back a lot to the organization. I'm going to stay a few years and keep supporting the women's organization back in Nepal. I hope that when I go back, the women will respect me because I was not just working for my personal concerns. In addition, some of the money that I am investing . . . goes to help the kids of poor families. The kids can get scholarships to study in the university. I feel like I have contributed to the Nepalese society.

Several women reported that they regularly sent money to support Nepali NGOs and schools. Like Binta, they expressed the hope that they would be respected for their contributions when they returned. Faced with downward mobility and jobs that offer few opportunities for self-fulfillment in the United States, they have turned to building transnational assets, taking advantage of the transfer of capital across countries. Abha was vocal about this matter: "I think my self-respect has been most affected. The job that I hold now solves my economic problems. But when I helped needy people back home, I was proud of myself and my job. But performing this job has made me stronger internally. Yes, this process has definitely made me courageous. If women gather their courage and act accordingly, then they can do anything."

Anita, a fifty-one-year-old live-in nanny, is working hard to save some money so that she can open a school in Nepal. She is also quite involved in the Nepalese community in the United States. She works to raise funds to help and support poor children in Nepal: "I am a member of Greater Boston Nepalese Community organization, and I am really involved in that. Recently, each of us donated fifty dollars to a public school back in Nepal. I am also involved in the one-dollar program; the money we collect primarily goes to the needy and poor children back home."

We did not find a direct, clear correlation among our interviewees between higher education, higher earnings, and giving to civil society organizations; however, Abha and other women who are more visible as leaders are more apt to be college educated. These remittances appeared to build a path that would result in higher status when or if these women returned to Nepal. While their giving was always humanitarian in nature, their earnings, however meager, appeared to create spaces for them as women in the public arena. From this perspective, they are deploying their earnings to challenge a gendered system where men have traditionally been the participants in the public arena. Gendered shifts, though not always apparent from our current theoretical perspective, were resulting from these women's earnings in the United States.

Thus, Nepali women use their U.S. earnings to acquire social capital in family, community, and civil society settings in Nepal. And their overlapping patterns of giving suggest that we think about their remittances in terms that go beyond the gendered racialized expectation that these poorly paid women are simply enmeshed in their families.

Conclusion

A significant body of work has documented that care work is difficult, strenuous, and organized in ways that offer very few rewards to the women (and occasionally men) who perform this labor in the informal economy. This study supports these earlier conclusions. However, the two trends we identified raise additional theoretical issues.

First, the Nepali women appeared to work in a niche of the domestic work labor market. This finding appears to indicate that this labor market is segmented. These women were hired by affluent Indian families, and key employment qualifications were cultural characteristics—food, religion, and some linguistic familiarity. While we are convinced that education gave these women a significant edge over their less educated peers, college degrees are not typically the qualifications these employers sought or rewarded.

Since the mid-1960s, when they began to come in large numbers, Indian migrants to the United States have consistently been among the top median income earners among immigrants (see, e.g., Purkayastha 2005). Indian American families have developed the economic power to pick care workers whose culture most closely approximates their own. In other words, Indian American nonassimilation in matters of religion, food habits, willingness to speak other languages at home, and cultural retention creates a segment defined by cultural match. The experience of Latinas and Caribbean women suggests that the stereotypes of these women lead to their opportunities in mainstream white households. Nepalis, partially because of their invisibility and the larger society's lack of understanding about who they are, do not appear to be able to access these care-work opportunities in mainstream homes. But the affluence of co-ethnic South Asians makes Nepali culture the human capital for this segment of the labor market. With nonwhite Americans poised to become the new "minority majority" in the twenty-first century, this issue has potential long-term consequences for the informal labor market.

Second, most studies of transnationalism have not looked systematically at informal workers' ability and practice of sending money back to build community institutions and social capital. While many studies have tracked the huge sums transferred back to home countries, few examine the meanings and directions of women's contributions. Among transnational studies, Levitt (2001) did not differentiate by sex, and Purkayastha (2005) focused on middle-class and affluent South Asian groups. Here we find evidence of women building institutional links outside family spheres. So, women appear to be creating transnational social capital—clout, resources—by virtue of being members of a group. Equally important, women appear to be supporting education, peace efforts, and women's groups—that is, strengthening the institutional arenas in which they had been active prior to migration—in ways that challenge existing gender barriers. Future research should move beyond the idea that "traditional Third World women" are enmeshed only in gendered (read: subordinated) family relationships and examine their transnational involvements even though they are poor and marginalized in the United States.

Notes

1. Ray and Qayum (2009) also found that domestic workers were ill treated in New York City.

2. All names used in this chapter are fictitious, and data from two cities have been merged to ensure confidentiality.

3. The first wave included interviews of twenty women in 2005–6. In the second wave, which occurred during the summer of 2009, Hamal Gurung interviewed fifteen new participants and conducted follow-up interviews with five of the earlier participants.

4. Historically, India has been the main destination for Nepali labor migrants. Male international labor migration, particularly for British and Indian army soldiers, has a long history.

5. Female labor migrants who work in domestic service in the Arabian Gulf nations have been frequently reported to suffer simultaneously from labor and sexual exploitation. During a 2008 visit to Kathmandu, Hamal Gurung read of three such cases.

6. Our informal impression is based on Hamal Gurung's position in the community. The University of Connecticut has promoted scholarly work on Nepali groups, and Hamal Gurung was previously located on this campus, where she initiated this study. The North American Nepali women's conference—the first of its kind—was held at the university, and Ranjeet and Purkayastha's (2007) work on domestic violence was conducted there.

7. In addition, some women had overstayed their visas, while others who were in the country legally lacked visas that permitted them to obtain employment.

References

Central Bureau of Statistics. 2001. *Statistical Year Book of Nepal.* Kathmandu, Nepal.

Diner, Hasia. 1983. *Erin's Daughters in America: Irish Immigrant Women in the Nineteenth Century.* Baltimore: Johns Hopkins University Press.

Ehrenreich, Barbara, and Arlie Russell Hochschild 2002. Introduction to *Global Woman: Nannies, Maids, and Sex Workers in the New Economy,* ed. Barbara Ehrenreich and Arlie Russell Hochschild, 1–13. New York: Henry Holt and Company.

Hamal Gurung, Shobha. 2003. "Women in Factory-Based and Home-Based Carpet Production in Nepal: Beyond the Formal and Informal Economy." PhD diss., Northeastern University.

———. 2009. "Growing Up Hindu: Mapping the Memories of a Nepali Woman in the U.S." In *Living Our Religions: Hindu and Muslim South Asian American Women Narrate Their Experiences,* ed. Anjana Narayan and Bandana Purkayastha, 195–210. Sterling, Va.: Kumarian.

Hondagneu-Sotelo, Pierrette. 2001. *Doméstica: Immigrant Workers Cleaning and Caring in the Shadows of Affluence.* Berkeley: University of California Press.

Hondagneu-Sotelo, Pierrette, and Ernestine Ávila. 1997. "I'm Here but I'm There: The Meaning of Latina Transnational Motherhood." *Gender and Society* 11:548–71.

Ignacio, Emily. 2005. *Building Diaspora: Filipino Community Formation on the Web.* New Brunswick, N.J.: Rutgers University Press.

Kofman, Eleonore. 2000. "Beyond a Reductionist Analysis of Female Migrants in Global European Cities: The Unskilled, Deskilled, and Professional." In *Gender and Global Reconstructing: Sightings, Sites, and Resistances,* ed. Marianne H. Marchand and Anne Sisson Runyan, 129–39. New York: McGraw Hill.

Levitt, Peggy. 2001. *The Transnational Villagers.* Berkeley: University of California Press.

Louie, Miriam Ching Yoon. 2001. *Sweatshop Warriors: Immigrant Women Workers Take on the Global Factory.* Boston: South End.

Parreñas, Rhacel Salazar. 2001. *Servants of Globalization: Women, Migration, and Domestic Work.* Palo Alto: Stanford University Press.

Pessar, Patricia. 1999. "Engendering Migration Studies." *American Behavioral Scientist* 42:577–600.

Portes, Alejandro. 1997. *Globalization from Below: The Rise of Transnational Communities.* http://www.transcomm.ox.ac.uk/working%20papers/portes.pdf.

Purkayastha, Bandana. 2004. "Skilled Migration and Cumulative Disadvantage: The Case of Highly Qualified Asian Indian Immigrant Women in the U.S." *Geoforum* 36:181–96.

———. 2005. *Negotiating Ethnicity: Second-Generation South Asian Americans Traverse a Transnational World.* New Brunswick, N.J.: Rutgers University Press.

Ranjeet, Bidya. 2009. "At the Cross Roads of Religions: The Experiences of a Newar Woman in Nepal and the U.S." In *Living Our Religions: Hindu and Muslim South Asian American Women Narrate Their Experiences,* ed. Anjana Narayan and Bandana Purkayastha, 86–90. Sterling, Va.: Kumarian.

Ranjeet, Bidya, and Bandana Purkayastha. 2007. "A Minority within a Minority: Nepalese American Women and Domestic Violence." In *Body Evidence: Intimate Violence Against South Asian Women in America,* ed. Shamita Das Gupta, 38–42. New Brunswick, N.J.: Rutgers University Press.

Ray, Raka, and Seemin Qayum. 2009. *Cultures of Servitude: Modernity, Domesticity, and Class in India.* Palo Alto: Stanford University Press.

Romero, Mary. 1992. *Maid in the U.S.A.* New York: Routledge.

Sassen, Saskia. 2006. *Cities in a World Economy.* Thousand Oaks, Calif.: Pine Forge.

Schiller, Nina Glick, Linda Basch, and Cristina Blanc-Szanton, eds. 1992. *Towards a Transnational Perspective on Migration.* New York: New York Academy of Sciences.

Ward, Kathryn. 1990. "Introduction and Overview." In *Women Workers and Global Restructuring,* ed. Kathryn Ward, 1–22. Ithaca: Cornell University Press.

Waters, Mary, and Peggy Levitt, eds. 2002. *The Changing Face of Home: Transnational Lives of the Second Generation.* New York: Sage.

Wichterich, Christa. 2000. *The Globalized Woman: Reports from a Future of Inequality.* New York: Zed.

5

Paradoxes of Patriarchy

Contradicting Experiences of South Asian Women in Ethnic Labor Markets

PALLAVI BANERJEE

Sufia is a twenty-eight-year-old Pakistani woman who works in an ethnic jewelry store owned by her brother-in-law in the South Asian ethnic labor markets in a large midwestern city. She lives with her brother-in-law's family in a neighborhood close to the ethnic market and earns between five hundred and one thousand dollars a month, depending on how well the business is doing. Her husband lives in Pakistan after being deported from the United States for overstaying his tourist visa. She has two children, aged four and two, and is their primary caregiver and provider. Her workday begins at around 6:00 in the morning, when she prepares lunch for her children and her employer's children, gets them ready for school, and then drives her employer's children to school and her children to day care. She then opens the jewelry store, puts the jewelry on display, opens up the account book, processes the orders for the day, and waits for her brother-in-law and his wife. When they arrive, she leaves to pick up all the children and bring them to the store, where she feeds them. The store is busier in the evening, so she alternates her work with taking care of the children. When she is dealing with customers, her employers often take care of the children. At about 8:30 in the evening, she cleans the store, puts the jewelry away, and drives home with her children. She helps with dinner, puts the children to bed, and finally ends her day.

This story is typical for South Asian women who work in the South Asian labor market in the United States. Not all such women work in businesses owned by their relatives, but many of their lives nevertheless resemble Sufia's. Most of the women are engaged in low-wage work within the ethnic labor market, employed by male-owned businesses and with little separation between the private and public spheres. The women and their families often live in same ethnic enclaves where they work.

In the past two decades, research on low-wage-earning immigrant women in the labor markets has focused primarily on Latinas and Hispanics (Greenlees and Saenz 1999; Hondagneu-Sotelo 1992; Hondagneu-Sotelo and Ávila 1997; Portes and Borocz 1989; Portes and Rumbaut 2001; Segura 1989). Little attention has been paid to other low-income immigrant minority women, such as those from South Asia. The few U.S. sociologists who have studied South Asian women have focused on sociocultural aspects of the lives of high-income Indian or Pakistani women (George 1998; Greene 1997; Kurien 2001). Low-wage-earning South Asian women remain an understudied group.

Previous research has shown that South Asian societies follow a model of classical patriarchy (Kandiyoti 1988). The women in this structure have no economic independence and are not part of the production system in any way other than reproductive work (Toro-Morn 1995). They are provided for economically by the men in the family. In this system, women have been found to secure some power within the family by playing the patriarchal system and making the best they can of their situation (Kandiyoti 1988). As heterosexual families migrate from a patrilocal and kinship-based societal structure to Western society, their social worlds change (Baluja 2003; Espiritu 2003; Yang and Ebaugh 2001). This shift causes intense renegotiations among men and women in a new power structure, followed by important shifts in the resources available to both men and women (Espiritu 2003; Kibria 1993).

Migration often demands that women share and shoulder economic responsibilities for the family. They often find work in the low-wage labor markets in their ethnic enclaves (Hondagneu-Sotelo 1992, 2003; Hondagneu-Sotelo and Ávila 1997; Raijman and Semyenov 1997; Segura 1989; Zhou and Logan 1989). This change in the status of women from subordinate economic dependency to employment often leads to renegotiations within the family, reframing the forms of patriarchy and male domination as both men and women try to adjust and become acculturated to the host society. One interesting question concerns whether alterations in the interactions between men and women (where both are employed in low-income labor markets) have any significant effect on women's bargaining power and reduce men's authority and domination within the household. In this essay, I explore whether South Asian immigrant women's entry into a structurally stratified ethnic labor market creates a paradox in the lives of these women. I specifically examine whether employment increases the women's bargaining power within the household and whether the close proximity between work and home facilitates working longer hours for little pay.

I explore these questions by conducting ethnography of South Asian women in low-wage ethnic labor markets. I find that these women's structural and cultural circumstances make them more vulnerable to exploitation. The women often choose to work in ethnic labor markets to be close to their homes. However, this proximity blurs the division between the public and private spheres, increasing the women's overall working hours. The women also negotiate many contradictions. The ethnic markets' familial/patrilineal structure creates social capital and a safe space for the women but also affords exploitation of the women in terms of reduced wages and increased work hours.

Paradoxes of Immigration and Gendered Labor in Ethnic Enclaves

The literature on international migration contends that immigrants often experience considerable hardships when entering the labor market of a new country (Boyd 1989; Hondagneu-Sotelo and Ávila 1997; Raijman and Semyonov 1997; Segura 1989). Raijman and Semyonov (1997) use King's (1988) concept of multiple disadvantages to suggest that "recent immigrant women from Asia and Africa are at a 'triple disadvantage,'" first as women, second as recent immigrants, and third as immigrants from less developed traditional societies" (Raijman and Semyonov 1997, 119).[1] Many immigrants, especially those with low human capital (that is, little education, little or no English proficiency, and nontransferable professional skills), often can find only low-paying employment in ethnic labor markets. Ethnic enclaves and labor markets are parallel economic systems, often based on informal market interactions and fostering the founding and growth of ethnic businesses, which provide employment opportunities for co-ethnics.

Decades of debate about how ethnic labor markets affect immigrant workers has resulted in two distinct arguments. One camp (Portes 1987; Portes and Jensen 1987; Portes and Manning 1986; Portes and Sensenbrenner 1993) argues that ethnic labor markets offer better opportunities for recently arrived immigrant workers by providing social support networks that generate "bounded solidarity" and "enforceable trust" (Portes and Sensenbrenner 1993). The other camp (Gilbertson 1995; Kwong 1997; Sanders and Nee 1987; Waldinger 1986; Zhou 2004) argues that ethnic labor markets are mobility traps because they do not provide opportunities available in the formal economy, such as job training, wage increases, and labor protection. Ethnic labor markets thus afford more labor exploitation. With the exception of studies like those of Gilbertson (1995) and Zhou and Logan (1989), these discussions completely overlook how gender plays out in the ethnic labor markets. These two studies, however, find that despite being more educated than men, women working in ethnic labor markets get less return on their human capital.

Similarly, Dallalfar's (1994) case study of Iranian women in ethnic labor markets in Los Angeles shows that though ethnic labor markets provide opportunities for women to own businesses and employ co-ethnic women, the outcomes vary because of differential access to these resources. For example, women with less education face clear constraints on employment. Women were also excluded from many retail and service industries where most owners and shopkeepers were men. Most Iranian women were employed in homes or by businesses run from home by other women, making these women's work not publicly visible. Dallalfar also hints at the possibility that for the women who own businesses as well as the women who work in these businesses, the distinction between the public and private spheres disappears.

Bao's (2001) study of garment sweatshops in U.S. Chinatowns finds that although these shops employed numerous women, the division of labor on the shop floor was ascertained by traditional gender expectations: the higher-paying jobs, such as pressing and sorting, went to men, while the lowest-paying jobs, such as trimming and sewing, went to women. Bao also finds that since the garment shops were located in the ethnic enclaves where most of the workers lived, women who had family responsibilities, such as taking care of small children, often worked from home. Living in a close-knit community afforded these women relationships with their employers that resulted in employers allowing the women to bring sewing machines home. The women liked this arrangement because it allowed them flexible work hours and preserved the traditional household setting, with women staying home and allowing other members of the family, especially men, to work outside. Such arrangements, however, blurred the division between the public and the domestic sphere, and the women's work was often devalued because it was done at home. The garment shops were familial and paternalistic, and employers and employees frequently formed emotional ties and used kinship terminology with regard to one another. This managerial style created an informal collegial relationship among employers and employees, allowed flexible work schedules, and offered opportunities for family-type recreation, such as celebrations of the Chinese New Year; in addition, however, employers developed expectations of unquestioned allegiance and loyalty among their employees. Hiring and firing were informal processes, thereby making employees particularly vulnerable. Nevertheless, the paternalistic structure also provided employees with some agency to use the system to garner benefits.

Some of the paradoxes can be explained by Ong's (1991) theory that labor regimes in Asia and Mexico are often despotic (state controlled) and paternalistic (local institutional control). Ong argues that one of the reasons for Third World immigrant women's oppression in the workplace is the lack of development of feminist consciousness in developing countries. According to Ong (1991, 412), local labor regimes are neither exclusively paternalistic nor despotic but "involve different disciplinary schemes institutionalized by local capitalist and cultural practices." To analyze the complex and changing relations of domination and subordination in different labor regimes, Ong uses the idea of cultural struggle, arguing that the way labor regimes use culture to wield power over workers and the ways workers defend themselves against modes of control by using cultural tropes show the importance of cultural struggles in understanding power and agency in labor regimes. Ong uses the example of Asian workers in export industries, where women are addressed as "working daughters," thus emphasizing their junior status. This strategy justifies paying the women less for their work than the men. Thus the "daughter" status at home is reproduced in the workplace, generating tensions between new feelings of personal freedom on the one hand and the claims of family and society on the other. The women often use this vulnerable status to their advantage by performing gender in ways that give them opportunities to renegotiate power relations. The women in these labor regimes also sometimes exercise self-surveillance (Foucault 1979) because the disciplinary practices of the labor markets (which often resemble Foucault's prison) produce docile bodies that self-police into a performance of femininity. This self-surveillance or policing, Foucault argues, is a form of obedience to patriarchy.

The contexts of patriarchy vary, however, in different societies. Kandiyoti's (1988) theory of classical patriarchy points at culturally specific gendered practices that immigrants might carry to the United States. Classical patriarchy, prevalent in the Middle East and in South and East Asia, has a strict hierarchy in which men are the heads of household and the providers, while women remain at the bottom both in society and in the family. In addition, classical patriarchy features the complete separation of the private and the public spheres and patriarchal surveillance of women. Kandiyoti suggests that in the classical South Asian patriarchal model, women maximize resources within patriarchal systems through the use of rational agency in the form of strategies they deem necessary to survive the system. She calls these strategies "patriarchal bargains," by which she means the ways that women negotiate and adapt to the norms that guide and constrain gender relations. "Bargaining with patriarchy" implies that both men and women possess resources with which they negotiate to maximize power and options within a patriarchal structure.

However, migration alters interactions between men and women in the migrating families (Espiritu 2003; Kibria 1993; Yang and Ebaugh 2001). While alterations may occur in the interactions between men and women, virtually no significant shifts take place in men's power and authority (Kibria, 1993; Min 1998; Pessar 1995). As my research on Bangladeshi women in Chicago (Banerjee 2008) and Predelli's (2004) research on South Asian Muslim women in Europe show, while South Asian women are cultural products of the classical form of patriarchy, migration to the United States with their husbands has altered this form of patriarchy. My interviews with Bangladeshi women show that women now identify their husbands as the heads of household, and that instead of subjugation to their fathers and later fathers-in-law, women are now subordinate only to their husbands, a phenomenon I call conjugal patriarchy (Banerjee 2008). Another important change that occurs with migration is that women often have to act as coproviders in the household for the economic survival of the family (Glenn 1992; Kim and Hurh 1985; Min 1998; Moon 2003; Segura 1989). Also, nonwhite men, especially recent immigrants with low human capital, can rarely earn enough to support their families, forcing women to enter the labor force for subsistence as their wages are critical to the household (Glenn 1992). Moreover, studies have shown that the growth in female-intensive labor markets and a bias for racialized female labor make Asian women more employable than men both in low-wage jobs and in white-collar jobs (Chai 1998; Espiritu 1997, 2003; Glenn 1992). This employability often reflects existing patriarchal and racist ideologies about work and workers, whether in the electronics industry (Hossfeld 1994) or in service-related industries (Chai 1998). As Chai (1998) concludes, the patriarchal and racist ideologies that consign women of color to subordinate positions also provide such women with an employability advantage, possibly increasing their bargaining power in their families.

In some cases, women's employment status affects their negotiation and bargaining power within the household (George 2005; Menjivar 1999; Min 1998; Moon 2003; Park 1997). Moon (2003, 841) argues that when immigrant women increase their financial contribution to their household income through paid employment, they acquire more power within the household to "renegotiate their power vis-à-vis their husbands, demanding a more equitable share in decision making and housework from their husbands." Min's (1998) study of Korean families in New York provides another insightful account of how migration alters the lives of Korean families and how both men and women negotiate changed gender relationships within the household. Min finds that Korean men carry patriarchal ideologies; husbands expect even working wives to be obedient and to do all the housework, which is seen as "women's work." As a result, the women suffer from overwork, stress, and frustration. However, as they gain economic and social independence, women begin to demand that their husbands share in the housework. Conflicts result because while the economic roles of men and women have changed in the new society, men's gendered expectations of women have not changed, and doing housework is seen as a loss of masculine authority as master of the household.

These studies show that while employment status gives the perception of independence and even has real consequences in changing gendered practices within the household, the ideologies of gender do not change much, especially for men. Women's employment also results in some increase in their ability to negotiate male domination within the household, but such changes are often inconsistent with women's ideologies of gender and family.

These findings lead to important questions about how South Asian women negotiate the paradoxes in their lives that emerge from their migration process and their employment status in the ethnic labor markets. Does moving away from the traditional gendered expectations for women in their home countries give South Asian women a different perception of their negotiation abilities within their households? Does women's employment status and subsequent economic independence change their acceptance of subordination in patriarchal (now conjugal) families? Does the idea of what constitutes work in ethnic labor markets take on a different meaning for men and women? How do these perceptions compare to the material realities of South Asian immigrants' lives?

Methodology

This study is based on in-depth interviews and observations at the homes and places of employment of twenty women who migrated to the United States from five different South Asian countries—Pakistan, Bangladesh, Nepal, Afghanistan, and India—that are part of what Kandiyoti (1988) calls the "classical patriarchy" belt. The women are now employed in different South Asian ethnic labor markets. My interview questions sought to determine whether the women's employment status contributed to their empowerment or constituted an added form of male domination and oppression, reinforcing gender and socioeconomic inequality. The interviews and the participant observations were conducted over a long period beginning in April 2007, with follow-up interviews conducted in 2008 and some new interviews conducted in 2009. The interviews were conducted either at participants' homes or at their workplaces during breaks. Most of the interviews took two to three hours, with frequent breaks to play with the interviewees' children or to eat. I generally observed the women at the stores where they worked for one or two hours a week over a period of six months. My interviewees constituted a nonrandom convenience sample from among employees with whom I had conversed at various stores I patronized. I asked each woman if she would like to participate in a study about immigrant women in ethnic labor markets and scheduled interviews with those who agreed.

My status as a South Asian woman who spoke the employees' language and was a customer made me an insider, facilitating my entry into the community. However, my position as a researcher and a customer also made me an outsider, a status that conferred both advantages (because the women did not feel threatened by me) and a disadvantage (because some members of the community, especially men and business owners, viewed me with suspicion). As a researcher, I am also aware of my power over my participants. To ensure interviewees' confidentiality, I checked with them about how they were represented in this study and accepted any suggestions they offered to conceal their identities and maintain their confidentiality.

INTRODUCING LOW-WAGE SOUTH ASIAN WOMEN WORKERS

All of the women in my study moved to the United States within the past ten to fifteen years. They either came with their husbands (most of whom possessed diversity visas)[2] or joined husbands who had come five to fifteen years earlier, found jobs, and could now afford to bring their families. The husbands generally worked in other ethnic markets, were cab drivers, or owned small businesses and employed their wives. The women ranged between twenty-five and thirty-five years of age. Most of the women came from lower-middle-class or working-class backgrounds, though three women described their families as middle class. These three women were the only ones in the group who had high school and college degrees. Most of the women came from either Bangladesh or Pakistan, with two from Nepal, three from Afghanistan, and three from India. The two Nepali women were Hindu; all of the other women were Muslim. Eight participants worked part time at the checkout counters of ethnic grocery stores; one woman ran an ethnic grocery store owned by her husband; two worked in an ethnic restaurant; one worked in a clothing store; two worked in an ethnic jewelry store; three worked in a travel agency; and three worked in an ethnic hair salon. Two of the women were unmarried; all of the rest had children between ages five and fourteen. Only the three women working at the travel agency had college degrees; nine of the others had completed high school; the rest had either never gone to school or dropped out before high school. Only fourteen women could speak and understand English; the other six could use phrases such as "How are you?," "Thank you," and "Have a good day."

BIRYANI RICE TO BOLLYWOOD MOVIES: DESCRIPTION OF THE ETHNIC LABOR MARKETS

Like most ethnic labor markets, the market where I conducted my study is located in a South Asian ethnic enclave in a large midwestern city. Located on a busy street, this enclave is bustling with people, mostly South Asians, and has a localized economy with community-based resources to sustain it. Businesses include restaurants, snack and sweet shops, clothing stores, beauty salons, electronics stores, luggage stores, jewelry stores, grocery stores, a travel agency, pawn shops, dollar stores, media (video and CD) stores, immigration lawyers, accounting firms, insurance agencies, health centers with South Asian doctors and nurses, nonprofit organizations, social service agencies, and banks. Most of the businesses are owned and run by South Asian men, mainly Indians and Pakistanis. Most of the employees in these businesses live in the area. Though most of the businesses are formally registered with the state, business is carried out in a way that can be categorized as informal. Most employees are hired through personal and familial contacts, and no formalized hiring or firing systems are followed. No standard salary or compensation structures exist. Jobs offer no leave or benefits. Most products and services have no fixed prices, and consumers are expected to haggle. Hence, I view this ethnic labor market largely as an extension of the informal economy on which 92 percent of the South Asian communities (India and Pakistan) depend (Baruah 2004).

According to the ethnic business owners, they choose to employ these immigrant women in large part because they can be hired cheaply and are inclined to be obedient workers. The employers, especially single-owner enterprises run by men, also cast themselves as benevolent feudal patriarchs. In my participant observations, these owners often described feeling a moral obligation to employ these women so that they can earn money that their families and children need. Employers also often used familial metaphors, especially when compensating the women for their work or when paying them less than the agreed-upon salary.

The women generally offered three reasons for working in these markets. As is the case for many other low-paid immigrant women, the primary reason that these women work was that their families needed extra income. All of the women said that their families had difficulty surviving on only their husbands' income, which often was very low. In a typical statement, Farah said, "My husband earns six hundred dollars every two weeks as a chef. We have four kids. We pay seven hundred dollars in rent, buy food, and send three hundred dollars back home to Bangladesh. We barely have any money left for food, and then there is going to the doctor for the kids, my husband's travel costs. We were almost starving, so I started looking for jobs in the area and got one, helping in a clothing store. It does not pay much, but we survive."

Having decided that they needed to work, these women chose to find employment near their homes so that they could more easily take care of their children. Many of the women often brought their children to work after school. Zoya, a mother of two who worked in a hair salon, said, "If I worked in another salon somewhere, I would probably make more money. But I can't work away from home. Who will get the kids from school? . . . My husband is a taxi driver. I never know which part of town he is in. I can quickly go home and fix my kids a meal. I often bring them here. It helps to work near where you live, especially if you are a woman."

A third reason highlighted by the women is the fear of mainstream America. At least sixteen of these women told me that they were "afraid to work outside the enclave." They also reported that "it feels safer to work among our own people." The only women who said that they would be willing to work outside the enclave were two of the three college-educated women working in the travel agency. Most of the women feared racism and worried that white American businesses would not hire them. The women were also aware of their low human capital, which rendered them unemployable in the mainstream formal economy. Finally, they said that the informality of the ethnic labor markets also made it easier for the women to become employed. According to Reba, "I never thought it would be so easy. I walked into a store and I asked for a job, and they gave it to me. No forms to be filled out, no interview. . . . They asked me if I can talk well in Hindi, and I said yes, and whooosh, I was employed."

Women Workers' Dilemmas

Three broad themes emerged from my analysis of the women's narratives. These themes are contradictory and perhaps indicate the dilemmas that these women face in their everyday lives.

THEME 1: DERIVED SENSE OF SELF-ACTUALIZATION, EMPOWERMENT, AND DEMARGINALIZATION

Women from South Asia belong to a traditional patriarchal structure that enforces a strict separation of the public (work institutions) and the private (family and the home) spheres. Women are thought to belong strictly in the private sphere. The migration process not only altered their family structure to conjugal patriarchy but also changed their social location and ultimately their employment status. These changes led to a feeling of self-actualization among many of the women. Many participants felt that employment had helped them discover their talents, learn new life skills, and become more productive. Razia, a salon employee, said, "I had done a training in hairdos and threading when I was nineteen, back in India. Then I got married and never thought I would ever use what I learned. I was really happy when I got this job. I am considered the best threading person here. All the customers want me for threading. It makes me very happy. For the first time I feel I am worth something." Farida told me, "Since I have started working, I have become so much smarter. I can even speak a little bit of English, and I even travel in the city on my own." The process of self-actualization also provides a sense of demarginalization, enabling the women to feel that they can better negotiate mainstream America, which was completely foreign to them before they began interacting with the world outside their household walls.

Another prominent emotion expressed by the women as a result of their employed status was a sense of pride and indispensability. The women felt that their income provided stability to their families. The women also said that they felt that their families could survive in the United States because of their income as much as that of their husbands. Parvati said, "I feel happy to be able to help with running the family. My kids know that today if Dad loses his job, Mom can support the family." According to Ayesha, "Since I got the job at this grocery store, my husband sleeps better at night. He now knows that we will not be evicted tomorrow and that he can still send money home for his sick dad."

Another empowering aspect of employment was the formation of new social networks and a new social support system in the workplace. Many of the women said that at their workplaces, they have friends of different races, religions, and socioeconomic statuses. They learned a lot about America from their friends at work. Most women in the study regard their women coworkers as their confidants, especially because workplace friends had no access to the women's husbands, meaning that the women could share secrets and family troubles without feeling vulnerable to exposure. Rokiya reported, "I have made so many friends at work. If something goes wrong at home, I can at least come and talk to them. And don't say this to my husband, but when we have breaks, we even discuss strategies of how to get our husbands to do more housework without them knowing they are doing it."

The women felt safe talking to female friends at work and thought of them as a social support network. All of the married women said that their husbands controlled the finances, and most interviewees said that they did most of housework in their homes. However, a few women reported that their employment status had raised their bargaining within the household in aspects of control over finances, household decision making, and distribution of household labor. Sania, who worked in an ethnic salon, had a deal with her husband that he would take care of weekday dinners and put their two children to bed: "He is a cab driver, and he works night shifts, so he is home all day. In the morning, I come to work at 11:00. I make lunch, do all the cleaning, send the kids off to school while he is sleeping. When I come back home, I am dog-tired. I can hardly stand on my feet. It was getting to be too much for me. One day, I sat him down and told him that we are no longer in Pakistan. I don't have the luxury of staying home. Since we both work, he needs to help me at home, or I need to stop working. So far, it has worked."

This statement shows that while Sania was still doing most of the housework, she used her employment status as a leverage to get her husband to help her with housework. Another woman, Samita, who worked in a grocery store, said that working has enabled her to send money to her sick mother in Nepal: "My husband is in charge of all the money in the family. He decides how to spend it and all. But since I started working, I told him that I will send money to my mother in Nepal. He always sent money to his family since we came to the United States. My mother is a widow and sick, and my brother's family in Nepal does not have enough to support her. Before this job, I had no way of helping her. Now I do, and I will. My husband understands that I work like a donkey for our family, and this is something he has to allow me to do. I won't budge from this."

Kamaldeep had migrated to the United States five years earlier with her husband and two children from a rural village in northern India and began working at a packaging company to get health insurance for her family while also working in her husband's electronic store in the ethnic enclave. Her daughter, Jassi, was graduating from high school and wanted to go to college, but Kamaldeep's husband saw no sense in sending a girl to college. Kamaldeep told her husband, "I think we should let Jassi go to college so that she does not end up like me or even you. If I had gone to college, I would probably be working in a more respectable job. And it cannot be just your decision. She is my daughter, too. I earn too now. I can pay for her college. If Parmit [their son] wants to go to college, will you say the same thing? I think girls need to be independent, and the best way out for Jassi is to go to college. I will send her to college." Jassi went on to study pharmacy science at a community college. Samita's and Kamaldeep's statements suggest that working has given them some control over household finances and decision making. They can now demand money for personal use, make important decisions about their children, and ask for things that are important to them, an agency they lacked before they began working.

THEME 2: SENSE OF DISADVANTAGE BOTH AT HOME AND AT WORK

While the women felt empowered by and benefited from their employed status, they also expressed a deep sense of disadvantage. They talked about extreme fatigue, a visceral fear that their husbands would suspect them of engaging in illicit affairs at work, a sense of not being compensated enough for their hard work, a sense of being devalued at work, and deep psychological dissatisfaction and guilt at being bad wives and mothers. Most of the women in my study were extremely tired as a result of working double shifts at their places of employment and at home. Ayesha, who worked at a grocery store, said, "Life in America is just backbreaking. See, I wake up at 4:00 in the morning, cook, clean, get my kids ready for school, make lunch for my husband, walk them to school, and then come to work. I work here until 8:00 in the evening, constantly standing. I go back home, cook dinner, and get ready for work the next day. During tea break, I go pick up the kids from school and leave them with my friend. My husband picks them up when he gets back home." She continues, "I get back home and it's the same grind. . . . I am so tired that I can't even provide much pleasure to my husband (you know what I am talking about). He gets frustrated, and I feel really bad about it. I always feel I am not a good wife." Ayesha's lament not only shows her sense of fatigue but also expresses the deep psychological trauma and guilt that she negotiates in her everyday life. Her struggles are embedded in the oppressive working conditions that normalize exploitation of women's labor and a deep-seated patriarchal ideology at home that makes housework and child care the sole responsibility of the woman, and frames providing sexual pleasure to her husband as part of a woman's wifely duty.

All but four of the women told me that they feel constant pressure to present themselves in nonsexual ways in the workplace so that their husbands and the community do not perceive them as promiscuous. Noori, who works in a travel agency, reported, "We had never really worked or interacted with men outside our families before we came here. But our work is about dealing with customers, and you know how the men in this country are, especially the Africans. They'll say anything. Like, 'You are so beautiful. Want to come with me to Africa?' and I shudder. There are Pakistani folks all around. This is sure to reach my husband. He'll then raise hell. He already thinks I am sleeping with everyone." She continues, "I never dress up when I come to work. I sometimes don't even do my hair. I look like I am crazy. So I can't help it if these customers still say nonsense. This is so much stress, you can't imagine. I'd much rather not work than go through trying to prove that I am not a whore every day. . . . But, see, I also get a lot of customers because they find me pretty—that increases my pay, and then [my husband] is happy."

The women also felt that they were not being good mothers in the traditional sense, though they knew that employment was important for their children's well-being. Many of the women expressed concerns about not being able to devote enough time to their children. Farah, who worked at a salon, brought the nuances of this paradox to light. After a phone conversation with her nine-year-old son, she told me, "He just got back from school. He wants me to come back home. I feel like I am such a bad mother. He needs me, and I can't be with him. How can I make him understand that Mama needs to work, to keep the family running. . . . I wish my husband would help a little with the kids, but he thinks that is not a man's job. I understand why he feels that way, but I have a job, too. I am doing a man's job, too. How much and how many hours can a human being work without dropping dead?"

These women fight an ideological battle. While Farah does not refute the claim that men should not do housework because they are men (a direct cognitive schema developed from patriarchal ideology), she recognizes that it is only logical for her husband to help at home. But she lacks the authority to make these changes. Another woman who worked in the same salon, Zoya, felt a more self-imposed guilt: "Life is so hard here that my husband often offers to help me with housework. Last night I was so tired, I left the dishes undone. My husband said I should not worry about them, he'd do it in the morning. But I felt really bad about it, so I woke up early and did the dishes. My husband got mad at me—he says I overdo and then overwork myself, but I feel really bad. My mother, my aunts never let the men lift a finger around the house, and I feel I should be able to do the same for my husband or I am not an able wife." She continues, "Not that he expects me to be perfect. He knows I am also working and trying my best. It's more my issue—I feel really guilty. Ideally women should be able to manage everything well." This narrative suggests an internalization of gendered expectations and the patriarchal ideology. It also suggests that women conduct a degree of self-discipline in accordance with gendered norms. However, it also indicates that migration might have or is likely to alter the traditional form of household division of labor if the husband is ready to relinquish some power.

The women feel equally disadvantaged at work. Munira, a checkout clerk at a grocery store, said, "The hours here are long and pay very little. The work is backbreaking, too. And we get yelled at a lot. The pay is not fixed either. The employer just reduces pay without warning. The problem is that we have no education, and we can't even speak English. The employers think they have done us and our families a huge favor by giving us a job. They did not ask for any papers, credentials, or interviews. I guess this is the price we pay for it." According to Sufia, a distant cousin and the sister-in-law of the owner of the jewelry store where she worked, "I enter this building at 9:00 in the morning and return home at 8:30 at night. I take no breaks, and I don't even get paid ten dollars a day. I stay at my employer's house because I am alone in the United States and have two little children. My husband has been deported. So I go back home, cook for the family, and put [my and my employer's] children to bed. By the end of the day, I feel like every bone is broken, and every morning when I wake up, I feel so tired, I wish I was dead." She continues, "And my brother-in-law justifies everything by saying I am family, but in fact what they have is a bound laborer. I know I have to work hard to get my husband back to the United States, and it is hard for me to find a job because I am not educated. But this life just kills me." Sufia summed up, "Life is very hard, but there is some satisfaction in knowing that everything I am doing, no matter how hard and cruel it is on me, is for my kids and for the family I love so much."

Sufia brings out a poignant paradox. While she is exhausted and feels disempowered by the amount of work she must do to survive, she also feels empowered to be able to raise and support her family by herself. She has agency to decide what is best for her children despite her extremely restrictive and exploitative circumstances. Most of the women in my study negotiate similar contradictions arising from their transnational experiences, the lived realities of working in patrilineal ethnic markets in low-wage jobs, and the new context of conjugal patriarchy.

THEME 3: EMPLOYER AS THE BENEVOLENT PATRIARCH

Like Chinatown garment shops (Bao 2001), the South Asian ethnic labor market in this study features familial, paternalistic businesses where the employers tend to establish emotional ties and kinship terminology with their employees. Male employers often address the women as "daughter" or "sister," automatically placing them in a subordinate familial status. This relationship also demands a familial loyalty and allegiance from the women workers. Some weeks Radhika, a single mother of two who worked in a clothing store owned by an Indian family, would receive less money than her informal agreement with her male employer called for. When Radhika demanded her full pay, the employer said, "Beti [daughter], stop crabbing. I am like your dad: When I earn more I will give more. I love your kids like my own. I buy them candies and gifts every day. If you count how much I spend on them, you'd know that I am not paying you less or cheating you out of your salary." Despite its drawbacks, Radhika, too, sees benefits to her employment situation: "This work does not pay much, but it provides a safe place for my children. My employer is crazy when it comes to pay—he tries to cut all corners with pay. But he lets my children hang around in the store and sometimes even does homework with them. I would hate if they were just hanging outside. They'd get into gangs and the bad stuff." She reasons, "Here at least they are under my watch. . . . My kids also get to celebrate Holi, Diwali, and other festivals at the store and in the other stores—at least that way, they are in touch with their culture. These are important things. My boss here also helped me with my Illinois Link Card [state-sponsored food assistance/food stamps]. I did not know how to get them, and he walked me through it." Radhika's case offers a good example of the paradox of the exploitative employer who is also a benevolent patriarch. Radhika knows that she is being exploited, but she chooses to put up with the situation because her workplace becomes an extension of the familial unit she lacks in the United States.

Similarly, when asked why she works despite knowing that she is being exploited, Sufia says, "I want my children to get a good education and better life than me or their father has had. If I worked somewhere else like at 7/11 or Walmart, I would make more money. But I couldn't bring my children to work. At least here, my brother-in-law and his wife watch them when I am working. They do homework with them. They helped me to admit my daughter to kindergarten. My babies can play with their kids. This is big thing for me." She continues, "I couldn't live with the guilt of doing any less than what I am doing for my kids now. I already feel I am not doing enough. . . . If I did any less, that would kill me." The employer and his family have become Sufia's surrogate family, a situation that has benefits but also allows for the exploitation of her labor in multiple ways, such as long work hours and unpaid care work for the employer's family.

Similarly, Sehra, a Pakistani mother of two who works in an ethnic insurance agency and whose husband spends long periods of time in Pakistan, where he has another family, and does not contribute to the family income, recognizes that her workplace is "different . . . from the rest of America. The people here want to get the most work out of you for less money. But they also help you out in other ways. My boss here treats me like his sister. He also pays me as if I was his sister—nothing. But he took my daughter to the hospital when she was sick and bailed my son out when he got picked up by the cops for speeding. What employer would do that?" She says, "With the pressures, I often lose my head, but he has never asked me leave. I also do a lot for them. When his wife goes back [to Pakistan], I cook them meals and make sure the kids are taken care of and fed. I guess as a mother, that is my calling. I don't take credit for it. He tells me I am second mother to his kids. That makes me feel appreciated." Here Sehra very clearly articulates the paradox of living and working in an ethnic labor market that is structured like a family. Being treated like the boss's sister means that she is paid very little, and she is expected to perform the work traditionally assigned to women in a patriarchal household. Sehra accepts this as her calling as a woman and a mother. The erosion of the boundary between public and private spheres means that gendered expectations in the family are reproduced in Sehra's work relations. Sehra recognizes that she is being exploited, but she also sees value in having a boss who is involved in her personal life and who does things for her family. A family is not a power-neutral unit; thus, the reproduction of family relations is a reproduction not only of intimacy but also of inequality.

Discussion and Conclusion

These narratives suggest that women who work in the South Asian ethnic markets constantly negotiate and wrestle with the contradictions and paradoxes that complicate their lives. These paradoxes also provide an alternative perspective from which to examine Third World women's immigrant experiences, complicating Western feminist concepts of the public and private spheres, ideas of family and work, and the meaning of being a low-wage woman worker in an ethnic enclave. These women's accounts can be illuminated by theories of black feminist thought (Collins 1990) and Third World feminism (Mohanty 2003), in that they show how the material experiences of being an immigrant woman from the Third World, a low-wage immigrant worker in an informal economy, and a wife and a mother differ substantively from the experiences of other U.S. women, including more privileged women of color.

These women's experiences and the paradoxes that emerged were shaped by conjugal patriarchy, particularly the notions of what it means to be a woman and a mother. They felt guilty and ashamed when they perceived their life circumstances as preventing them from being good mothers or dutiful wives in the traditional sense. However, the work that pulled them away from their homes also enabled these women to contribute to their families' financial well-being, creating paradoxical feelings of pride and guilt. In addition, these women regulated their public interactions and appearances to nullify their sexuality in the public sphere, thus engaging in self-surveillance (Foucault 1979) of gendered expectations to keep intact the systems of traditional patriarchy.

Apart from dealing with the oppression of a patriarchal gender ideology perpetuated by self-surveillance, the women also felt disadvantaged by the structural conditions of work—long hours, low pay, and unpaid caregiving work for employers' families. The ethnic market replicated the patriarchal structure of the household in work relations, creating another paradox. The ethnic markets' patrilineal and kinship-based structure rendered the economy informal, and arrangements about compensation and work duties were verbal and hence changeable. The women thus became more vulnerable to exploitation and faced even more strenuous demands on their labor. For example, employers often expected the women workers to do unpaid care work, such as cooking and caring for the employers' children. They justified this by saying that the worker was like a woman kin—a sister or daughter, and thus the expectation. While the patrilineal structure of the markets created exploitative conditions, at the same time, employers viewed the women as needing a safe space to work and assumed responsibility for them and for their children. In these and other ways, employers adopted the role of benevolent patriarchs, showing affection while maintaining power and exploiting the women's labor.

Western feminism has long questioned and problematized the idea of separate spheres for men and women (Ferree 1990; Greenstein 2000; Jacobs and Gerson 2004). The women in this study have experienced the dissolution of the divide between the private and public spheres, and one merges into the other. The structure of the markets forced the women to do unpaid caregiving work for their employers, just as they did for their families. Caregiving work was not characterized as work. At the same time, the women used the public sphere to navigate their private sphere, bringing their children to work and arranging for informal child care in their workplaces. Employers also provided help with familial work, such as obtaining food stamps and celebrating ethnic festivals. The women at times used the kinship rhetoric to make themselves indispensible, a practice that may be seen as a form of covert resistance that slightly challenged power relations (Ong 1991).

Many of the women used their employment to make their household positions more visible. While conjugal patriarchy left men as heads of household and women remained lower in the hierarchy, employment somewhat increased women's bargaining power within their households and compelled a renegotiation of power relations. They could now make decisions about their children's future or gain some financial independence to use the money for things they view as important. Women often threatened to quit work as a tactic in negotiations with their husbands about housework. Such an approach may be seen as a first step toward challenging the patriarchal gender ideology. Employment status also gave the women access to a wider network and a social support system. Women who worked in skilled jobs, such as in salons, found a new sense of self-actualization—and bargaining power with employers—through customer appreciation.

However, poor immigrant women of color embedded in a structure of conjugal patriarchy both at work and at home lack the space in which to develop feminist consciousness. The women negotiate the situation and gain some residual power only by performing gender in ways that will make them important in the structures of which they are part (Ebaugh, Fuchs, and Chafetz 2000; Kandiyoti 1988)—that is, their families, the workplace, and the community.

Given that this study was done in a South Asian ethnic enclave and is based on a small sample of women, it does not speak to the experiences of all immigrant women who work in informal markets. However, my research raises some theoretical questions about informal work, patriarchy, gender ideology, and the experiences of low-wage immigrant women in ethnic enclaves. What are the implications of the contradictions that the women must negotiate? How do the experiences of the women in this study compare to the experiences of other immigrant women of color under similar circumstances? This begs for theoretical frameworks to better explain the paradoxes that the women experience in their lives. Given the contradictory nature of these women's lives, how can they improve their circumstances? Do the answers lie in enforcing labor laws in the ethnic labor markets to make employer–employee transactions more formal, leaving less room for exploitation? What would happen to the informal social support system if the economy were to become more formal? Does the state need to change its incorporation policies for immigrants? Would it help if there were local social services instituted to develop human capital among the women to secure better jobs, to help families with child care, to raise feminist consciousness among both men and women, and to regulate how ethnic markets treat their employees?

Notes

1. The women in my study face multiple disadvantages, but I do not find race to be a factor in their lives, probably because of their limited contact with people of other races.

2. Diversity visas are issued to residents of countries whose population is underrepresented in the United States. Each of these countries has a quota for its citizens, and green cards are awarded to applicants based on a lottery system.

References

Baluja, K. F. 2003. *Gender Roles at Home and Abroad: The Adaptation of Bangladeshi Immigrants*. New York: LFB.

Banerjee, Pallavi. 2008. "Religious Gathering of Immigrant Bangladeshi Muslim Women in Chicago." M.A. thesis, University of Illinois at Chicago.

Bao, Xiaolan. 2001. *Holding Up More Than Half the Sky: Chinese Women Garment Workers in New York City, 1948–1992*. Urbana: University of Illinois Press.

Baruah, Bipasha. 2004. "Earning Their Keep and Keeping What They Earn: A Critique of Organizing Strategies for South Asian Women in the Informal Sector." *Gender Work and Organization* 11(6): 605–26.

Boyd, Monica. 1989. "Family and Personal Networks in International Migration: Recent Developments and New Agendas." *International Migration Review* 23:638–70.

Chai, K. 1998. "Competing for the Second Generation: English-Language Ministry at a Korean Protestant Church." In *Gatherings in Diaspora: Religious Communities and the New Immigrations*, ed. R. Stephen Warner and Judith Wittner, 295–331. Philadelphia: Temple University Press.

Collins, Patricia Hill. 1990. *Black Feminist Thought: Knowledge, Consciousness, and the Politics of Empowerment*. New York: Routledge.

Dallalfar, Arlene. 1994. "Iranian Women as Immigrant Entrepreneurs." *Gender and Society* 8: 541–61.

Ebaugh, Helen Rose Fuchs, and Janet Saltzman Chafetz. 2000. *Religion and the New Immigrants: Continuities and Adaptations in Immigrant Congregations*. Walnut Creek, Calif.: AltaMira Press.

Espiritu, Yen Le. 1997. *Asian American Women and Men: Labor, Laws, and Love*. Thousand Oaks, Calif.: Sage.

———. 2003. "Gender and Labor in Asian Immigrant Families." In *Gender and U.S. Immigration: Contemporary Trends*, ed. Pierrette Hondagneu-Sotelo. Berkeley: University of California Press.

Ferree, Myra Marx. 1990, "Beyond Separate Spheres: Feminism and Family Research." *Journal of Marriage and Family* 52: 866–84.

Foucault, M. 1979. *Discipline and Punish*. New York: Vintage.

George, Sheba Mariam. 2005. *When Women Come First: Gender and Class in Transnational Migration*. Berkeley: University of California Press.

Gilbertson, Greta A. 1995. "Women's Labor and Enclave Employment: The Case of Dominican and Colombian Women in New York City." *International Migration Review* 29: 657–70.

Glenn, Evelyn Nakano. 1992. "From Servitude to Service Work: Historical Continuities in the Racial Division of Paid Reproductive Labor." *Signs* 18:1–43.

Greene, Patricia G. 1997. "A Resource-Based Approach to Ethnic Business Sponsorship: A Consideration of Ismaili-Pakistani Immigrants." *Journal of Small Business Management* 35:236–87.

Greenlees, Clyde S., and R. Saenz. 1999. "Determinants of Employment of Recently Arrived Mexican Immigrant Wives." *International Migration Review* 33:354–77.

Greenstein, Theodore N. 2000. "Economic Dependence, Gender, and the Division of Labor in the Home: A Replication and Extension." *Journal of Marriage and Family* 62:322–35.

Hondagneu-Sotelo, Pierrette. 1992. "Overcoming Patriarchal Constraints: The Reconstruction of Gender Relations among Mexican Immigrant Women and Men." *Gender and Society* 6:393–415.

———. 2003. *Gender and U.S. Immigration: Contemporary Trends.* Berkeley: University of California Press.

Hondagneu-Sotelo, Pierrette, and Ernestine Avila. 1997. "I'm Here but I'm There: The Meaning of Latina Transnational Motherhood." *Gender and Society* 5:548–71.

Hossfeld, Karen, J. 1994. "Hiring Immigrant Women: Silicon Valley's 'Simple Formula.'" In *Women of Color In U.S.. Society*, ed. Maxine Baca Zinn and Bonnie Thornton Dill, 65–94. Philadelphia: Temple University Press.

Jacobs, Jerry, and Kathleen Gerson. 2004. *The Time Divide: Work, Family, and Gender Inequality.* Cambridge, Mass.: Harvard University Press.

Kandiyoti, Deniz. 1988. "Bargaining with Patriarchy." *Gender and Society* 2:274–90.

Kibria, Nazli. 1993. *Family Tightrope: The Changing Lives of Vietnamese Americans.* Princeton: Princeton University Press.

Kim, Kwang Chung, and Won Moo Hurh. 1985. "Ethnic Resources Utilization of Korean Immigrant Entrepreneurs in the Chicago Minority." *International Migration Review* 19:82–111.

King, Deborah K. 1988. "Multiple Jeopardy, Multiple Consciousness: The Context of a Black Feminist Ideology." *Signs* 14:42–72.

Kurien, Prema. 2001. "Religion, Ethnicity and Politics: Hindu and Muslim Indian Immigrants in the United States." *Ethnic and Racial Studies* 24:263–93.

Kwong, Peter. 1997. "Manufacturing Ethnicity." *Critique of Anthropology* 17:365–87.

Menjivar, Cecelia. 1999. "The Intersection of Work and Gender: Central American Immigrant Women and Employment in California." *American Behavioral Scientist* 42:601–27.

Min, Pyong Gap. 1998. *Changes and Conflicts: Korean Immigrant Families in New York.* Boston: Allyn and Bacon.

Mohanty. Chandra Talpade. 2003. *Feminism without Borders: Decolonizing Theory, Practicing Solidarity.* Durham: Duke University Press.

Moon, Seungsook. 2003. "Immigration and Mothering: Case Studies from Two Generations of Korean Immigrant Women." *Gender and Society* 17:840–67.

Ong, Aihwa. 1991. "The Gender and Labor Politics of Postmodernity." *Annual Review of Anthropology* 20:279–309.

Park, Kyeyoung. 1997. *The Korean American Dream: Immigrants and Small Business in New York City.* Ithaca: Cornell University Press.

Pessar, Patricia R. 1995. "On the Homefront and in the Workplace: Integrating Immigrant Women into Feminist Discourse." *Anthropological Quarterly* 68:37–47.

Portes, Alejandro. 1987. "The Social Origins of the Cuban Enclave Economy of Miami." *Sociological Perspectives* 30:340–72.

Portes, Alejandro, and Jozsef Borocz. 1989. "Contemporary Immigration: Theoretical Perspectives on Its Determinants and Modes of Incorporation." *International Migration Review* 23:606–30.

Portes, Alejandro, and Leif Jensen. 1987. "What's an Ethnic Enclave? The Case for Conceptual Clarity." *American Sociological Review* 52:768–71.

Portes, Alejandro, and R. D. Manning. 1986. "The Immigrant Enclave: Theory and Empirical Examples." In *Competitive Ethnic Relations*, ed. S. Olzak and J. Nagel, 47–68. Orlando, Fla.: Academic.

Portes, Alejandro, and R. G. Rumbaut. 2001. *Legacies: The Story of the Immigrant Second Generation*. Berkeley: University of California Press.

Portes, Alejandro, and Julia Sensenbrenner. 1993. "Embeddedness and Immigration: Notes on the Social Determinants of Economic Action." *American Journal of Sociology* 98:1320–50.

Predelli, L. N. 2004. "Interpreting Gender in Islam: A Case Study of Immigrant Muslim Women in Oslo." *Gender and Society* 18:473–93.

Raijman, R., and M. Semyonov. 1997. "Gender, Ethnicity, and Immigration: Double Disadvantage and Triple Disadvantage among Recent Immigrant Women in the Israeli Labor Market." *Gender and Society* 11:108–25.

Sanders J. M., and Victor Nee. 1987. "Limits of Ethnic Solidarity in the Enclave Economy." *American Sociological Review* 52:745–73.

Segura, Denise A. 1989. "Chicana and Mexican Immigrant Women at Work: The Impact of Class, Race, and Gender on Occupational Mobility." *Gender and Society* 3:37–52.

Toro-Morn, Maura. 1995. "Gender, Class, Family, and Migration: Puerto Rican Women in Chicago." *Gender and Society* 9:712–26.

Waldinger, Roger D. 1986. *Through the Eye of the Needle: Immigrants and Enterprise in New York's Garment Trades*. New York: New York University Press.

Yang, F., and H. R. Ebaugh. 2001. "Transformations in New Immigrant Religions and Their Global Implications." *American Sociological Review* 66:269–88.

Zhou, Min. 2004. "Revisiting Ethnic Entrepreneurship: Convergencies, Controversies, and Conceptual Advancements." *International Migration Review* 38:1040–74.

Zhou, Min, and John R. Logan. 1989. "Returns on Human Capital in Ethnic Enclaves: New York City's Chinatown." *American Sociological Review* 54:809–20.

6

Changing Expectations

Economic Downturns and Immigrant Chinese Women in New York City

MARGARET M. CHIN

> The first and only time I stayed in a hotel was in Guilin. . . .
> The maids were servants. They just cleaned, and no one spoke
> to them. . . . The teachers tell me that in American hotels, the
> customer speaks to the maids and asks for all kinds of help. It
> is customer service. Why do [customers] do that? All I want is a
> cleaning job.
>
> *Linda, student in hotel training program, 2009*

This chapter elaborates on the evolving New York City Chinese ethnic economy, the changing job market, and the strategies that Chinese women use to find and keep jobs. In the aftermath of the September 11, 2001, terrorist attacks and during the recession that began in 2008, at least a quarter of Chinatown's workforce was unemployed. Most of these workers were women, who were less protected by their enclave affiliations than were their husbands. These workers looked for jobs in the remaining enclave garment factories and subsequently in other service industries—first restaurants in the enclave, then out of the enclave in the home health attendant industry and in the hotel and hospitality industry. Working in garment factories had offered unionized jobs with benefits, a rarity for low-skilled immigrant women. Since garment industry jobs are no longer available, Chinese immigrant women looked for jobs in industries that offered health, vacation, and pension benefits. Such jobs were available in the home health attendant and hotel and hospitality sectors. Yet Chinese immigrant women faced obstacles as they moved into these low-wage-sector jobs outside of the Chinese enclave because they require customer service skills these women have not developed. Community centers are stepping in to help Chinese women develop new job skills and customer service expertise as well as the basics of on-the-job rights.

Community organizations initially stepped in to assist these workers in acquiring unemployment benefits. Soon, however, community organizations began to take a far more aggressive role in response to the devastation in their ethnic enclave communities. They became training centers and became central in workforce development. They worked to increase the skills (human capital) among these immigrant women and collaborated with nursing aide and senior aide associations to certify trainees. Many community organizations similarly trained Chinese immigrant women in hotel and hospitality work, teaching such basics as hygienic food preparation and cleaning and maintaining hotel rooms.

These new strategies put in place by community organizations helped create a more professional low-wage worker by teaching the importance of customer service along with quick and flexible thinking to handle customer inquiries. In a changing economy, community organizations must emphasize the importance of serving the customer and teach this new skill. Customers, especially Americans, expect to be able to obtain assistance from anyone in a uniform. Community organizations also teach Chinese women workers about their rights and serve as clearinghouses for information not only about work but about balancing home and work life.

As Chinese women's work hours and locations change, their home schedules change as well. New jobs that take women outside of the enclave also take them outside of the informal support system for children and household demands. A more formal eight-hour workday is less supportive of the balanced family life to which these women were accustomed while working in the enclave garment factories, where close proximity to work, easy access to child care, and flexible hours were the norm. Work in these new industries made life more hectic for these women. Finally, with workers now more isolated in their workplaces, community organizations and their office space became an arena in which women could gather to share information about how to adjust to their new work lives and how to organize to claim rights as workers.

New York City's Chinatown and the Enclave Model

New York's Chinatown community has changed tremendously since the turn of the twenty-first century. Chinatown has always been supported by the workers in the garment, restaurant, retail, and service industries. While Chinatown is home to only 56,000 Asian residents, as recently as 2002 it housed close to 250 garment factories that employed 14,000 Chinese workers and 250 restaurants that employed upward of 3,000 workers (Asian American Federation New York 2002).[1] Estimates put the number of workers in Chinatown's industries and shops (including specialty stores selling jewelry, gifts, and food/tea as well as those offering services, such as banks, insurance agencies, travel agencies, and beauty salons) at more than 33,000. Half of these workers lived outside of Chinatown, mostly in Brooklyn and Queens, and commuted to work five days a week, spending some of their wages in the community.[2] The Chinatown enclave survived because co-ethnics who worked there spent money they earned in the local economy.

New York City's Chinatown is still the largest Chinese neighborhood in the United States. Scholars have depicted it as a classic immigrant ethnic enclave, an alternative economic system that specifically supports ethnic businesses and co-ethnic employees (Portes and Bach 1985; Wilson and Portes 1980; Zhou 1992, 2009). Immigrants can attain upward mobility in an ethnic enclave economy by using ethnic resources to find work that is equal to or better than the jobs available in the secondary labor market and do not require knowledge of English or "American ways."

Chinatown has also been described as a mobility trap, where workers are exploited on a daily basis (Kwong 1997; Sanders and Nee 1987). According to Kwong (1997) the arrival of undocumented immigrants drives wages down and worsens work conditions. Workers in Chinatown face deteriorating conditions because easy access to a cheaper and more vulnerable labor force allows employers to exploit workers, documented and undocumented alike. Kwong also argues that because both documented and undocumented immigrants stay in the enclave, they do not have a chance to learn English, thus limiting their ability to leave for better jobs. Thus, Kwong disagrees with his academic predecessors (e.g., Portes and Bach 1985; Wilson and Portes 1980; Zhou 1992, 2009) who viewed the reduced necessity to learn English as an amenity that benefits immigrants in enclaves. Although enclaves benefit immigrants who might otherwise remain unemployed, Kwong argues that enclaves also undermine immigrants' ability to obtain language skills that are crucial to their ability to work outside of the enclave. In this sense, he views the enclave as a trap rather than a refuge. In keeping with the ethnic enclave model proposed by Wilson and Portes (1980), Portes and Bach (1985), and Zhou (1992, 2009), Chinese immigrants stuck in Kwong's trap do not learn English; however, they fail to do so for different reasons. In the ethnic enclave model, they never acquire English-language skills because they can achieve mobility without doing so; in Kwong's model, they are trapped in low-paying jobs without access to opportunities to learn English.

Before the 2008 recession, Chinatown provided jobs and promoted the mobility of Chinese women workers. The economic enclave—specifically, the co-ethnic hiring and recruiting that were encouraged—was particularly important for these immigrant workers. Immigrants who come to New York with little money and education depend on family and friends to help them adjust to their new homes.

Social networks lead new immigrants to ethnic neighborhoods where they will live and work alongside co-ethnics.

In Chinatown, the ethnic enclave offers a venue for economic mobility without the need to interact with or depend on the outside population (Portes and Jensen 1989; Zhou 1992, 2009). Even though they are not fluent in English, many Chinese who have worked in Chinatown have saved money and purchased homes in Brooklyn or Queens, thereby acquiring one of the major symbols of success and upward mobility (Zhou 2001). However, the recession hit Chinatown's ethnic economy hard. The community has not fully recovered from September 11. As Chinatown's garment shops and restaurants have closed or relocated, immigrant workers are less attracted to the neighborhood as a source of jobs. Neighborhood businesses such as hair salons, banks, travel agencies, and groceries that depended on workers' patronage found their customer bases dwindling. Today, the ethnic enclave is in trouble. At a June 1, 2009, meeting of New York's Chinatown Working Group, job creation, preserving housing, and maintaining small businesses remained major areas of concern.

The vulnerability of ethnic enclaves during recessions raises questions about the positive gloss so frequently painted in the literature, dramatically demonstrating the limits of such enclaves. During economic downturns, Chinatown can no longer provide jobs for low-skilled, non-English-speaking immigrants, and the dependence on co-ethnic social networks that the ethnic enclave nurtured becomes a liability. All Chinese neighborhoods, even those outside the enclave, suffer trickle-down effects. More than half of the displaced garment workers in my study lived outside of Manhattan, with many residing in Chinese neighborhoods in Queens (Flushing and Jackson Heights) and Brooklyn (Sunset Park and Bensonhurst). With less income, these workers spend less in their neighborhoods.

Members of these displaced workers' social networks have few, if any, leads to work opportunities outside of Chinese neighborhoods. For example, most of the women knew only other women who worked in the garment industry, and a few knew others who worked in hotels or as home health aides. Also, these jobs were located for the most part in Midtown or Upper Manhattan, with a few in Brooklyn and Lower Manhattan.

Not only did working in the Chinatown enclave limit workers' social networks, but enclave workers were not exposed to the skills necessary to find jobs outside of the enclave. Most workers do not speak fluent English. While many had taken English classes, few became fluent, because their everyday life did not require them to converse or read in English.

Many of the Chinese workers in this study had never filled out job application forms or interviewed for jobs. Most relied on word-of-mouth recruiting and hiring. Few had ever been to an employment agency. Hardly any had awareness of the skills required in jobs in non-enclave industries such as health care or hotel and clerical work. During economic good times, the enclave provided many benefits for Chinese workers and entrepreneurs, but when disaster hit, these benefits became liabilities that hampered Chinese workers' ability to get jobs outside of the enclave.

Interviews with women workers show the liabilities of the ethnic enclave during the recession by exposing shortcomings that affected women more than men. Women workers' networks are still there, but they are no longer useful. Most displaced Chinese women garment workers get information about jobs from other family members, but this information pertains primarily to industries hurt by the recession that no longer have the capacity to absorb new workers. For example, although many women workers retrained for jobs as home attendants or in the hotel service sector, their social networks offered little help in finding jobs in those industries.

In contrast, men who retrained for hotel service jobs already knew other men who worked outside of Chinatown and even outside of New York State. Thus, men had knowledge about what working outside of the community entailed and about job conditions. Moreover, none of the men considered the effect that moving away for long periods would have on their families. Caring for their families long distance was assumed to be possible.

When women heard about jobs outside of Chinatown, they rarely heard about the experiences of full-time mothers and wives without other family support. In addition, obtaining a job in the home health aide industry or in the hotel industry required less reliance on social networks, with employment agencies or interviewers serving as gatekeepers. These jobs required a different skill set, including that of conversational English. The women also had to be knowledgeable and skilled in basic health care and cardiopulmonary resuscitation, or in the intricacies of hotel work and customer service. Finally, the health care agencies looked for home attendants who were certified, and the hotel industries searched for women who could also handle hotel guest inquiries.

Screening was much more difficult, with many more requirements. The hiring process was much stricter and had set formal rules. Friendly references helped but proved no guarantee that one could get a job. This process was very different from that of the garment industry, where a personal reference guaranteed a job.

Data

For this study, I conducted two sets of interviews with residents of Chinatown during periods of economic downturn. The first phase of interviewing took place during the summer of 2002, while the second phase took place during the winter of 2008–9. I interviewed a total of thirty women and ten men, all of whom were recruited from various job finding and training centers. I was able to locate six women from the first phase to participate in follow-up interviews during the second phase. All of the women and three of the men had previously worked in the garment industry. My interviews indicated that unlike many New York City neighborhoods and economic sectors, the Chinatown enclave never recovered from the post–September 11 downturn.

All participants in the earlier sample and in the second phase of interviews were either working part time or were unemployed. All interviewees were looking for better jobs that paid at least minimum wage and provided health and other benefits, such as sick leave and vacation. If they could not get health benefits with the job, they wanted some way of qualifying for New York State–sponsored health insurance.

Old Garment Work versus New Kinds of Work

At one time, garment factory jobs were the main base of labor organizing as well as an employment clearinghouse for Chinese immigrant women. Garment factories were located in ethnic communities, and information on wages and conditions could easily be shared by word of mouth on the streets, in schools, in grocery stores, or even on the shop floor. The importance of health insurance, unions, good working conditions, and balancing home and work life were part of the everyday discussion among women in the ethnic community. Women who did not work in the industry had mothers, sisters, aunts, or cousins who worked there and shared information. Within this industry, women often found jobs via word of mouth. A factory owner might tell workers that there was a vacant seat, or workers might ask employers for jobs for relatives on their way over from China. As the industry declined, the old ways of searching for jobs disappeared.

Garment work was most often a Chinese immigrant woman's first job in the United States, and some Chinese immigrant men also found themselves in the industry. Because they worked with dozens of co-ethnics, social communications and networks were easily maintained. Social networks also helped ease daily life on the factory floor. In addition to providing information about job openings, co-ethnics could provide introductions to bosses, explain floor routines, and smooth over any other issues. As Wei, a former garment worker, reported, "I knew where I would try to find a job a month before I arrived in New York City. My aunt promised to bring me to the meet her boss in a garment factory. I never thought there was any other way to get a job. Everyone I knew got their job this way." She and other interviewees told me that on the job floor, they learned about one another, how to work efficiently, and about their rights and benefits. Coworkers often shared important information about sewing shortcuts and about how to ask for time off. Sandy, another former garment worker, said, "We all work by the piece, and of course we want to make a much as we can and leave. When your cousin or your friend works next to you, you can always show them how to sew a dress quicker, and you can ask them to show you. Sometimes you need to sew the short seams to put together the dress and sew it all together, instead of piecing the little pieces. Other times, another way is faster."

Workers particularly enjoyed the camaraderie, eating lunch together and socializing on the job floor. Ling told me that all of the women with whom she worked "knew about the wedding of our friend Lan's daughter. Every day, we would hear news about the restaurant, the food, the guests, the dresses, and eventually the honeymoon plans. It was like we were all planning the wedding together." In some cases, many years had passed since my interviewees worked in garment factories, but the experience of working in a large social group continued to influence what they wanted from a job.

Finally, the garment industry was for the most part unionized and offered health benefits, which was particularly important for families with young children. Another former garment worker, Linda, sought another job that would provide health coverage: "The health insurance was the most beneficial for my family. If I could find any job, my only requirement would be health insurance. I like being with people, but health insurance for my family is worth more."

Moving to New Kinds of Work

With globalization and the growth in manufacturing in newly modernized countries such as China, the local garment industry lost its viability. Many U.S. manufacturers moved their operations to less expensive foreign factories. After September 11 even the remaining garment work in New York City, which was based on high style and quality or time-sensitive production, lost its advantage. As the garment factories closed, the whole social system changed. Social networks were no longer helpful in getting jobs. Although social networks still provided information about jobs, these were frequently located outside of Chinatown and required more than a word-of-mouth recommendation. New York's immigrant Chinese women needed to learn new ways to look for work and new ways of handling work.

In the Chinatown enclave, any acquaintance could be counted on for assistance in the job hunt. This process provided openings with Chinese-owned firms, many of which were located in other Chinese communities in Manhattan, Brooklyn, or Queens. Family members or friends who worked outside of Chinese neighborhoods were usually men, so many women knew very little about outside jobs for women. As a result, women knew primarily about jobs within the enclave in industries suffering in the wake of September 11 and the recession. Few of those opportunities qualified as "good" jobs.

One thirty-eight-year-old woman had been living in the United States for sixteen years. She and most members of her family lived in Flushing, Queens, while most of her family members worked in Manhattan's Chinatown or in one of the Chinese communities in Brooklyn or Queens. Her sister, two cousins, and three sisters-in-law worked in the garment industry; her husband, three cousins, two brothers-in-law, and a sister-in-law were employed in restaurants; and her husband's uncle and his wife worked in Chinatown as a doctor and a pharmacist, respectively. Two other family members in New York City did not work in Chinese communities. Both her sister, a pattern maker, and her brother-in-law, a hotel electrician, worked in Midtown Manhattan in jobs for which the old methods of word-of-mouth job referrals were not reliable. As a result, this woman knew few people, especially other women, who could introduce her to jobs outside of the Chinese neighborhood.

Moreover, the women I interviewed had little information about how other women balanced their work and family schedules. These women were accustomed to the social supports and services available in Chinatown (babysitters, relatives, doctors, banks, after-school programs, grocery stores, prepared meals from restaurants). Flexible hours in the garment industry allowed these women to take advantage of Chinatown's services. Working outside of the enclave without flexible hours often meant rearranging child care and errands, lengthening their days with before- and after-work tasks. A few women needed to stop in Chinatown to drop off children in programs or with grandparents before heading to work in Midtown or in another borough.

In contrast, the Chinese men worked in restaurants outside of the enclave. Many of the men and women I interviewed knew other men who traveled outside of the New York area to work in restaurants. Many men boarded near their jobs and returned to New York City only once a week. Immigrant workers' already scarce family time grew even rarer.

The Most Recent Downturn

By 2008, jobs in the service economy were really the only ones available for the displaced garment workers. The recession further reduced these opportunities. Organizations in Chinatown opted to train unemployed Chinese women in growth industries (Chin 2005a, b). For immigrant Chinese women, these new jobs were as health attendants in private homes, and as maids, kitchen staff, and service workers in hotels. Such jobs represented a wholly new kind of work organized in a wholly different way.

Home health employment agencies and hotels usually hire through a formal application process. Word of mouth could only get the women to the employment office. Each person had to fill out a job application, have an interview, and demonstrate her knowledge of English and other relevant skills. By the winter of 2008–9, most interviewees no longer relied on social networks for job information but instead focused on getting retrained to move to jobs outside of the enclave. Such training not only means learning how to perform jobs in another sector but also learning English thoroughly.

Many of the women I interviewed had left the garment industry in the preceding five years because they were no longer able to sustain their families with that type of work. Some had been laid off, while others left voluntarily for restaurant work or to help relatives in other businesses. These women realized, however, that they needed to move out of the enclave sector because small entrepreneurs within the Chinese community were struggling—wages were not increasing, and jobs were becoming more and more scarce, with increasing competition from undocumented immigrants.

Friends who worked as home attendants or in hotel service jobs steered these women to those sectors. Although social networks could not help the women find jobs, since those doing the hiring were firms that often required certified training and held higher standards, friends could help applicants maneuver through the process. According to Sim, a friend "told me to go to the same training program as the one she went to. . . . I could see that she learned a lot of English . . . and she explained all the different hotel jobs to me . . . so I enrolled there too. She also told me that I can get some money to pay for the course." In many cases, friends had received training but had not yet found jobs, and these women gradually realized that training did not guarantee employment, especially for women who had received little more than an elementary-school education in China.

Most of my interviewees enrolled in training classes with their friends. For many, this was their first classroom experience since elementary school. One thirty-five-year-old woman had worked in the garment industry for about a year. She was not a union member, but her family wages were so low that the family qualified for New York State's health insurance program. She attempted to find work in the hotel sector, but when she went to the human resources office at a Midtown hotel, she could not complete the application. She left disappointed but determined to return and enrolled in a training class that would enable her to become a hotel housekeeper.

It may seem surprising that women need training for an "unskilled" position such as a housekeeper, but most Chinese immigrants lack the English skills necessary to fill out job applications. Moreover, even women who manage the application process and learn how to make beds and clean bathrooms have difficulty finding jobs because they do not know enough English to handle hotel guests' requests or complaints, a skill that must be demonstrated in the interview process. Said Cindy, "I have been cleaning and making up beds for over thirty years [for my family]. I can work in a hotel. My cousin works as a hotel maid in Guangzhou, and I know I can do what she does. All she does is clean. But here, they want you to do more. In training, it is always about helping the person staying in the hotel. They told us that they can ask us anything, and we should be able to help them. It will take me forever to learn that much English."

Chinese women who obtain housekeeping jobs often find the position very difficult. According to my interviewees, a maid or housekeeper cleans an average of fifteen rooms per day, with each room taking about thirty minutes to clean. Housekeepers usually change linens, clean bathrooms, vacuum, and generally straighten up. This pace allows very little time for socializing.

The hotel training programs discussed realistic expectations for housekeeping jobs and provided participants with information about other hotel jobs, including working at the front desks and in restaurants. The lucky few who learned or relearned English had incredible opportunities. Po An "learned English in China as a child and teenager, but I rarely used it during the twelve years that I have been in the United States. I worked in the garment industry like all the rest of my family, and only now that my son can walk home from school, I decided that I needed to find another job. . . . I took the hotel training program and was qualified to work in the front desk as a trainee. They liked that I was bilingual."

During the recession, the only other growing economic arena available to Chinese immigrant women was the home health aide sector. The elderly still need care, even during an economic downturn. Most of my interviewees' home health attendant jobs were arranged by agencies, although a few women had obtained their jobs by word of mouth and were paid in cash. These are two different employment sectors. Those working for agencies had customers of every race, while those who worked via personal references mostly had Chinese customers. Those paid in cash had neither benefits nor health insurance. Some agencies also did not provide benefits, especially for assignments requiring fewer than thirty hours a week of work.

In both cases, formal training programs were necessary. Women initially took classes in English and in filling out applications and interviewing, followed by job-specific training regarding the care of an elderly patient—CPR, massage, bathing, feeding, and general care of the infirm. My interviewees cited learning to speak English as a key skill; otherwise, they would be ignored when they applied for jobs. Moreover, they pointed out the importance of contextual language skills for career advancement.

Home health jobs can be very intense, particularly when patients need constant care. A typical day lasts from 8:00 A.M. until 8:00 P.M. and might include cleaning, cooking, feeding, bathing, and giving medicines to the patient. Although patients are often cooperative, some can be difficult, screaming at attendants. May, who worked as an attendant for an eighty-one-year-old man confined to a wheelchair as the result of a stroke, described her day:

> When I get there in the morning, I check in with his wife, who is getting ready to leave. She tells me what kind of breakfast he has had and how much he has eaten. She reminds me about his medication change, and she leaves for the day to run errands and to visit with her friends. I understand—she can't be home with him every day, every minute either. I check up on him and read to him from the Chinese newspaper. I think he understands because he nods and tries to talk to me. I clean up the breakfast and change him and his clothes. I give him his first round of medicines and give him a leg massage and an arm massage. I wheel him outside for some fresh air. After a thirty-minute walk, I return and start getting lunch ready for him. I feed him, which takes a long time.
>
> When he finishes, I go clean up the lunch preparation. I then clean up the apartment a bit while he watches a bit of TV; sometimes he naps. When he is done, I change him again and get him ready for a sponge bath. I give him a massage on his body and arms. I give him his medicines again. I dress him again, and I go prepare dinner for him and his wife. When dinner is ready, I read to him some more. It is almost time for me to leave.

Isolating Work Conditions

Working either as a home health aide or in a hotel can be much lonelier than working in a garment factory. Most housekeepers have little occasion to talk with their coworkers, since they encounter other maids only occasionally. They can still make friends and learn shortcuts, but little socialization takes place during the workday. Home health aides are even more isolated, often alone with their patients for between eight and nine hours each day. Rarely do such aides have opportunities for extensive interactions with others, besides their patients, in person or on the phone during that time. Moreover, home health workers are usually instructed not to discuss their clients or the conditions of the homes in which they work. Thus, workers cannot learn from one another. The women tend to return home exhausted at the end of the day, leaving them with little time or energy to talk with others and organize. Wendy, a home health worker, told me, "Only at church do I see other home health aide workers like me. When I was in training, I made all of these friends, but since I started working, I never see or speak to them. We don't even bump into each other on the subway. We are all so busy at work. The jobs can be anywhere in the city, and when we get home, we have so much to do with our families."

Home health aides must be independent and responsible. Very often, they travel by themselves to and from their assignments. Some women have multiple assignments. Winnie, for example, goes to two different jobs, each for two days per week. The assignments "are very different. One person received a new hip and is very independent and cannot wait to walk by herself again. The other person is elderly, too, but can't remember anything. I shouldn't tell you, but their apartments are so different. The person with a broken hip has a really nice apartment. The other person keeps everything. His apartment is a mess, and I don't know what to do when I'm supposed to straighten up. I can't tell anyone how much of a mess he makes. I would like to speak to anyone who has ideas for me."

Many of the women I interviewed did not have regular and consistent contact with other workers but did have contact with the organization that trained them. The organization, in turn, became a clearinghouse for information and helped link the workers to one another.

The Ongoing Role of Community Organizations

Community organizations have taken up the challenge of providing programs that support new workers. My interviewees often received follow-up phone calls from administrators, who occasionally offered suggestions for job openings and interviewing tips. Community organizations also keep tabs on their graduates to assess organizational performance. Many organizations need to report to funders about the efficiency and placement rates of their training programs.

Such monitoring provides an unintentional benefit for trainees and experienced workers in the form of a support system that links them both to information and to other workers. The next step would be organizing the workers, but this area is a sensitive topic, since funders of worker training and education may not support worker organizing. Organization staff report that they walk a fine line to avoid crossing the boundary between helping workers and organizing them. However, these groups can educate workers so that they can make informed choices.

With workers in the hotel and home health industries so isolated, community organizations are often immigrant women's only contact. According to one teacher in a hotel training program, "Before we graduate the students, we discuss how much pay one is supposed to receive in these jobs, how much work they are supposed to have, vacation, sick days, and even health benefits. We do this because there are many fewer home health aides and hotel housekeepers than there were garment workers. Our graduates might never learn this information from someone they know—they might not know anyone in the industry. Moreover, the information sinks in over time; we need to reinforce this new information.

In the beginning, the workers do not believe how difficult it can be." More important, the training programs give the workers a context for asking for better wages and conditions. Just having the facts about the conditions of their new work allows many workers to ask questions. As the director of a hotel training program explained, "We tell the trainees what they should expect to be paid. We don't want our trainees to be taken advantage of. We also tell them what kind of work is expected. And of course, we tell them which jobs are unionized."

The workers often come to realize that their fellow participants in training programs are their best resource for questions about work since old friends from other industries cannot offer concrete suggestions. Rosie, a recent trainee, said, "I never really made friends with others in my training program. Since I can't seem to find a job, I go back to the center to help out. Now, I'm making friends, and I can keep learning about the work conditions." The training programs and the continuing support programs also contribute to the growth of the community organizations. As individuals join the classes, they learn about the variety of presentations, programs, and events hosted by the organization and frequently become more involved. Others, like Rosie, who choose not to get involved while in training later become involved. Women in isolated workplaces may seek additional training to make contact with others who are in or who understand similar situations. Such connections benefit the community, the organizations, and the women workers.

Conclusion: Women and The Liabilities of the Enclave

Mae, a home health aide, said in 2009, "I just started working over a month ago. I'm very happy with what I learned in the training program, but now that I'm working, I don't go back to Chinatown for much of anything. I don't need to go there to meet co-ethnics to tell me about the jobs, nor do I need to go there to socialize."

The collapse of the ethnic economy means that Chinatown has stopped serving as a central location from which to find work. Consequently, fewer and fewer Chinese immigrants go to the community for their shopping, banking, and cultural needs. Although women workers used community organizations as a training resource, the programs did not result in an infusion of money into the local economy. The consequences for the Chinatown community are not yet fully clear. The number of workers who go daily to Chinatown has decreased dramatically. Until the number of jobs in the enclave increases, those who ventured away will have little interest in returning to work there.

For workers, the benefits of Chinatown's enclave may at one time have outweighed the drawbacks, but the reverse now seems to be true. Nevertheless,

Chinese community networks remain strong. However, they often seem useless in helping women find jobs. Community organizations have stepped in, but they are not the same as friendship and family networks.

Notes

1. Twelve thousand of the employees in Chinatown's garment shops were members of a union, UNITE (Asian American Federation New York 2002). Many undocumented garment workers do not join the union because they work too few hours, do not need access to health insurance, or are being paid cash off the books. Only thirty-five nonunionized shops existed, and some of their workers would be undocumented.

2. Based on my interviews with UNITE officials, garment-shop owners, and garment workers, about half of all garment workers lived in Manhattan; however, a higher proportion of workers interviewed for this study lived outside of Manhattan.

References

Asian American Federation New York. 2002. "Chinatown One Year after September 11th: An Economic Impact Study." Report.

Chin, Margaret M. 2005a. "Moving On: Chinese Garment Workers after 9/11." In *Wounded City*, ed. Nancy Foner, 184–207. New York: Sage.

———. 2005b. *Sewing Women: Immigrants and the New York City Garment Industry*. New York: Columbia University Press.

Kwong, Peter. 1997. *Forbidden Workers: Illegal Chinese Immigrants and American Labor*. New York: New Press.

Portes, Alejandro, and Robert L. Bach. 1985. *The Latin Journey: Cuban and Mexican Immigrants in the United States*. Berkeley: University of California Press.

Portes, Alejandro, and L. Jensen. 1989. "The Enclave and the Entrants: Patterns of Ethnic Enterprise in Miami before and after Mariel." *American Sociological Review* 54:929–49.

Sanders, Jimy M., and Victor Nee. 1987. "Limits of Ethnic Solidarity in the Enclave Economy." *American Sociological Review* 52:745–73.

Wilson, Kenneth, and Alejandro Portes. 1980. "Immigrant Enclaves: An Analysis of the Labor Market Experiences of Cubans in Miami." *American Journal of Sociology* 86:295–319.

Zhou, Min. 1992. *Chinatown: The Socioeconomic Potential of an Urban Enclave*. Philadelphia: Temple University Press.

———. 2001. "Chinese: Divergent Destinies in Immigrant New York." In *New Immigrants in New York*, ed. Nancy Foner, 141–72. New York: Columbia University Press.

———. 2009. *Contemporary Chinese America*. Philadelphia: Temple University Press.

PART 3

Informal Economies

7

From Street Child Care to Drive-Throughs

Latinas Reconfigure and Negotiate Street Vending Spaces in Los Angeles

LORENA MUÑOZ

> This street is where my job is. . . . I sell tamales, . . . elotes, . . . y champurrado. I have been working here since I arrived in Los Angeles. I live and work here; this is my neighborhood.
>
> *Maria, Street Vendor in Los Angeles*

"¡Tamales! ¡Elotes! ¡Champurrado!" Maria's voice makes a perennial imprint on a particular noisy Los Angeles intersection. Donning a long, floral print skirt, she seldom changes her ten-hours-a-day, seven-days-a-week routine: selling home-cooked tamales, steamed corn, and fresh champurrado from a red grocery cart. Like thousands of Latino street vendors, her style (that is, her dress, behavior, and language) transforms the physical space that she occupies into that of a gendered, street-vending landscape. The result is an embodiment of her originating culture, a method by which street-vending immigrants carve a place in the urban landscape.[1]

Most research on this informal economy describes it as an economic activity of last resort, a survival strategy adopted because formal avenues of employment are not possible. Whatever the merits of this view, Latina vendors exercise a great deal of agency, not only in terms of their formal and informal employment choices but also through their economic strategies that reconfigure the urban landscape. This aspect of street vending lies at the core of this chapter.

This chapter focuses on how street vending is practiced and organized in Garment Town,[2] a Latino immigrant–receiving neighborhood in South Central Los Angeles. More specifically, the chapter examines and documents how street-vending spaces are organized, supported, and created through the daily practices of Mexican and Central American immigrant women vendors. This examination sheds light on how the informal economy is organized at the street level in developed economies (particularly in global cities with a high influx of immigrants) and allows us to understand street-vending landscapes as not only racialized but also gendered. Thus, Latina vendors perform, transform, and reorganize public space in ways that facilitate their business strategies and assist them in negotiating the demands of everyday life. Such actions include transforming street corners into drive-throughs, adapting car trunks to serve as markets, and providing child care on the streets.

Economic Context of Immigrant Vending Practices in Los Angeles

In the early 1990s southern California transformed, moving from heavy manufacturing to light manufacturing, a shift that increased demand for unskilled service workers, a labor pool later filled in large part by Latino immigrants—in particular, immigrant women (Hondagneu-Sotelo 2001; Tyner 2003). In this particular labor sector, Latino immigrants, especially women, have been overrepresented in southern California. According to Sassen (2003, 44): "Global cities are key sites for the specialized servicing, financing, and management of global economic processes. These cities are also a site for the incorporation of large numbers of women and immigrant activities that service the strategic sectors. These workers are not represented as a vital part of the global economy. Therefore, there is a devalorization of this labor force, partly because of the feminization of the service sector that genders these particular jobs as 'woman's labor' in global cities."

Sassen (2003), Tyner (2003), and others suggest that complex, global economic processes have helped to restructure local demand for unskilled labor. In these low-wage labor employment sectors, poverty wages and scarce benefits often force workers to take additional jobs to survive. This process produces spaces of informal work wherein additional employment is found outside the formal sector. There are several advantages to supplementing income by working in the informal economy: income is nontaxable, work hours are flexible, and in some cases, laborers do not have to report to anyone (Hamilton and Chinchilla 2001; Zlolniski 2006).[3] Furthermore, women can take care of their children while working on the street.

In a social context, female street vendors use informal economic opportunities to create a sense of place and transform public spaces into vending landscapes.[4] These landscapes reflect power inequalities and reify gender roles among men and women, thereby normalizing patriarchal and cultural values in public space (Monk 1992). As such, street-vending practices are one way in which complex relationships among low-wage labor, gender, immigration, and informal economic practices are articulated in space.[5]

Street Child Care, Labor, and Choice

Street child care is a nuanced way Latina vendors reconfigure public space. Street child care arrangements allow Latina vendors to meet work and family obligations. Recent literature that focuses on how female immigrants' negotiations of labor, family, and gender highlights the blurred boundaries that exist between home and workspace, particularly among immigrant entrepreneurs and home-based workers (Bao 2001; Park 2005; Parreñas 2001, 2005). However, this literature has seldom focused on how blurred boundaries between home and work also are blurred for women who work on the street. Thus, Latinas taking care of their children on the street genders these vending landscapes. These vending landscapes often are perceived as dangerous, unfriendly, and illicit. However, the presence of children in the landscape transforms that perception. These spaces become gendered, family-friendly, and unthreatening.

Lisa Sun-Hee Park's (2005) work on children of immigrant entrepreneurs elucidates the complexities of growing up and working in adult spaces of labor. She finds that even though second-generation immigrants were raised within an adult work environment, their parents carved out childhood spaces. Thus, children were able to be with their parents, a situation the children perceived as positive. Most of these children of immigrants went to work in the family business as soon as they were able. Similarly, street vending incorporates children as additional labor, which in turn strengthens the business. Latina vendors primarily bring their infant children to work because of child-care constraints; however, having older children with them helps some Latina vendors with their jobs. Lupe, for example, brings her youngest son with her while selling traditional Mexican food out of the trunk of her car. Similarly, Lidia, another Latina food vendor, has no one with whom to leave her daughter since all her relatives work and she cannot afford child care; after school, therefore, her daughter helps her sell.

The Latina street vendors in this study prove that the boundaries between street vending and home life are fluid and dynamic and that simplified dichotomies are inadequate when understanding how street vendors (re)create vending landscapes. Estrada and Hondagneu-Sotelo's chapter in this volume (chapter 8) provides an understanding of how Latina youth street vendors are part of an established system of parental supervision and gendered practices. In this system, these girls negotiate their identities at home, in the street, and in school. Estrada and Hondagneu-Sotelo find that the gendered divisions of household labor extend to street labor. Girls assist with the cooking and chores at home and sell food in the street, fulfilling very different expectations and representations than their brothers. Their work provides groundbreaking analyses of Central American and Mexican immigrant female adolescent street vendors' experiences that challenge the ways we understand immigrant childhood and adolescence as well as immigrant child labor.

Two Latina street vendors, Lupe and Lidia, affirmed that children become an economic advantage when they are old enough to help. Therefore, bringing their children to work not only eliminates the need for child care but also helps mothers with their vending tasks. In addition, according to some women vendors having jobs in the formal workplace would not allow them to care for their children, and child care outside family or friend networks would be unaffordable.

Immigrant women workers in the United States have a long history of problems with child care. Previous research has focused on the scarcity of child-care choices for immigrant women workers. Bao's (2001, 187) work on Chinese women garment workers in New York City between 1948 and 1992 highlights the struggles women garment workers faced. On the one hand, some garment factories allowed workers to bring along their children; on the other hand, the dangers of unsafe work environments often pushed some women workers to leave their children at home unattended. The inability for either the state or employers to provide child care became a launching pad for union organizing among these women, and a union day-care center was established in 1977. Chinese immigrant garment workers did not find factory work to be an advantage in fulfilling their child-care needs. Latina street vendors, conversely, choose street vending because it offers child-care flexibility.

Street vending for Latina immigrants in Garment Town is a viable alternative to employment in other service-sector work. Vendors' ability to take care of their children while working is not only a perk but also a necessity, since most Latina vendors have few child-care alternatives. As geographer Ruth Fincher (2004) states, local labor markets and the local state are complicit in how gender and class are experienced by residents and workers in urban centers. The lack of child-care provisions by the local state often complicates women's ability to undertake paid work outside the home. While the lack of affordable child care and the need for women to have choices regarding economic sustainability do not exactly push Latina vendors into the informal economy, working in the informal economy as vendors does carry a tangible benefit. Like Lupe, who provides street child care while vending, most Latina vendors interviewed echoed the view that flexibility in caring for their young children is an important benefit of street vending. Thus, Latinas engender public spaces by transforming them into labor and child-care spaces.

Kang (2010, 120) elucidates the gendered processes that shape Asian immigrant women's decision to find employment in nail salons because it affords them greater flexibility in managing childcare. Similarly, Latina street vendors in my study who provided street child care while vending cited this as the most important reason they chose this occupation over wage work. The majority of the women vendors I studied reported that they were unable to afford child care and lacked family networks that could provide it. For Renata, street child care has been a pathway to building a gendered network in her neighborhood. After her arrival in Los Angeles two years prior to my study, she started working for her cousin's street-vending business. She found street vending easy, although the preparation was at first overwhelming. She later decided to work in the garment industry, since she had experience in Mexico working for a seamstress. She also worked briefly as a domestic before discovering that she was pregnant and then returning to street vending. She obtained her own cart, causing friction with her cousin. She came to feel isolated in a city that was large and difficult to navigate; she was considering returning to Mexico when she found a way to join a group of women who sell together and take care of their children at the same time. Renata found it much easier to sell while other people were watching out for her child: "You don't know what great help are my *comadres* with Andrecito. . . . Of course, here all of us help each other, and I even come with joy to work, knowing that I can bring my son with me. If I had another job—well, impossible. Who would take care of Andres?" Thus, working in groups provides Latina vendors with young children a nuanced way of street vending that re-creates public space into spaces of entrepreneurship, labor, and child care (Hamilton and Chinchilla 2001).

Women Organizing the Informal Economy in the Streets

In addition to providing child care, Latina vendors engender vending landscapes by what they sell, whom they sell it to, and how they sell. Most Latina street vendors sell Mexican and Central American foods and wares that are both traditional and region-specific, including herbs, fresh fruit and vegetables, flower arrangements, and new and used garments. Holidays such as Mother's Day, Valentine's Day, Easter, Christmas, and Halloween, along with other Latin American national holidays, are essential for seasonal, part-time, and some full-time vendors.

At Halloween, for example, vendors sell not only homemade costumes but also secondhand clothes that could be used as Halloween *disfraces* (costumes). Handmade *lucha libre* (Mexican wrestling) costumes are also sold by street vendors. Women design and create these costumes at home. Vendors also utilize the sidewalk as retail space for their products, arranging them on plastic crates, cardboard boxes, and blankets. Vendors also sell stuffed animals, used shoes and clothes, and a variety of household products. Women usually tend the "store" while their male relatives or employers drive the vans and help unload the merchandise. Once the merchandise is unloaded, the male employer leaves the area, returning in the evening to pick up the merchandise and the van. In most street-vending operations, a vendor/owner employs other vendors and places them strategically around the city. It is not uncommon for women to be employed by other vendors to sell during the day. This is one of the ways in which traditional gender roles are maintained; however, it also means that the streets are a female space where the women navigate, organize, and exercise agency.

The most popular way in which vendors display and sell their food is by using shopping carts, converting some streets into informal markets. Karina, a Mexican street vendor, sells tamales out of her red grocery cart in Garment Town. She describes her cart as functional: "How else would I carry the food if I did not have this?" She has extended her cart by adding a blue plastic crate in which she keeps napkins, plastic forks, plastic bags, and cups. Karina carries two hot containers in the cart, a red thermos of *champurrado* (chocolate-based atole) and a large metal pot for the tamales. She also uses a black plastic crate to support the load and hangs plastic bags from the cart's handles. She is a stationary vendor who sells at a busy and popular Garment Town intersection.

Colorful patio umbrellas are a functional signifier in the vending landscape. Karina, like many other vendors, use these umbrellas not only for protection from the elements but also as a way of advertising. The umbrellas are a recognizable and standard element of vending, and vendors use them as part of a conscious effort to increase their visibility and sales in Latin America as well as in Los Angeles. Several vendors noted the similarities between how street vendors sell items in Los Angeles and in their home countries. Street vending transcends borders in recognizable ways.

Spatial Organization of Latina Street Vendors

Street vending in Los Angeles is systematically organized. These vending strategies break down myths about informal vending just popping up in unregulated spaces. The simplistic notion that vending is an unorganized economic survival strategy practiced by people operating at the margins of society, as is the case in Latin America, does not explain vending practices in Los Angeles. In fact, the way in which vending is organized at the street level varies by block. Some vendors in Garment Town pay "rent" to male gang members for use of sidewalk space and for protection from business owners, neighborhood residents, other gangs, and code enforcers. Ximena, a Mexican street vendor, pays five dollars every day to gang members for protection and security whenever she sells on a specific block.

It is unclear how many vendors pay rent to gang members, because most vendors do not want to discuss the subject. A lieutenant of the Los Angeles Police Department (Los Angeles Police Department, Alvarado Corridor Project 2005) calls this practice illegal, a form of extortion. Yet Ximena says that it is a matter of convenience, since paying rent helps her when the police raid the streets or when she has a conflict with a local resident or business owner. Ximena does not consider the gang members dangerous because she knows most of them from the neighborhood. It is not entirely clear specifically how the gang members intervene on behalf of the vendors whom they protect: neither Ximena nor a supposed gang member volunteered that information. However, Ximena described a male gang member as part of her extended family, and she attended family parties with him, complicating the way in which gang regulation and control over vending space is understood. Thus, simplistic notions that male gang members regulate and control female vending spaces does not explain women's agency as vendors. Ximena and other vendors who pay rent to local gang members for protection navigate spaces layered with restrictions from the local government, and enact resistance to the state (by getting gang members to provide protection from police raids and potential competition). Thus, Latina street vendors claim public space as their own.

Perhaps most beneficial to established vendors is the gang's barrier to entry, which occurs when competition tries to open in a paying vendor's location. For this reason, some new vendors choose to push their food carts around the neighborhood instead of parking in specific spots. Lizette, a Mexican immigrant, stated, "I go to my customers, instead of waiting for the customers to come to me." For approximately six months, Lizette has moved through the neighborhood, announcing, "¡Tamales! ¡Tamales! ¡Tamales!" She does this only from 5:00 to 9:00 A.M., before she goes to her full-time job later in the day. She makes a good living from her job in the formal economy and uses vending as a supplement, providing her with about fifty dollars a day. The four hours she spends each morning as a mobile vendor provide the same income she would receive in a full day stationed on a street corner. She has regular customers who buy tamales from her almost every day for breakfast, and new customers are always willing to try them. However, she has learned to avoid certain streets where she has been slightly harassed by *cholos* (gang members) and other vendors. She believes that she has built her clientele by starting early in the day, before people go to work, and she considers herself successful.

As Lizette's description illustrates, vendors follow varying schedules and devote varying amounts of time to their work. Some vendors are newly arrived immigrants, working the streets only until they find alternative employment, while others have worked in the trade for years. Latina immigrants often find street vending a viable, profitable street business. Vendors with seniority stake out their territory and have unspoken rights to their particular site. If a new vendor tries to sell the same product on the same block or street corner, the senior vendors quickly tell the new vendors that they must move. However, new vendors are accepted if they are not in direct competition with established vendors. For example, if an established vendor sells tamales or other prepared food, a new vendor who sells nonfood items will not cause conflict and may in fact attract customers.

Vending spaces are systematically organized at the street level in Los Angeles, particularly in Garment Town. Unspoken, unofficial street rules delineate where vendors can sell, what they can sell, and how they can sell it. Based on understandings of these unofficial rules, vendors constantly re-create and reorganize vending to fit their own priorities and schedules. Most important, vendors decide why they sell their products on a particular street. Teresa, a Mexican immigrant, sells tamales and champurrado out of a red grocery cart on a coveted corner of a busy intersection. Throughout her five years of selling on that particular street corner, many other vendors have come and gone, but she reports that she has been the only one selling tamales and champurrado. Other vendors typically sell flowers, fresh vegetables and herbs (such as nopales and flor de calabaza), fruit (either cocktails or whole fruit), and holiday paraphernalia, among other nonfood items. One vendor who occasionally sells fresh-fruit cocktails on that corner reported, "Teresa thinks that it's her street, that she owns it, but she is also respected because she has been here a long time. People expect her to be here. When people come to do their laundry, they usually eat her tamales." According to Teresa, even the police have stopped giving her tickets, instead just telling her to clear out and go home.

Finally, family networks are important for entering vending in the streets of Los Angeles. Ana recently graduated from high school and is a U.S. citizen, though her family is from Mexico. She speaks fluent English and Spanish and is thinking of taking business courses at a community college in hopes of eventually owning her own business. She works part time at her uncle's food cart, one of five he operates in the neighborhood. For Ana, this is a temporary job: "I only work Saturdays and Sundays, maybe one day during the week. . . . I have been working for four months. I started before I graduated from high school. . . . My uncle needed someone to work the days. My aunt takes care of my cousin's kids, so they asked me to work. . . . I get bored sometimes, but it's OK, I guess . . . easy work." Ana does not want to work as a domestic, like her mother.

Mainstream perceptions hold that street vendors are not only undocumented immigrants but also are struggling to get by, locked outside of traditional employment. The Economic Roundtable reports that immigrants become informal laborers in Los Angeles as a consequence of economic desperation and extreme poverty. But this assessment does not always hold true. Vendors choose to participate in street vending for various reasons. Ana has incorporated herself into a family business while she figures out her next steps. Other street vendors operate multiple carts. Working in the informal economy is sometimes preferable to formal employment opportunities, providing unique benefits, both illicit (for example, untaxed wages and profits) and legitimate (flexible hours, no supervisor, and the possibility of rapid income growth). Rosario is an undocumented Mexican immigrant who does not speak English and who has worked full time as a street vendor for about two years. As is common for people from her hometown, who leave school as soon as they are old enough to earn money, she has only a fourth-grade education and has never worked in the formal sector; she began selling hot empanadas from a tweed basket because she was related to another street vendor in the area. She says she likes selling empanadas, because she meets new people and the time passes quickly. Unlike other vendors in the area, Rosario did not seem to have plans to grow her business. Her husband has a full-time job, which allows them to send most of her earnings to her three children in Mexico.

Night Vending

Garment Town's mixed-use zoning provides multiple opportunities for vending not only during the day but also at night. Night vending, however, consists of semipermanent taco trucks attended mainly by men. Women generally are present only in the background or in collaboration with men. Night vending becomes gendered male not only by the workers who sell during the nighttime but also by the consumers. During late evening hours, most of the customers (except people coming back from work) are patrons of bars and liquor stores or attendees of Alcoholics Anonymous and Narcotics Anonymous meetings. Vendors situate their carts or taco trucks in strategic locations in the evenings to target the nighttime consumer population, especially on weekends. This shift attests to perceptions of public space being dangerous at night and safer during the day. Thus, vending strategies are organized around perceptions of day vending as a safe space for women and children without male supervision or caretaking.

Conclusion

Latina vendors in Garment Town negotiate and navigate complex layers of a vending system. Latina immigrants as vendors exercise choice and agency among patriarchal structures that reify gender roles in the streets. Latina vendors are entrepreneurially savvy in the ways they reconfigure public space into spaces of work, networking, and child care. Vendors blur the boundaries between home and work, with women maintaining responsibility in such traditional areas as child care. Work as a street vendor is a viable employment choice for women with young children.

Where, what, and how selling take place are also gendered. Latina vendors usually sell prepared *comida típica* (regional traditional food) out of grocery carts or car trunks during the day, while men sell tacos out of a more or less stationary stand at night. Such practices are consistent with the social stereotypes of traditionally female roles of cooking in the kitchen. For the majority of Garment Town's Latina vendors, participation in the informal economy is not an economic activity of last resort or a survival strategy as a result of lack of opportunities in the formal economy. It is a complex, systematic way in which the vendors claim and reconfigure space and place through the agency they carve out in the urban landscape.

Notes

This research was made possible by partial funding support from the Ford Foundation and the Low Wage Work, Migration, and Gender project at the University of Illinois at Chicago.

1. In this sense, place, according to McDowell and Sharp (1997), is enacted through social and cultural displays as well as interactions.

2. Garment Town is a pseudonym. Because of the legal issues surrounding street vending in Los Angeles, I do not disclose the exact location of this site.

3. According to the Economic Roundtable (2005), on any given day, Los Angeles has approximately 670,000 informal workers. It is unclear, however, how many informal workers are street vendors because studies on the informal economy of Los Angeles have not included street vendors. The focus has been mainly on informal employment in the manufacturing and service sectors, including household and landscape services. Immigrant or noncitizen participation in informal employment is at the forefront of these studies, highlighting the fact that 65 percent of this informal labor force is comprised of immigrants.

4. Sense of place emerges from places, wherein individuals or a group of people experience deep connections or emotive feelings attached to a place. Sense of place is a personal as well as a collective phenomenon that is experienced through a sense of attachment and meanings to a place. It is created by people's memories, experiences, and desires. The end result is often ultimately articulated by the way people use, understand, and create a specific place. Sense of place is constructed through unbound and unfixed feelings that are constantly informed by memories, images, photographs, stories, personal histories, and experiences. Sense of place is a subjective psychosocial process triggered by feelings of familiarity—the smell of food; the sounds of music; the expressed forms of language, dress, and behaviors, among many other phenomena. Thus, these concepts are vital elements of informal vendor landscapes.

5. Street vending is a female-dominated economic practice around the world. In Latin America, 65 percent of street vendors are women, and the number is much higher in other developing economies in the global South (Chen 2006).

References

Bao, Xiaolan. 2001. *Holding Up More Than Half the Sky: Chinese Women Garment Workers in New York City, 1948–92*. Chicago: University of Chicago Press.

Chen, Martha. 2006. "Rethinking the Informal Economy: Linkages with the Formal Economy and the Formal Regulatory Environment." In *Unlocking Human Potential: Concepts and Policies for Linking the Informal and Formal Sectors*, ed. Basudeb Guha-Khasnobi, Ravi Kanbur, and Elinor Orstrom, 3–33. Oxford: Oxford University Press.

Economic Roundtable. 2005. *Hopeful Workers, Marginal Jobs: LA's Off-the-Books Labor Force*. Los Angeles: Economic Roundtable.

Fincher, Ruth. 2004. "Class and Gender Relations in the Local Market and the Local State." In *Reading Economic Geography*, ed. Trevor J. Barns, Jamie Peck, and Adam Tickell, 304–15. New York: Blackwell.

Hamilton, Nora, and Norma S. Chinchilla. 2001. *Seeking Community in a Global City: Guatemalans and Salvadorans in Los Angeles*. Philadelphia: Temple University Press.

Hongdagneu-Sotelo, Pierrette. 2001. *Domestica: Immigrant Workers Cleaning and Caring in the Shadows of Affluence*. Berkeley: University of California Press.

Kang, Miliann. 2010. *The Managed Hand: Race, Gender, and the Body in Beauty Service Work*. Berkeley: University of California Press.

Los Angeles Police Department. Alvarado Corridor Project. 2005. "Talk in the Park: Public Forum about the Past, Present, and Future of MacArthur Park." October 29.

McDowell, Linda, and Joanne P. Sharp, eds. 1997. *Space, Gender, Knowledge: Feminist Readings*. London: Arnold.

Monk, J. 1992. "Gender in the Landscape: Expressions of Power and Meaning." In *Inventing Places: Studies in Cultural Geography*, ed. Kay Anderson and Fay Gale, 123–38. New York: Wiley Halstead.

Park, Lisa Sun-Hee. 2005. *Consuming Citizenship: Children of Asian Immigrant Entrepreneurs*. Stanford: Stanford University Press.

Parreñas, Rhacel Salazar. 2001. *Servants of Globalization: Women, Migration, and Domestic Work*. Stanford: Stanford University Press.

———. 2005. *Children of Global Migration: Transnational Families and Gendered Woes*. Stanford: Stanford University Press.

Sassen, Saskia. 2003. "Strategic Instantiations of Gendering the Global Economy." In *Gender and U.S. Immigration: Contemporary Trends*, ed. Pierrette Hondagneu-Sotelo, 43–62. Berkeley: University of California Press.

Tyner, James. A. 2003. "The Global Context of Gendered Labor Migration from the Philippines to the United States." In *Gender and U.S. Immigration: Contemporary Trends*, ed. Pierrette Hondagneu-Sotelo, 63–80. Berkeley: University of California Press.

Zlolniski, Christian. 2006. *Janitors, Street Vendors, and Activists: The Lives of Mexican Immigrants in Silicon Valley*. Berkeley: University of California Press.

8

Living the Third Shift

Latina Adolescent Street Vendors in Los Angeles

EMIR ESTRADA

AND PIERRETTE HONDAGNEU-SOTELO

Adriana is a thirteen-year-old middle school student in East Los Angeles. During the day, she attends school, but on selected weeknights and on weekends, Adriana and her parents sell food at La Cumbrita, a small street in East Los Angeles where other street-vending families congregate to sell food from their home country, such as pupusas, tamales, atole, and tacos. Adriana has been street vending with her parents since they came from Puebla, Mexico, when she was five years old. Like Adriana, other children and teens sell food items with their parents after school and on the weekends to generate extra income for the family. While both girls and boys work alongside their parents on the street, girls are disproportionately present in street vending in Los Angeles.

Second-wave feminist scholarship taught us to see the invisible private sphere of household work (Oakley 1985) and alerted us to the "second-shift" work obligations faced by many employed women (Hochschild 1989). The ideal family type now includes breadwinner but "involved" dads, working moms, and children who are supported by adults. Children and teens in postindustrial societies are normatively sentimentalized, thought to be dedicated to school and play, and shielded from the public sphere of work by their parents, although it is generally thought appropriate and desirable for children to have "chores" or household tasks that teach them responsibility (Zelizer 2002). While middle-class children are indulged and provided with consumer items (Pugh 2009), their public lives have shrunk, leading to what Barrie Thorne (2004) calls "the privatization of childhood." Street-vending girls such as Adriana thus contradict this normative image of non-income-earning, "cared for" children. These girls are not shielded from adultlike responsibilities and public interactions. Rather, they do considerable housework, and they are earning money at a site (the street) that is normally considered a dangerous place for children, and girls in particular.

This pattern is particularly vexing because many Latino parents go to great lengths to keep their daughters confined at home when not in school or chaperoned by a family member. Parents generally try to protect girls from dangerous streets, neighbors, and especially boys. In New York City, for example, Smith (2006) found that Mexican immigrant parents restricted their daughters' spatial mobility, keeping them home "on lockdown" (like a prison) while boys were allowed to roam the streets.

Many Latino parents believe that protecting their daughters' virginity is important. Sociologist Gloria González-López (2005) conceptualizes virginity as *capital femenino*, a strategic, life-enhancing resource that will allow girls to have a better future and marry better husbands. Some Mexican immigrant parents are changing these views on the necessity of maintaining their daughters' premarital virginity (González-López 2003), but many still want their daughters monitored at home. This idea holds true for immigrant parents from other countries with strong Spanish Catholic traditions, including the Philippines. As Espiritu (2001) has noted, Filipina girls in the United States are expected to be family-oriented, chaste, and willing to serve the family. While some parents push these girls to strive for education, achievement, and elite college admissions, others have then forbidden their daughters to go away to college (Wolf 2002). These parents think of their daughters as morally superior to their white, Anglo counterparts, but this emphasis on the family burdens the girls with unpaid reproductive work and domestic confinement (Espiritu 2001). Morality is expressed through dedication to family and protection from public streets and sexual danger.

The daily practices of street-vending daughters of Central American and Mexican immigrant parents call into question current ideas about childhood and adolescence in the United States in the early twenty-first century as well as about the lives of working-class Latina girls. Not only do these daughters of Latino immigrant workers attend to their school work, but they are saddled with significant household-work responsibilities—cleaning, cooking, laundering, and looking after younger siblings. In addition, they dedicate time to income-generating street-vending work. In other words, these Latina girls negotiate a triple shift—street vending, household work, and schoolwork.

This paper extends the feminist literature on intersectionality by exploring the world of Latina/o teenage street vendors from a perspective that takes into account gendered expectations resulting not only from the familiar intersecting relations of race and class but also from the age as well as the inequality of nations that gives rise to particular patterns of international labor migration. As Thorne et al. (2003) suggest, raising children in transnational contexts may involve competing and clashing definitions of the meaning of being a child or adult. Parents may assume, for example, that young children will continue to be income-contributing members of the family (Orellana 2001). Many of these parents were poor in their countries of origin: among the poor in Mexico and Central American nations, having children contribute to household sustenance is normative (Bunster and Chaney 1989; Estrada Quiroz 2000; González de la Rocha 1994, 2006; Murillo López 2005).

As Mexican and Central American immigrants make their way in subordinated and saturated Los Angeles labor markets, many of them find that their best economic options are to utilize the possible labor from all family members (Dyrness 2001). Yet curiously, among the street-vending families in this study, the girls are preferred over boys. Based on nine months of ethnographic observations and twenty in-depth interviews with adolescent street vendors (sixteen girls and four boys), we address three research questions: (1) Why do more girls than boys do street vending with their families? (2) How do the girls experience this activity? and (3) Do the girls see this "third shift" as a burden or as a source of empowerment?

First Shift: School

For many children today, school is like work. Children and teens, especially in the middle class and affluent social classes, are highly scheduled, monitored, and subjected to what Annette Lareau (2003) calls the practice of "concerted cultivation." Parents want to reproduce their familial class status or seek mobility for their kids and do so by attempting to structure their children's high achievement in education and extracurricular activities (music lessons, sports, tutoring, enrichment programs, and so forth).

This intensive focus on educational achievement is not only class based but also a comparatively recent historical construction. The elite aristocracy of feudal times, for example, did not require their children to prepare for competitive college placements (Ariès 1962). The United States has undergone rather dramatic changes in conceptions of childhood in the last century. Sociologist Viviana Zelizer (1985) analyzes the transformation of notions of childhood that took place in the United States between 1870 and 1930, using the term *useful child* to refer to the nineteenth-century child who actively contributed to the family's economic survival through labor. In the twentieth century, she notes the emergence of the productively "useless" yet emotionally "priceless" child. Philip Ariès (1962), Zelizer (1985), and others have noted that this ideal of the sacred, sentimentalized child emerged in the context of industrialization, urbanization, and the concomitant rise of compulsory schooling, prevalent first among the middle class and later spreading to working-class and immigrant families. Zelizer (1985, 6) estimates that by the 1930s, "lower-class children joined their middle-class counterparts in a new nonproductive world of childhood, a world in which the sanctity and emotional value of a child made child labor taboo." These notions of childhood—that children must be educated, "developed," and "raised"—today prevail in most Western, postindustrial nations (Thorne 2004). In fact, children's protected, sacred status in part defines modernity. As one scholar has observed, "The dissociation of childhood from the performance of valued work is considered a yardstick of modernity" (Nieuwenhuys 1996, 237). The dominant view is that school and work are antithetical spheres.

Many children of Latino immigrants grow up in working-class circumstances but also face strong parental expectations to do well in school. They do not have access to tutors, prep schools, or, in many cases, even a quiet desk at which to do their homework, but they are expected to achieve educationally. Parents often underscore their own migration sacrifices and hard work at low-paying jobs as reasons the children must study. Some scholars have referred to this as part of the "immigrant bargain" that second-generation U.S.-born children must make with their parents (Smith 2006; Suarez-Orozco and Suarez-Orozco 1995). The idea is that parental sacrifice will be redeemed by the children's American success story.

Yet many low-income immigrant families depend on the economic contributions of all family members (Dyrness 2001) and thus are unable to maintain the level of normative child-rearing practices where children are indulged in the private sphere of home and dedicate effort only to school. Does this mean that the immigrant parents support the neglect of children's education? Our answer, based on the research for this paper, is no. Yet a good deal of the literature on children and informal-sector street vending remains predicated on the idea that work detracts from children's appropriate focus, education (Basu 1999).

Second Shift: Household Work

Household work has for centuries been identified as women's domain. This is true across all social classes, but women with money can outsource or buy out of some of the gender oppression by paying poor, racialized women to do housework (Ehrenreich and Hochschild 2005; Hondagneu-Sotelo 2001; Torres Sarmiento 2002). What happens when Latina immigrant women go into the public sphere for paid work? How do they manage their cleaning, cooking, and caregiving? Since they lack the resources to hire help for their household work, they turn to family members, typically female kin, including their daughters.

These gendered transitions reinforce the gender division of household work among Latino children. Many studies in Mexico show this pattern, with girls expected to assume more household responsibilities than boys. Liliana Estrada Quiroz (2000, 238), for example, has found that while both boys and girls are expected to perform household chores, these chores are gendered, with girls at a young age relegated to domestic activities (*quehaceres*) inside the home, and boys seldom performing such chores. These household burdens on female children seem to increase with migration. Ethnographic observations by Orellana (2001) in Central American immigrant households showed that girls as young as seven do numerous household chores (for example, unpacking groceries, bathing and dressing a younger sibling, and cleaning) without being asked to do so by their parents. This demand for young girls to help out in the home increases not only when their mothers go to work but also "when families are detached from the support networks of extended kin" (Thorne et al. 2003, 252).

Third Shift: Working the Streets of Los Angeles

Children today are not supposed to work, and when they do, they violate Western norms (Song 1999). The notion of children working is often seen as backward and anachronistic, and as a Third World child-labor practice rejected by developed nations such as the United States (Edmonds and Pavcnik 2008; Song 1999; Zelizer 1985). However, the reality is that children in the United States today do engage in paid-work activities and that such activities are not restricted only to immigrant children of color. Zelizer (2002, 2005) has noted that some jobs are seen as desirable for children and teens in particular contexts (for example, household chores and babysitting). Ong and Terriquez (2008) have found that white middle-class youth engage in paid economic activities more than do black, Asian, and Hispanic youth, a finding the authors attribute to the resources available to white middle-class kids, such as access to better transportation (including owning a car to take them to and from work) and the ubiquity of appropriate jobs near their places of residence. Inner cities, such as in Los Angeles, conversely, have very few jobs available for the youth.

The city of Los Angeles has begun to address this concern.[1] However, ethnic business enclaves have historically provided employment opportunities for children of color who must juggle school, home, and work responsibilities, not for résumé building or "experience," but to keep their family's business afloat. These family arrangements are often gendered, with daughters experiencing unequal divisions of labor. In her study of Chinese immigrants in southeastern England, Miri Song (1999) finds that children are a fundamental part of their families' takeout restaurants. According to Song (58), "Children not only did labor-intensive kitchen work or took orders at the counter, but they also acted as translators and intermediaries for parents who knew little or no English. As a result, some young people grew up with a great deal of responsibility and became privy to adult concerns from a young age." Song also found that girls worked more than their brothers, but these girls failed to acknowledge this unequal division of labor, using age justifications instead of gender inequality rationales. In addition, the girls dealt with sexism and sexual harassment from customers. The gender hierarchy in these families also placed mothers in subordinate positions to the patriarchal father, with mothers usually assisting fathers in the kitchen.

Similarly, in a U.S. study, Lisa Sun-Hee Park (2005, 73) has observed that Korean entrepreneurs employ family members, including children, in their restaurants, liquor stores, laundries, dry cleaners, and more. Park notes that respondents were "conscious of their gender division of labor." Girls started working at younger ages than their male siblings and were usually relegated to "mother's helper" positions. The work that girls performed with their mothers was seen as appropriate and natural, in large part because "immigrant work has historically been gendered as 'female'" (98). In contrast, boys who worked with their parents were demasculinized. Working with their parents caused children, boys in particular, to experience a prolonged childification (104).

Some street-vending businesses, like other ethnic businesses, rely on the work of children, but street vending complicates the work kids do because the practice is illegal in Los Angeles (Cross and Morales 2007; Hamilton and Chinchilla 2001; Muñoz 2008) and is performed in open visible spaces. Unlike the children who work in formal-sector family ethnic enclave businesses, such as Korean dry cleaners or Chinese restaurants, the Latina street-vending kids lack safety, protection, and respect from the larger society and government authorities. Not only the appropriateness of the work comes into play but also the appropriateness of the place where this work is performed: the street.

The work that girls do as street vendors both perpetuates and challenges gendered expectations. On the one hand, they are performing a type of work that has been gendered as feminine (preparation of food); on the other, they are doing this gendered work on the street, a space that has been gendered as masculine and inappropriate for *señoritas* (virginal women). Thus, an analysis of gender in this type of ethnic business allows us to see how gendered beliefs are not only enforced by societal norms but also internalized, reinforced, challenged, and adjusted by family members to meet the needs of the family business while still providing protection for their daughters.

Methods

This study is based on nine months of ethnographic fieldwork at various sites in the Los Angeles area and on twenty in-depth interviews with adolescents who sell items on the street with at least one parent. The sample included nineteen youths aged between ten and eighteen and one twenty-one-year-old who had been street vending with her mother since she was four years old. All of the interviews were

completed during the summer of 2008, and ethnographic observations continued for six months thereafter. Most children in this study and their families were
approached in the street while they were working, and consent forms were filled
out by all respondents as well as by their parents.

All of the children and their parents were aware of the strict laws against both
street vending and child labor. Some parents described the children's work as
"help," while others lied about having kids. Parents feared that the researchers
were undercover police, health inspectors, or social workers looking for child
labor abuse. These are common fears of respondents recorded by other scholars
who have conducted studies with street vendors (Muñoz 2008) or family businesses that rely on children's work (Song 1999).

Nevertheless, the researchers established a rapport with some families and
their children, a process eased by our ability to speak fluent Spanish, since all of
the parents spoke only that language. Estrada established trust by sharing her
background with the families: she spent her early years in Mexico and worked
alongside her parents as a child in Los Angeles, helping her father flag down cars
at a parking lot and accompanying her mother on paid domestic-work jobs. Estrada also brought her young daughter, husband, and mother along on several
site visits. Her family members bought and ate a variety of food from the street-
vending families.

Estrada was known in the field as *la estudiante de USC* (the student from USC).
The young street vendors, who were students themselves, related to her and
sympathized that she had to do "homework" late at night and on the weekends.
Hondagneu-Sotelo was known as *la profesora* (the professor). Her visits to the
field helped to reassure parents, reinforcing their trust in our project. Parents and
children asked *la profesora* questions about the university where she worked. They
were also impressed that she would take time off from "regular" school hours to
help her student with her project.

The respondents selected an interview site that they found convenient and
comfortable. Five interviews took place at the respondents' homes, three took
place inside Estrada's car (in close proximity to street-vending parents), one took
place in a coffee shop, and the rest took place on sidewalks, in parks, and in parking lots while parents or siblings briefly relieved the respondents from their work.
The interviews ranged between about thirty and ninety minutes long. All of the
interviews were conducted and transcribed by Estrada. Transcripts were read by
both authors several times and coded for themes.

Our sample was not equally distributed by gender. Sixteen of the respondents
were girls, and four were boys. We had originally planned to interview ten boys
and ten girls, but our time in the field showed that more girls were engaged

in this activity. Respondents were not able to recommend boys for our study, echoing our observations that this was a predominantly female activity. Twelve of the kids did not receive regular monetary remuneration for their work; the others received between five and thirty dollars per day. Four girls and one boy sold merchandise alone while their family members did street vending at other sites, while the others sold alongside their parents, though they were left alone at times while their parents ran errands. Thirteen of the respondents were second-generation, U.S.-born citizens, an important characteristic because previous literature on street vendors has focused on first-generation immigrants from Mexico and Central America (Dohan 2003; Hamilton and Chinchilla 2001). Nineteen of the respondents were attending school, and three attended private Catholic schools.

Most of the ethnographic fieldwork took place at a street we call La Cumbrita, a small side street just off a main avenue in the heart of East Los Angeles. By day, it is an isolated strip. Two large parking lots take up most of the space. One parking lot belongs to a supermarket; across the street is a parking lot for Bank of America customers. By night, both parking lots are filled with hungry customers who seek "authentic" Mexican and Central American food. As soon as the sun sets, this street transforms into a lively open market where predominantly Mexican, Guatemalan, and El Salvadoran families sell prepared food from their home country—tamales, pupusas, champurrado, tacos, pozole, and platanos fritos. They also sell candies, gelatins, pirated DVDs and CDs, toys, clothes, cosmetics, and much more. The families at La Cumbrita typically sell from 7:00 to 11:00 every Friday, Saturday, and Sunday evening. However, our observations took place as early as 6:00 P.M. and as late as 12:30 A.M., allowing the researchers to witness interactions among street vendors, family members, customers, and gang members in a more informal setting. The street vendors gabbed about fights, the police, gang intervention, children's education, and an alliance that was forming to settle street-vending disputes with the city.

In addition to spending time at La Cumbrita, Estrada attended a Halloween party organized by a group of street vendors, went street vending with a sixteen-year-old girl, and conducted three home visits. One home visit included meeting the family at 4:00 A.M. to collect cardboard boxes in downtown Los Angeles. Estrada prepared and sold *raspados* (cylinder-shaped donuts and snow cones) and *elotes* (corn on the cob), took apart cardboard boxes, and danced at the party.

None of the respondents and their families received payment for their interviews. In exchange for the children's time, Estrada offered educational support, such as filling out applications for financial aid and college, and helped them write résumés.

The Gendered Division of Labor in the Household and the Street

BOYS SLACK OFF: HOUSEHOLD RESPONSIBILITIES

These girls carry substantial loads of housework. Almost all of the girls listed household responsibilities that included a combination of cleaning, cooking, and taking care of their younger siblings. Twelve-year-old Esmeralda, who had two younger sisters and three younger brothers, said, "I do the beds, I do the dishes, and sometimes I [clean] the balcony with my other sisters. [My brothers] just stay there and watch TV and do *tiradero* [a mess] and everything, and [my sisters and I] have to sometimes pick it up." Gloria, a fourteen-year-old who sold tacos with her parents, similarly reported, "I go wash with my mom at the Laundromat. . . . I have to help her because it's my clothes also. My [ten-year-old] sister sometimes goes too, and then my [twelve-year-old] brother, he doesn't go. He stays with my dad. But it is usually me, [my mother], and my grandma."

Ten of the sixteen girls in our sample also had some type of responsibility for caring for their siblings or extended family members. According to Mariana, a sixteen-year-old who sold fruit with her parents, "Pos yo entro a las siete y salgo como a las dos. . . . Mi hermana los cuida [a mis hermanos] cuando yo estoy en la escuela y luego yo llego de la escuela y los cuido yo. . . . Yo soy las que los cuido cuando llego a la casa [I start school at seven, and I get out at around two. . . . My sister takes care of [my siblings] when I am in school, and then when I get home from school, I take care of them. I am the one that takes care of them when I get home]." These responsibilities shift as the children grow. Eighteen-year-old Carmen, for example, is no longer required to take care of her eight-year-old brother, though she did so when he was younger: "Cuando [mi hermano] tenia tres o cuatro años yo lo cuide. Pues lo cuide, le di de comer de mientras que mi mama trabajaba. Pero ahorita ya que mi mamá ya tiene tiempo ella lo cuida [When (my brother) was three or four years old, I took care of him. Well, I took care of him, I fed him while my mother worked. But now that my mom has more time, she takes care of him]." Carmen still bore the brunt of household cleaning responsibilities, however: "Mis hermanos nomás se paran y bueno trabajan pues y yo no, yo tengo quehacer—tender las camas, barrer, y bueno muchas cosas [My brothers just get up, and well, they work and all. But me, I have household work—make the beds, sweep the floor, and well, many things]."

Some of the girls in this study cooked for their entire families or prepared food for family businesses. Street vendors who sell prepared food spend a good deal of time purchasing ingredients and making the food at home. Monica, an eighteen-year-old who sold tamales with her parents, reported, "My responsibilities [were] to get home from school and help my mom do the tamales and clean the leaves and do everything you're supposed to do [for] the tamales and help around the house and then clean everything in the house."

By contrast, both the boys in this study and the brothers of the girls in this study relied on sisters, mothers, or sisters-in-law to do household domestic work. Eric, an eighteen-year-old boy who sold raspados on his own, lived with his three older brothers and his sister-in-law: In their household, cleaning and cooking was his sister-in-law's job. Other boys in this study simply looked puzzled when asked if they had any household responsibilities. For example, Juan, a ten-year-old boy who sells homemade jewelry with his father, responded "No" to this question, but his sister, just a few years older and also involved in selling jewelry with her father and two brothers, was in charge of cleaning the house. She laughed at the idea that her brothers would clean the house. But when she was asked how she felt about having to do more household work than her brothers, she answered in an annoyed way, "Well, not good, because they don't do anything. They slack off." Many of the girls we interviewed echoed the idea that boys avoid doing household work, consistently reporting that their brothers were expected to do very little if any household work. Doing household work was a task that fell to daughters.

BOYS CAN ALSO SLACK OFF ON STREET VENDING

The boys' ability to avoid work extended to the sphere of public street vending. Even boys who did not have sisters at home to pick up the household workload had light responsibilities. Edgar, a thirteen year-old who sells *tejuino* (a corn-based Mexican drink) with his mother, is an only child. Edgar reported that when he was not selling tejuino, he worked out at a local gym with his friend. When asked about his responsibilities at home, he replied, "Pos mi mamá me deja el día libre. O si no ya cuando termino [de trabajar] aquí me voy al gimnasio [Well, my mom leaves me free the rest of the day. Or when I finish (working here), I go to the gym]." Edgar was not only free from household work but he was also able to leave street-vending work to pursue leisure with friends.

Many girls faced a different situation. Katia, age twenty-one, sold fruit with her older brother and mother when she was younger. She recalled that her brother "was more wild. He used to go help [my mother] and then go home. He was not like us. [My cousin and I were] stuck to my mom." Katia did not resent the fact that her brother went home while she had to work with her mother, attributing such arrangements to "natural" gender differences: "[I am] a girl, he is a guy. I guess he ha[d] a girlfriend already? *Él se iba más temprano* [He would leave much earlier] with his friends. *Le ayudaba un ratito [a mi mamá] y se iba con sus* [He would help my mom for a while and then he would take off with his] friends. *Y yo me tenía que quedar ahí* [I had to stay there] because I was a girl. I was with my mom. And he is a guy. Guys, they just leave with their friends."

Other girls sang a similar refrain. They were typically brought to the street-vending site by their parents or by an older sibling. Once there, they were allowed to return home only when escorted by a family member at the end of the day. This strategy was predicated on the belief that girls required family protection to maintain their virginity and family honor, a belief that is widely shared in Mexican Catholic culture (González-López 2003, 2005) as well as in Filipino society (Espiritu 2001). This strategy yielded an added family economic benefit, as the girls were required to put in many hours of work. Yet the parents were then faced with the dilemma of protecting the girls while they were working in the streets.

STRATEGIES FOR PROTECTION

Some street-vending girls worked alongside family members, but others were un-accompanied as they sold food. In these cases, the families and the girls employed other protection strategies. One strategy was to have the girls stationed in public parks where a familial environment prevailed—for example, at a playground. In another family, the daughter sold cut-up fruit alone at a park. While these girls sold at relatively safe parks or busy street corners on their own, their parents often sold at more dangerous spots and/or sold merchandise that was considered more dangerous than food (pirated DVDs, for example). While Adriana was selling fruit by herself at a popular park in East Los Angeles, her mother sold fruit and flowers by a freeway entrance, a location perceived as more dangerous for a young girl, and her father sold pirated CDs and DVDs. Even though Adriana lacked a permit, selling fruit inside a park was perceived as safer than being near the free-way or selling products that would merit jail time if police chose to intervene. In addition, Adriana used the family's only "official-looking" metal cart, while her mother used a shopping cart. Similarly, Lolita, a sixteen-year-old who sold corn on the cob, mangos, and churros at a park south of Los Angeles, was dropped off by her father early every Saturday and Sunday. Her father then would sell the same items, but he did so while walking down the street, a practice that made him more visible and vulnerable to police harassment. Lolita, however, sold in a more controlled environment where many Mexican immigrant families went to spend their weekend days.

Another parental strategy was to monitor the girls via cell phone. The girls were instructed to use the phone in case of an emergency, and they received instructions from their parents via telephone. During one of the fieldwork observations, Estrada accompanied Lolita's seventeen-year-old sister, Martha, who sold corn on the cob, churros, and raspados, to a park and also to gathering spot in front of a church. Martha used her phone to obtain business-related instructions from her father. For example, Martha's father called and told her to walk to a nearby park, where his friend was having a big party and wanted to buy a sizable order of corn on the cob and raspados for his guests. She called her father to notify him that she was on her way and phoned him again after arriving. Cell phones allow the girls to remain tightly tethered to parental instruction and monitoring.

Gendered Justifications

"GIRLS ARE MORE CLEAN THAN THE GUYS"

Gendered beliefs that girls sold more than boys came up repeatedly in conversations. Girls were associated with being clean and nonthreatening to customers. According to Katia, "Some people think, 'Oh, she is more clean because she is a girl,' and [when they see] a guy, [they think], 'Oh no.' They say that a lot. Like people don't think about it, but they do see it—'Oh, she is a girl. She is clean.'" It was in this light that Katia viewed the family's decision to have her rather than her brother do street vending: it was better for business.

Accordingly, girls are associated with cleanliness, soap, and purity, while boys were associated with dirtiness and dubious hygiene. As Verónica, an eighteen-year-old girl who sold tejuino with her father on the side of an isolated highway near a running track, said, "I feel bad for the guys, because they're in the sun too, and they don't sell as much as girls because we see guys as more dirty. They think that girls are more clean than the guys. That's what some of the customers told me before, too. Because they say that the guys don't even clean their hands—they don't wash their hands when they get the money or they [prepare the tejuino]. So I think that's why they buy more from the girls." Verónica said, "If I don't come, I don't think that [her father and brothers will] make that much money." Young "virginal girls" and "maternal, nurturing women" are socially constructed as natural purveyors of food. They are seen as clean, and their "natural" service in the kitchen is extended to the public sphere of street vending.

Ethnographic observations with Verónica and her family affirmed that customers did indeed prefer to have a girl prepare the tejuino. On one occasion, a customer specifically asked Verónica, rather than the older man her family had hired, to prepare the tejuino because he liked the way she prepared it. Verónica rinsed her hands with water from one of their jugs and then grabbed a large cup, put ice and salt inside the cup, and began to cut and manually squeeze about five limes into the cup. She then filled the cup with tejuino and covered it with a lid. Placing one hand over the lid and the other under the cup, she began to mix the tejuino, lime, salt, and ice. When I asked if such instances were common, she said, "Yes, because sometimes [customers] say that . . . they like how I mix it. . . . They say that they like how I make it. Because last time [the man] was by himself, . . .

the customers were complaining [because] it tastes good but not as good. . . . So then after [that], my mom [said], 'No, then I'm just going to put you with that guy because [otherwise] the customers are not going to want to come no more.'"

Verónica and Katia's experiences were not isolated. Street vendors were acutely aware of presenting themselves as clean cooks and their work as involving hygienic routines. Street vendors constantly cleaned their stands while customers lingered nearby. They also made sure that their surroundings were clean at all times. Women often used hairnets and plastic gloves. Families with more children had the luxury of assigning one of the children to handle the cash transactions, so that clean hands could remain in contact with the food. Boys or fathers usually had charge of cash transactions, while mothers and daughters prepared food. It was also common to see jugs of water near street-vending stands so that vendors could constantly wash their hands. Bottles of water were also available so that customers could wash their hands.

The street vendors' hygienic performances mattered, but so did their gender. On one occasion, a boy was selling tamales alone from a grocery pushcart. He was modestly dressed in a black cap, black sweatshirt, and blue jeans. Even though his clothes were not new, he looked clean. Like the rest of the vendors, he used plastic gloves when putting the tamales into plastic bags or on plates for the customers. Even though he followed the same routines as the other street vendors, one customer asked him, "Did you make the tamales?" The boy responded, "No, my sister did, but she asked me to come sell them for her. I only sell them." He attempted to reassure the potential customer. The customer ended up not buying the tamales and instead purchased two pupusas from two sisters, sixteen-year-old Linda and fourteen-year-old Susana. While it is possible that this customer's decision to buy pupusas rather than tamales was simply a desire for a particular type of food, the customer may also have been concerned about whether the boy made the tamales and/or was clean enough to sell them.

"GUYS BUY MORE FROM GIRLS"

Attractive young girls were a good asset for family businesses. When Katia was fourteen or fifteen and she and her cousin were left alone to tend the fruit stand, they sold more than when her mother or brother was in charge. Katia explained, "You're a girl, and you are growing up, and you know how guys are, *que quieren mirar a las muchachas* [that they want to see the girls]?" She continued, "Guys *les compran más a las muchachas que a* [buy more from girls than they do from] ladies or guys."

Mariana and her teenage sister enjoyed playing games and bantering with male customers. Doing so not only made the time pass quickly but also enabled them to sell more fruit. In Mariana's words, "Pasan unos guys y los guys les dicen 'Hi' a mi hermana verdad, y mi hermana les contesta pa' tras a los guys [Some guys will pass by, and the guys will say 'Hi' to my sister, right, and my sister will say 'Hi' back to them]." Customers would often try to pick up Mariana and her sister, encounters that they enjoyed because "se siente a gusto porque no nos aburrimos allí y así vendemos más [it feels good because we don't get bored there and we sell more]."

These flirtatious encounters were very frequent and were often initiated by the clients. The encounters were also normal for teenage girls. In small towns throughout Latin America, youth commonly meet at the town plaza, where they chat, laugh, and flirt. While the girls enjoyed what they called *travesuras* (pranks), they also were aware of the dangers they faced. To protect themselves from male customers, they gave false names and claimed to be older.

Parents either were not aware of these flirtatious games or looked the other way. Mariana and her sister said that their father was unaware of these interactions, and if he had seen them talking with young men, "Pues a lo mejor sí [se enoja] pero va a pensar que está comprando fruta [Well, he might (get upset), but he will think that (the customer) is buying fruit]." Other parents were more vigilant. Linda and Susana's mother, for example, reprimanded them and made it clear to the customers that she disapproved of them flirting with or disrespecting her daughters. When a local gang member and customer called Susana over and she started walking toward him, her mother intervened and told her to sit down, angrily telling the girl that she was not to go near the guy.

Contesting the Gendered Roles

Although street vending takes place in an open space where girls are exposed to many dangers, girls are seen as more apt for these kinds of jobs. While the girls prepared the food at home and later sold it on the street, most of the brothers helped with tasks the girls were unable to do, such as peeling coconut and driving. Mariana frequently woke up early to peel fruit; her sister helped with all the produce, but her brother "would just help peel the coconut." Before Linda and Susana began selling pupusas with their parents at La Cumbrita, they sold the pupusas door-to-door from a basket and shopping cart. Their brother was older and did not accompany them, although, according to Linda, "He would just drive us there. . . . And when we finished, we used to call him. So, he'll be like the driver."

Like Linda, other girls attributed their brothers' failure to do street vending with their parents to the fact that the boys were either too old or too young. The tasks with which the boys helped, such as peeling hard fruit and driving, did not require long workdays. The boys put in less time and effort than the girls.

Some girls also referenced their brothers' lack of skills. For example, when I asked Adriana if her brother helped cut the fruit, she laughed and explained, "Él deja echar más [fruta] con la cáscara [he leaves more fruit on the skin he cuts off]." Because he was careless and wasted fruit, he was released from this duty.

Other girls were less amused about their brothers' slacking off and contested the unequal gendered division of labor. Verónica, for example, believed that it was unfair that she worked more than her brothers simply because she was a female: "So then I'm the one [who cleans because] *las mujeres limpian, no los hombres* [women are the ones that clean, not men]. And I get mad, too, and I tell them, 'No, guys could do the same thing. All humans are the same. . . . Guys could clean, too, and everything.' And [my brothers mock me by saying], '*Ay ay muy trabajadora. ¡Cállate!* [Ay, ay, what a hard worker. Shut up!]."

Verónica not only was required to do more domestic work but also was the only child who helped her parents with their street-vending business. She was annoyed that her brothers were unwilling to share their male privilege, mocking her and ignoring her plea for domestic gender equality.

Other girls, too, were unhappy about the tasks they were assigned or expected to do simply because they were female. In Martha's case, her father rather than her brother reinforced the gendered division of labor at home: "My dad is like old Mexicans, and [he thinks that] guys are not supposed to do anything. . . . Once my brother was ironing his pants, and [my dad] yells at [my sisters and me] and says, 'Why aren't you ironing your brother's pants?'" Martha replied, "He irons his own pants. He doesn't like the way we iron." Martha's father responded, "Well, he's not supposed to iron." Martha challenged the gendered position she had been assigned by her father, labeling him an "old Mexican" for thinking that ironing was a task not suitable for males.

Even though girls believed it was unfair that their brothers shirked domestic and street-vending work, this unequal gendered belief materialized itself on the street when the girls generated greater sales and were preferred by customers, as discussed earlier. In such instances, girls internalize these gendered justifications and even pity male street vendors for failing to sell as much as females do, and so girls see their labor as an asset to the family business.

The Third Shift: Burden or Empowerment?

The third shift these girls experienced is tiring, and some of the respondents complained about the workload. Lolita works about twelve hours each Saturday and Sunday with her father and older sister. Her day usually starts at eight o'clock in the morning, as she spends about two hours getting ready, having breakfast, and bagging the peanuts she will sell that day. She starts street vending at eleven o'clock at a park in a neighborhood about twenty minutes away from her home. At the end of the day, usually around eight o'clock in the evening, her father picks her up.

The other girls in this study followed similar schedules, devoting their entire weekends to street vending. Adriana, for example, worked alone selling fruit from ten o'clock in the morning until five o'clock in the evening, while her parents sold at other spots. The family later regrouped at seven o'clock at La Cumbrita, selling CDs and DVDs until midnight.

Even though these girls and their families worked very hard, the girls saw their work positively. Although Lolita found her long work hours "tiring," she added, "I like helping my parents." Many of the respondents echoed these sentiments. Said Monica, "You are doing it because you have to help your parents out, but it's fun at the same time because you have fun seeing different people every day."

While it may appear that girls in this study are constrained, most girls obtained as much benefit from their work as did their families. Some, like Monica, expressed feelings of freedom. According to Gloria, "Every Friday there is something different going on. . . . Before we sold tacos, I was at home Fridays and . . . it would be boring. Like just watching TV and going on the computer and the same things." Unlike her brother, who played soccer, Gloria did not participate in extracurricular activities that would give her a reason to be out of the house; thus, before her family decided to street vend, she was more confined to the home, similar to the girls in Smith's (2006) study.

In addition to experiencing a relief from boredom and more physical freedom from their work, the girls also acquired purchasing power. Those who were paid by their parents liked having the freedom to buy things. Carmen said, "Sí, sí me alcanza [el dinero que me pagan], pues yo no soy una persona que quiero todo pero compro lo necesario. . . . Pues compro mis cositas [Yes, (the money I get) is enough, because I am not a person who wants everything, but I buy what is necessary. . . . Well, I buy my own things]." These girls also helped invest in their families' businesses. When I asked Adriana what she did with her wages, she said, "Lo guardo y embebes cuando ellos no tienen [dinero] para comprar fruta les presto [dinero] [I save it, and sometimes when they don't have (money) to buy fruit, I lend them (money)]." Being able to help their parents financially made the girls feel proud and like they were valuable economic contributors.

In addition to seeing their work as beneficial for their entire family, these girls saw their work as preparation for the future. Katia and others believed that street vending provided them with the skills, strength, and courage to do any other type of work: "Selling fruit, . . . you know how to work—how to be in the sun, how to run from the cops, or whatever. And if you get another job, [it will be] easy. [Selling fruit also teaches you] how to get along with people, because you have to talk to people."

The girls also saw their third shift as a strategy to further their education. Three of the youth attended private schools and recognized that their work helped pay for their education. Carmen and her brothers did not go to private school, but their work helped them pay their tuition at a local California state university. When Carmen was nearing graduation from high school, her parents gave her a choice between helping to street vend or staying at home. She decided to street vend because she knew that going to college would cost money. Carmen said that her parents "me dijeron que si quería quedarme en la casa podía quedarme a estudiar y yo le dije no porque voy a entrar al colegio. Y dije, 'No yo mejor te quiero ayudar paque cuando vaya al colegio vaya un día y un día te ayudo . . . paque le ayude a pagar las cuentas del Cal State' [told me I could stay home and study if I wanted, and I told them no because I am about to start college. And I said, 'No, I want to help you, because when I go to college I will help you one day and . . . this way I can help pay for the Cal State expenses']."

While some of the girls complained about their heavy workloads and very full schedules, the majority of them saw the work as opening new opportunities. Street vending made them feel useful and responsible, it ended the boredom that many felt at home, and it offered what the girls perceived as useful socialization experiences for their future. Most important, the girls saw tangible benefits, as their street-vending labor brought more money into the household and thereby allowed their parents to buy them special items—trendy jeans or simply school supplies. On the whole, the girls saw street vending as an empowering experience that opened doors to new possibilities and better life opportunities.

Conclusion

While Zelizer saw distinct historical periods corresponding to the "economically useful" child and "emotionally priceless" child, the girls in this study experience a paradoxical situation. As economically useful girls, they are gendered as "little women," attending to household work and street vending. Yet they are simultaneously gendered as "little girls" who require protection, surveillance, and dedication to their studies. One might say they are also overprotected, as their parents employ various strategies to keep them safe on the street.

While the girls in this study may appear constrained, restricted, and overburdened, they thought they received as many benefits from their work as did their parents. Parental appreciation and recognition of the girls' contributions filled them with feelings of pride, achievement, and family belonging.

Shedding light on the labor contributions of these Latina adolescent street vendors opens a window for us to see how economically useful girls can transform household dynamics and alter parent-child relations, a topic that merits further research. So much of the research on work and family has been devoted to understanding spousal work-family balance (González de la Rocha 1994; Torres Sarmiento 2002). It is now time to focus on understanding how innovative income earning strategies, particularly in immigrant occupational niches and the informal sector, affect parent-child relations.

Moreover, the vast literature on the second generation—the children of immigrants—has been both illuminated and constrained by segmented assimilation (Portes and Zhou 1993). The literature has focused on the relationship between different modes of cultural assimilation and economic mobility, but it has largely ignored an important facet of reality in many poor and working-class immigrant families: many children work alongside their parents. This study has shown how street vendors in Los Angeles work as part of a family unit. The labor contributions of children—and especially girls—are vital for the family's economic mobility, and complicated gendered beliefs are drawn upon and elaborated to support these practices. Other Latino occupational niches also incorporate children into family work arrangements (for example, suburban maintenance gardening, domestic work, garment work, and agricultural work), and these other immigrant occupational family gender dynamics should be explored.

We have highlighted how Latina adolescent street vendors negotiate triple shifts, the continuities between gendered household divisions of labor and street vending, and the gender belief systems and practices that support these work-family arrangements. Rather than bringing to light yet another instance of women's and girls' oppression, the research suggests better life opportunities for the girls.

Notes

This research was made possible by partial funding support from the Diversity Placement Research Fellowship in the USC College Office of Graduate Programs.

1. In 2009, in response to this "new" problem, Mayor Antonio Villaraigosa joined with the Los Angeles Community Development Department to sponsor a Summer Youth Employment Program that sought to provide work experience opportunities for up to five thousand students not attending school during the summer (summer school had been cut due to the California state budget crisis). The target population was students between the ages of fourteen and twenty-four, especially eleventh- and twelfth-grade students who had not passed the California High School Exit Exam. This program was designed to keep kids busy in school or at work and off the streets. Although the immediate focus was getting youth summer jobs, the overarching focus remained improving academic performance and providing work experience (as well as pocket money).

References

Ariès, Philippe. 1962. *Centuries of Childhood: A Social History of Family Life*. New York: Vintage.

Basu, K. 1999. "Child Labor: Cause, Consequence, and Cure, with Remarks on International Labor Standards." *Journal of Economic Literature* 37:1083–119.

Bunster, Ximena, and Elsa M. Chaney. 1989. *Sellers and Servants: Working Women in Lima, Peru.* New York: Praeger.

Cross, John, and Alfonso Morales. 2007. "Introduction: Locating Street Markets in the Modern/Postmodern World." In *Street Entrepreneurs: People, Place, and Politics in Local and Global Perspective,* ed. John Cross and Alfonso Morales, 1–14. New York: Routledge.

Dohan, Daniel. 2003. *The Price of Poverty: Money, Work, and Culture in the Mexican American Barrio.* Berkeley: University of California Press.

Dyrness, Grace R. 2001. *Policy on the Streets: A Handbook for the Establishment of Sidewalk-Vending Programs.* Los Angeles: University of Southern California.

Edmonds, Eric V., and Nina Pavcnik. 2008. "Child Labor in the Global Economy." *Journal of Economic Perspectives* 18:199–220.

Ehrenreich, Barbara, and Arlie Russell Hochschild. 2005. "Global Woman." In *Gender though the Prism of Difference,* ed. Maxine Baca Zinn, Pierrette Hondagneu-Sotelo, and Michael A. Messner, 49–55. 3rd. ed. New York: Oxford University Press.

Espiritu, Yen Le. 2001. "'We Don't Sleep around Like White Girls Do': Family, Culture, and Gender in Filipina American Lives." *Signs* 26:415–40.

Estrada Quiroz, Liliana. 2000. "Familia y Trabajo Infantil y Adolescente en Mexico." In *Jovenes y Niños: Un Enfoque Sociodemografico,* ed. Martha Mier and Teran Cecilia Rabell, 203–47. Mexico City: Porrúa.

González de la Rocha, Mercedes. 1994. *The Resources of Poverty: Women and Survival in a Mexican City.* Cambridge, Mass.: Blackwell.

———. 2006. "Vanishing Assets: Cumulative Disadvantages among the Urban Poor." In *Out of the Shadows: Political Action and the Informal Economy in Latin America,* ed. Patricia Fernandez-Kelly and Jon Shefner, 97–123. University Park: Pennsylvania State University Press.

González-López, Gloria. 2003. "De Madres a Hijas: Gendered Lessons on Virginity across Generations." In *Gender and U.S. Immigration: Contemporary Trends,* ed. Pierrette Hondagneu-Sotelo, 217–40. Berkeley: University of California Press.

———. 2005. *Erotic Journeys: Mexican Immigrants and Their Sex Lives.* Berkeley: University of California Press.

Hamilton, Nora, and Norma S. Chinchilla. 2001. *Seeking Community in a Global City: Guatemalans and Salvadorans in Los Angeles.* Philadelphia: Temple University Press.

Hochschild, Arlie Russell, with Anne Machung. 1989. *The Second Shift: Working Families and the Revolution at Home.* New York: Viking.

Hondagneu-Sotelo, Pierrette. 2001. *Domestica: Immigrant Workers Cleaning and Caring in the Shadows of Affluence.* Berkeley: University of California Press.

Lareau, Annette. 2003. *Unequal Childhoods: Class, Race, and Family Life.* Berkeley: University of California Press.

Muñoz, Lorena. 2008. "'Tamales . . . Elotes . . . Champurrado': The Production of Latino Vending Landscapes in Los Angeles." PhD diss., University of Southern California.

Murillo López, Sandra. 2005. "Ethnicidad, Asistencia Escolar y Trabajo de Niños y Jóvenes Rurales en Oaxaca." In *Jóvenes y Niños: Un Enfoque Sociodemográfico,* ed. Martha Mier and Teran Cecilia Rabell, 249–88. Mexico City: Porrúa.

Nieuwenhuys, Olga. 1996. "The Paradox of Child Labor and Anthropology." *Annual Review of Anthropology* 25:237–51.

Oakley, Ann. 1985 (1974). *The Sociology of Housework*. Oxford: Blackwell, 1985.

Ong, Paul, and Veronica Terriquez. 2008. "Can Multiple Pathways Offset Inequalities in the Urban Spatial Structure?" In *Beyond Tracking: Multiple Pathways to College, Career, and Civic Participation*, ed. Jeannie Oakes and Marisa Saunders, 131–52. Cambridge, Mass.: Harvard Education Press.

Orellana, Marjorie. F. 2001. "The Work Kids Do: Mexican and Central American Immigrant Children's Contributions to Households and Schools in California." *Harvard Educational Review* 71:1–21.

Park, Lisa Sun-Hee. 2005. *Consuming Citizenship: Children of Asian Immigrant Entrepreneurs*. Stanford: Stanford University Press.

Portes, Alejandro, and Min Zhou. 1993. "The New Second Generation: Segmented Assimilation and Its Variants." *Annals of the American Academy of Political and Social Science* 530:74–96.

Pugh, Allison J. 2009. *Longing and Belonging: Parents, Children, and Consumer Culture*. Berkeley: University of California Press.

Smith, Robert Courtney. 2006. *Mexican New York: Transnational Lives of New Immigrants*. Berkeley: University of California Press.

Song, Miri. 1999. *Helping Out: Children's Labor in Ethnic Business*. Philadelphia: Temple University Press.

Suarez-Orozco, Carola, and Marcelo Suarez-Orozco. 1995. *Transformations: Immigration, Family Life, and Achievement Motivation among Latino Adolescents*. Stanford: Stanford University Press.

Thorne, Barrie. 2004. "The Crisis of Care." In *Work-Family Challenges for Low-Income Parents and Their Children*, ed. Nan Crouter and Alan Booth, 149–58. Hillsdale, N.J.: Erlbaum.

Thorne, B., M. F. Orellana, W. S. E. Lam, and A. Chee. 2003. "Raising Children, and Growing Up, across National Borders: Comparative Perspectives on Age, Gender, and Migration." *In Gender and U.S. Immigration: Contemporary Trends*, ed. P. Hondagneu-Sotelo, 241–62. Berkeley: University of California Press.

Torres Sarmiento, Socorro. 2002. *Making Ends Meet: Income-Generating Strategies among Mexican Immigrants*. New York: LFB Scholarly.

Wolf, Diane L. 2002. "There's No Place Like 'Home': Emotional Transnationalism and the Struggles of Second-Generation Filipinos." In *The Changing Face of Home: The Transnational Lives of the Second Generation*, ed. Peggy Levitt and Mary C. Waters, 255–94. New York: Russell Sage Foundation.

Zelizer, Viviana. 1985. *Pricing the Priceless Child: The Changing Social Value of Children*. New York: Basic Books.

———. 2002. "Kids and Commerce." *Childhood* 4:375–96.

———. 2005. "The Priceless Child Revisited." In *Studies in Modern Childhood: Society, Agency, and Culture*, ed. Jens Qvortrup, 184–200. London: Palgrave.

9

Reinventing Dirty Work

Immigrant Women in Nursing Homes

LUCY T. FISHER AND MILIANN KANG

Paula, a fifty-nine-year-old widow who emigrated from the Philippines in the mid-1980s, has worked at the same nursing home in California for sixteen years. When asked to describe her work as a certified nursing assistant, she joked that she refers to herself not as a CNA but as a "PAW—professional ass washer." While she highlighted the dirtiness of the job, she also regarded it as caring, skillful work, and she took pride in performing it. She elaborated: "Giving a bath like that, cutting their nails. Everything, do everything. . . . CNA is a big responsibility. Not in bed making—it's easy to do the bed. If you're taking care of people, you have a big responsibility, because their life depends on you. It's hard. Like those who are working in the office [can] just leave the papers. . . . But I'm not considering this a hard job because it depends upon your technique and routine. . . . Of course, if you're very picky, you cannot be successful CNA. You have to be practical. . . . I supported my niece for nursing school. . . . Now she can find work anywhere—Saudi, Canada, Australia—anywhere. I'm proud of her." Paula's description revealed the multiple and contradictory dimensions of a CNA's job. On the one hand, it is low-status, poorly paid, and physically demanding "dirty work" that requires attention to intimate parts of the human body. On the other hand, the fact that others "depend on you" for their lives, and that the job is a "big responsibility" can lend it meaning and importance. As Paula asserted, not everyone can be a CNA, as the job necessitates developing "technique and routine" that encompass a range of physical, emotional, and communication skills learned only through experience. Furthermore, this job allowed her to support herself and her extended family; in addition to putting her niece through nursing school, she sponsored visas for family members and regularly sent money back home to the Philippines.

Immigrant women like Paula, who make up a large part of the CNA workforce, accommodate themselves to the various demands of low-wage, low-status service jobs by engaging in "boundary making" (Lamont 2000, 3), processes that circumscribe and redefine the performance of "dirty work" (Stacey 2005). This study builds on these concepts and expands them based on distinct processes related to the provision of long-term care in nursing homes. According to Lamont, boundary making refers to material and symbolic processes in which providers of low-wage work impose limitations on its performance while redefining the work as skillful and important. For CNAs, boundary making also includes negotiating the interface between hands-on work in long-term-care institutions and their own social worlds, especially reformulating the stigmatization of this work as unskilled and low status. While these processes can give CNAs and other service workers some control over both the material and symbolic aspects of the work, boundary making also has significant structural limitations. CNAs' ability to create better working conditions and higher status for this job is limited by the institutions that employ them, their status as immigrant women performing low-wage work, and the downgraded status of both elderly people and elder care in the United States.

Drawing on the literature on care work, nursing, and the body, we define *dirty work* as physical labor that involves cleaning and caring for the human body, its products, and its environs, particularly where doing so involves handling body parts or products that are intimate, messy, or possibly contaminated. Several aspects of the CNA job contribute to its characterization as dirty work: contact with the human body and detritus; sexualization of interactions involving intimate physical contact with patients; and dealing with dead or dying patients. This work also involves extensive emotional labor (Hochschild 1983) and body labor (Kang 2010), in which the management of feelings and bodies is an essential part of performing service work. By recognizing the embodied and emotional dimensions of their work as requiring important skills, CNAs reinvent dirty work as having greater dignity. Like Stacey's (2005, 849) study of home-care work, which found that aides derive a "sense of pride that comes from doing 'dirty work,'" our study shows that CNAs find meaning through their mastery of work that others shun. However, this work is performed under less-than-ideal conditions that constrain CNAs' ability to redefine it in empowering ways. Yet institutions do not always take unfair advantage of the emotional labor of CNAs and other care workers, and they can also provide support for the provision of effective, high-quality physical and emotional care. As Lopez (2006, 133) argues, "Care organizations can be plotted on a continuum with emotional labor at the coercive end and organized emotional care at the other." Thus, organizations such as nursing homes in some instances extract care from workers under coercive conditions, but in other instances can facilitate the provision of care in ways that benefit both the patients and providers. Furthermore, CNAs and other care workers actively negotiate how they interface with the multiple forces shaping their work—from the patients, to the families, to administrators, to the larger community in which these institutions operate.

By presenting data from fieldwork in three California nursing homes, this chapter shows how immigrants working as CNAs make meaning of work that is often construed as dirty work through the social processes of boundary making and in the context of particular social institutions and structures of what Lopez terms "organized emotional care." We show not only how CNAs try to establish their social worth as workers who do dignified work but also how they do so by transforming their work spaces and ultimately their social worlds within the work setting as well as in their homes and communities. Care organizations both facilitate and constrain workers' attempts to provide high-quality care and to construct this labor as meaningful, rewarding work. Together, these processes allow workers to bring some measure of dignity to a low-wage, low-status job, and shape their identity formation as workers and immigrants within constraining institutional contexts. The chapter concludes with an analysis of how this reinvention enables CNAs recognition and acceptance of their employment situation, while also illuminating this meaning-making process as a consequence of and adaptation to the low status and low social value scripted by other actors and organizations for this work.

CNAs and Elder Care in the United States

The U.S. Census Bureau reports that by 2019, for the first time in history, older people will outnumber young people across the globe (Kinsella and Wan 2009). In the United States, the number of older adults is projected to increase by 135 percent between 2000 and 2050 (U.S. Census Bureau 2008). This demographic shift contributes to a shortage of direct-care workers to provide personal care to frail and disabled older adults living in private homes and in institutions (U.S. Department of Health and Human Services 2004). CNAs, also known as nursing assistants or aides, provide this hands-on care in nursing homes. This work is termed "activities of daily living" and refers to tasks most of us take for granted: eating, bathing, toileting, dressing, and physically moving from place to place. However, when people can no longer perform these tasks themselves and must rely on others for assistance, these activities are no longer easy or taken for granted but require hard work to fulfill. While helping to complete these essential functions, nursing assistant work is poorly compensated, physically and emotionally taxing, and demands daily contact with noxious sights and smells. It has one of the highest on-the-job injury rates (U.S. Department of Labor 2011). Positioned at the lowest rung of the nursing home organization in training, authority, and pay and benefits, CNA work is located within institutions characterized as bureaucratic, heavily regulated, and profit-driven (Diamond 1992; Foner 1994; McLean 2007).

As in the past, the current long-term-care workforce is heavily dependent on women from racial/ethnic and minority backgrounds and increasingly relies on the transnational migration of women seeking work (Montgomery et al. 2005; Redfoot and Houser 2005.) In fact, the percentage of foreign-born nursing assistants in long-term care settings increased from 6 percent in 1980 to 16 percent in 2003 (Redfoot and Houser 2005). In major cities, CNAs are primarily minority and immigrant women (Wilner and Wyatt 1998). Given the rising number of older Americans needing paid care, the difficulty in attracting stable, qualified workers to provide this care, combined with mounting health-care costs, make it critical to understand how transplanted workers find, perform, and remain in a job with few obvious rewards and many challenges.

Design of the Study

This study is based on a constructionist approach to grounded theory (Charmaz 2006; Glaser and Strauss 1967) and on a symbolic interactionist theoretical perspective (Blumer 1986). Specifically, this "theory/method package rooted in Symbolic Interactionism" (Clarke 2005, 2) assumes that knowledge is co-created by the researcher and study participants interacting in particular contexts and aims toward interpretive understanding of meanings. The primary researcher (Fisher) collected the data for her dissertation, drawn from seven months of field observations and interviews in three nursing homes in northern California.

After approval by the university institutional review board and the administrators of the facilities involved, directors of nursing introduced the researcher either to individual CNAs or to the staff as a group. Initial weeks in each home were spent on the day and evening shifts, observing staff and residents in public areas, such as activity rooms, hallways, and dining rooms. Recruitment was primarily by snowball sampling or through aides approaching the researcher after seeing her in the home. The interviews were semistructured and were conducted in a private area of the facility or in private homes. Each participant was both interviewed and observed for at least one shift while providing personal care to residents. Interviews were recorded and field notes written shortly after each observation. In all, twenty-seven people met the inclusion criteria: being a full-time worker, speaking English, and being certified as a CNA. All were people of color; twenty-four were immigrants; and twenty-two women. Sixteen of those interviewed were born in the Philippines, while others emigrated from Mexico, the South Pacific islands, and Asia and Africa. The sample closely reflected the ethnic/racial background of those employed at the facilities.

The three nursing homes in the study represent the three major payer types in the United States: (1) proprietary, usually national for-profit chains; (2) nonprofit organizations; and (3) government-sponsored institutions. The three homes, which are identified by pseudonyms, were located in urban and suburban areas in different counties. The first home, Chain Elder Care, has 140 beds on three floors and is part of a for-profit chain. Located on a major thoroughfare in a large city, it is housed in a nondescript building with narrow halls and cramped rooms. Some public areas were undergoing refurbishing. The dining room is too small to accommodate all residents, so several line the hall waiting for meals in wheel-chairs. Except for the home's administrator, a white male, all other upper-level staff members were people of color, mostly Filipino immigrants. Most CNAs also were immigrants from the Philippines, save for a woman from Mexico and two from China. This home was unionized; CNAs with two years' experience were paid $11.17 per hour and had recently received a $1.30 hourly raise.

The second home, Golden Haven, has 67 beds and is part of a nonprofit residential care community in a small, upper-class town. The home and grounds are spacious and well kept, and most of the residents have private, well-appointed rooms. A chef serves a variety of entrées at each meal, and residents eat at small, cloth-covered tables. Most members of the upper-level staff are white women, as are most of the residents. CNAs in this home migrated to the United States from all over the world: Africa, the Philippines, the South Pacific islands, and Mexico. Workers in this home were not unionized and earned about $13.75 per hour, with generous vacation and retirement benefits.

The third home, County Nursing Home, is government owned and licensed for 281 beds. It is situated near a commuter train station in a midsized suburban community. The three-floor building appears institutional, and the interior is in need of refurbishing. Residents eat either in their rooms or, if they need assistance, in small "feeder" rooms. Like those living in Chain Elder Care, most residents were immigrants and reliant on Medicaid/Medicare for their health insurance. All upper-level staffers were immigrants from Russia or the Philippines, and CNAs were primarily born in the Philippines, with a few from India and the Pacific Islands. CNAs at this site were unionized and had just negotiated their contract to about $18 per hour with health and retirement benefits.

These three sites illuminate various patterns of work performed by CNAs, their strategies for reinventing dirty work as a meaningful occupation, and the limitations on their attempts to transform their work and workplaces.

CNA Work as Dirty Work

Several aspects of the job of a CNA characterize it as dirty work. In addition to direct contact with the body and its by-products, CNA work involves dealing with dead or dying patients. Furthermore, baths and cleaning can necessitate contact with genitalia, which can be fraught with sexualized overtones. Dirt, death, and sex and the stigmatization of contact with them create an underlying sense of dirtiness associated with CNA work. The dirtiness of this work is further exacerbated because it is often performed under less-than-ideal conditions. Carol, a thirty-two-year-old Filipina CNA who came to the United States in 1991, when she was fifteen years old, has worked at Chain Elder Care for ten years. She captured the dirty work aspects of her job in one word: "Vomit." She elaborated, "I rather clean B[owel] M[ovement] than vomit. Vomit is just so—ugh, that sour smell. I think that's more disgusting than anything. I rather clean poop than vomit. I think most of the CNA, I ask them, they agree with me, they rather clean BM than vomit." Carol took for granted these dimensions of her work, which others rarely acknowledge or discuss. However when she was away from work for even a short period, she had to reacclimate herself upon returning. She says, "Being here every day . . . I think your nose gets used to the smell. But then if you're gone for a couple weeks, you come back and say, 'Oh, that's the smell. I haven't been here for a while.'" Her comments reveal how CNAs are challenged by but eventually adapt to work requiring contact with the human body and its detritus.

Care of patients is further complicated by the need to satisfy expectations of the patients' family members, who are often removed from the daily reality of caring for their loved ones. Carol described the difficulties she faced in caring for a patient with permanently shortened muscles whose family members asked that she be dressed up for their visits: "Her family would like to dress her up in this long-sleeved dress that they bought her, and all I see is this arms that won't open, the arms and legs, and I felt like, 'Oh my god, I just want to cry and go home.' It was hard. I even thought about quitting. I say, 'Oh my god, I don't think I can do this anymore,' because I was sweating. And usually what's hard is residents that is just dead weight, and then they make it more harder because they fight. Even now, even after ten years, that's still hard. When they're heavy and they insist on going to the restroom, and even though there's just like two or three of you, you're either going to break your back or you're going to drop the resident, so that's hard."

Thus, the dirty work of attending to their patients' bodies also subjects CNAs to labor that is literally backbreaking and dangerous, both for themselves and their charges. When large and heavy residents are unable to walk or stand or turn in bed, as many as two or three CNAs may be needed to pull them up if they have slid down in bed. During a typical eight-hour shift, CNAs change clothes and diapers, brush teeth and hair, shave and put makeup on patients, lift residents from bed to chair and back again. Twice a week, each resident is scheduled for a shower and shampoo, which can be challenging even if the resident is cooperative. In addition to these physical challenges, some patients have dementia and become belligerent or fearful of their caregivers.

In performing this work, CNAs not only must attend to the dirtiness of their patients but also can become dirty in the process. Carol described sweating from the physical exertion of changing her patient without dropping her. In other instances, CNAs internalize feelings of dirtiness from contact with patients. Juan, age thirty-six, came from Mexico in 2002 and has worked as a CNA for four years. During his first days on the job, he recalled, "I can't go to eat my lunch time. I wash my hands 3 to 4 time [from his fingertips to his upper arms]. I see the other CNAs. They go to eat, wash their hands, but I can't. I go to my house right away, take a shower, everything." CNAs, especially those new to the job, thus absorb a sense of degradation from the performance of dirty work. These feelings are exacerbated when patients, families, and institutions do not value this work and even penalize those who do it. Workers reported that verbal and physical abuse by residents and family members was more disturbing than performing hands-on care. Spitting, swearing, and hitting were mentioned, as were overt and coded sexual comments.

Sexualization of caring work adds another dimension to the sense of its dirtiness and makes for particularly charged interactions with patients, especially because many CNAs are women and must care for men. Even when the process does not take on sexual overtones, Carol was initially shocked at having to clean genitalia: "I started when I—I think I was twenty-one. First it was like, 'Oh my god, this is what I'm going to do?' But then, I don't know. I think cleaning vagina, it wasn't [as] hard for me [as] cleaning a male resident's [penis] because, you know, it's not like I clean male before. So it was different—'Oh my god, what I'm going to do?' I remember Room 1, the room used to be male residents, and I used to have this one resident in 1B and [his wife] has to teach me how to clean her husband because his penis is not circumcised, . . . so she told me, 'You have to do like this.'"

In such cases, gender differences can pose difficulties simply as a consequence of lack of familiarity and a sense of embarrassment. In other instances, patients' behavior reflects gendered power differences and crosses over into overt sexual harassment. Regina, a thirty-five-year-old Filipina, emigrated in 1989, when she was eighteen years old. She has worked on the evening shift at County Nursing Home for eleven years. In one instance, she reported telling her husband about a distressing sexualized encounter with an elderly male patient. Regina came home in the evening and her husband noticed that she was upset and asked her, "'What's wrong?' 'I'm stressed,' I said that to him. 'Why?' Because of my patient, this patient, he calls me, and then he wants [me] to check every time his balls. He says, 'Can you check my butt? Can you put ice between my groin?' Every time and every time I pass by, 'Regina, Regina,' and everybody knows I'm stressed with him. . . . Same thing with his roommate. He's very abusive to sex. He talks about, 'Come sleep with me. Hold [me], make me come.' That's the second one. Same thing. Especially when he will have a shower, he plays. And then he's going to say, he's telling to the female CNA, 'Stroke me, stroke me.' I don't know. It's not good for us, too."

Incidences such as these reveal how the sexualization of caring work performed by CNAs exacerbates their already vulnerable position as immigrant women in low-wage jobs. While they find strategic ways to draw boundaries around such encounters, these sexualized encounters nonetheless illustrate multiple inequalities of gender, class, and immigrant status that coalesce in subjecting women to these advances. Furthermore, the women are far more likely to be blamed for or stigmatized by these advances than are the men who perpetrate them. Much attention has been focused on the abuse of patients by caregivers, and while this is a serious issue (as discussed later in the chapter), the opposing problem of caregivers being abused by patients, particularly the often invisible dynamics of sexual harassment, also deserve serious consideration.

Another difficult and stigmatizing aspect of CNA work is the contact with dead or dying patients. This dimension of the work imposes physical and emotional demands to which CNAs learn to respond over time. Gloria, a forty-two-year-old Filipina, traveled back and forth from the Philippines beginning in 1997 but settled permanently in the United States in 2002, and has worked at Chain Elder Care for four years. She explained how CNAs sometimes know that a patient is going to die "in a few hours, so we just clean them before it happens. But [when] they pass away, we still have to check to make sure, because usually they pass a bowel. [We] make sure they're clean, and if their family will come, just make them look presentable. But usually their mouth open, usually we tie it and stuff . . . but we don't bag them here. The guy [from the mortuary] comes and pick them up."

Gloria and other CNAs generally adjust to this aspect of their work dealing with end-of-life care, but many experienced feelings of fear and aversion during their initial dealings with dying patients. According to Nona, a twenty-four-year-old Filipina who immigrated when she was seventeen and has worked at Chain Elder Care for two years, the first time she was working with a dying man, "every time I change him, every time I go in that room, I have to call somebody—'Oh, Ata, can you go with me? Oh, Kuya, go with me. I'm scared.' And every time there's something touching my skin [she screamed]. But after a month or two months it's just like, 'Oh, never mind. Don't think about that.' So now I'm OK, I'm not scared with dying people, of dead people."

Although Nona and other CNAs learned not to be frightened by dead and dying patients, contact with dead bodies still carries a heavy social stigma. Thus, even as CNAs adjust to the "dirtiness" of their work, the stigma that accompanies sex and death undermines their own sense of comfort and dignity in performing this work.

Hughes (1971) has noted that work is one of the more important aspects of one's social identity. Since language about work is loaded with prestige judgments, he proposes that individuals attempt to revise conceptions of themselves and their work through "collective pretensions" and "dignifying rationalizations" (Hughes 1971, 340). In the Hughesian sense of dirty work, the mundane and repetitive nature of the work provides an opening for people to develop collective pretensions to give their work, and consequently themselves, "value in the eyes of each other and of outsiders" (340). However the low status of their work combined with their marginalized status as immigrants and racial minorities makes it difficult to maintain these dignifying rationalizations. Thus, many immigrant CNAs appeal to previous or separate aspects of their identities in order to draw boundaries around and construct a sense of moral worth that distinguishes them from their performance of stigmatized work and their association with others who engage in similarly degraded work.

Erecting Boundaries for Moral Worth

In her study of working-class men, Lamont (2000, 2) examines "how workers construct similarities and differences between themselves and other groups" to construct a sense of moral worth. Workers, she says, use moral standards to define who they are, why what they do matters, and, just as important, who they are not. According to Lamont, culturally specific notions of morality are at the center of workers' sense of selves and the worlds that they construct. We found that immigrant CNAs' boundary work simultaneously appeals to multiple constructions of the self that allow them to assign meaning and dignity to their work and make judgments that set them apart from others.

CNAs engage in various strategies of boundary making that are particular to their gender, class, occupation, and immigrant status. These strategies include appealing to their previous status prior to immigration, reframing dirty work as skillful and important work, and identifying with their workplaces and constructing them as respectable places of employment. The workers established boundaries in three areas: between themselves and other CNAs; between themselves and others higher in authority and influence; and between their nursing homes and those of others. These workers craft differences, reconstituting their identities and re-creating environments to both understand and elevate their social positions as low-status workers and new arrivals to America.

Certain CNAs make clear that they differ from their fellow workers by their elevated status in their country of origin. Before coming to the United States, they pointed out, they were accustomed to a privileged life. Banita, age forty-four, described herself as "a queen" in her home country, Fiji: "We had a big house, a big property, many people to help us. Now I have to wipe butts." Fifty-year-old Myra similarly recalled her life of leisure: "When I was in the Philippines, we have maid, we have driver. We don't cook, we don't wash our clothes, because we have maid. But here I must learn a lot of things, like clean your house, do your marketing, everything, everything." Both women held two jobs, waiting to return "home" sometime in an uncertain future. The economic and social parameters defined by Banita and Myra set them apart from other workers, but their former way of life was invisible and had little bearing on their day-to-day living and working conditions. However, their previous status lingered in their imagination, providing a vivid reminder of the differences between then and now. In an interesting paradox, they invoked their past status as a way of ameliorating the sting of dirty work, but this appeal to their higher-class background also increased their resentment and dissatisfaction.

A second demarcation emerged around evaluations of the quality of work performed by other aides. Throughout interviews and observations, aides focused on lapses in care by unnamed others. Aides did not want to be accused of mistreating a resident and so were attentive to who succeeded them at the end of a shift. Regular staffers were more likely to be seen as "good workers" and could ease this worry, but per diem employees represented an unknown link in the smooth handoff of work. Specifically, CNAs were concerned about assessing the condition of "their" residents during the shift before a day off (bruises or breaks in skin reported, complaints allayed), and when the CNAs returned, they scrutinized their charges from head to toe. CNAs' detailed inspections of their patients' bodies reveal that they take pride in their work even as they disdain it.

This sense of valuing the performance of dirty work can allow some CNAs to reverse the nursing hierarchy by claiming that their work is the most important aspect of care and that only they are qualified to do it well. Although CNAs acknowledge that they are below nurses in authority and responsibility, they create an identity that transcends official ranking by asserting that certified nursing aides are the only staff able to perform hands-on care. Ellie, a fifty-year-old Filipina who had worked for three years as an aide, contends that although it's "hard to explain" the job of a CNA, and she provides an example of how they can be more skilled than nurses in providing essential care. She asserts that when residents need help "to go to the bathroom, [a CNA's job is] to assist the residents; [nurses] can't do that." Regina agreed that aides, not nurses, provide essential care. Confirmatory evidence comes not only from her own belief but also from the residents' families, whose favorable assessment of her work she proudly recounts. Regina stated, "Some people say without CNA, nurses cannot do this job. Nurses cannot clean poo-poo. That's why [families] say 'Without you guys, my mom cannot be like this.' That's the comment they're giving me sometimes, the family. Yes, they appreciate us." Thus, CNAs sense that they provide the most crucial care, bolstered by supportive comments from families, allows them to reframe the stigma of dirty work as well as to challenge workplace hierarchies. However, their ability to redefine the meaning of dirty work relies not only on their constructions of self but also on the kind of facility in which they work and the conditions and policies associated with it.

CNAs must contend with a double stigma—both what they do and where they work. Thus, they seek to redefine both aspects of this stigma, by reframing first the work itself and second the particular institution where they work. They understand from media reports and their friends' reactions that the public widely views nursing homes as providing poor-quality care. Aides counter this prevailing notion by providing detailed accounts of how "their" nursing home is substantially superior to other places of work. Forty-five-year-old Helen, who is married and has three children, came to the United States in 1995 from the Philippines, where she was a hairdresser. When the man who had sponsored her was picked up and jailed by the FBI, and her electronic assembly job was outsourced to Costa Rica, she learned about CNA training from a friend. She proudly describes her workplace, Golden Haven, in terms that allow her to take pride both in her work and in her place of employment, and to articulate this sense of pride by making visible rather than hiding concrete dimensions of dirty work, such as the incidence of bed sores and the frequency of changing diapers: "I like it here. Clean. That's why I work just only like two months the other facility. Oh my god, the residents, when I see them over there—bedsore, big sores. . . . One resident bring here the first day, we saw it like big, after that, in a few weeks, months, it's getting smaller. They take good care here. Every three hours they check. They always tell the CNA, 'Did you clean, or did you change the diaper every hour, two hours?' They really take good care of the resident. So we didn't see any sores here. I've been here almost three years." Likewise, Paula, age fifty-nine, cited another concrete measure of the cleanliness of her facility—the lack of offensive smells: "The first time you walk into [a nursing home] you can see, because there's some facility you can smell. And for all the facilities [in this for-profit chain], this is the cleanest. Our place . . . this is the cleanest. That's what they say, people say."

Aides at all three research sites made comparisons to showcase their particular nursing home by emphasizing rather than concealing its attentiveness to different aspects of performing dirty work. Those in the small, nonprofit home Golden Haven pointed to the abundance of tools of the trade (diapers, sheets, mechanical lifts) and available patient services, such as physical and occupational therapies, while aides working for the national chain focused on surpassing their numerous local rivals. CNAs in the third home run by the county government spoke of how the new owners (a government entity) had made positive changes to the facility, including improved pay and benefits, a refurbished environment, and sufficient sheets and towels. "We used to hide sheets and blankets for later," one said, and several recalled purchasing shampoo and hand lotion for residents.

CNAs thus rewrite the language of dirty work to emphasize their own caregiving skills and to showcase the superiority of their own places of employment. In so doing, they draw boundaries around their identities in ways that redefine not only their jobs but also the social worlds that they inhabit. However, they are constrained in these boundary-making efforts by the organizational structures of the job and the workplace.

Structural Limitations of Boundary Making

While CNAs redefine their work through boundary-making processes, these efforts are constrained by the structural conditions of the work as a low-wage, low-status, unstable occupation that is dominated by women and for the most part lacks benefits and collective representation. Within the nursing home hierarchy of caregivers, CNAs are on the bottom rung in terms of pay, power, and prestige.

Direct-care workers hold the lowest-paid jobs in long-term care (U.S. Department of Labor 2010). Whether they are born or trained in the United States or overseas, CNAs' wages and benefits are determined by nursing home ownership. Few homes are unionized. Many CNAs work part time, and the median hourly wage of $9.56 for these workers in 2010 was significantly lower than that of the average hourly wage for U.S. workers (of $14.15) (U.S. Department of Labor 2010). As a result of low wages and part-time work, 19 percent of home-care aides and 16 percent of nurse aides are poor by the U.S. Census definition (Montgomery et al. 2005).

Labor unions and other organizing efforts have helped to improve wages and benefits in unionized nursing homes. At the same time, other market forces, such as the need to minimize turnover and reduce the high cost of orienting and training new employees, have put pressure on nonunionized homes like Golden Haven to improve wages and working conditions. Golden Haven maintained a stable, skilled workforce by addressing the needs not only of the home's owners and residents but also of the workers, offering a living wage, decent benefits, and respectful worker-owner relations. Workers felt appreciated by management and more often treated nursing home residents and their families like kinfolk. To create an appealing, familiar setting and provide attentive service to attract wealthier clients and their families, private homes like Golden Haven need to attract and keep skilled CNAs. Satisfied workers produce satisfied consumers who provide positive testimony to others about quality of care and are less likely to complain to home administrators or government regulators. Thus, larger, unionized homes were not necessarily the most-desired workplaces for CNAs, as small, private, not-for-profit homes in affluent neighborhoods also were forced by market pressures to improve working conditions for CNAs.

Certified nursing assistants are the largest job classification in nursing homes but are ranked at the bottom of the nursing hierarchy, below licensed vocational nurses and registered nurses. At the top of the pyramid is the director of nurses, who has authority over all nursing activities. Nearly 70 percent of nursing homes are privately owned, and most are affiliated with for-profit, multisite corporations (Wunderlich and Kohler 2001). Although federal and local authorities regulate the entrance of workers into this field, the requirements and training are minimal. California requires twice as many hours of training to obtain a manicurist license as it does for nursing assistants. The California Department of Public Health, Licensing and Certification Division specifies that applicants need only be at least sixteen years old, be free of "hazardous" health conditions, and never have been convicted of a serious crime ("Health and Safety Code" 2011). In 1987, the federal government required CNAs to have a minimum of seventy-five hours of training and pass a competency test within four months of employment. Federal standards for CNA training have not changed significantly since then.

The low standards for competency are a mixed blessing. On the one hand, they allow easy entry into the field. On the other hand, they contribute to the low status and poor compensation for the work, since workers are viewed as unskilled and easily replaceable. These dynamics produce workers who are spread thin among multiple jobs and have little incentive or power to change conditions. Unless they were caring for a parent or child at home, workers in this study held second or third jobs. Most worked in other nursing homes, while some supplemented their salaries with a home-based business, such as catering, hairdressing, tailoring, or taking in boarders.

While CNAs were troubled by the general lack of respect for the work they perform, more disturbing was the perception that facility administrators favored the interests of residents and their families over the ability of nursing aides to perform their jobs adequately and safely. Myra, age fifty, came to the United States in 1992 from the Philippines, where she attended nursing school. She started working as a live-in companion to a woman, deciding to work as a CNA after the woman died. Myra described fear of being accused of "patient abuse" as a subtle but daily presence in CNAs' thoughts and actions. She explained that patients can be "very abusive. Here we are always talking about the patient rights, but our rights? Sometimes patients, they are scratching us, but then, what can you do? So it's a patient rights, that's what they're always telling us. Patient rights." The state of California requires ongoing training in patient rights and elder-abuse recognition and reporting ("Report Abuse" 2011; "Health and Safety Code" 2011), and CNAs were aware of the serious consequences of allegations of mistreatment. Possible outcomes were public exposure, an investigation by the director of nursing and state officials, and suspension or termination from work. Each day, CNAs inspected residents' skin for redness and breakdown and for bruises and discoloration, reporting any findings to a nurse. This notification requirement seemed to relieve the anxiety of an accusation of "patient abuse" but also created an atmosphere of surveillance. According to Ellie, "You have to react, you have to report: 'Did you tell the nurse?'"

In addition to fears of accusations of neglect or abuse, as well as the sexual comments and harassment described earlier, CNAs' low status also subjected them to insulting comments or insensitive, demanding, and dismissive treatment by nurses, residents, family members, and administrators. Despite the higher pay at one home, Karen left the job because she felt demeaned by nurses: "I feel like I'm just—they can just throw me anything." For fifty-six-year-old Barbara, the main source of her negative feelings about her job was residents' disrespect, as she asserted that residents "get ruder by the minute and more demanding. Each one is under the impression that 'I'm paying their salary.' 'You're not a nurse's aide, you're a maid,' and I've had them refer to me, 'You're my girl.' I've heard, 'Asian girls—go back to your country. Where did you learn to speak English?'" Such comments, which reflect a combination of gender, racial, and anti-immigrant discrimination, undermine the already difficult and degrading aspects of CNA work.

Fraught with indignities, the job of a nursing aide entails work that others would prefer not to do or even know about. In addition to the material dirtiness of the work, the sense of symbolic pollution (Douglas 1966) plays a major role in the structure of inequality. This physical and psychic sense of degradation motivates workers to transform their job into something not merely palatable but also rewarding. Yet the conditions of understaffed, low-paying work in a niche dominated by immigrant women of color impose limitations on the degree to which CNAs can reinvent this work. Nevertheless, this work enables fluid constructions of gender—both masculinity and femininity—that open new possibilities for immigrant workers to define positive identities as CNAs, and more broadly as care providers. While most CNAs are women, the gendered construction of the work poses particular challenges for men in giving positive meaning to their performance of feminized work.

Gendered Constructions of CNA Work

The effort that men exert in redefining highly feminized work to conform to acceptable notions of masculinity reveals how immigration and labor-market segregation shape fluid constructions of gender both in CNA jobs and in care work more generally. The men in the study explicitly challenged hegemonic constructions of masculinity, citing "feminine" attributes of patience, gentleness, and equanimity as essential to their sense of identity and ability to perform quality work. While they regarded themselves as possessing these features, they believed that other men in their social networks who were not CNAs lacked these positive caring attributes. These men's performance of CNA work altered their views of masculine norms, as they viewed themselves more favorably than they did other men who conformed more to traditional models of masculinity. Thus, their workplace identities in some ways redefined their notions of masculinity both inside and outside of the nursing homes. Juan, a thirty-six-year-old immigrant from Mexico who has worked as an aide for four years after being a janitor in a nursing home, assessed how men must conform to perform the work of a CNA. Juan's sense of what constitutes "good care" not only countered mainstream American perceptions about those who perform this job but also challenged notions of masculinity within Latino communities: "I see people who went to aide school and speak good English and work many years but don't like their work and don't give good care. I don't think its school but your *costumbre* [customs] and your life. . . . Not all mens can work CNA. I have a lot of friends working hard, they [earn] $7.00 for hour, $7.25, more, $8.00, and [they work] hard and [they are] tired, but they can't work CNA. The personality is different. The mens need to have clear . . . *limpia mental* [mental hygiene], no think nervous. Clean thinking about the old ladies. Gentle to the older people, especially to the woman. I know sometimes they like work hard, but I see when his girlfriend or his wife, machismo, you know? These people can't work CNA. When you work CNA, you need to calm down so everything is gentle." Thus, Juan's employment as a CNA has taught him to value qualities of gentleness and respect for women and the elderly, and to question norms of machismo. Similarly, Eduardo, a thirty-year-old who emigrated from the Philippines in 1998, when he was twelve, reformulated his views of masculinity through the requirements of his job. He was not accepted into an RN program and completed the shorter licensed vocational nursing (LVN) training but decided not to take the exam. His mother signed him up for CNA training because he was "partying a lot." According to Eduardo, "Only a few CNA

I think do this type of job. People [must] have patience. . . . None of my [male] friends are in the nursing business. I mean nursing environment. They're all in business or accounting, and I don't think they can do this type of thing, cleaning up and stuff. I don't think they can do that. They get disgusted by it. But for me, it doesn't bother me."

While some men reconstructed the gendered meanings of their work in positive ways, they nonetheless expressed frustrations about their disempowerment as wage earners and lack of authority in their workplaces. Twenty-eight-year-old Andy, an Eritrean immigrant who has worked for two years as a CNA, explained, "I'm working two jobs. I'm working seven days [a week]. I have two days, only eight hours off. I'm working here five days, I'm working there five days. In the middle of those, I have two days off here, two off over there, and I work eight hours, and the rest of the hours I'm off. Just like that. Now I have about two and a half years working here. . . . I'm thinking of going to the higher state, LVN, from LVN to RN, you know? I like to learn, but it's a family problem. I have to take money, send back [to] my country, my father, my brother." The necessity of sending money back to his family tempered his willingness to jeopardize his job by complaining. In addition, he appeals to the hierarchy in his workplace, recognizing that he is at the bottom. He desired to become an LVN and eventually a registered nurse, both higher-paying positions that act as supervisors to CNAs such as himself. Thus, his inability to fulfill certain roles as a breadwinner or to exercise leadership or power as a CNA motivated him to seek other work. Rather than fighting for the rights of CNAs, he aspired to a higher-status position.

Both men and women struggle to redefine this work in positive ways. In addition to drawing boundaries and reframing the stigmatized aspects of the work, they also make the work palatable by bringing their own cultures into the workplace, re-creating potentially alienating and dehumanizing social worlds as familiar and homelike, although again, these efforts are limited by institutional structures and the larger cultural devaluation of CNA work.

Re-creating Social Worlds

Nursing homes are bound by government regulations, American cultural values, and economic forces, but are also shaped and influenced by the immigrant CNAs who give meaning to a low-wage/low-status job by transforming the nursing home from an unfamiliar organization into the intimate and comfortable world of home. Reinventing a home culture takes on different forms depending on the mix of the countries of origin and the context of the particular institution. In the small, nonprofit nursing home, CNAs came from many countries. They crafted a staff room as a communal place and found common ground in home-cooked meals. In this lunchroom, a Vietnamese CNA and Nigerian CNA compared the heat of peppers mailed from home, while other CNAs discussed how soy sauce crossed geographic borders. In this facility, the residents, upper-level staff, and the surrounding community were predominantly upper-middle-class Caucasians, and no place of birth dominated among the CNAs. The social worlds were small, varied, and fluid, and in the communal lunchroom, cultural differences came together and were openly acknowledged.

In the Chain Elder Care nursing home, staffed primarily by immigrants from the Philippines, management and CNAs reconstructed the Filipino social world. The power, appeal, safety, and comfort of the familiar were evident throughout the facility. The facility featured photos of scenic sites in the Philippines, the smells of Filipino meals wafted through the building, and CNAs conversed in Tagalog while bathing, feeding, and dressing residents, and during break times. The staff members transformed their work space into the home space Espiritu (2003) calls "home making" in "the space between." The attraction of memories of the home country were sometimes even stronger than sentiments deriving from the nursing "home" of residents. American holidays such as Thanksgiving, Halloween, and Easter were observed with seasonal decorations, but the celebration of the Philippine Independence Day was the largest event of the year.

On one occasion, the researcher attended the birthday party of the twelve-year-old son of a Filipina CNA. She arrived at the suburban home, gift in hand, and saw several youth playing basketball in the driveway. Inside were CNAs from Chain Elder Care as well as their spouses and some retired CNAs. This birthday party centered on planning a Philippine Independence Day celebration to be held at the nursing home. The children came in to fill their plates and left for their own activities in the backyard. There was no cake, no games, or opening gifts. Instead the event focused on the re-creation of the holiday consistent with its celebration in the home country. In planning for the event, the researcher and other adults watched a videotape of a local dance troupe, listened to CDs of dance music, and discussed the possibility of elaborate dresses and costumes for the nursing home's celebration. The Independence Day party at the nursing home ultimately became an all-day affair throughout the facility.

This event not only brought CNAs together outside of the nursing home in their own community but also served as an impetus for them to plan an event that allowed them to bring aspects of their community into the nursing home. This was one of CNAs' many efforts to create their own social world in their workplace. While a certain kind of generalized camaraderie develops among CNAs within a nursing home based on common complaints about the work and the residents, in this instance, immigrants from the same country fashioned an expanded and culturally specific "space between" that encompassed work, home, and homeland.

At other times, home and work were remade into a seamless community through concrete connections between individuals. For Carol, coworkers and the workplace became a substitute form of family: "They're just like my extended family. Even my husband tells me that, because even when I'm not at work, I still hang out with them, go to dinner or birthday parties whatever. I always hang out with them. They're like sisters, and Paula is our big sister or like our mother hen. Three or four of them, they know my problems. Even though they can't do anything about it, they're always willing to listen to you, whether I'm at work or I'm out of work. My husband says, 'Aren't you already tired of talking to them? You just talked to them at work.' But I forgot to tell them something!"

At times, this reproduction of home at work through close relationships involved bringing actual kin into the workplace. At all three study sites, participants pointed out that some of their relatives were their coworkers. Both Sepela and Regina worked with their sisters; Barbara's children volunteered at her workplace; and Nick and his aunt shared the same work schedule. When obtaining a job through word of mouth was not possible, ties with a common homeland were sufficient. Gloria said she was initially turned away because she lacked work experience, but "when then the [nursing] director heard me and we have the same dialect, she called me in." According to Mila, the fact that a Filipina was doing the hiring helped Mila get a job: "Maybe because I'm Filipina, she's a Filipina, maybe it's easy for me to get in, because same thing with my sister." Thus, the blurring of boundaries between home and work facilitated labor recruitment and retention through the creation of a positive work environment and the willingness of workers to assist each other formally and informally, even without pay.

"Home" at Chain Elder Care expanded during off hours to include friends and family. On weekends and during the evening hours, when the Filipina management was not at the worksite, off-duty CNAs brought their families to the nursing home. The researcher was proudly introduced as a university affiliate, and met workers' daughters, sons, and husbands. A few older, more experienced CNAs were godparents to these children, whose mothers instructed them to show appropriate respect. Rather than goofing off when their family members visited, CNAs enlisted their kin's assistance with work, thereby providing their workplaces with additional unpaid workers.

Making Meaning of Low-Wage Work, Gender, and Migration

What are the dimensions of the work that CNAs perform on a daily basis? How do CNAs negotiate the demands of this job, and what factors constrain these negotiations? This chapter has illuminated both the dirty work involved in this job and the boundary-making processes through which those who perform it imbue it with a sense of purpose and dignity. At the same time, it has emphasized the limitations imposed by the organizational structures of low-wage work, gender, and migration on these efforts to define the work more positively.

Nursing assistants acknowledge their devalued status and reformulate their identities to minimize stigma. These processes are influenced by their status as immigrants, particularly their marginalization as noncitizens and speakers of limited English. Immigrant CNAs engage in boundary-making processes to bring meaning and dignity to their work and their lives. Through the process of boundary making, they reconstruct identities to give themselves a sense of purpose and moral worth. In addition, immigrant aides re-create work spaces into familiar and comfortable social worlds by incorporating home culture(s). Moreover, for some workers and the settings they work in, the borders dividing home, work, and homeland are blurred, creating an unbounded territory for everyday community. This reinvention of identity and place evolves as a necessary adaptation to the performance of a job that they—and the public—acknowledge as dirty work.

Exposure to dirty work is constant; there is no beginning, no end, and often no escape. The work of a CNA is physically arduous, and pay and benefits can be at or near poverty levels. The work takes place in nursing homes with elderly clients who struggle with disabilities and dementia. CNAs do work that families cannot or do not want to do. While this job involves giving care, the actual tasks are repetitive and at times repulsive. This work is even more challenging when the person receiving care cannot interact in a meaningful way because of language barriers or cognitive failings. Rather than shunning the challenges of dirty work, some aides reconstruct attentive physical and emotional care as the starting point in an evaluation of meaningful work. CNAs claim a sense of accomplishment and even superiority from their ability to perform work that others cannot stomach. They redefine the dirtiness of their work as a badge of honor rather than a stigma, but this badge only carries meaning within their own social worlds.

Most workers, whether they are well-paid executives or poorly paid nursing assistants, need to feel good about themselves and the work they do. Work gives meaning to lives. Given the unpleasant aspects of CNA work, why does it continue to attract workers? CNA jobs are readily available, with minimal requirements and training. These jobs are particularly appealing for immigrants, since these positions do not require fluency in English. Hiring often occurs through informal word-of-mouth channels, so newcomers may feel more at home with similar others. The large number of Filipina CNAs results from several factors, chief among them a legacy of Filipina economic, political, and social support that pushes workers toward transnational migration, particularly in health-care fields (Espiritu 2003; Guevarra 2009; Rodriguez 2010). For workers in the United States who see this position as a stepping-stone to the more prestigious (and higher-paying) RN and LVN roles, having friends and family in the field provides a network for future job possibilities (Lledo 2010).

CNAs stay in their jobs because they have few options: they lack the skills for other jobs; their education and knowledge of the English language may be poor; and the ever-growing elderly population means that CNAs are always in demand. CNAs find meaning and adjust to the work, but these processes are necessary because of the demanding nature of the work and the conditions under which it is performed. In response to this work, immigrant CNAs import the solidarity and comfort of the familiar by crafting the workplace as a substitute family and home. In so doing, they create better working conditions that benefit themselves as well as their patients and institutions.

Interviews with CNAs and observations at worksites and social settings reveal a complicated story about how CNAs transform their identities and work spaces to bring dignity to this type of low-wage/low-status work. Although individuals are altered by their occupations, their transnational locations bring an added dimension to meaning-making processes. CNAs transform nursing homes by incorporating home cultures into their work spaces as a means to make their work more palatable; and in doing so, they are able to provide more stable, efficient and quality care. Simultaneously, they transform their own identities through their experiences as immigrant workers and their engagement with the organizational structures of their workplaces. Together, these processes are a unique reinvention of low-wage labor that reflects both immigrant women's agency in re-creating a gendered-service niche and the structural limitations they face in constructing work that is meaningful, respected, and rewarded.

References

Blumer, Herbert. 1986 (1969). *Symbolic Interactionism: Perspectives and Method.* Berkeley: University of California Press.

Charmaz, Kathy. 2006. *Constructing Grounded Theory: A Practical Guide through Qualitative Analysis.* London: Sage.

Clarke, Adele E. 2005. *Situational Analysis: Grounded Theory after the Postmodern Turn.* Thousand Oaks, Calif.: Sage.

Diamond, Timothy. 1992. *Making Gray Gold: Narratives of Nursing Home Care.* Chicago: University of Chicago Press.

Douglas, Mary. 1966. *Purity and Danger: An Analysis of Concepts of Pollution and Taboo.* London: Routledge and Kegan Paul.

Espiritu, Yen Le. 2003. *Home Bound: Filipino American Lives across Cultures, Communities, and Countries.* Berkeley: University of California Press.

Foner, Nancy. 1994. *The Caregiving Dilemma: Work in an American Nursing Home.* Berkeley: University of California Press.

Glaser, Barney G., and Anselm L. Strauss. 1967. *The Discovery of Grounded Theory*. Chicago: Aldine.

Guevarra, Anna Romina. 2009. *Marketing Dreams, Manufacturing Heroes: The Transnational Labor Brokering of Filipino Workers*. New Brunswick, N.J.: Rutgers University Press.

"Health and Safety Code Section 1337–1338.5." 2011. California Department of Public Health, Licensing and Certification Division. http://www.leginfo.ca.gov/cgi-bin/displaycode ?section=hsc&group=01001–02000&file=1337-1338.5. Accessed March 22, 2011.

Hochschild, Arlie. 1983. *The Managed Heart: Commercialization of Human Feeling*. Berkeley: University of California Press.

Hughes, Everett C. 1971. *The Sociological Eye: Selected Papers on Work, Self, and the Study of Society*. Book 2. Chicago: Aldine Atherton.

Kang, Miliann. 2010. *The Managed Hand: Race, Gender and the Body in Beauty Service Work*. Berkeley: University of California Press.

Kinsella, Kevin, and He Wan. 2009. *U.S. Census Bureau, International Population Reports, P95/09-1, An Aging World: 2008*. Washington, D.C.: U.S. Government Printing Office.

Lamont, Michele. 2000. *The Dignity of Working Men: Morality and the Boundaries of Race, Class, and Immigration*. New York: Sage.

Lledo, Lolita. 2010. Interview by author. June 11.

Lopez, Stephen. 2006. "Emotional Labor and Organized Emotional Care: Conceptualizing Nursing Home Care Work." *Work and Occupations* 33(2): 133–60.

McLean, Athena. 2007. *The Person in Dementia: A Study of Nursing Home Care in the U.S.* Peterborough, Ont.: Broadview.

Montgomery, Rhonda. J. V., L. Holley, J. Deichert, and K. Kosloski. 2005. "A Profile of Home Care Workers from the 2000 Census: How It Changes What We Know." *Gerontologist* 45:593–600.

Redfoot, D. L., and A. N. Houser. 2005. *"We Shall Travel On": Quality of Care, Economic Development, and the International Migration of Long-Term Care Workers*. Washington, D.C.: AARP Public Policy Institute.

"Report Abuse." 2011. California Department of Social Services. http://www.dss.cahwnet. gov/cdssweb/PG20.htm. Accessed March 22, 2011.

Rodriguez, Robyn. 2010. *Migrants for Export: How the Philippine State Brokers Labor to the World*. Minneapolis: University of Minnesota Press.

Stacey, Clare L. 2005. "Finding Dignity in Dirty Work: The Constraints and Rewards of Low-Wage Home Care Labour." *Sociology of Health and Illness* 27:831–54.

U.S. Census Bureau, Population Division. 2008. *U.S. Population Projections*. Washington D.C.: U.S. Census Bureau. http://www.census.gov/population/www/projections/summary tables.html.

U.S. Department of Health and Human Services. 2004. *Nursing Aides, Home Health Aides, and Related Health Care Occupations—National and Local Workforce Shortages and Associated Data Needs*. Washington, D.C.: U.S. Department of Health and Human Services.

U.S. Department of Labor, Bureau of Labor Statistics. 2010. "Occupational Employment Statistics. National Occupational Employment and Wage Estimates." http://www.bls.gov/ oes/current/oes_nat.htm#31-0000. Accessed February 16, 2011.

———. 2011. *Nonfatal Occupational Injuries and Illnesses Requiring Days Away from Work, 2011.* U.S. Department of Labor (USDL-12-2204). http://www.bls.gov/news.release/osh2. nro.htm. Accessed January 10, 2013.

Wilner, M. A., and A. Wyatt. 1998. "Paraprofessionals on the Front Lines: Improving their Jobs, Improving the Quality of Long-Term Care." Paper presented at the AARP Long-Term Care Initiative Conference, September 10–11.

Wunderlich, Gooloo S., and Peter O. Kohler, eds. 2001. *Improving the Quality of Long-Term Care.* Washington, D.C.: National Academy Press.

10 Extending Kinship

Mexicana Elder Care Providers
and Their Wards

MARÍA DE LA LUZ IBARRA

In the context of economic globalization, all postindustrial societies have experienced a dramatic growth in their elderly populations. In 2009, for example, three nations—Italy, Germany, and Japan—determined that more than 20 percent of their citizens were over the age of sixty-five (Sokolovsky 2009, 5). In North America, seniors now make up almost 14 percent of the population in Canada and 13 percent in the United States (Schellenberg and Turcotte 2007; U.S. Census Bureau 2010). In the United States, there are at present more than 37 million people age sixty-five or older. Moreover, as this population continues to grow as a result of the maturation of the baby boomer generation, the senior population is predicted to reach 71.5 million by 2030. This unprecedented demographic shift—in both the United States and in the world as a whole—carries important consequences for aging individuals, for their kin, and for their nation-states.

Not surprisingly, different societies have different approaches to the evolving needs of their elderly populations. A growing academic literature addresses these differences and looks at the scope and parameters of formal-sector care in institutions (Foner 1995) and private homes (Lyon 2006; Parreñas 2001; Solari 2006), as well as family-based (Lamb 2009) and community-based care (Sanjek 2009; Stafford 2009). Less qualitative or quantitative research exists, however, on paid private care within the informal sector, wherein work is not regulated by the state and workers are paid directly by employers. Consequently, the labors of migrant women, who predominate in this sector, remain relatively invisible outside of their local context.

I focus here on Mexican migrant women—Mexicanas—employed as informal-sector, private elder-care providers in Santa Barbara, California. Specifically, I focus on the case study of a worker who forms part of a family care group and who literally and figuratively "extends" kinship to her ward. Here a worker's words shed light on the socioemotional ties and practices that engender relatedness and create what she perceives to be a mutually beneficial relationship. The case study, moreover, highlights one of the key recommendations made by workers to improve the occupation: employers—typically the adult children of the ward— should respect workers' labors and knowledge of their wards (see appendix).

Before focusing on the case study, however, I address the different elder-work contexts within the informal private-care sector in Santa Barbara. Doing so helps to contextualize the family-unit work strategy and how its particular organization constitutes an effort by some workers to create better conditions for themselves and their wards. The family-unit strategy, however, is often highly personalistic. In this regard, I briefly review the literature on domestic employment and the role that personalism continues to play within the occupation, especially as it pertains to workers' expressed desires for closer "family" relations with their employers. If we take workers' words seriously, what does family mean to them? I address insights from contemporary studies in anthropology to place private elder care in a broader context of constructed kinship relations.

Santa Barbara, California: The Evolving Range of Elder Care

I have conducted long-term ethnographic research focused on Mexican migrant women employed as housecleaners and care providers in Santa Barbara. This is an ideal location for studying elder care and elderscapes because, since the nineteenth century, the city has been a retirement community and has historically attracted many seniors. Today, people aged sixty-five or older represent 15 percent of the population, creating a significant demand for a range of care services in this affluent city (U.S. Census Bureau 2010). In the formal sector, care options include assisted-living homes, board-and-care homes, elder "day-care" sites, nursing homes, and private nursing. Moreover, each care category contains a variety of options based on the financial possibilities of employers.

Similarly, the informal sector features many care arrangements within private homes. The primary typologies within informal-sector employment are live-in and live-out work, and each is in turn differentiated by the presence of other workers who may help care for a ward.

LIVE-OUT, PRIVATE INFORMAL WORK

Workers generally prefer live-out jobs for a variety of fairly straightforward reasons: live-out work allows women the ability to break away from what may be physically and emotionally exacting labor; it allows them to maintain their own affective family and friendship relations; and it generally commands higher wages than live-in work. Moreover, live-out elder-care jobs are not homogenous but rather highly flexible in terms of personnel, hours, and tasks. The work may be performed by one or more individuals—paid employees, unpaid family members of a paid worker, and unpaid family members of the ward. Likewise, the workday itself and/or the workweek may vary. Some workers may come in for part of a day (anywhere from two to six hours), while others work for a whole or extended day (from six to twelve hours).

Case 1: Claudia, who is thirty-six years old, was hired to come in one day a week for four hours at a rate of ten dollars an hour. During work, she is asked to accompany her eighty-four-year-old employer, Betty, on errands or on medical visits. A typical shopping excursion involves Claudia helping Betty to get dressed, walk down a flight of stairs, and get in her car, and then driving her to the specified location. Claudia then unloads Betty's walker from the car, carries purchases, helps Betty use the public bathroom, helps Betty get back into the car, drives back home, and assists with the unloading and organizing of purchases. During this time, Claudia and Betty talk about a range of things, including Betty's health, plants, and family. Claudia has been working for Betty for almost two years, and Betty would like for Claudia to begin working an eight-hour day, since Betty gradually needs more assistance with her daily household tasks.

Case 2: Francisca, who is forty-one years old, cares for eighty-nine-year-old Catherine six days a week, from eight o'clock in the morning until two in the afternoon. She earns twelve dollars an hour. Catherine has mobility problems and needs help exercising as well as performing basic tasks. She is, however, mentally cognizant and relatively healthy, and she lives in an assisted-care apartment complex that has an on-call nurse and doctor. When Francisca arrives, she helps Catherine get out of bed, go to the bathroom, and get dressed in comfortable clothing, and then she prepares breakfast. Francisca then picks up around the house and makes up the bedroom while Catherine reads the paper or watches television. When Francisca is done tidying up and Catherine has had time to warm up, they go on a half-hour walk and then spend as long as an hour doing floor exercises at home. Thereafter Catherine rests while Francisca prepares a healthy lunch. The two women have lunch together, talking about a range of topics, including Catherine's adult kids and deceased husband. When they finish eating, Francisca cleans up the kitchen while Catherine continues to chat with her. Francisca then asks Catherine if there is anything special she would like to have done—perhaps washing a load of laundry, fixing a button on a shirt, watering the plants, getting something down from a top shelf. At two o'clock, Francisca hugs Catherine and gives her a kiss on the cheek before leaving, reminding her that if she needs help, she can call Francisca at home. Francisca anticipates that sometime in the next year Catherine will require more help in the afternoon and into the evening. Francisca believes that one of her female cousins may take the second shift.

Case 3: Fifty-four-year-old Erica cares for ninety-two-year-old Charley, who has Alzheimer's disease. She was hired a year ago by Charley's daughter, who pays Erica eight dollars an hour. Erica originally worked Monday through Friday from seven o'clock in the morning until six in the evening, but for the three weeks preceding the interview, she had also been working weekends after the weekend nurse quit. To provide Erica with some time off, Charley's daughter, who lives out of state, arranged for him to be picked up twice a week by an adult day-care center. Erica describes Charley as a sweet man with occasional lucid moments. He has had some bouts of violence (throwing things, pushing her away), which she ascribes to his fear about not knowing what is happening around him. When Erica arrives, she is careful to speak in soothing tones so that Charley, who is often still in bed or sitting in a chair, is not startled. She asks him how he feels, and he may respond in some way. She says she pays more attention to his expression than his words, because what he says may not often accord with the context. She then walks him to the bathroom, where she begins the extended process of removing his diaper and bathing him, although the room is not set up to ease the process. (Erica suggests a specialized chair in the tub and enough room for her to stand next to him.) After he is bathed, newly diapered, shaved, and combed, she walks him over to a comfortable chair and turns on the television while she prepares his breakfast. He eats very lightly, so she gives him small amounts of food throughout the day. She is also concerned about him getting enough physical exercise, and she often takes him on long walks around his neighborhood, taking many rests and providing him with water and snacks. When they return to the house, she helps him use the bathroom and then sit outside or lie down while she prepares lunch. They eat together, and she talks to him, whether or not he responds. During the afternoon, she undertakes other exercises with him, and at around four o'clock, she begins the process of winding him down to sleep so that by six, when she leaves, he is diapered, in pajamas, in bed, has taken his medications, and has a remote control for the medical alert service by his side. She always leaves some crackers and water for him next to the bed, but she worries about him at night. Charley's daughter does not want him to be in a nursing home, but given his extensive needs, he may need to move into one soon. Erica thinks that if she can recruit one of her brothers-in-law to work on the weekends, the move to the nursing home may be postponed for a few months.

FLEXIBILITY AND THE CREATION OF KINSHIP SUPPORT

These three case studies underscore the flexibility of the job: workers constantly adapt their routines and hours to the changing needs of an aging person. Caretaking activities hinge on the health and physical abilities of the individuals for whom workers care and the amount of time workers are on the job. Straightforward routines involve helping with some daily activities for a short period, but they can also involve greater responsibility for physical care or, as in Charley's case, serious responsibility and full-time care. As we move from case 1 to case 3, we see examples of an increased need for care. Increased care needs may either require a change in the private care-work arrangement or a move into the formal sector. Private informal care is often one phase in the caretaking spectrum.

In cases where people require full-time care, shift work is generally considered best because it allows the sharing of the physical and emotional labors among several workers. This is a fairly common practice within the formal sector. Sometimes within the informal sector as well, workers consciously create such arrangements by recruiting female and male kin as well as friends. Some workers find the idea of recruiting kin desirable because they feel that family members are more likely to share a care ethic and/or that using family members will allow better control of care practices (Ibarra 2003). In one case I observed, a worker recruited her husband to sleep at her dying ward's home so that he would not be alone; in another case, a worker recruited her daughter and other kinswomen to help with the physical care of a ward on her days off and when she needs to be away from the city (Ibarra 2010). In another instance, a worker recruited her son to help lift her heavy ward (Ibarra 2003). I also encountered a case in which a woman recruited her niece to work for several months so that the woman could spend time with her family in Mexico (Ibarra 2008).[1] In such cases, the worker consciously seeks out help so that she is able to perform a job that she might not otherwise be capable of performing without physically harming herself or her ward, to give what she considers the best care possible to her ward without hurting her affective relations, and to extend her relations with a ward toward her own kin group and thus break up what some workers perceive as a false dichotomy between their work and family.

In all of these examples, workers literally extend kinship to their wards by bringing in family members to help care and thus create better work conditions for themselves and better care for their wards. Occasionally, however, workers also figuratively extended kinship to their wards, claiming them as family members. This literal and figurative extension of kinship requires an understanding of the literatures on personalism within domestic employment and on kinship in anthropology, thereby helping to illustrate what family may mean in the context of elder-care work.

Personalism in Domestic Employment

Historians of domestic service emphasize a few strands of European history to explain personalism, or personal intimacy, in the occupation. For some scholars, the roots of American domestic service and personalism lie in European agrarian societies, where serfs depended on feudal lords for their livelihoods (Coser 1975; Horn 1975; Rollins 1985). In this power-laden relationship, lords could exercise very detailed control over their dependents, and thus servants gave loyalty and work in hopes of receiving good favor. In this socioeconomic arrangement, a lord as the paterfamilias should ideally "have a fatherly care over his servants as if they were children" (Meldrum 2000, 37). And at least rhetorically, as Meldrum notes, fatherly care included such things as a lifelong obligation to provide guidance—and, when necessary, correction—on the moral path of life.

As feudalism eventually gave way to capitalist wage relations, personalism persisted but in changing and abbreviated forms in different historical moments and places. In the late-nineteenth and early-twentieth-century United States, for example, female employers who supervised their domestic workers continued to believe that workers owed loyalty and service, but did not worry about long-term obligations to these workers. Sometimes, too, employers felt they had the right to tell workers how to lead their lives in an effort to mold their moral characters or gendered identities (Katzman 1978). Employers may also have referred to workers as being "like family" with the intent of having workers do more (Palmer 1990). Personalism was thus a cause for concern among both occupational reformers and workers themselves. Not surprisingly, therefore, various responses—including the call for more contractual relations as well as workers living outside the residence of the employer—were proposed and implemented in the United States over the twentieth century.

Personalism, however, was never completely eliminated. As late as the 1980s, some employers continued to claim that their live-out workers were family members, though employees may have disagreed. Said one worker, "I don't think you can feel like one of the family. I'm not white, or Jewish. I'm not adopted. We're friends. And I don't expect her to say, do something without pay" (Romero 1992, 124). In this case, differences in race and religious background as well as the absence of legal ties lead this employee to the unequivocal conclusion that she is not kin to her employer. Thus, a clear disconnect exists between one employer's perception and an employee's understandings about what constitutes family. The historical literature has many such examples—employers impose kinship terms on their employees, but workers do not reciprocate the implied sentiment behind the family designation (Clark-Lewis 1994; Dudden 1983; Katzman 1978). The desire for personalism consequently is often construed as a one-way proposition from the employer to the employee.

Yet in some instances, employees have perceived their employers as kin-like. Evelyn Nakano Glenn (1986, 156) writes that for many Japanese women in domestic employment, "the relationship with particular employers was analogous to family ties." Moreover, for some war brides, such ties were charged with emotional significance, substituting for kin ties that had never existed or had been lost when the women left Japan. Thus, in spite of the inherent race and class inequities embedded in domestic service, some workers at times perceived their long-term, elderly employers as something analogous to kin.

In more recent scholarship, Pierrette Hondagneu-Sotelo (2002, 206) finds that some Latina domestics in late-twentieth-century Los Angeles want more personal relations with their employers. The desire for personalism among Latinas in contemporary Los Angeles is, in turn, related to the nature of the work performed. Those who care for children contrast with those workers who solely clean. Whereas house cleaners may desire more contractual, "professionalized" relations (Romero 1992), those who care for children—who nurture and even love their charges—want not only verbal recognition from their employers but also closer relationships. Employees want to feel like family or friends (Hondagneu-Sotelo 2002, 206). However, today's female employers, who are themselves employed, may not wish to expend time and energy on creating a more personalistic relationship with employees and may in fact prefer more contractual relations. Hondagneu-Sotelo (2002, 208) argues, however, that while personalism alone is not enough to upgrade the occupation, "its absence virtually ensures that the job will be experienced as degrading."

In the case of formal-sector elder care in private homes, some employers may wish to uphold the ideal of family care (Lyon 2006), and personalism may be cause for concern when employers use family terminology in reference to workers. But the scope of private elder care is very broad, and workers at times actively strive to create close affective ties to their wards (Martinez-Buján 2008), also upholding the ideal of family care. In some cases, workers come to refer to their wards as being "like family," or even more strongly as simply being "family" (Solari 2006).

Making Kinship

Who fits into what is considered family and how family is made are two key questions in anthropology. In the United States, the answer to the first question is guided by two key symbols: blood and choice. If one shares blood with others, then one may be considered family. However, choice is also important. And as David Schneider (1980) and Marilyn Strathern (1981) have noted, "There has always been an element of choice in the degree to which blood ties become relationships in any given family" (cited in Hayden 1997, 45). Among blood relatives, choice may thus mean either restricting membership or the quality and depth of interaction.

But anthropologists have also convincingly demonstrated that the privileging of blood and kinship is not a human universal (Schneider 1984). Anthropologists thus discuss kinship constructed along lines other than biology across time and place, including the reckoning of kinship through residence, ritual, adoption, fostering, material transactions, and "proper" behavior. For example, in New Guinea, people became members of descent groups through common residence and food sharing (Strathern 1972). Similarly, the Nuyoo from the coastal Oaxacan region of Mexico made kin through nourishment and nurturing (Monaghan 1995). Among working-poor African Americans, Carol Stack (1971, 60) has found that "friends are classified as kinsmen when they assume recognized responsibilities as kinsmen." Stack (61) goes on to say that in a community of long-standing poverty, the "extension of kin relationships to non-kin allows for the creation of mutual aid domestic networks." Similarly, in Mexican and other Latin American societies, friends may also be classified as kin through relations of *compadrazgo*—a coparent or godparent relationship that is associated with Roman Catholic Church rituals such as baptisms and confirmations that establish a set of obligations of godparents to their godchildren and of mutual obligation between the coparents. *Compadrazgo* strengthens existing ties of kinship or expands ties to friends (Kemper 1982); among the urban working poor, *compadrazgo* helps individuals deal with the tensions of daily poverty (Lewis 1969). In sum, kinship can be constructed along lines other than blood ties.

The privileging of choice—or love—as opposed to blood has also become the focus of much recent anthropological writing in First World countries. Here, technological innovations, evolving sexual mores, and social contexts create new means for kin construction. Scholars propose that kinship relations might be conceived as "a set of flexible interpersonal relations negotiated and made through specific practices by individual agents in response to social changes" (Yan 2001, 226). Individual agency is in turn structured by relations of power (Ginsburg and Rapp 1995).

In these studies of choice, "intentionality" is often key to resolving a lack of biological relatedness as well as to setting guideposts for future practice. For example, in *Families We Choose*, Kath Weston's (1991) study on lesbian and gay families in San Francisco, coparents intend to conceive and raise children and maintain lifelong obligations to those children. The promise of time and endurance are here the bases of kinship (Carsten 2004, 149). In Helena Ragoné's (1994) work on surrogacy, intentionality refers to the desire to have a child, a desire that in turn brings a surrogate relationship into being. Without the intention—the "conception in the heart"—the birth of the child would not have been possible. What is important, then, is not the biogenetic substance but the agency of the individual in wanting to conceive with the promise of time, effort, and endurance.

But while intention, with its attendant time and endurance, serves as the base for kinship, specific "kinning" practices are what make people into kin (Howell 2001). In the case of lesbian and gay families, these practices include claiming an active role in the creation of the child (literally and figuratively), hyphenating parent names, and having parents and siblings (from the couple's biological families) on both sides participate and use kinship terms (Weston 1991). One study of Norwegian adoption found that parents create symbolic pregnancies and birth events and embed their adopted children into their biological and social networks. For example, parents have children engage in "healthy outdoor activities" with grandparents and other kin biologically related to the adopted parents as a way to bond the child to people, places, and ideologies of Norwegian identity (Howell 2001). Howell (215) emphasizes that "adoptive parents work extremely hard at making themselves and their adopted children conform to their notion of a normal family." Thus practices of care and effort, of enduring solidarity, help make kinship (Carsten 2000).

Kinship is also susceptible to continuous adaptations and transformations over the life cycle of individuals and their families as a result of changing social reproductive needs, economic realities, physical distance between individuals, and constantly evolving choices (Robertson 1991). Kinship is in this sense an adaptive process rather than a frozen snapshot.

Case Study: Cecilia Ramos

When I interviewed Cecilia Ramos in 2009 she was forty-six-years old and had migrated to the United States ten years earlier. Cecilia left a large city in Mexico because both she and her husband, postgraduate professionals, were having financial problems and because she felt that her family was too scattered. For a long time, she had a foot on either side of the border, and the decision to come and settle in Santa Barbara was greatly influenced by her desire to be near her sister, Sara; Sara's husband, Tómas; and their three children. Cecilia wanted her two daughters to grow up knowing that they were not alone—that they had family. Cecilia's mother had died when she and her sister were very young, leaving them orphans. This experience of loss combined with other factors to bind Cecilia tightly to her sister. On this migration to Santa Barbara, Cecilia's cousin, Sonia, joined them.

After she arrived, Cecilia began working alongside Sara, caring for two women. When Cecilia began to understand each of the two women's needs, Cecilia and

Sara divided the work into shifts. But then the husband of one of the women suffered a stroke, and round-the-clock care became necessary. The wife asked Sara to stay and care for them. Sara and Cecilia and their families met to decide how best to perform the work of caring for three people, two of whom needed constant care. Factored into the decision was the information that the second woman had also begun to require more attention, and her daughter was making plans to move her mother to her home. According to Cecilia, "This decision we made as a family, what would be best for everyone—for them and for us. . . . We decided that it would be best if my sister and Tómas were responsible [for the couple], and I could continue with the other señora until her daughter was able to pick her up." Subsequently, Cecilia "would look for another private job that was not full time so that I could help Sara and Tómas should they need it." Cecilia was not worried about finding another job because she and her sister and brother-in-law had "recommendations—we are known as honorable people." Ultimately, Cecilia found her current ward, Nancy, after receiving a recommendation from one of the first two women.

Nancy was eighty-seven years old at that time and in good physical and mental health. However, she had tripped and fallen several times and wanted companionship and assistance with her everyday activities. Nancy did not initially present herself as an effusive or tender person. Cecilia described her as being very careful, guarded, authoritative, and intelligent. She had previously dismissed aides whom she felt were "speaking down" to her. When Cecilia first met Nancy, she said something like, "I need some help, but do not treat me like an idiot. I expect you to behave professionally, and I, in turn, will treat you professionally." Cecilia described this conversation as "respectful but firm."

According to Cecilia, Nancy is very wealthy and lives in an exclusive neighborhood. Cecilia consequently asked for and received a higher hourly rate than she had previously earned. She was hired by Nancy's eldest daughter, Lillith, who is generally responsible for her mother's overall care, and began employment at fourteen dollars an hour in 2005. By the time I interviewed her in 2009, she was earning twenty-one dollars an hour. Cecilia's job was circumscribed by Lillith from the beginning: Cecilia was to be in charge of Nancy's personal needs and space but did not need to perform any serious cleaning since the family also employed a housekeeper. Cecilia was also not required to cook anything other than breakfast, as she was told that food could be ordered and brought in from any restaurant. Likewise, she was not required to drive Nancy to doctors' appointments, a task that was the responsibility of the weekend nurse. She could buy anything that was needed at the house and provide receipts for reimbursement or leave a list so that the housekeeper could purchase any necessities. The situation was thus unique because a relatively large number of individuals were hired to support the caretaking of one person.

Cecilia's first three years of employment as a caretaker for Nancy were "not work for me—it was a pleasure to be with her. Sentiment began to grow, and I gave my heart. She also began to have affection for me. . . . How does love grow? The treatment one receives, time, compassion." She offered a description of the work routine that illustrates both good reciprocal treatment and the importance of time—of repetition, of growing familiarity. After arriving at eight o'clock in the morning, Cecilia begins preparing breakfast.

> [Nancy] doesn't like a heavy breakfast when she first gets up, but she likes her coffee and bread and jam. I prepare the tray and take it into her room at about 8:30. She is still in her pajamas, and I greet her. . . . "Good morning. It's a beautiful day outside. Do you want to see?" I put on her bathrobe, I give her a hug or a kiss. . . . She drinks some of her coffee, sometimes some bread . . . and [then I] help her move to the living room so that we can talk and look at the view. I wonder aloud, "What kind of day is it going to be? It's going to be a beautiful day," I say, "and you have to take a bath." . . . I also ask her what she wants for her breakfast and provide her with options. I have to please her. . . . So if she says, "I'm fat," I say, "I'll give you something light" and offer her yogurt and fruit.
>
> [After breakfast, medicines and vitamins are dispensed]. I have to watch her while she drinks them so that she doesn't choke. She then watches the news and often wants to talk about what she's watching. She asks me questions, and I say, "I don't know. Let me sit with you." So I sit next to her, sometimes Nancy holds my hand, and we comment on this or that story. [Then] I walk her to the bathroom, where she brushes her teeth. . . . She can still do it, but later I will have to. Then she rests and reads the newspaper. She is a person who likes to be informed. While she's doing that, I warm the [bath]room and put towels in the dryer so they are warm. I take care of her as if she were my mother. While bathing her, I don't look straight at her, because she doesn't like that. . . . After the bath I put on her robe, I dry her, I comb her, I dry her hair, I put on her makeup. I use a small towel to dry beneath her breasts and bottom. I make it a little joke and say [in a high-pitched voice], "Excuse me!" so that she knows this is a respectful touch. She asks me all the time, "How did you learn to be such a good nurse, Honey?" And I tell her, "Necessity first and then affection." She likes that and sometimes says, "I love you too." . . . One day she said, "I can't imagine what it would be like to live without you," and that moved me. . . .
>
> After the bath, Nancy wants a cocktail, but I distract her—I say, "Let's go out for a walk and get some sun," for example. Or to make her laugh and give her encouragement, I say, "Maybe one of your boyfriends is out there." After a walk, Nancy returns tired and takes her nap. Sometimes it takes her a very long time

for her to wake. . . . She takes so long at each thing; sometimes she is asleep, and I don't know what to do to wake her. It worries me that she sleeps so long, that she has not eaten. Eventually she wakes and has her lunch, sometimes as late as two or three P.M. I don't order from a restaurant. . . . There's too much salt in the food. . . . I will always make what she likes with fresh ingredients. . . . We eat together and talk about everything. She is a very intelligent person and likes to analyze everything, including her children. I can't tell you how many hours we've spent talking about why her children are the way they are.

Nancy treats Cecilia with respect and appreciation and eventually love, and in return, Cecilia grew to love Nancy, in part because of the younger woman's compassion for Nancy's vulnerability as a result of her age. Cecilia explained to me that, unlike children, who have their whole lives before them, Nancy's life is coming to a close. Nancy recognizes this end and needs many things, especially love and security. Cecilia and other Mexicana care providers mark this last stage of life as significant (Ibarra 2010).

Until a year before my interview, Cecilia would finish the daily work routine by cleaning up in the kitchen and getting Nancy into her pajamas and settling her in a chair in front of the television. Nancy would then take care of herself in the evening. On those occasions when Nancy seemed nervous, Cecilia would let Lillith know, and then Cecilia would return with her daughter, sister, or niece to check up in the early evening. She did not tell Nancy that the visit was for Nancy's benefit but phoned and explained that Cecilia and her family needed Nancy's advice about something. Cecilia did not want Nancy "to feel that she could not be trusted to care for herself. . . . I thought about how she likes to be useful [and how] she is very considerate, especially to women." If Nancy agreed to the visit, an advice session would ensue. According to Cecilia, as she and her family member explained their problems—marital misunderstandings, high school homework assignments, or worksite issues—the conversation evolved into something real. Nancy gave herself to the task of listening and helping figure out a resolution. In so doing, these women came to know each other—Cecilia and her kinswomen sincerely appreciated Nancy's advice. Likewise, Nancy showed appreciation by asking about Cecilia's family during the day: "She had them present in her mind."

About a year before my interview, full-time care became necessary. Nancy fell one evening and hurt herself, and Lillith decided that someone needed to stay the night. However, Nancy was adamant that she did not want strangers sleeping in her house. She asked Cecilia, "Can you help me, Honey?" The request had great emotional impact on Cecilia: "I could not say no to her. Imagine, she didn't even ask her own daughter. . . . But I did say to her that alone I could not do it. I would have to get my family's help. And she was fine with that, because she knew how strongly I feel about my children and my husband, and also she had already gotten to know my family."

PRIVILEGING LOVE AND KNOWLEDGE AND EXTENDING FAMILY

Cecilia says of Nancy, "I feel love for her. She is like a family member. When I don't see her, I miss her. I felt an obligation to make the end of her life the best it can be, as one would do for their parent. [But] no, it's not that I feel she is my mother—more like an aunt, someone who is not there all the time but who helps you, who loves you, who takes responsibility if it is required." Love for Nancy, which Cecilia had developed over the course of three years of intimate physical and emotional contact, helped engender ties of relatedness analogous to those known within Cecilia's kinship circle. Cecilia's sense of obligation to an older woman in her kin circle is fluidly transferred to Nancy. Privileging love and its attendant obligations then leads to concrete actions, which would result in a new work arrangement.

Cecilia brought her family together to discuss Nancy's need for full-time care and to recruit their help. She remembers that part of the discussion revolved around the contrast between her family's knowledge and concern for Nancy and that of Nancy's biological kin. Said Cecilia, "It is sad that my family knows her better than her own. We know her because we are with her every day. We take care of her. She doesn't know her own grandchildren; their parents do not teach them the value of their family. My daughters visit her at least half an hour every week; they accompany us on our walks; they bring her her favorite gelatin. Love comes from knowing her now in the present, interacting with her, . . . knowing about her needs."

Given this love for and knowledge about Nancy, Cecilia took it as a given that her family's labor would be recruited and that changes to their current employment would have to be made. She discussed the possibility of an ideal schedule where the women could divide the workweek in some equitable way so that no one had to regularly be on night shift. She initially thought, "If it's a twenty-four-hour need, that means that somehow between the three of us, we should try to have an eight-hour job apiece." At this point, the weekends were staffed by an agency nurse.

The work and financial obligations of all of Cecilia's family members needed to be taken into account before a decision could be made. At this juncture, Tómas was employed full time by a physically incapacitated elderly ward, Sara had three part-time charges, all of who were relatively healthy, and Sonia was employed in a nursing home. Determining how to handle Nancy's care was thus complicated, and their solution would require several weeks to put into practice. Sonia would quit her job at the nursing home after she was trained to take over Sara's three charges (who would be consulted). Sara and Cecilia would reorganize the workweek so that they could switch day and night shifts caring for Nancy. Until the new arrangement could be implemented, Sonia would take on some of the night shifts, since she was unmarried and young. On these occasions, Cecilia's husband would drive Sonia to Nancy's house in the evening, since Sonia did not have car. Everyone agreed to help Cecilia care for Nancy. "With the support of my family, I felt empowered. I had the warm covering [*abrigo*] of my family to be able to accept Nancy. A person alone cannot do it—you need the support and backing of your family." Speaking about her current schedule and working with her sister, Cecilia said, "When she's there, I feel as if I'm there. We share information and think through changes that are taking place with Nancy."

VOICING OF INTENTIONS: COMMITMENT TO PERMANENCE AS WELL AS FEARS

Cecilia says, "I wanted to, I want to now, take care of [Nancy] until she no longer needs me. What makes this job different is that you have to involve your heart; you suffer, but you have to involve your heart. I am lucky that she is wealthy and is able to pay us well, but even if she did not have the money, I would still do what I had to do to care for her. We've become fond of each other. My love comes from her treatment of me—she is loving to me and concerned about me. She is a good person. She has lived her life well, raising six children."

Cecilia thus made a commitment to Nancy that involved both time and permanence. Here, however, "permanence" is circumscribed by the knowledge that Nancy is at the end of her life. "Permanence" thus means caring for her until her death. This commitment, however, was tinged with fear, not unlike that felt by some prospective parents who want to adopt children (Ragoné 1994). Cecilia feared that Nancy's biological family could simply dismiss Cecilia: "I fear that I could do something wrong."

Cecilia feared not that she would be physically unable to perform the job, but rather that she would somehow overstep her place and offend Lillith or one of Nancy's other children. Cecilia expressed two overriding concerns. First, she did not like that Lillith made decisions without first consulting Nancy. The weekend nurse, for example, had been hired because she had a nursing degree, but Nancy did not like her. Cecilia saw this action as personally hurtful to Nancy as well as disrespectful to her as a mother: "The daughter doesn't understand that Nancy does not like things imposed upon her. This upsets her. She wants to know what is going on. She is an intelligent person . . . but her daughter doesn't try to find the way." Second, Cecilia dislikes that one of Nancy's grandsons encourages her to drink alcoholic beverages. Cecilia believes that "drinking for Nancy at this age is a poison. Her body takes days to recover. The days she drinks, she sleeps all the rest of the day. She doesn't eat."

Cecilia felt that she needed gently to encourage both the daughter and the grandson to behave in ways that were better for Nancy but feared the consequences of such an action: "I see her as my family, I take care of her as if she were family, but I am not her family—I have no authority. Her grandson has authority." Cecilia felt obvious anger at the situation and questioned whether the young man was motivated by Nancy's long-term well-being or by short-term and selfish concerns: "What does he care? They get drunk, he takes her to the Biltmore, and she pays. That is not love: That is a vulture. He's waiting around for his inheritance like a vulture. . . . I'm sorry, I'm usually more positive—I focus on the positive. But it really affects me."

Conclusion

In the context of transnational labor flows fomented by economic relations of inequality between the United States and Mexico, new types of work environments flourish. Sliced into this socioeconomic reality is a dramatic demographic change that creates a range of care needs in U.S. households. The case study of Cecilia Ramos demonstrates how in an intimate care setting, a worker may not only desire personalistic relations on the job but may also extend kinship to her ward.

"Extending" kinship here has two meanings. First, Cecilia literally extends her own close kin relations into the workplace and facilitates friendships among her biological female kin and her ward, Nancy. Thereafter, when both love and recognition of Nancy's stage in the life cycle serve as the basis for permanent commitment, these kinswomen are recruited to provide round-the-clock paid care. In recruiting her kin, Cecilia enmeshes Nancy in one affective sphere of common goals and people. The recruitment of Cecilia's family thus becomes a key kinning practice. Moreover, Cecilia considers both planning and working as a family unit desirable because she is able to trust that someone is taking good care of her ward and to know that she has the moral and physical support to do a good job. Extending kinship also has a second meaning. Cecilia behaves in a manner concordant with her understanding of what family members do for each other, and she declares her intention to provide time and permanence. In this regard, she commits herself and her family to provide care until Nancy dies.

This latter aspect of extending kinship is, however, fraught with insecurity. Even in a relatively positive work environment where an employer's wealth removes many of the burdens and costs associated with full-time care by one worker, Cecilia expresses fears of being dismissed. She is concerned that she will overstep her boundaries as a paid employee by presuming relations that are too familiar. Contested practices of kinship and obligation create what she perceives as a discordant environment in which her ward's needs are not adequately considered. This sense of discord is in turn interpreted as disrespect for her labors and personhood. If she is intimately responsible for the care of another, should she not be able to exercise some authority? Whether one ultimately agrees that Cecilia and her kin group are socially constructing family with Nancy, the insights derived from the case study complicate our understandings about personalism within domestic employment and the nature of kin relations in the twenty-first century.

Appendix

Over the course of two short fieldwork visits to Santa Barbara funded by the Ford Foundation in 2009, I asked workers what they thought was needed to improve the occupation. The following is a list of their recommendations.

1. ACCESS TO TRAINING AND CERTIFICATION

Workers said that training provides protection for them and their wards. Through training, workers learn how to protect their bodies from injury as well as how to be cognizant of the physical ailments of and treatments for wards. Likewise, "home health aide" certifications, available through some city colleges, provide access to higher-paying jobs. In this regard, workers cited examples from the formal sector, where nursing homes pay people without certificates minimum wage while those with certificates earn more.

2. ACCESS TO ENGLISH-LANGUAGE CLASSES

Workers stressed the need to effectively communicate not only with their wards but also with other care providers and/or coordinators of care. However, long shifts and limited transportation make taking English-language classes difficult. One suggestion within the formal sector is for classes to be provided during lunch breaks. For informal sector workers, the ideas proposed included holding classes at public libraries or through bookmobiles that regularly park in different sites throughout the city.

3. DRIVER'S LICENSES FOR ALL, WHETHER DOCUMENTED OR UNDOCUMENTED

Workers emphasized the need to drive themselves to the job and to transport wards to various sites.

4. ACCESS TO HEALTH CARE INSURANCE / MEDICAL CARE

Workers repeatedly expressed their fear of injury or spoke of past injuries that were still unresolved as a consequence of the lack of access to affordable health care.

5. THE SUPPORT OF THE WARD'S FAMILY MEMBERS

Workers repeatedly said that a ward's family members need to recognize that what workers do is valuable. Their labors and knowledge of their wards should be respected, and others should not undermine what workers do.

6. WORKER AND WARD PROTECTIONS

Basics for Employees

Workers said

(a) Don't accept gifts from elderly wards, and document all gift offerings with the persons responsible for finances. (For some elder-care workers, professionalization means that acceptance of gifts, especially from those who are mentally or physically challenged, would constitute a moral lapse.)

(b) Protect your body.

(c) Don't do this job unless you have patience.

(d) Remember that wards are old and sick—they are suffering. Put yourself in their place and ask, "What would I want?"

(e) Treat wards with respect and love.

Basics for Employers

(a) Ask for recommendations.

(b) Pay for a health screening for a potential employee.

(c) Provide proper equipment/facilities for care.

Note

1. While more research is necessary to ascertain the prevalence of the family group strategy, two of the participants in my 2009 nonrandom purposive sample of six workers had created kin-based work groups.

References

Carsten, Janet, ed. 2000. *Cultures of Relatedness: New Approaches to the Study of Kinship*. Cambridge: Cambridge University Press.

———. 2004. *After Kinship*. Cambridge: Cambridge University Press.

Clark-Lewis, Elizabeth. 1994. *Living In, Living Out: African American Domestics in Washington, D.C., 1910–1940*. Washington, D.C.: Smithsonian Institution Press.

Coser, Lewis. 1975. "Servants: The Obsolescence of an Occupation Role." *Social Forces* 52:31–40.

Dudden, Faye. 1983. *Serving Women: Household Service in Nineteenth-Century America*. Middletown, Conn.: Wesleyan University Press.

Foner, Nancy. 1995. *The Caregiving Dilemma: Work in a Nursing Home*. Berkeley: University of California Press.

Ginsburg, Faye, and Rayna Rapp, eds. 1995. *Conceiving the New World Order*. Berkeley: University of California Press.

Glenn, Evelyn Nakano. 1986. *Issei, Nissei, War Bride: Three Generations of Japanese American Women in Domestic Service*. Philadelphia: Temple University Press.

Hayden, Corinne. 1997. "Gender, Genetics, and Generation: Reformulating Biology in Lesbian Kinship." *Cultural Anthropology* 10:41–63.

Hondagneu-Sotelo, Pierrette. 2002. *Doméstica: Cleaning and Caring in the Shadows of Affluence*. Berkeley: University of California Press.

Horn, Pamela. 1975. *The Rise and Fall of the Victorian Servant*. New York: St. Martin's.

Howell, Signe. 2001. "Self-Conscious Kinship: Some Contested Values in Norwegian Transnational Adoption." In *Relative Values: Reconfiguring Kinship*, ed. Sarah Franklin and Susan McKinnon, 203–33. Durham: Duke University Press.

Ibarra, María. 2003. "The Tender Trap: Mexican Immigrant Women and the Ethics of Elder Care Work." *Aztlán: A Journal of Chicano Studies* 28:87–109.

———. 2008. "The Social Imaginary and Kin Recruitment." In *Gender in Asia and the Pacific: Method, Theory, Practice*, ed. Kathy Ferguson and Monique Mironesco, 161–75. Honolulu: University of Hawai'i Press.

———. 2010. "My Reward Is Not Money: Deep Alliances, Spirituality, and End of Life Care." In *Intimate Labors: Cultures, Technologies, and the Politics of Care*, ed. Rhacel Salazar Parreñas and Eileen Boris, 117–31. Stanford: Stanford University Press.

Katzman, David. 1978. *Seven Days a Week: Women and Domestic Service in Industrializing America*. New York: Oxford University Press.

Kemper, Robert. 1982. "The *Compadrazgo* in Urban Mexico." *Anthropological Quarterly* 55:17–30.

Lamb, Sarah. 2009. *Aging and the Indian Diaspora*. Bloomington: Indiana University Press.

Lewis, Oscar. 1969. *A Death in the Sanchez House*. New York: Random House.

Lyon, Dawn. 2006. "The Organization of Care Work in Italy: Gender and Migrant Labor in the New Economy." *Indiana Journal of Global Legal Studies* 13:227–42.

Martinez-Buján, Ráquel. 2008. "Bienestar y cuidados: El oficio del cariño." Ph.D. diss., University of Coruña.

Meldrum, Tim. 2000. *Domestic Service and Gender, 1600–1750: Life and Work in the London Household*. Essex: Pearson Education.

Monaghan, John. 1995. *Covenants with Earth and Rain: Exchange, Sacrifice, and Revelation in Mixtec Sociality*. Norman: University of Oklahoma Press.

Palmer, Phyllis. 1990. *Domesticity and Dirt*. Philadelphia: Temple University Press.

Parreñas, Rhacel. 2001. *Servants of Globalization*. Stanford: Stanford University Press.

Ragoné, Helena. 1994. *Surrogate Motherhood: Conception in the Heart*. Boulder, Colo.: Westview.

Robertson, A. F. 1991. *Beyond the Family*. Berkeley: University of California Press.

Rollins, Judith. 1985. *Between Women: Domestics and Their Employers*. Philadelphia: Temple University Press.

Romero, Mary. 1992. *Maid in the U.S.A.* London: Routledge

Sanjek, Roger. 2009. *The Gray Panthers*. Philadelphia: University of Pennsylvania Press.

Schellenberg, Grant, and Martin Turcotte. 2007. *A Portrait of Seniors in Canada*. Ottawa: Statistics Canada.

Schneider, David. 1980 (1968). *American Kinship: A Cultural Account*. Chicago: University of Chicago Press.

———. 1984. *A Critique of the Study of Kinship*. Ann Arbor: University of Michigan Press.

Sokolovsky, Jay. 2009. "Aging, Center Stage." *Anthropology News* 50:5.

Solari, Cinzai. 2006. "Professionals and Saints: How Immigrant Careworkers Negotiate Gender Identities at Work." *Gender and Society* 20:301–33.

Stack, Carol. 1971. *All Our Kin: Strategies for Survival in a Black Community*. New York: Harper and Row.

Stafford, Phillip. 2009. *Elderburbia*. Bloomington: Indiana University Press.

Strathern, Marilyn. 1972. *Women in Between; Female Roles in a Male World: Mount Hagen, New Guinea*. London: Seminar.

———. 1981. *Kinship at the Core: An Anthropology of Elmdon Village*. Cambridge: Cambridge University Press.

U.S. Census Bureau. 2010. "Quick Facts: Santa Barbara (City)." http://quickfacts.census.gov/qfd/states/06/0669070.html. Accessed January 11, 2013.

Weston, Kath. 1991. *Families We Choose: Lesbians, Gays, Kinship*. New York: Columbia University Press.

Yan, Yunxiang. 2001. "Practicing Kinship in Rural North China." In *Relative Values: Reconfiguring Kinship*, ed. Sarah Franklin and Susan McKinnon, 224–45. Durham: Duke University Press.

PART 4

Grassroots Organizing and Resistance

11

Immigrant Women Workers at the Center of Social Change

Asian Immigrant Women Advocates

JENNIFER JIHYE CHUN, GEORGE LIPSITZ, AND YOUNG SHIN

In early 2003, two Korean immigrant women, Chung Hee Cho and Hung Ja Kim, traveled from San Jose to San Francisco to lead a workshop on the topic of English-language dominance. This workshop was part of a core set of leadership trainings developed by Asian Immigrant Women Advocates (AIWA), a grassroots community-based organization aimed at improving the living and working conditions of Asian immigrant women employed in low-paid and socially devalued jobs. By linking the insistence on speaking English-only to a longer history of racial and colonial domination, AIWA's English-language-dominance workshop sought to combat the stigma and humiliation that nonnative English speakers experience in their everyday lives. It also attempted to empower devalued and disenfranchised groups to take leadership roles in engaging in social change, regardless of their language ability or marginalized socioeconomic location.

As "senior trainers" (that is, experienced members of the organization that led leadership development trainings to newer members), Cho and Kim had facilitated this training on numerous occasions. However, this particular workshop was noteworthy both for the trainers and the organization. Unlike previous workshops, which were spearheaded and conducted by AIWA, this workshop occurred at the request of a separate organization, Mujeres Unidas y Activas (Women United in Action). Like AIWA, Mujeres Unidas is a grassroots community-based organization aimed at empowering low-income immigrant women workers, in this case in the Latino community. Given their shared mission and constituency, Mujeres Unidas requested that AIWA lead a workshop for twenty of its Spanish-speaking members, utilizing Korean-to-English and English-to-Spanish interpreters. In addition to serving as a rare opportunity for immigrant women workers to cross racial and language barriers and share their experiences, the workshop broke with a familiar and conventional organizing mold. Limited-English-speaking immigrant women themselves, rather than native-English-speaking and college-educated staff members or external consultants, were responsible for leading every aspect of the workshop, from set up and facilitation to discussion and evaluation.

The workshop on English-language dominance embodied many of AIWA's core principles and organizing philosophy. Senior trainers Cho and Kim initially came to the organization as a consequence of their desire to learn English. Under AIWA's Community Transformational Organizing Strategy, a systematic model of organizing developed by the organization to promote immigrant women as their own advocates of change, Cho and Kim deepened their involvement in the organization on multiple levels, becoming public leaders of the organization in the media and in campaigns as well as doing the behind-the-scenes work of recruiting, teaching, and developing strategy—activities typically reserved for paid staff organizers.[1] Their training equipped them with the critical perspectives, specialized knowledge, and organizing skills needed to challenge hostile employers, government officials, and social service providers. The workshop also promoted investment and engagement with activism by providing opportunities and incentives for new forms of individual and collective agency and new frames of identity and identification among individuals who were typically not involved in social movement work or were averse to the risks of social contestation (Della Porta and Diani 2006, 103).

In addressing the problems that immigrant English-language learners face because of language discrimination, anti-immigrant English-only initiatives in politics and education, and the failure of monolingual individuals and institutions to respect the rights and meet the needs of a multinational and multilingual workforce, the workshop displayed important dimensions of social movement practice. It provided an opportunity for an organized collective response to language discrimination by recasting private troubles as a public issue (Mills 2000, 18). It turned a problem into a project, a complaint into a cause. It also situated the daily humiliation that limited-English-speaking immigrant women experienced in a longer history of colonial domination and cultural violence against enslaved blacks and Native Americans. By rejecting the second-class status attributed to a lack of English-language ability, the Asian and Latina women turned hegemony on its head (Nagel 1997, 70). The immigrant women who participated in the workshop were transformed from people belittled for their accents and their not-yet-fully-developed skills in English into multilingual critics against language oppression in all spheres of society, from their workplaces to movement communities. By creating the conditions for immigrant women whose first language was not English to be positioned as sources of authority about language discrimination and experts in intercultural communication, AIWA's English-dominance workshops could be described as what Chela Sandoval (2000, 53) calls a "methodology of the oppressed." It established "a set of processes, procedures, and technologies for decolonizing the imagination" that enabled "individuals and groups seeking to transform dominant and oppressive powers [to] constitute themselves as resistant and oppositional citizen-subjects" (68).

By reaching across linguistic and racial lines to offer their training to Spanish-speaking Latina workers, the AIWA workshop created new affinities and affiliations based on the families of resemblance that made their experiences similar (but not identical) to those of another aggrieved group. The women in Mujeres Unidas y Activas were not Asian immigrants and did not speak Chinese or Korean. Cho and Kim were not Latinas and did not speak Spanish. Yet both Mujeres Unidas y Activas and AIWA had experience forging panethnic solidarity among people from different national backgrounds. Both groups faced exploitation and antagonism as a result of their immigrant and limited-English-speaking status. The Latina and Asian women in both groups occupied common ground as low-wage workers, immigrants, and victims of various kinds of sexual harassment and sexism. Differences in language and national origin created obstacles to be overcome; speaking to each other through Spanish–English and English–Korean translators slowed the pace of conversation and generated possible misunderstandings and miscommunications. Yet the similarities between AIWA and Mujeres Unidas y Activas women exposed the systemic global origins of problems that otherwise might seem personal and particular. It created a shared "psychic space" in which women from different racial, ethnic, national, class, and cultural backgrounds could "recognize one another as 'countrywomen' of a new kind of global and public domain" and assert "coalitional consciousness" that transformed overlapping oppressions into alternative social movement praxes (Sandoval 2000, 70).

Locating Immigrant Women Workers at the Center of Social Change

How and under what conditions have organizations such as AIWA created new methods and new visions for organizing individuals considered marginal in almost every sense (that is, employed on the margins of the economy and disenfranchised by their language and cultural ability)? Why did the organization emphasize a human-development approach to grassroots community organizing that prioritized the self-activity of immigrant women in social change efforts over more pragmatic concerns about organizational efficiency and winnable victories? What role does grassroots leadership development play in tackling social and economic inequalities along multiple axes of difference, including race, gender, immigration status, and language ability?

The initial answers to these questions can be found in AIWA's self-reflexive approach to community organizing. Based on twenty-five years of organizing workers situated on the bottom rungs of the United States's racialized, gendered, and classed hierarchy, AIWA pioneered a grassroots approach to leadership development called the Community Transformational Organizing Strategy (CTOS). As the organization's "methodology of the oppressed," CTOS combines a multilingual and multiracial approach to community organizing with a comprehensive model of grassroots leadership development that provides low-income, limited-English-speaking Asian immigrant women with the skills, knowledge, and opportunities to advocate on their own behalf at every level of social movement practice, from identifying problems and mobilizing constituencies to educating broad-based constituencies and pioneering new solutions. In contrast to the conventional view of organizing that treats leadership as the embodiment of "naturally endowed" qualities among a select few, AIWA argues that racial, gender, economic, and language inequalities thwart meaningful forms of influence and decision-making power for marginalized sectors of society. Thus, to subvert these barriers and hierarchies, the CTOS model aims to generate a paradigm shift that transforms immigrant women workers' everyday lives from a subordinated state of voicelessness and devaluation to an empowered state of self-representation and meaningful participation at every level.

AIWA's emphasis on grassroots leadership development reflects the politics and practices of a new generation of social movement organizations. These organizations generally can be categorized as progressive nonprofit organizations with a mission of social change. They "aim to address systemic problems in a way that will increase the power of marginalized groups, communities or interests" (Chetkovich and Kunreuther 2006, 14). Not all such organizations see themselves as part of a cohesive social movement unified by shared principles and goals, as was commonly thought to be the case during the 1960s and 1970s civil rights, antiwar, and women's movements. However, many social-change-oriented nonprofits that have been directly influenced by the antiracist, feminist, and social justice politics of previous movements have pursued an alternate trajectory of community organizing that is rooted not in specific neighborhoods but rather in the "identities and subsequent attacks faced by the marginal—immigrants, youth, women of color, and the very poor" (Sen 2003, i).[2] As such, they are important empirical sites for examining the development of new organizational forms and strategies in the 1980s and 1990s that have innovated community organizing beyond pragmatic, neighborhood-based concerns, and reinvigorated a longer and more radical history of grassroots struggle from below (Anner 1996; Delgado 1997; Louie 2001).

AIWA is a particularly revealing case among this new generation of community organizations. Founded in 1983, AIWA was one of first worker centers and earliest community-based organizations established for low-wage Asian immigrant workers, a group that was particularly difficult to organize as a consequence of the flexible system of subcontracting that was dominant in the garment and electronics industries and was commonly neglected as a result of the xenophobia and racism of existing unions. The jobs and lives of AIWA's two primary constituencies—Chinese immigrant women working in Oakland's Chinatown garment shops, and Korean immigrant women working in Silicon Valley's high-tech assembly factories—have also been intimately intertwined with broader demographic, economic, and political shifts characterizing the post-1960s era: explosive immigration from Asia and Latin America; global economic restructuring; the dismantling of the welfare state; and a burgeoning sector of nonprofit and nongovernmental organizations. AIWA was also established in what has become one of the most dense social movement communities in the world, benefitting from a shared base of organizational resources, networks, and synergies, as well as the passion, commitment, and experience of students and activists involved in multiple movements. AIWA staff and volunteers have been involved in various forms of regional activism, from struggles for Black Power and Third World liberation to immigrant rights and environmental justice campaigns. They have also participated in political education and community-organizing trainings run by the Oakland-based Center for Third World Organizing that are explicitly designed to train people of color in antiracist grassroots-organizing methods. AIWA has also attracted a steady stream of second-generation Asian American students, not only from the neighboring University of California at Berkeley and San Francisco State University but also from private liberal arts universities from around the country, such as Carleton, Oberlin, Harvard, and Yale. These students were politicized through ethnic studies classes and were eager to gain on-the-ground experience in grassroots community organizations that united Asian Americans and people of color in broader panethnic and multiracial social formations.

The interlocking dimensions of race, class, gender, immigration status, and language oppression in the lives of low-income Asian immigrant women workers have made an intersectional organizing approach central to AIWA's work. An intersectional organizing approach rejects the subordination of one oppression to another (such as racism to sexism or classism to racism) and recognizes that the dynamics of power and inequality are inscribed and reproduced on multiple scales, from the body and household to the workplace and the broader community (Crenshaw 1989). Commonalities of experience across history and axes of social inequality also highlight families of resemblance among oppressed and disenfranchised groups, laying the basis for collective political strategies for social change. A relational organizing approach emphasizes the necessity of building relationships rooted in community networks and sustaining participation among grassroots actors (Warren 1998). Key to this approach is the ability of groups to develop political capacity over time (as opposed to mounting issue-driven campaigns), so that grassroots actors connect community organizing to more broad-based forms of political transformation. A relational organizing approach also challenges the binary between participatory democracy and concrete organizing victories, viewing differences in skills and capacities as sources of mutual learning and organizational innovation rather than impediments to organizational efficiency and success (Polletta 2002).

To better understand the dynamics of growth and dynamism fueling AIWA's organizational trajectory, the chapter is organized into three main sections. First, we discuss the academic-community research collaboration that is the foundation of this study. Second, we examine the process of organizational reflexivity that has guided the development of AIWA's intersectional and relational organizing approaches. In particular, we examine the philosophy, structure, and implementation of the CTOS model in relation to AIWA's programs and campaigns. Finally, we consider the significance of our findings in the context of the changing terrain of social movement organizations, particularly regarding the role of community organizations in revitalizing democratic practice in the post-1960s era.

Analyzing AIWA's Theory and Method of Change: The Research Collaboration

The initiative to conduct a collaborative research project came from AIWA's executive director, Young Shin, who was eager to evaluate the organization's impact after two decades of community organizing. In particular, Shin was interested in analyzing the strengths and weaknesses of AIWA's CTOS leadership methodology, assessing what has worked, what has not, and why. Conducting a comprehensive overview of its grassroots approach to leadership development was not only important for AIWA's internal assessments but also crucial to establishing enduring organizing models that could be undertaken and adapted by similar groups locally, nationally, and globally. According to Shin (2010), AIWA had reached a critical point of reflection: "Some [community organizations] survive, some don't. There is lots of good stuff, but it's what survives that is crucial." Of particular importance was the necessity of documenting how AIWA has developed the mechanisms and infrastructure to facilitate the more full and active participation of low-income Asian immigrant women in everyday civic and political life.

To begin this self-reflective evaluation of its history and the lessons that can be learned from it, AIWA collaborated with Jennifer Jihye Chun, a longtime volunteer and former staff member who researches labor and politics and is part of a cohort of second-generation Asian American activists who became politically active, in part, due to AIWA's Justice for Garment Workers campaign, and George Lipsitz, a longtime supporter of AIWA whose activism and scholarly background reflect the organization's commitment to antiracism and social justice. The research in this chapter draws primarily on the first two rounds of focus groups conducted with twenty-eight member leaders in 2007 and 2008. Focus groups led by Chun were conducted in AIWA's Oakland and San Jose offices. Each focus group lasted approximately two hours; they were conducted in Korean, Cantonese, and English, with a Cantonese–English interpreter included when necessary. In addition to focus groups, the chapter draws on AIWA's twenty-five-year archive, including organizational newsletters, program reports, training materials, campaign documents, and newspaper coverage.

The research project is guided by a spirit of mutual collaboration and shared political commitments. Unlike sociological research that is narrowly theory-driven or motivated by the desire to solve a research puzzle as delineated and circumscribed by the academic literature, this project can be described as beginning "at a point prior to the moment that organizes the detached scientific consciousness" (D. Smith 1989, 11). It follows in the tradition of participatory and feminist research methods that seek to destabilize unequal power relations between the researcher and the researched and generate outcomes that "lead one small step further towards self-determination" and a collective project of social justice and social change (L. Smith 1999, 128). Research findings are shared, discussed, and disseminated in a variety of public and academic formats. As the evaluative study progressives, AIWA hopes to initiate a series of public conversations, placing its members in dialogue with social movement scholars and practitioners about what can be learned from the organization's history.

AIWA's Intersectional Organizing Approach

POPULAR EDUCATION AS A PATH
TO AWARENESS AND EMPOWERMENT

AIWA's organizational beginnings predate the rapid growth of worker centers.[3] In the early 1980s, few organizations existed that addressed the concentration of Asian immigrant women in low-paid and hazardous work. In places such as Oakland's Chinatown, garment factories were one of the most common entry points for Chinese immigrant women (particularly from the southeastern Guandong and Fujian Provinces) in the U.S. labor market (Louie 2001). One of AIWA's members explained that in Hong Kong (where she had emigrated from) people used to say that if you moved to the United States, you should be prepared to do one of two things: sew or wash dishes. In San Jose, the slogan "small, foreign, and female" was Silicon Valley's "simple formula" for recruiting immigrant women workers into low-paid electronics assembly jobs (Hossfeld 1994). Korean immigrant women were among the earliest and most visible population of workers in industry, along with women from Mexico, Vietnam, Taiwan, and the Philippines. San Francisco's hotel industry also had become a highly racialized and gendered workplace, with Asian and Latina immigrant women workers concentrated in the "back of the house" as room cleaners, and with white, college-educated waitresses, waiters, and receptionists at the "front of the house" (Louie 2001, 204).

In 1983, the vulnerability of Asian immigrant women workers to a wide range of abuses and violations as garment workers, hotel room cleaners, and electronics assembly workers created the impetus for the establishment of a community-based organization with an explicit mission of improving the living and working conditions of low-income, limited-English-speaking Asian immigrant women in the San Francisco Bay area.[4] The lack of union attention to the specific needs of this population further accentuated the need for a separate community-based organization that acknowledged the specific needs and interests of immigrant women workers. Miriam Ching Yoon Louie (2001, 205) explains that although the Hotel Employees and Restaurant Employees Union (HERE) Local 2 was one of San Francisco's largest unions, it did not employ any organizers fluent in the Korean language, leaving the Korean hotel workers at exclusive establishments such as Nob Hill's Fairmont Hotel with no access to participating in union activities or learning about the union's bargaining contracts.[5]

Given the significance of language access to the employment vulnerability of Asian immigrant women, one of AIWA's first program areas was teaching "survival English." While English-language classes are certainly an important service for nonnative English speaking immigrants in a monolingual English society, AIWA's rationale for providing English classes was directly linked to the group's role in subverting existing hierarchies in the everyday lives of immigrant women of color. Shin recalls that when she asked a group of Korean immigrant women employed as hotel room cleaners in one of San Francisco's most luxurious hotels why they wanted to learn English, they responded, "So we can tell the boss to stop yelling at us. We are not machines but human beings who deserve some respect"[6] This explanation presents learning English primarily as a form of self-defense and self-affirmation, not necessarily as a mechanism for individual upward mobility and assimilation.

Cognizant of the potential dangers of reproducing client-patron relationships in service provision, teaching survival English quickly became subsumed under a larger umbrella, workplace literacy (WPL) classes, which drew directly on Paolo Freire's (1993) principles of popular education. AIWA staff developed curricula with political content, such as the Rosa Parks story and an alternative history of immigration through Angel Island. Popular-education principles were also applied to the class format and structure. To subvert top-down, hierarchical approaches to learning, WPL classes were team-taught by a volunteer teacher (usually a student from a nearby university, such as UC Berkeley, San Francisco State, Stanford, or UC Santa Cruz) and an AIWA member. Although socially ingrained values about status and authority were difficult to unsettle, the team-teaching model tried to highlight the contributions of different backgrounds, experiences, and skill sets to the classroom. When AIWA began offering computer classes, it continued to apply the principles of popular education to the teaching and learning format.

The WPL classes offered valuable concrete knowledge and skills but did not do so in isolation from the complex lives of the students. Learning English through stories about Rosa Parks and early-twentieth-century Asian immigrants to Angel Island located students inside a historical continuum, revealed families of resemblance between today's immigrants and those of the last century, and encouraged students to see themselves as inheritors of a rich tradition of struggle and achievement by working women of all races.

AIWA's WPL and computer classes played especially important roles as sites for women to challenge culturally entrenched values regarding gender and the family. By emphasizing self-education, AIWA's classes required that women prioritize taking time for themselves outside their household obligations. One WPL member in San Jose recalled that when she first attended the WPL classes, "I used to go back and forth between home and church, and work. That was it. . . . On Wednesdays [the night of class], I'd rush home to prepare meals, much better than usual, wrapping the plates in plastic wrap, setting the table, and even folding napkins. . . . But one day I got too tired. As soon as I was done at work, I picked up the children [and was about to] make dinner really fast and go. My children knew it was too much, and my husband knew it, too, so husband said, 'You don't have to worry too much . . . because [the children] could just order pizza or go buy burgers.' [I said,] 'But how can I let you eat McDonald's after long hours of work?' He just replied, 'One doesn't die from eating McDonalds once in a while.' . . . So now I take it easy on Wednesdays. I leave home with confidence."

According to another woman from AIWA's Korean component in San Jose recalled, "I think I discovered what 'woman' is after coming here. And that empowers me. If I tell people to educate themselves and hear them reply that they should stay home to cook, I tell them, 'Put aside only two hours a week for your sake. Come for your own good.' We are too full with our families, children. . . . Yes, of course we have our duties. I don't mean you should neglect them. But if you can spare just two hours for yourself, life will be more beautiful. 'Find yourself,' is what I always tell people. And when they do, they tell me they feel so good. To come here for two hours' English lessons, for their own sake. Learning English is not necessarily the only purpose. When you come here, you discover yourself."

AIWA's WPL classes were also crucial for changing the power imbalance between immigrant mothers and their children. Many AIWA members spoke about the social devaluation they felt in their children's eyes as a result of their limited English-language ability. They also talked about "feeling dumb" if they did not speak English or know how to use computers, an emotion that was particularly alienating for electronics assembly workers, who were often directly involved in manufacturing computers. Enhancing their knowledge and skill base through AIWA's classes thus became a path toward earning the respect of their children. One woman taking computer classes in Oakland explained, "My sons in the past always teased me for being a dummy, knowing nothing. Then, I told them that I am learning computer on Sundays. They are excited to know that I am learning to use the computer. AIWA has changed the family life of the women."

Another woman taking computer classes in San Jose echoed this sentiment: "The first story we learned in the English class was Rosa Parks's story. And of course my English wasn't that good in the beginning. Now, we did typing as well in the class. So they asked us to type something up at home, and when I did that, I asked my daughter to check for typos. She read it over, and asked, 'Do you always read stories like these in class?' And I said, 'Oh, so you know Rosa Parks?' It was shortly after I heard what the story meant to her that I felt really warm inside. My daughter saw that her mom was learning about such good stories and has backed me up since then. Till then, my husband didn't really care, but my kids now got to see it differently. So then the kids gave me support and then my husband started to show support."

Just as AIWA's English-language-dominance workshop provided an opening for immigrant women workers to renegotiate their relationships with employers, WPL classes encouraged the creation of new relations with home and family. Getting men to accept changes in domestic responsibilities; winning new respect from children for developing new knowledge and skills; viewing their roles as mothers, wives, daughters, and sisters as important conditions of their existence rather than their total identities; and developing trusting, purposeful, and caring relations with people outside their families all contributed to building a new sense of personhood and possibility. This intersectional approach to challenging hierarchies and forging affinities laid the basis for AIWA's subsequent political mobilizations.

MORE THAN EDUCATION AND SERVICE PROVISION: DEVELOPING COLLECTIVE STRATEGIES FOR CHANGE

AIWA's English classes also served as an important site for providing information to immigrant women workers about their rights in the workplace. AIWA's "right to know" curriculum focused on the legal right of all workers to a minimum wage, a regulation that most of Oakland's garment shops seemed to ignore during the early 1980s. AIWA's experience with minimum-wage education, however, decisively shifted the organization's focus from workers' rights education to leadership development and collective organizing. Shin (2002) recalled, "When we first started in 1983, the story goes, workers did not always receive minimum wages in the garment districts. And when we started talking about that, the workers would go and say, 'Why don't you pay me?' And the minute they said that, they got fired. Certainly, we told them that they have a right to ask that question, but they have to work with other women to advocate for their rights so that they don't get into that difficult position. We talked about the fact that if you do it alone, you basically will lose. You have to work together."

The role of service provision as an organizing tool complicated the notion that services and organizing represented separate and distinct activities, yet AIWA was keenly aware of the tensions between service provision and organizing. Job training was one area of contention. AIWA members cited limited labor market opportunities as a consistent barrier to improving their working and living conditions. Shin used to say that clerical jobs are an entry-level position for English speakers but are nearly unobtainable for limited-English speakers. Rather than pour time and resources into job-oriented English-language training, AIWA decided to focus on the industries where immigrant women were already employed, such as garments and electronics. AIWA also discontinued its citizenship classes after the organization decided to take a more active and participatory approach to promoting citizenship rights. AIWA's citizenship classes had focused on familiarizing members with the citizenship exam to facilitate their efforts to obtain formal citizenship. However, its efforts revealed that obtaining citizenship status required much more than just passing the exam; it involved helping limited-English immigrants navigate the entire application process, which would heavily weight the organization's activities toward direct service provision and advocacy rather than organizing and collective action.

When AIWA expanded its organizing efforts to San Jose in 1990, its popular-education approach to teaching English classes continued to serve as an important avenue of organizational learning about the needs and issues facing Korean immigrant women working in Silicon Valley's high-tech factories. More than low wages, women talked about the constant headaches, nausea, skin rashes, and body aches they experienced as a result of handling toxic chemicals, working in poorly ventilated spaces, and engaging in repetitive work for long hours. Many women also highlighted the industry's culture of silence and neglect regarding workplace health and safety. Most workers had no idea what specific chemicals they worked with, let alone the toxic impacts of those chemicals. Although signs were posted in English, companies made no effort to translate health and safety hazard signs into the workers' primary languages. Also, if women raised questions about health issues, their supervisors would retort, "Then go home or go find work at another company." The vulnerability of women to the industry's rampant health and safety violations was exacerbated by their institutional vulnerability. Silicon Valley employers were notoriously antiunion, and employers quickly squashed attempts to form unions, particularly among low-wage assembly workers. Language and cultural barriers also made it difficult for women to navigate existing channels such as California's State Occupational Safety and Health agency.

To challenge the culture of silence and neglect in the industry, AIWA began its Environmental Justice Project in San Jose. This project consisted of a series of trainings on health and safety hazards in the workplace and basic health and safety rights in which a group of women leaders were first trained themselves and then trained other women about the dangers of toxic chemical exposure in the workplace. One of AIWA's first participants in health and safety trainings explains that this was a transformative process: "Through AIWA, I learned how my work affects my health. At first, I started to attend English classes in the evening. We exchanged some practical resources and received training on workplace health and safety. In addition, we learned about the labor laws and human rights. Along with other coworkers, we [began asking our company for improvements such as] a ventilation system. Through AIWA, we can continue to fight for better working conditions, labor laws, and human rights with the belief that we must take care of our own health and create a better society."

AIWA's grassroots approach sought to provide women with the tools and knowledge to educate themselves and others about their everyday working conditions. It also aimed at promoting the active participation of immigrant women workers in demanding policy and institutional changes, first in their workplaces and then more broadly in the garment industry.

An incident at the Lucky Sewing company, a Chinese-owned garment subcontractor, catapulted Asian immigrant women workers to the center of policy change in the garment industry and to the forefront of the emerging anti-sweatshop movement. In May 1992, twelve female Lucky employees showed up at AIWA's Oakland Chinatown office. Their paychecks had bounced after Lucky had filed for bankruptcy, and the workers were seeking advice about how to recover a total of fifteen thousand dollars in lost wages. AIWA's research on the structure of accountability in the garment industry revealed that these women had little legal recourse against the bankrupt company, especially since it was a subcontractor that produced clothing for larger manufacturers. However, AIWA's knowledge about things such as the Farm Labor Organizing Committee and its efforts to hold Campbell's Soup accountable to agricultural contractors provided a model for how to hold clothing retailers who outsourced to smaller subcontractors responsible for wage and employment conditions (Delgado 1996, 83). When the former Lucky employees learned that Jessica McClintock Inc. was selling the evening gowns that they had sewn in its exclusive San Francisco boutique for upward of $175, they launched what would become a three-and-a-half-year public campaign against Jessica McClintock. Although Jessica McClintock was not legally responsible for compensating the former Lucky employees, AIWA's Justice for Garment Workers campaign emphasized that the company profited from sweatshop labor and was thus fiscally and morally responsible for paying workers' unpaid back wages.[7]

The Justice for Garment Workers Campaign resulted in many precedent-setting victories, including a model for waging community-based corporate campaigns in the garment industry.[8] AIWA not only used the media to try to shame Jessica McClintock into doing "the right thing" but also mobilized a strong secondary support network of students, community members, religious leaders, and social justice activists at the local and national levels. Asian American students and community activists, many of whom had mothers and grandmothers who had worked in garment sweatshops and had become politically activated after learning about events such as the 1968 ethnic studies strike at San Francisco State University and the struggles of Filipino farmworkers in the Central Valley, were particularly crucial in sustaining the public protests in the second and third years of the campaign. The support of third parties was especially important in light of the fact that many garment workers themselves, including the women from Lucky Sewing, feared blacklisting if they chose to participate in public rallies. Not only did public support provide personnel for the picket lines as the campaign dragged on, but outsiders' support gave protesting garment workers the courage to publicly protest without covering their faces and to reject compromise deals in which Jessica McClintock attempted to shirk formal responsibility for labor violations by offering workers a "charitable donation" instead of their unpaid back wages. Through consistent and escalated public pressure, AIWA and Jessica McClintock finally came to a cooperative agreement in February 1996, with the assistance of Robert Reich in the U.S. Department of Labor, in which a Garment Workers Education Fund and a toll-free multilingual and confidential hotline for garment workers was created to help them report workplace violations. In 1997, AIWA secured the participation of three more clothing retailers, Esprit de Corp, Byer California, and Fritzi of California, to establish hotlines that allowed garment workers employed by subcontractors to report labor violations.

Although the direct actions and community mobilizations during the Justice for Garment Workers Campaign set important precedents in changing garment industry policy and the landscape of garment worker organizing, they also highlighted a widening gulf between the garment workers who directly experienced the workplace violations and the community allies who publicly supported the struggle. The courage and resilience of the immigrant women workers from Lucky

Sewing certainly formed the heart of the campaign, providing inspiration to the hundreds of supporters who joined; however, AIWA became increasingly aware of the limited role of immigrant women themselves in resolving their dispute. Although AIWA organized public hearings at which workers and contractors testified about their experiences to relevant public authorities, reliance on outside advocates and allies reduced the role of rank-and-file women workers in public mobilizations and legal mediations. Moreover, given the crisis-driven and reactive elements of the campaign, much of AIWA's time and resources were spent on propelling the overall campaign, not on developing the capacity of immigrant women to advocate on their own behalf.

As AIWA moved out of this period of crisis-driven organizing, these tensions generated internal discussion about how and where to refocus AIWA's priorities. The extensive network of external allies and supporters made AIWA the site of immense interest and inquiry, creating additional pressures on the small grassroots organization. While AIWA recognized the benefits of advocates and secondary supporters, it also became concerned about the tendencies in social justice organizing to foreground issue-based campaigns and tangible policy outcomes over the self-organization and leadership development of the workers involved. AIWA leaders also worried about the potential of tokenizing immigrant women in social movement practice. While many people talked about the importance of grassroots participation, how many immigrant women workers, especially limited-English speakers, were directly involved in influencing society's decision-making structures?

To ensure that its constituents had the ability to begin more directly advocating on their own behalf, AIWA returned to its organizational mission—promoting the self-empowerment of low-income Asian immigrant women workers. AIWA refocused on developing the grassroots leadership capacity of immigrant women workers to mobilize collectively and politically on their own behalf. AIWA also established the Youth Build Immigrant Project to broaden the group's organizing base. The children of Chinese immigrant garment workers, who had become heavily involved in the Justice for Garment Workers campaign, were asking for opportunities to continue their activism. Although AIWA did not immediately set up a youth component during the campaign, it did expand its mission to include multigenerational organizing in 1997 with a commitment to developing the leadership and organizing skills of youth from low-income Asian immigrant families in Oakland's Chinatown.

By strengthening and expanding its commitment to empowering low-income Asian immigrant women, their families, and their communities, AIWA fortified its relational approach to organizing. As Mark Warren (1998, 86–87) explains in his analysis of the Industrial Areas Foundation, the relational organizing approach does not prioritize "mobilization on issue campaigns" but rather involves the deliberate building of relationships and the sustained participation of community actors "for the purpose of finding common ground for political action." This approach seeks to strengthen community organizations' ability to "build their political capacity over time so that they have the potential, however partially realized, of addressing a broad range of issues." Shin reiterated this principle in the February 1998 issue of the *AIWA Newsletter*: "AIWA has been transformed into an organization with internal strengths and external visibility. With their organizing and leadership skills, immigrant women are ready to accept the challenge of taking on leadership roles in the broader community. All of us at AIWA are committed to bringing the concerns of low-income immigrant women workers to public debate and consciousness. In 1998, we envision low-income immigrant women working in solidarity with other disenfranchised populations, and possessing confidence and leadership to bring justice to all communities in struggle, both within the United States and abroad."

Shin's statement offered a clear indication of the organization's commitment to empowering immigrant women to become their own advocates and agents of social change. It also highlighted the importance of building relationships based on affinities and solidarities. Much of the impetus for focusing on grassroots leadership was related to the life of activism and the importance of creating enduring change in the society's structures of power and decision making. Shin (2010) clarified, "In the past people used to [think] that most movement activists were college graduates who eventually moved on [to grad school or law school]. The question is, 'How do we make our human investment and capital continue? We can't continue to raise money [from foundations]. People affected need to be the main drivers of change.'" For Shin, prioritizing a relational organizing approach meant allowing the marginalized and disenfranchised to truly speak for themselves and to participate autonomously and actively in democratic society on the issues that most affected their lives. This principle provided the basis for the shift in AIWA's organizing work from reactive and issue- and campaign-based organizing to proactive, collective, and relational organizing.

AIWA's Relational Organizing Approach

GRASSROOTS EXPERTS IN INDUSTRY
HEALTH POLICY AND REFORM

The next phase of AIWA's organizing involved strengthening the voice and visibility of low-income Asian immigrant women as health experts in the garment and electronics industries. This effort involved more than providing firsthand testimony to win health policy changes at the legislative level; it involved changing familiar patterns of social movement practice in which immigrant women workers were the voices but not the agents of social change. Innovative collaborations between Asian immigrant women workers and health professionals provided an important basis for reconfiguring these patterns so that immigrant women workers could serve as experts in changing workplace health and safety policies.

AIWA used its peer training approach to establish the Peer Health Promoter Network, whose main thrust was the direct participation of immigrant women workers in diagnosing occupational health and safety problems in the garment industry. At meetings in Oakland's Chinatown, where the majority of the organization's members were Chinese immigrant women who worked as seamstresses, garment workers began working directly with health professionals such as doctors, nurses, and occupational therapists to identify which repetitive actions at work resulted in chronic pain and injury. According to one Peer Health Promoter Network trainer who started working as a seamstress almost immediately after immigrating to the United States from China in 1990, "99 percent of all garment workers never thought that the neck, shoulder, and back aches [they experienced] were related with sewing. Besides, [since] they didn't have health insurance, many just ignored it and endured it until they couldn't take it anymore." The fear of losing their jobs if they reported pain and injury was also a powerful deterrent against the filing of workers' compensation claims.

Through its Garment Workers' Clinic in Oakland's Chinatown, which was established in 2000 to provide basic health services and screening of occupational injuries to immigrant garment workers, AIWA continued to uncover extensive pain and injury resulting from working conditions. Clinic patients reported spending between eight and ten hours a day at work in garment shops, sitting on metal chairs that did not rotate. According to clinic research, 99 percent of garment workers had at least one chronic injury related to work, a list that included back, neck, and shoulder sprains or strains. Approximately 94 percent of clinic patients also reported ergonomic-related problems related to their workstations, including inadequate seating (90 percent) and awkward bending and twisting (67 percent) (Lashuay et al. 2002). Wendy Yeung told the *Oakland Tribune* that her pain reached such an intense level that she could no longer stand upright (Casey 2004). Others talked about permanent injuries to their necks, shoulders, and backs as a consequence of their work.

From the data they collected in conjunction with health professionals, AIWA members developed a curriculum to train garment workers about the relationship between their working conditions and their chronic pain and injury. AIWA members were directly involved in the self-education, outreach, and training process about ergonomic health and safety. According to one leader, "First, five of the committee members trained to be trainers. Then, we divided into three groups to train fifteen trainers to be trainers. Each group consists of five trainees. Each group receives four hours of training and two hours of practice. Then fifteen new trainers divided into seven groups. In the same way, we have thirty-five more trainers. Altogether we have fifty trainers. Each of the trainers can teach other women at work about the relationship [between their injuries] and their working conditions."

Core trainers conducted health and safety outreach and education to more than 125 other workers in Oakland's garment shops about ergonomic health and safety. Through this process, AIWA's organizing approach created the conditions for its members to become the primary agents in disseminating information about ergonomic safety in the garment industry, an issue that was very rarely, if ever, addressed by their employers or doctors.

Involving garment workers directly in the education and training process laid the foundation for them to become leaders in developing health policy and engaging in health-care reform. After AIWA created a space for discussing the extent of chronic pain and injury, the need to change the ergonomic conditions of garment shops became a central campaign issue.

AIWA worked with the state occupational health and safety department and the University of California, San Francisco Schools of Medicine and Nursing to design a "model garment shop." One of the most important features of the model shop was the use of adjustable chairs and footrests to improve workstation conditions. In 2002, AIWA leaders took their self-advocacy one step further by identifying five Oakland garment factories to participate in a new Ergonomics Improvement Project (Ergo Campaign).

The Ergo Campaign combined key elements of AIWA's grassroots organizing approach. After women identified ergonomics reform as the main issue, they were responsible for studying the topic and carrying out the campaign from beginning to end, a task they often found daunting. However, their direct participation in brainstorming and strategic planning helped build their confidence and leadership skills. One woman recalled, "Well, you can't do it alone. And you see it's tiring . . . for women really . . . because they have their hands full with too many things. But as I come here, sit on the membership board, and see how one person comes up with an idea and then another person brings in another idea until things become one concrete work. . . . I am drawn to that and I really like it that I can lead it on."

Through their committee meetings and planning retreats, women discussed various options for improving ergonomics in the garment industry. Based on the model shop research, women decided that installing ergonomic-friendly workstations was a key route in improving workers' health. Given the industry's cost-squeezing structure, however, persuading garment shop owners to invest in new equipment proved difficult. After much discussion and deliberation, women decided to target the city of Oakland.

The experience of several key AIWA members with city officials during the 1999 Community Equity campaign was pivotal in preparing AIWA members for a campaign to pressure the city to change occupational health and safety policy. AIWA's WPL classes, which taught English to more than 120 workers every term, were held at the Oakland Asian Cultural Center (OACC) at no cost until 1998, when the OACC board cited financial reasons for refusing to continue allowing AIWA to use the space. AIWA collaborated with an intermediary organization, Just Economics, to conduct research and develop curriculum materials about city government accountability. After learning about the tax benefits that OACC received to contribute to community development in Oakland's Chinatown, women began to ask, "Where is the 'community' in community development?"

To pressure OACC to follow through on its commitment to low-income workers in the community, Oakland WPL members began a campaign to pressure OACC to change its decision. AIWA members met directly with then Oakland District 2 council member John Russo and participated in a public hearing, sponsored by Russo, on OACC's access and management issues. According to one campaign leader, "Since OACC was funded by $1.5 million of taxpayer money, we as taxpayers should have equal rights to use the city's property." Although AIWA was unable to secure community access space at the OACC, AIWA members worked with the city of Oakland and the Redevelopment Agency to obtain access to classroom space in another city-owned facility.

Building on their experiences with direct action and local political pressure as well as research and education about how to develop collective solutions to workplace problems, AIWA members worked with local public officials and businesses to cultivate a relational approach to community organizing and political transformation. In February 2004, AIWA members negotiated a twenty-five-thousand-dollar grant from the Oakland City Council to expand the group's Ergonomic Chair Library, which loaned height-adjustable and rotating chairs to garment factories through an application process in which garment shops paid 10 percent of the cost of the chairs and committed to using the chairs, with proper monitoring, for one year. Through their direct outreach with employers, the committee elicited the participation of a dozen factories and trained almost two hundred garment workers in the value of using ergonomic chairs.

Although the chair library did not challenge some of the larger systemic abuses in the industry by holding the retailers and manufacturers responsible for providing healthy work environments, the Ergo Campaign resulted in important changes in the lives of the women leaders involved as well as the broader community of garment workers. Its ongoing monitoring of participating garment shops revealed that the use of ergonomic chairs reduced injury rates by more than 50 percent—and enhanced productivity rates by 10 percent. The Ergo campaign also profoundly changed garment workers' awareness regarding the issue of ergonomic health and safety. Campaign leader Kwti Fong Lin stated, "We've done something we never thought we could do. The workers in Oakland now know there's an ergonomic chair that's good for their health. Everybody's talking about the chair" (Romney 2004, 126). Few AIWA staff organizers imagined that at the beginning of their health and safety work AIWA members would become the experts and innovators who improved ergonomic conditions in garment shops, yet through the self-education, strategic planning, outreach, and training of campaign leaders, garment workers made ergonomic reform a key change in the local industry.

The Ergo Campaign challenged expert knowledge, enlisted other experts with technical training as allies, reinforced the dignity of workers by making management listen, and skillfully pushed at management prerogatives without defying them. Like many successful social movement actions, it turned bystanders into upstanders, drawing elected officials, state functionaries, physicians, and scientists into negotiations between workers and employers and eventually crafting a solution that protected the health and safety of workers while increasing productivity. It also linked community organizing directly with political action, eliciting the support and participation of city officials, local employers, and health professionals in a common agenda to improve health for immigrant women in the garment industry.

CREATING SUSTAINABLE SYSTEMS
FOR DEMOCRATIC TRANSFORMATION

The focus on peer training and women's direct self-advocacy and participation in social change helped clarify and strengthen AIWA's approach to grassroots leadership development. Through a series of brainstorming sessions by staff organizers, AIWA began outlining and clarifying the philosophy, mechanics, and implementation of CTOS. In particular, AIWA was interested in reflecting on its previous three campaigns—the Justice for Garment Workers Campaign (1992–96), the Community Equity Campaign (1999–2000) and the Ergonomics Improvement Campaign (2002–6)—and analyzing what specific systems and mechanisms they had developed to ensure that immigrant women spearheaded social change. The result of these discussions was the CTOS model.

AIWA's CTOS model (figure 1) identifies seven levels of individual and collective social transformation. AIWA recognizes that leadership development is not a simple, narrow, direct, or linear process. The group emphasizes, however, that given existing barriers to such participation posed by language ability, racial and ethnic oppression, sexism, and exploitation, clear, concrete, and transparent organizational systems must be created to ensure that all immigrant women have the potential and the right to exercise full and meaningful participation in society. The premise behind the CTOS model is that immigrant women cannot exercise their rights without the opportunity to acquire the skills, knowledge, and capacity to advocate on their own behalf as fully informed and active citizens. Levels 1 and 2 highlight that community organizing begins at the moment of initial contact, when immigrant women become aware of the existence and activities of AIWA in their workplaces and communities through outreach efforts and social events. Level 3, self-education, is the foundation of AIWA's leadership-development strategy. In contrast to the divisiveness and fear that often pervades immigrant workplaces and communities, women active in AIWA meet each other in a supportive social space where they share information and experiences and learn about their rights as workers, women, and immigrants. After women begin the process of self-education, they are encouraged to participate in leadership training activities (Level 4), where various workshops explain AIWA's experiences waging direct action campaigns, the history of the civil rights movement, and the legacy of the deployment of the English language as a tool of colonial domination and worker exploitation.

Leadership development training serves as a vehicle for recruiting members to become more actively involved in the organization through participation in AIWA committees related to such issue areas as health care, immigration, and special events. Participation in these committees leads to Level 5: leadership on AIWA's Membership Board, which is the central body for deciding on programs and activities for each component. At Levels 5 and 6, members have the opportunity to take skill- and capacity-building training programs that facilitate their ability to run meetings and engage in strategic and campaign planning. Members at Levels 5 and 6 exercise leadership skills as peer trainers and peer teachers and coordinators in AIWA's classes (Level 3) and serve as public leaders in direct actions and coalition-building activities. This wealth of experience, combined with targeted skills and capacity building, lays a solid foundation for preparing immigrant women to motivate others to bring about change in their workplaces, their ethnic communities, and the broader society in the struggle for social and economic justice (Level 7).

While empirical research is still ongoing regarding CTOS's impact on immigrant women workers' leadership, preliminary findings suggest that the CTOS structure is promoting more engaged forms of participation. Turning students into teachers and leaders into organizers of new recruits inhibits the development of an entrenched bureaucracy inside AIWA and discourages the emergence of cults of personality around charismatic leaders. It disperses rewards and responsibilities widely within the organization, enacting and instantiating in everyday life activities the egalitarian practices envisioned by the group's ideology. While the time and resources required for grassroots leadership development often inhibit quick returns on human investment, the process has also changed internal values related to the culture of advocacy. Staff organizers play more of a role as facilitators and program coordinators than do community organizers, and AIWA members take more of a leadership role in all stages of the organizing process, from outreach and recruitment to campaign planning and organizational strategic development. While the emphasis on member development has often taken precedence over staff and volunteer development, AIWA has prioritized a kind of organizational discipline with regard to the group's primary mission. Hiring staff organizers who respect the centrality of AIWA's mission to organizational decision making and strategic planning has been an important component of its commitment to grassroots leadership development.

The CTOS model also provides an important relational context for AIWA women who participate in various programs and activities. One woman explained that learning about the CTOS levels gives her a way to understand her relationship to other women at AIWA. Though she first started attending AIWA to learn English, she quickly became more involved in the leadership structure, attending trainings on health and safety and then training other women on the topic. She explained, "By seeing the CTOS model, I can see a clear path for how I can become a strong leader at AIWA." In other words, by visualizing her relationship to others in a broader organizational structure, she can see what is possible if she commits more time and energy to the organization.

Conclusion

The development of AIWA's CTOS model reflects a process of organizational reflexivity in the face of dynamism and change. AIWA has pursued a path similar to other social change organizations that prioritize individual and collective empowerment as a legitimate and necessary building block for social transformation. The research findings from the initial round of focus groups reveal that understanding how this process takes place requires recognizing the overlapping dimensions of women's lives, particularly their struggles to assert voice and visibility in asymmetrical structures in the family and community as well as the workplace and broader society. Because inequality and injustice are produced and inscribed in many different areas of people's lives—including the body, household, workplace, community, psyche, and imagination—struggle must take place on multiple planes and in multiple ways. Barriers to participation for limited-English-speaking immigrant women also create the need to develop concrete mechanisms and organizational support to facilitate their full and active participation in civic and political life. While investment in human development is time- and resource-intensive, it is central to cultivating the political power of disenfranchised and disempowered groups to lead community-driven efforts for social change over the long term.

THE SEEDS OF SUCCESS

By placing immigrant women workers at the center of the struggle, AIWA produces new kinds of politics, polities, and personalities. Low-wage immigrant women workers possess unique optics on power. Their experiences with exploitation and exclusion imbue them with powerful desires for democratic participation in the decisions that shape their lives. Their self-activity affirms the existence and potential of the multinational, multiracial, and multilingual nation that took to the streets on May 1, 2006, to defend the dignity and protect the livelihoods of immigrants. AIWA's practices turn hegemony on its head, transforming socially subordinated and devalued individual women into a self-active collectivity. Pursuing intersectional and relational approaches to organizing creates important avenues for supporting collective and sustained forms of political participation at the grassroots level.

AIWA's actions and campaigns draw previously uninvolved bystanders into their own struggles. Its popular-education approach to English and computer classes, as well as its political education curriculum, highlights shared experiences and identities, creating new affinities and solidarities among immigrant women workers. Team teaching at WPL classes, which pairs college student volunteers with rank-and-file workers, and innovative campaigns involving workers, health professionals, public officials, and businesses, reveal the potential of cross-class cooperation and collaboration. AIWA's recognition of the potential dangers of reproducing client-patron relationships in its organizational practices leads the group away from simple service provision and toward the creation of transformative experiences that empower the rank and file in hierarchically organized workplaces and political structures. The CTOS system's success in turning students into teachers and rotating decision-making positions works against the dangers that sometimes turn social movement organizations into social clubs, hierarchical bureaucracies, or passive followers of charismatic leaders. The CTOS's success in making immigrant women the experts in industry and health policy also subverts conventional expectations regarding who is the expert and who is the client. These practices distribute rewards and responsibilities throughout the group, enacting the egalitarian principles that AIWA's ideology envisions. Perhaps most important, whatever gains are won in specific struggles matter to the organization mostly as steps toward developing the long-term potential for leadership and the realization of solidarity and full social membership by working-class immigrant women. Because AIWA recognizes that macrosocial injustices shape and reflect microsocial experiences, the group's projects go beyond the workplace and the political system to produce new social relations within families and between families and the broader social world. Women's time takes on new meaning when attending classes or meetings takes precedence over putting dinner on the table for husbands and children. Power relations within families take on new dimensions when children see their mothers mastering new skills and husbands recognize their domestic responsibilities.

AIWA has won important victories for women workers at the point of production and in the community. Yet even tangible victories have led the group to change course when it discovered that the specific concessions won through struggle depended too much on outside allies and not enough on the continuous development of new knowledge, new leaders, and new possibilities. The group is now engaged in a large-scale retrospective and reflexive study of its history, engaging outside experts, staff members, and veterans of the CTOS system to conduct a critical evaluation of the strengths and weaknesses of its organizing methods. An organization less dedicated to democratic principles might try to leverage its past successes with outside philanthropic institutions and allies in the political system to secure more funding, influence, and power for itself. AIWA, however, proceeds by other principles. While open to outside support, it affirms its core commitment to the difficult and relentless work required to place immigrant women workers at the center of social change. It takes the more difficult path, because as the great organizer and activist Ella Baker used to say, "We who believe in freedom cannot rest."

Notes

1. Community organizations, which were influenced by the dominant paradigm of community organizing in the 1960s—i.e., the Alinsky model—often created a distinct division between the role of the community leader and the staff organizer. According to Sen (2003, xvi), "in Alinsky-style organizations, the unpaid volunteer leader, who should be indigenous to the community in which the work is taking place, represents the organizations, gets in front of the media, and negotiates with the power structure [whereas] the organizer works behind the scenes—recruiting, coordinating, doing research, taking notes, buying donuts."

2. For a discussion of the shift from geography-based to identity-based community organizing, see Delgado (1997).

3. The number of worker centers, defined as "community-based mediating institutions that provide support to and organize among communities of low-wage workers," grew from five in 1985 to more than thirty-five in 2005, with the majority of growth occurring in the mid-1990s (Fine 2006, 9–11).

4. Along with Young Shin, Elaine Kim of the Korean Community Center of the East Bay (KCCEB) and Chinese American Hotel and Restaurant Employees Union Local 2

organizer Patricia Lee played key roles in the formation of AIWA. AIWA started under the auspices of KCCEB, and Young was hired as its first project director.

5. The Chinese Staff and Workers Association (CSWA), the first worker center in the Asian American community, was established in response to the union's disregard of Asian immigrant workers in New York City. After his disappointment with HERE's role in organizing Chinese workers at one of the largest restaurants in New York's Chinatown, the Silver Palace, Wing Lam, who worked as a staff organizer of the International Ladies Garment Workers Union and then HERE realized that unions were not equipped to address the needs and concerns of Chinese immigrant workers in the city and established a separate organization, the CSWA, in 1980.

6. Speech given by Young Shin (2000) to the Tri-Agency Asian Pacific Council and the Federal Women's Program.

7. For more on the Justice for Garment Workers campaign, see Delgado (1996); Louie (2001).

8. The Justice for Garment Workers campaign influenced the formation of the Los Angeles Garment Workers' Center and its campaign against Forever 21 from 2001 to 2004. In social movement struggles, no aggrieved group is ever strong enough to win gains entirely by itself. Yet victories are contagious, and prevailing patterns of power mean that no group wins gains solely for itself because successes are quickly replicated by others in similar positions.

References

Anner, John, ed. 1996. *Beyond Identity Politics: Emerging Social Justice Movements in Communities of Color*. Boston: South End.

Casey, Laura. 2004. "Chinese Workers Fight for Safety on the Job: Immigrant Women Seek Better Conditions in Oakland Factories, Sweatshops, and Other Workplaces." *Oakland Tribune*, March 26.

Chetkovich, Carol, and Francis Kunreuther. 2006. *From the Ground Up: Grassroots Organizing Making Change*. Ithaca: Cornell University Press.

Crenshaw, Kimberle. 1989. "Demarginalizing the Intersection of Race and Sex: A Black Feminist Critique of Antidiscrimination Doctrine, Feminist Theory, and Antiracist Politics." *University of Chicago Legal Forum*, 139–67.

Delgado, Gary. 1996. "How the Empress Gets Her Clothes: Asian Immigrant Women Fight Fashion Designer Jessica McClintock." In *Beyond Identity Politics: Emerging Social Justice Movements in Communities of Color*, ed. John Anner, 81–94. Boston: South End.

———. 1997 (1993). *Beyond the Politics of Place*. Oakland: Chardon.

Della Porta, Donatella, and Mario Diani. 2006. *Social Movements: An Introduction*. Malden, Mass.: Blackwell.

Fine, Janice. 2006. *Worker Centers: Organizing Communities at the Edge of the Dream*. Ithaca: Cornell University Press.

Freire. Paolo. 1993. *Pedagogy of the Oppressed*. New York: Continuum.

Hossfeld, Karen J. 1994. "Hiring Immigrant Women: Silicon Valley's Simple Formula." In *Women of Color in U.S. Society*, ed. Maxine Baca Zinn and Bonnie Thornton Dill, 65–93. Philadelphia: Temple University Press.

Lashuay, Nan, Barbara J. Burgel, Robert Harrison, Leslie Israel, Jacqueline Chan, Catherine Cusic, Jane Chao Pun, Ken Fong, and Young Shin. 2002. *We Spend Our Days Working in Pain: A Report on Workplace Injuries in the Garment Industry*. http://aiwa.org/workingreport.pdf. Accessed December 13, 2012.

Louie, Miriam Ching Yoon. 2001. *Sweatshop Warriors: Immigrant Women Workers Take on the Global Factory*. Boston: South End.

Mills, C. Wright. 2000. *The Sociological Imagination*. New York: Oxford University Press.

Nagel, Joane. 1997. *American Indian Ethnic Renewal: Red Power and the Resurgence of Identity and Culture*. New York: Oxford University Press.

Polletta, Francesca. 2002. *Freedom Is an Endless Meeting: Democracy in American Social Movements*. Chicago: University of Chicago Press.

Romney, Lee. 2004. "Chairs Sit Well with Laborers." *Los Angeles Times*, May 26.

Sandoval, Chela. 2000. *Methodology of the Oppressed*. Minneapolis: University of Minnesota Press.

Sen, Rinku. 2003. *Stir It Up: Lessons in Community Organizing and Advocacy*. San Francisco: Jossey-Bass.

Shin, Young. 2000. Speech to Tri-Agency Asian Pacific Council and the Federal Women's Program. AIWA Organizational Archives, Oakland, California.

———. 2002. Profile. http://www.rwjf.org/en/about-rwjf/newsroom/newsroom-content/2006/10/young-shin-j-d.html. Accessed December 13, 2012.

———. 2010. Interview by Jennifer Jihye Chun. May 5.

Smith, Dorothy. 1989. *The Everyday World as Problematic: A Feminist Sociology*. Boston: Northeastern University Press.

Smith, Linda Tuhiwai. 1999. *Decolonizing Methodologies: Research and Indigenous Peoples*. London: Zed.

Taylor, Verta. 1989. "Social Movement Continuity: The Women's Movement in Abeyance." *American Sociological Review* 54:761–75.

Toney, Mark. 1996. "Power Concedes Nothing without a Demand: Building Multiracial Organizations with Direct Action." In *Beyond Identity Politics: Emerging Social Justice Movements in Communities of Color*, ed. John Anner, 17–28. Boston: South End.

Warren, Mark R. 1998. "Community Building and Political Power: A Community Organizing Approach to Democratic Renewal." *American Behavioral Scientist* 42:78–92.

12 Transfronteriza

Gender Rights at the Border and La Colectiva Feminista Binacional

MICHELLE TÉLLEZ

To better understand the ways in which women border dwellers are responding to transnational processes and the effects of neoliberal policies, this chapter focuses on woman-centered activism projects and innovative forms of political organizing and community formation at the U.S./Mexico border. Building on the idea of *transfronterismo* (Ruiz 1992), or transborderness,[1] I highlight how the actual border should be seen not just as a site of passage but also as a site for gendered transformation where a politicized *transfronteriza* identity can emerge. I look specifically at the transborder space of the twin cities of Tijuana and San Diego and the work of the Colectiva Feminista Binacional (Binational Feminist Collective),[2] which formed in 2004.

This work is part of a larger project in which Cristina Sanidad and I examine how grassroots organizations are collaborating, both binationally and locally, in the San Diego/Tijuana border region to create worker-centered spaces for change. Though the rapidly changing global economy causes constant shifts in production, stability, and worker conditions, the maquiladora (factory) industry has consistently drawn migrant workers north for more than forty years. The border economy arguably depends on the maquiladora industry, yet the lives of the workers are deemed disposable. The Colectiva Feminista Binacional (CFB), CITTAC (Support Center for Workers), and the San Diego Maquiladora Workers' Solidarity Network (SDMWSN, a binational support system for maquiladora workers based in San Diego) are the three grassroots, worker-centered spaces that challenge this disposability and have emerged as advocates for many workers seeking an improvement in unjust working conditions. Through the creation of an autonomous infrastructure, these groups offer legal support, workers' rights workshops, and the opportunity for cross-border actions to pressure the transnational companies for whom they work. By examining the strategies of meagerly funded community-based organizations that have created change in the lives of workers struggling to survive the gendered, class-based, and racialized sociopolitical structures at the U.S./Mexico border, I center the lives and experiences of the men and women of the maquiladora industry, who are overlooked.

In this chapter, I examine the conditions and effects of policies proposed and enacted by the neoliberal state, such as the North American Free Trade Agreement (NAFTA), to understand how women workers and their communities and families are responding to their predicaments. Through an analysis of the strategies, challenges and successes of the CFB, we will gain a better understanding of binational feminist organizing and the materialization of a politicized *transfronteriza* identity.[3] In my research, I found that the construction of this identity is determined by three factors: a shared geographical space, a collective consciousness based on mutual experiences and solidarity, and a feminist politics that looks at women's rights as fundamental to challenging the system.[4]

Methodology

The data from this paper were collected between September 2004 and March 2009. The data include participant observation, which entailed active involvement in the collective's activities (such as meetings, actions, and celebrations) for two years, extensive interviews with two current CFB members (one who has been involved since its inception and one who joined more recently and has become a vocal and active participant), and a follow-up focus group. To complement the ethnographic material, I incorporate textual data gathered by the CFB, such as meeting minutes, a ten-page summary of and reflection on a binational conference the CFB organized, and an analysis of the group's mission statement and supporting documents.

The interviews were conducted in March 2009 at the CFB's Tijuana office and followed a semistructured question format with three broad foci: the group's history and mission, current issues and organizing strategies, and the effects of recent political and economic changes on the interviewees' work as feminists, labor rights organizers, and border dwellers.

Tijuana y las Maquiladoras: Structural Violence and Worker Conditions

As a result of the intersecting power structures of capitalism, racial hierarchy, and patriarchy, Mexican border cities are fraught with infrastructural problems (lack of housing, health facilities, schools) that create a "structural violence" endemic to the region (Segura and Zavella 2007). Many scholars have examined the transnational maquiladora industry on the U.S./Mexico border within the context of globalization, migration, and the effects of global capital on the social and economic environments. More recently, this scholarship has included the ways in which globalization affects the day-to-day lives of workers, who are subject to exploitation by means of low wages, exposure to environmental risks, sexual harassment, and discrimination (Bandy 2000; Cravey 1998; Landau 2005; Muñoz 2004; Peña 1997). The multinational companies that own this industry thrive and maximize profits through the recruitment of cheap labor, the implementation of strict labor conduct rules, and noncompliance with safety, environmental, and labor standards. These business practices create catastrophic environmental, health, and social problems that affect both the workers' labor experience and life in their communities and are compounded by the underdeveloped public service infrastructure (Bacon 2004; Landau 2005; Lorey 1999; Martínez 1994). The consequences are exacerbated for border women and workers on whom the conditions of structural violence weigh heavily, as they bear the greatest responsibility for alleviating these effects. Their induction into the labor force in the border region has a particular history.

The development of the modern-day maquiladora industry began more than forty years ago. In 1961, the Mexican government launched the Programa Nacional Fronterizo (PRONAF, National Border Program), which sought to beautify border towns, build up their tourist infrastructure, and create favorable conditions for industrialization in the border region. In 1965, the Border Industrialization Program (BIP), an outgrowth of PRONAF, established the border zone corridor of export processing industries known as maquiladoras (Herzog 1990; Lorey 1999; Nevins 2002). Maquiladoras were the only firms exempt from Mexican law, which requires majority Mexican ownership (Lorey 1999). BIP also helped to fuel significant migration to border cities from other parts of Mexico. Between 1950 and 1990, the population of Mexican border states multiplied 3.6 times (Lorey 1999). Implemented in 1994, NAFTA and the growing liberalization of the Mexican economy have also facilitated a significant exodus from Mexico's countryside. From 1980 to 1990, for example, the population living in Mexico's rural areas declined from 36 percent to 28 percent of the total (Nevins 2002). In Tijuana, the population has grown by 70.5 percent, from 461,257 in 1980 to 1,274,240 in 2000 (Kopinak 2003). Furthermore, despite the rhetoric of a borderless global society, the border has become starker in this neoliberal context, which can be seen in strategies such as Operation Gatekeeper in San Diego and Operation Hold the Line in Texas. For numerous reasons, migrants who intend to cross the border stay in border cities such as Tijuana and seek employment in these maquiladoras.

Although some recent shifts have occurred, women historically have comprised the bulk of the maquiladora workforce through strategic recruitment efforts resulting from a presumed level of both manual dexterity and naiveté (Domínguez 2002; Fernández-Kelly 1983; Peña 1997; Sklair 1989; Tiano 1987). The city of Tijuana currently has forty-seven industrial parks, each of which employs two hundred thousand workers on two twelve-hour shifts (Pool 2008). The evidence of disparities becomes abundantly clear when the minimum wage is 54.80 pesos ($4) per day and a gallon of milk costs approximately 45 pesos. Most maquiladora workers do not make more than fifty dollars a week. The impact of the dangerously low salary on families is exacerbated by the humiliation they face at the factories. Workers are often required to agree to a set of rules related to dress code, bathroom use and breaks, and water consumption. Women's rights are frequently violated through use of random pregnancy tests (which can include requiring women to show their underwear to prove that they are menstruating), and sexual harassment by power holders such as supervisors. As Elvia Arriola (2000, 782) writes, "The younger women are encouraged to utilize their sexuality in the maquiladoras at the same time that their right of reproductive choice is actively repressed. This is manifested in the sexist attitudes of managers who equate job security with being pretty, ladylike, and the sexual object of attention, exploitation, and abuse."

For many migrant workers from the interior of Mexico who work at the border, the blunt realities they encounter when they arrived are shocking, since they have been enticed to Tijuana by what one worker described as stories of "money on the floor" or "an abundance of well-paid work." According to another worker, "They tell us that here one can get a good car for almost nothing, that one will have work, a house, everything. It was the American Dream, only without the risks of crossing to the other side—the American Dream in Mexico." Instead, they find that their rights as workers are constantly violated. They suffer physical, emotional, and sexual abuse; are subject to forced overtime and illegal hiring and firing practices, such as being fired without pay; and have no recourse if they are hurt on the job. Such violations limit workers' job security and their freedom to make decisions without facing drastic consequences. Despite the obstacles, workers and activists are seeking ways to fight back.

In Tijuana, the movement to organize independent unions has been unsuccessful (Bacon 2004); instead, various grassroots organizations (CFB, CITTAC, La Red) have devised a plan of action that draws on Mexican federal labor laws to hold the transnational giants accountable. The legal code provides appropriate parameters for workers, including eight-hour workdays, vacation time, and health and safety regulations. While these laws work in favor of the workers' rights advocates, the complex layers of power within the maquiladora industry make it almost impossible to enforce those measures. As one organizer stated, "Before, a worker would confront his boss and would fight with his boss and that was the struggle between them. . . . Today this is not the case. For example, we are not fighting just with the bosses. In one case, we had to fight against the authorities, because the authorities always were on the side of the boss. And then we had to fight with the union, because the unions are also on the side of the boss. Then we had to bring in the environmental protection agency, asking them to help us look into the chemicals that were being brought into Mexico. So then we had to fight with customs. So that each time we would move forward, we would confront someone else. It's like a monster, and the maquiladora workers do not confront just their boss. No, now we have to confront the entire system. . . . The enemy that is coming face to face with the workers is an enormous enemy which they alone cannot defeat. They need a strong alliance to be able to defeat it." Workers' rights advocates in the border region find themselves in this environment, which is made worse by the fact that federal law lacks a clause that addresses sexual harassment and gender discrimination. While CITTAC has addressed the needs of all workers, and in the early 1990s became the first group to combat and win a sexual harassment case for a maquiladora worker, the CFB remains the only group highlighting the needs of women workers and border dwellers.

Binational Organizing against Transnational Forces

Widespread abuses and corruption in the maquiladora industry have ignited activist networks that transcend the U.S./Mexico border. This transnational or transborder activism has been studied as a collective response to globalization, creating networks across borders and nations that challenge inequalities in working conditions and environments created by multinational corporations (Armbruster-Sandoval 2005; Bacon 2004; Bandy 2000, 2004; Keck and Sikkink 1998; Liebowitz 2002; Muñoz 2004; Staudt and Coronado 2002). As Bandy (2004) notes, creating solidarity between workers and organizations is based on four elements: workers' critiques of neoliberalism, their mutual concern for the creation and upholding of labor standards and collective participation in unions or other political arenas to affect change, the cultivation of communication and relationships that extend across borders, and the creation of a culture of hope. Developed in this way, solidarity transcends borders and is central to the success of activists' efforts. This notion of solidarity is also central in Staudt and Coronado's (2002, 51) characteristics of successful cross-border organizing, which involve activists' involvement on both sides of the border; relationships with other local, state, or international movements; and transparent and cooperative efforts that have measurable results. Transnational solidarity, then, is critical to the effectiveness of movements that challenge the practices of multinational corporations.

Similarly, Bandy (2004) argues that transnational activism can strengthen social movements, creating greater possibility for social change in power structures and environmental and social conditions. Bandy's examination of the Coalition for Justice in the Maquiladoras demonstrates that with increased solidarity between social actors through worker-to-worker exchanges, collective consciousness emerges. This increased solidarity allows workers to identify with each other in their common struggles and to address their needs, which are often absent from larger political debates for change (Bacon 2004). Finally, transnational activism creates hope. Though this hope may seem relatively unimportant, it fuels the movement: "This language of hope cannot feed or clothe workers in need, and it alone does not regulate capital. Yet, it cannot be underestimated since, in the absence of substantive reform, it is a primary source of workers' commitments to movement participation and international coalition" (Bandy 2004, 419).

The elements of solidarity and hope for the creation of a collective consciousness are integral to the work of the cross-border organizing that takes place in the San Diego/Tijuana region. While current literature on gendered cross-border organizing highlights the particular concerns of women and the importance of an intersectional analysis of the effects of political processes at multiple levels (Collins 2006; Domínguez 2002; Mattingly and Hansen 2006), my work focuses on how these elements contribute to the creation of what I call a politicized *transfronteriza* identity by border women activists.

La Colectiva Feminista

The CFB was formed in 2004; the group self-identifies its members—mostly Chicanas and Mexicanas—as activists, feminists, maquiladora workers, Zapatistas, environmentalists, students, artists, and organizers from the United States and Mexico. The collective comprises seven active members and up to thirty-five affiliates between twenty-five and fifty-five years old.[5] The members attend meetings, organize workshops, and contribute to the kitchen collective. An informational pamphlet describes the collective's mission as helping to "construct a new movement that supports and highlights the spiritual and human components to the diverse struggles experienced by women in the border region." Members of the group had been working on various political projects independent of each other, but as post-NAFTA conditions became more visible, they realized that these policies had created more pressure on women through lower salaries, sexual harassment, constant threat of unemployment, chemical contamination, and toxic waste from the maquiladora industry. These factors affect the women not only as community members but also as mothers and wives. By drawing from their diverse experiences, the women actively sought to move beyond their individual locales to have a broader reach through collective action.

While the collective works in tandem with the other groups, its focus ensures that women's issues are highlighted and recognized in the struggle for workers' rights. The binational collaboration has facilitated development of a politicized *transfronteriza* identity that promotes not only cross-border solidarity but also the blurring of the juridico-political demarcation of the U.S./Mexico border, where commonalities of needs and rights both drive and inform actions. Through its work, the CFB is not only fighting for workers' rights but also introducing a gendered consciousness.

Over the past six years, the collective has developed four organizing tactics. First, with the goal of building networks, in September 2004 the collective decided to organize an *encuentro* (meeting) with other activists working on issues affecting women in the border region. This was the first grassroots, binational, woman-centered meeting and was hosted at the women's center in the autonomous community of Maclovio Rojas (see Téllez 2005, 2006, 2008), situated between the cities of Tecate and Tijuana. According to the call for the *encuentro*, "Knowing each other gives us the opportunity to extend our own struggles and working together we can come up with strategies for better communication locally, regionally and binationally. With this kind of gathering, we'll focus on the specific gendered problems that we face and, also, we will put forward a perspective from women and by women." The *encuentro* sought to

- examine ties that already exist between organizations in Baja California, Mexico, and California, United States;
- share different organizing experiences and learn from each other;
- discuss solutions to our problems as women workers, community members, and organizers in this region;
- reflect on who we are and what are our struggles are; and
- formulate strategies for support.

The two-day meeting attracted more than forty organizations from California and Baja California and an organizer from Guatemala. *Encuentro* participants included migrants, academics, students, union organizers, maquiladora workers, community health workers, indigenous women, stay-at-home moms, and media workers. In light of the fact that the gathering was organized and led by workers, students, and activists without any institutional support or external funding other than participant donations, the turnout was extremely successful. Important conversations and critical exchanges began to take place, and the construction of a cross-border collective identity began to emerge.

The collective's second strategy for developing a *transfronteriza* identity is through workshops for maquiladora workers. These workshops have been made available with the help of contacts and resources both from the *encuentro* and from relationships developed over years of organizing and working along the border. Workshop themes include gender rights in the workplace, reproductive rights, safety issues highlighting the needs of women, and the patriarchy. The CFB has also collaborated with other grassroots organizations along the border to produce a video, shown during the workshops, that documents incidents of sexual harassment against women maquiladora workers. According to one member, at the workshops, "we can focus on how women's reproductive health is affected in the sense that, for example, the lead disrupts one's menstrual cycle and causes spontaneous abortions while inside the factory. The men's sexuality is affected also. Their libido is lowered, just like the women's. . . . We prepare ourselves better. It interests us to have women participate in the intellectual. . . . Activism is good and all, but we also know that [such work is] sometimes based in books." Another member explained that community is built at the workshops: "We come to listen to one another . . . to share our troubles and frustrations as women, as border dwellers, as youth, as stay-at-home moms, as women, etc."

The third strategy is the kitchen collective, a service that functions as an alternative to the unemployment that runs rampant in the border region. In the words of one member, "The kitchen collective is a cooperative, a group of women that get together to make different food for different events. We sell food to those on the maquiladora tours.[6] . . . Basically, it's for economic help. And apart from this, we share recipes. Cooking is an important part of our culture, and we are learning a lot. We cook for a lot of people."

The kitchen collective is a new dynamic space that provides women an opportunity to build relationships and creates an alternative way to make a limited income. The CFB also recently applied for and received a grant from the city of Tijuana to purchase cooking supplies such as frying pans and stoves.

The CFB's final strategy involves cross-border actions in support of the campaigns initiated by the maquiladora workers. These actions are organized and attended by members of CFB, CITTAC, and the San Diego Maquiladora Workers' Solidarity Network. According to one member, "One of the best examples is the case of the company owners who were living in San Diego, specifically in Chula Vista. What we did was organize a simultaneous protest in San Diego and Tijuana. While the workers in Tijuana were marching in front of the factory that had been closed and in front of other businesses of the owners and the sports club that the owners belonged to, here [in the United States], we were protesting in front of the house of the owners, and through their pure bad luck that day had . . . invited over all of their friends and family. . . . Then all of the people there were scared when groups of activists arrived. It created a big scandal!" Members of the CFB support these cross-border actions and participate in the protests as they are able; currently, more members live on the Mexican side of the border.

Discussion

POLITICIZED TRANSFRONTERIZA IDENTITY

In many discussions of transnationalism, the border is merely seen as a passage, as the division between two nation-states rather than a site for community formation. The CFB's work demonstrates that women border dwellers and activists are moving beyond this typification and beginning to create a broader definition of community. For example, the space created within the *encuentro* allowed women to discover their commonalities across the geopolitical demarcation. With the border divide momentarily erased, several common transborder issues affecting women were exposed, including land and housing concerns, access to public services, and the racialization of environmental health. Participants repeatedly named state and transnational companies as the powers that shaped their realities and shared similar experiences as laborers in the global political economy. A shared politicized *transfronteriza* identity emerges.

For example, Beatriz, a maquiladora worker in Tijuana, discussed her lack of employment security: "Our boss gives us three- to six-month contracts. So they'll fire everyone at once and then call us back with these short-term contracts, sometimes lasting only a month. In December, some don't even get their job back. We have no seniority rights and no security. In that factory, we made plastic boxes for televisions for Sanyo, Sony, Panasonic, Sharp."

Albina, a worker and organizer from Guatemala, explained, "I worked for fourteen years in a Korean garment factory. I started out as a minor, and when the owners came, they would hide us in the warehouse because [management] didn't want [the owners] to see us. They humiliated us in many ways, especially women who are pregnant. We couldn't eat inside because the clothes would get dirty. They wouldn't clean the bathrooms, and there were about six hundred workers with only two bathrooms for men and four for women. There was no light. We would preserve our water because there was so little of it."

As a garment worker in Los Angeles, Lupe "would get about ten- to fifteen-minute breaks for lunch. We could only go to the bathroom twice, and you would have to ask for the key. They threatened to not pay us constantly—they'd pay us late or too little. Hygiene is really bad, it is very dirty, there are rats and cockroaches in the refrigerator. Owners would also threaten us by telling us that La Migra [the immigration police] was coming."

These short narratives demonstrate that those devalued in the market (poor, Third World women) experience exploitation on both sides of the border; thus, the sharing and acknowledging of their experiences creates a collective *trans-fronteriza* identity. Furthermore, these workers and activists also shared their local victories (campaigns against transnational companies, coalition building); by exchanging models of change, participants learn elements of new strategies and how to implement them successfully. As Rivera-Salgado (1999a, 1999b) underscores in her analysis of indigenous migrant workers from the Mexican state of Oaxaca in northern Mexico and California, binational activism strengthens communities and creates shared identities and political alliances. At the very least, listening to each other's struggles creates the sense of solidarity and hope that Bandy (2004) highlights.

Also, dialogue enables the activists to come to a more nuanced understanding of the relationship between the United States and Mexico, an understanding that not all peoples living in the United States are rich and privileged. The *encuentro* also made visible the experiences of those living in the United States who are also subjugated, building links between them and creating a unique sense of mutual understanding and support.

While the BIP program has been in place since the 1960s and workers have previously voiced their concerns, the CFB's work is important primarily for two reasons. First, transnational companies and economic policies have forced activists to think beyond their own locales, giving way to the unintended consequence of cross-border collaboration. Second, the collective *transfronteriza* identity was created through woman-centered grassroots collaboration and supported through continued work via workshops, actions, and the kitchen collective. While there is a primary focus on the needs of maquiladora workers and their struggles, as evidenced in the workshops and cross-border actions, U.S.-based activists (members of the CFB or the San Diego Maquiladora Workers' Solidarity Network) and supporters (doctors, teachers, and other professionals) build solidarity as they build relationships. Furthermore, to continue shaping the initial goals of the 2004 *encuentro* and to further build a *transfronteriza* identity, a second gathering should take place. However, through their transborder activism, these critical actors in the San Diego/Tijuana region demonstrate an emerging consciousness that highlights not only women workers' and activists' agency but also the solidarity they are creating across the border, which is an important factor when the news we hear about the border often pertains solely to violence, crime, and exploitation.

CHALLENGES

Although the CFB's work has many strengths, there have been challenges as well. The collective initially had difficulty getting recognition within the workers' rights struggle, particularly from CITTAC, because some male members of the larger movement did not see the need for a separate organization focused on the needs of women. One woman challenged this perspective, saying, "There are so many demands placed on women within the movement. We have to work, study, be good organizers, good workers, good wives, good everything, and we said, 'Enough!'" Women organizers realized that they needed to step up to fill this void. They also found it difficult to become involved if their husbands or partners did not agree with their participation. Members thus found ways to secure child care at meetings and workshops as a way to alleviate some of the tension. Collins (2006, 20) explains that organizing is especially hard for women, who are often faced with a "double-day" during which they not only hold down paying jobs but also bear responsibility for tending to the private sphere (cleaning the home, preparing food, and caring for children). With so many responsibilities in the home and at work, women have little time to participate in politics. While the active members of the CFB found ways to remain involved, they are still working on creating a better balance for all women.

Furthermore, while cross-border alliances provide unique opportunities for an engaged solidarity against transnational companies, language and cultural mis-understandings create obstacles to the projects. Similarly, although a collective *transfronteriza* identity is created, the political demarcation cannot be ignored; U.S.-based activists are more freely able to cross into Mexico than vice versa, creating inequalities in terms of privilege and access.

The recent economic crisis has presented the CFB with another major challenge and has had catastrophic consequences in Tijuana. The media is focused on the wars among drug dealers, paying almost no attention to the long lines of anguished people who wait outside the maquiladoras looking for jobs. The Tijuana government avoids speaking about this topic. "We must be optimistic," said an (employed) government official on TV (Davalos 2009).

As of January 2009, between twenty-five thousand and forty thousand jobs had been lost (Davalos 2009). Companies such as Samsung, Sony, and Panasonic are cutting days. The companies take advantage of the recession to lay off workers, increase productivity, reduce salaries, and deny benefits such as membership in the public health system (Seguro Social). In addition, the companies are now requesting middle or high school diplomas before hiring workers.

These conditions have made organizers rethink their strategies. For example, according to one organizer, "There are workers who are in conditions that are so bad, and they go through things in their work, and they come to us to get help and I feel terrible having to recommend to them, 'Take care of your job. Hold on just a little longer. It's bad what you went through, but it's better than not having a job.'" Activists argue that they must do more than protest; they must also look at ways to survive, creating alternatives in the form of collective gardening and shopping to avoid becoming victims of the companies and market for which they work.

Conclusion

In an environment (maquiladoras) where women are stripped of humanity and encouraged to compete against one another, these workers not only attempt to restore humanity and rights in the workplace but support each other in their shared and individual fights. Their activism demonstrates both the power of communities coming together and women's roles in creating solidarity and strength in the face of globalization.

Despite these obstacles, women reinvent and reenvision alternative forms of resistance and activism that would allow their voices to be heard and better represent their struggles, finding power in organizing within the community. Through their actions, women demonstrate that they are not passive victims, constantly finding new methods of resistance in their daily lives in the maquiladora industry and in their communities.

As members of the CFB join in solidarity across the border to create strategies of resistance, they become activists, giving voice to the marginalized to survive the border's gendered, class-based, and racialized social structures. As Landau (2005, 359) argues, "On both sides of the border, residents understand globalization not as a theory, but as a result of living the experience." This analysis of the workers and woman-centered organizing projects in the Tijuana–San Diego region underscores this experience as well as the lived experiences of resistance and social change from below, producing a politicized *transfronteriza* identity.

Notes

This chapter would not have been completed without the help of my research assistants, Courtney Andersen, Elizabeth Miller, Katie Norberg, and Cristina Sanidad. Thank you for your dedication, insight, and hard work. I would also like to thank photographer Oscar Michel for his help with the documentation of pivotal conversations and events. Finally, special thanks to members of La Colectiva Feminista for allowing me to share their story.

1. Transborderism occurs in an area that is geographically delineated and refers to the activities of people, communities, and institutions of local origin and destination (Ruiz 1992, 2). I use *transfronteriz(a)* to underscore the gendered signifiers of this identity.

2. The correct usage of the word *collective* in the Spanish language is *colectivo*, but members of the group chose to change the word to a feminine ending to mark their women-centered framework. For more information on the group and its activities, see Colectiva Feminista Binacional 2004a, 2004b, 2005, 2009.

3. I use *binational* to differentiate between groups based in the United States and in Mexico; I use *transfronteriza* to describe the process in which an identity is formed that simultaneously embodies both sides.

4. Sonia Saldivar-Hull makes a similar argument in her analysis of Chicana writer Sandra Cisneros's story, "Women Hollering Creek." Saldivar-Hull (1999, 2) examines

the ways in which this literary text "enacts a practice of Chicana feminism that engages with a transnational, transfronteriza practice of *feminismo popular* (popular feminism) . . . that enables us to re-examine an emergent formation of feminism on the border, a formation characterized by specific types of movements of Mexican women across geopolitical boundaries and borders." While in this fundamental literary text and analysis we can only imagine "the socially nuanced global Chicana Mexicana coalitions" (2), the CFB demonstrates the lived experiences of this exchange, offering important insights into the practices of these feminist encounters.

5. Women who are actively organizing events, workshops, and actions are members; the affiliates are women who participate in events, form part of the list of contacts, and support the group's actions.

6. The Maquiladora Support Network offers border tours to U.S. activists, students, and others as part of its organizing project. The CFB supports these activities.

References

Armbruster-Sandoval, Ralph. 2005. "Workers of the World Unite?: The Contemporary Anti-Sweatshop Movement and the Struggle for Social Justice in the Americas." *Work and Occupations* 32:464–85.

Arriola, Elvia. 2000. "Voices from the Barbed Wires of Despair: Women in the Maquiladoras, Latina Critical Legal Theory, and Gender at the U.S.-Mexico Border." *De Paul Law Review* 49:729–815.

Bacon, David. 2004. *The Children of NAFTA: Labor Wars on the U.S./Mexico Border.* Berkeley: University of California Press.

Bandy, Joe. 2000. "Bordering the Future: Resisting Neoliberalism in the Borderlands." *Critical Sociology* 26:232–67.

———. 2004. "Paradoxes of Transnational Civil Societies under Neoliberalism: The Coalition for Justice in the Maquiladoras." *Social Problems* 51:410–31.

Colectiva Feminista Binacional. 2004a. "Call for Encuentro." Flyer. Tijuana: Colectiva Feminista Binacional.

———. 2004b. Event flyer. Tijuana: Colectiva Feminista Binacional.

———. 2005. Encuentro summary. Tijuana: Colectiva Feminista Binacional.

———. 2009. Informational pamphlet. Tijuana: Colectiva Feminista Binacional.

Collins, Jane. 2006. "Redefining the Boundaries of Work: Apparel Workers and Community Unionism in the Global Economy." *Identities* 13:9–31.

Cravey, Altha. 1998. *Women and Work in Mexico's Maquiladoras.* Lanham, Md.: Rowman and Littlefield.

Davalos, Enrique. 2009. "El Mexicano." *Boletin Maquilero.* http://casadeculturaobrera. org/centro-de-informacion-para-trabajadoras-y-trabajadores-a-c/. Accessed November 30, 2009.

Domínguez, R. Edmé. 2002. "Continental Transnational Activism and Women Workers' Networks within NAFTA." *International Feminist Journal of Politics* 4:216–39.

Fernández-Kelly, Maria. 1983. "Mexican Border Industrialization, Female Labor Force Participation, and Migration." In *Women, Men, and the International Division of La-*

bor, ed. June Nash and Maria Fernández-Kelly, 205–23. Albany: State University of New York Press.

Herzog, Lawrence. 1990. *Where North Meets South: Cities, Space, and Politics on the U.S.- Mexico Border*. Austin: Center for Mexican American Studies, University of Texas.

Keck, Margaret, and Kathryn Sikkink. 1998. *Activists beyond Borders: Advocacy Networks in International Politics*. Ithaca: Cornell University Press.

Kopinak, Kathryn. 2003. "Globalization in Tijuana Maquiladoras: Using Historical Antecedents and Migration to Test Globalization Models." *Papeles de Poblacion* 9(37): 219–42.

Landau, Saul. 2005. "Globalization, Maquilas, NAFTA, and the State: Mexican Labor and 'The New World Order.'" *Journal of Developing Societies* 21:357–68.

Liebowitz, Debra. 2002. "Gendering (Trans)National Advocacy." *International Feminist Journal of Politics* 4:173–96.

Lorey, David. 1999. *The U.S.-Mexican Border in the Twentieth Century: A History of Economic and Social Transformation*. Wilmington, Del.: Scholarly Resources.

Martínez, Oscar. 1994. *Border People: Life and Society in the U.S.-Mexico Borderlands*. Tucson: University of Arizona Press.

Mattingly, Doreen, and Ellen Hansen. 2006. *Women and Change at the U.S.-Mexico Border: Mobility, Labor, and Activism*. Tucson: University of Arizona Press.

Muñoz, Carolina. 2004. "Mobile Capital, Immobile Labor: Inequality and Opportunity in the Tortilla Industry." *Social Justice* 31:21–39.

Nevins, Joseph. 2002. *Operation Gatekeeper: The Rise of the "Illegal Alien" and the Making of the U.S.-Mexico Boundary*. New York: Routledge.

Peña, Devon. 1997. *Terror of the Machine: Technology, Work, Gender, and Ecology of the U.S.-Mexico Border*. Austin: University of Texas Press.

Pool, Emilia. 2008. "Tijuana's Maquiladoras: Producing Resistance." *Rebeldia* 5:25–35.

Rivera-Salgado, Gaspar. 1999a. "Binational Organizations of Mexican Migrants to the United States." *Social Justice* 26:27–38.

———. 1999b. "Mixtec Activism in Oaxacalifornia: Transborder Grassroots Political Strategies." *American Behavioral Scientist* 42:1439–58.

Ruiz, Olivia. 1992. "Visitas y Convivencias de los Norteamericanos de Ascendencia Mexicana en Baja California." Paper presented at the conference on Historia y Cultura, El Colegio de la Frontera Norte/Universidad Autonomía de Cuidad Juárez.

Saldivar-Hull, Sonia. 1999. "Women Hollering Transfronteriza Feminisms." *Cultural Studies* 13:251–62.

Segura, Denise, and Patricia Zavella. 2007. *Women and Migration in the U.S.-Mexico Borderlands: A Reader*. Durham: Duke University Press.

Sklair, Leslie. 1989. *Assembling for Development: The Maquiladora Industry in Mexico and the United States*. Boston: Unwin Hyman.

Staudt, Kathleen, and Irasema Coronado. 2002. *Fronteras No Más: Toward Social Justice at the U.S.-Mexico Border*. New York: Palgrave Macmillan.

Téllez, Michelle. 2005. "Globalizing Resistance: Maclovio Rojas, a Mexican Community in Lucha." Ph.D. diss., Claremont Graduate University.

———. 2006. "Generating Hope, Creating Change, Searching for Community: Stories of Resistance against Globalization at the U.S./Mexico Border." In *Re-Inventing Critical Pedagogy: Widening the Circle of Anti-Oppression Education*, ed. Cesar Rossatto, Ricky Lee Allen, and Marc Pruyn, 225–34. Lanham, Md.: Rowman and Littlefield.

———. 2008. "Community of Struggle: Gender, Violence, and Resistance on the U.S./ Mexico Border." *Gender and Society* 22:545–67.

Tiano, Susan. 1987. "Women's Work and Unemployment in Northern Mexico." In *Women on the U.S.-Mexico Border: Responses to Change*, ed. Vicki Ruiz and Susan Tiano, 77–101. Boston: Allen and Unwin.

13

Formalizing the Informal

Highly Skilled Filipina Caregivers and the Pilipino Workers Center

ANNA ROMINA GUEVARRA

AND LOLITA ANDRADA LLEDO

Angel Roxas is a forty-year-old Filipino woman whose dream job is to manage finances and do accounting work.[1] She holds a master's degree in business administration, and for several years before coming to the United States in 2001, she worked as an assistant to the dean of a college in the Philippines. She had a staff that supported her daily work and a personal assistant who ran her errands and was at her beck and call. She woke up every morning with the security of a job and the closeness of family. Now, she works tirelessly as a home-care worker, and her daily routine revolves around providing services to the elderly. Not only does she feed them and administer their medication, she also cleans and handles intimate parts of their bodies, often with disbelief and fear. She also ensures that her patients' houses are tidy and visitor-ready.[2] She has learned to work through her loneliness, fatigue, and loss of sleep. In addition to her broken heart as a result of the dissolution of her marriage and her estrangement from the children she left behind in the Philippines, she bears emotional scars inflicted when some of her patients lost their minds. Moreover, her downward occupational mobility sometimes renders her emotionally paralyzed.

Roxas's experiences are representative of those in the informal economy of home-care workers in southern California, which has resulted in an ethnic labor niche occupied by Filipino caregivers. Home-care workers—that is, personal attendants and home-care aides—are part of the direct-care workforce of frontline paid caregivers that is expected to be the second-fastest-growing occupation in the United States between 2006 and 2016 (Paraprofessional Healthcare Institute 2008). These figures do not adequately account for the "gray" market that profits primarily from the labor of immigrants, many of whom have residency and citizenship status that renders them ideal candidates for unscrupulous private home-care agencies or enterprising individuals who provide viable albeit precarious employment.[3] But Roxas and many other Filipinos in this informal economy are highly educated with experience in higher-paying and prestigious positions as teachers, nurses, engineers, and administrators before becoming caregivers.

In this industry, like any other, wages and employment arrangements are defined by one's level of training. What happens when teachers, engineers, nurses, and administrators become caregivers and perform work that is often considered to be demeaning? Many of them would simply say that they are *only* caregivers, as if to signal that they see themselves as having very little social worth. And even when they may internalize their added export value (Guevarra 2003, 2010) as "ideal," they may still envision themselves as unskilled caregivers. However, despite experiencing downward occupational mobility, these same professional backgrounds may lead them to approach their work skillfully. They may not have received formal training in doing home-care work, but how they perform and deliver caregiving suggests a different framework for viewing skill and which aspects of such performativity count as skilled work. Their stories certainly highlight the social construction of skill and challenge the naturalization paradigm (Collins 2002) that may label certain types of work as inherently appropriate for a particular gender.

Developing, cultivating, and performing such high-quality care is a skill, whether it is self-taught or derived from expert advice provided by social networks. This framework also governs the grassroots organizing of the Pilipino Workers Center (PWC) through its COURAGE campaign. As a key advocate of Filipino caregivers' rights that is dedicated to ridding the industry of unscrupulous profit-making actors, the PWC also provides a community of support where workers can systematically share knowledge and caregiving techniques that can be institutionalized and harnessed in the worker-owned caregiving cooperative that the PWC seeks to establish.

Caregiving in Demand

The demand for home-care workers is fueled by the aging U.S. population. The total number of people over age sixty-five is projected to double from 35 million in 2000 to 71.5 million by 2030, when it will account for 20 percent of the total U.S. population. In California, the cohort of adults age sixty and over is projected to grow from 4.7 million in 2000 to 12.8 million by 2050, a 172 percent increase. The number of people over age sixty in the Los Angeles Basin is projected to triple by 2040 (California Department of Aging 2005). Following these projections, it is not surprising to see the increased demand for direct-care workers, a category that includes home health aides, personal-care aides, and certified nursing assistants working in various settings.[4] In 2006, the United States had an estimated 3 million direct-care workers, a number that is projected to increase to 4 million by 2016. According to the U.S. Department of Labor, approximately 767,000 of these workers were personal attendants and home-care aides, and they are expected to be the second-fastest-growing occupation in the United States between 2006 and 2016 (Paraprofessional Healthcare Institute 2008). By 2016, approximately 64 percent of direct-care workers will also likely be employed in home- or community-based settings instead of facilities (Paraprofessional Healthcare Institute 2008).

Many caregivers, especially those who fall into the category of personal attendants and home-care aides, are employed as part of the informal economy. Workers may be hired through private home-care agencies, which are classified as providing nonmedical custodial care and whose patients may pay through their personal funds or long-term care insurance. Other personal-care attendants work in private facilities that provide residential care for the elderly. California currently has 8,173 such facilities.[5] Workers may also find employment through their social networks—for example, by relieving a friend from a job assignment for a day or so. The unregulated nature of this gray market leaves caregivers at the mercy of agencies and their patients with regard to wages, benefits, and employment arrangements.

Filipinos have increasingly found employment as caregivers in this gray market. In 2006, approximately 1.6 million foreign-born Filipinos lived in the United States, trailing only Mexicans among the largest immigrant groups in the country. Almost half of these Filipinos resided in California.[6] The migration of Filipinos to the United States has a long history that is largely a result of the colonial relations between the two countries (Choy 2003; Guevarra 2003, 2010). This colonial relationship imposed an Americanized curriculum and nursing training that has made the Philippines an ideal source of nursing labor for the United States. Thousands of workers each year arrive in the United States seeking various forms of employment. The presence of Filipino caregivers in southern California is partly a result of a culture of labor migration (Choy 2003; Guevarra 2010) shaped by a glamorized view of the United States as the "land of milk and honey." However, as Tung (1999, 2003) points out, the presence of Filipino caregivers as a low-wage workforce has received less attention and has led to an inaccurate picture of the state of labor force participation among Filipinos in the United States that defies the assumption that they are concentrated primarily in high-income professions.

This project is based on in-depth interviews conducted in 2008–9 with thirty Filipinos (eighteen women and twelve men) who have worked or are working as caregivers in southern California. The participants ranged between twenty-five and seventy-six years old, with an average age of 47.9. They had lived in the United States between two and twenty-nine years. A majority of them are college graduates with advanced degrees in a variety of fields, including nursing, education, business administration, and engineering. As caregivers, they have experienced downward occupational mobility from their earlier employment as specialized nurses, English teachers, zoning administrators, seafarers, business owners, and supervisors. As caregivers, they have worked in patients' homes (both as live-in and live-out caregivers) as well as in residential care facilities. Almost all of them began their work in the United States as caregivers within board and care facilities before finding employment through agencies. Their wages varied from $60 to $120 per day. Thirty-seven percent of the participants were single, three of them with children. Forty-three percent were married with children, while about 7 percent were involved in some form of an arranged marriage for the purposes of citizenship or legalization of status. Ten percent were separated and/or divorced or widowed. Of those with children, 43 percent were part of transnational families, with spouses and/or children living in the Philippines under the care of their parents, in-laws, or other caregivers.

Pragmatic and Survival Consciousness: Caregivers as Highly Skilled Workers

What constitutes "skilled" work has been a subject of debate within the literature (see Steinberg 1990). While some define *skill* in terms of a worker's level of craft or in relation to technological advances, others define it in terms of its social construction and specifically its relation to gender. This conceptualization of skill is useful for examining the work that caregivers do. Feminist conceptualizations of the social construction of skill point out that providing caring labor is a complex process that entails a certain level of skillfulness that may not necessarily be perceived as such. For example, Neysmith and Aronson (1996) powerfully show that the "help" provided by female home-care workers in Canada is a complex and negotiated phenomenon that entails a series of individual tasks that involved observing their patients, obtaining particular knowledge regarding the individuals in question, and using "common sense" in the absence of finding support for their work. In most cases, they also found that home-care workers do more than their prescribed duties and often become involved in their patients' social worlds, a level of work for which the caregivers are not necessarily compensated (Aronson and Neysmith 1996). Similarly, the elder caregivers in Maria de la Luz Ibarra's (2003, 102) work also demonstrate that the act of caregiving requires a level of routinizing work that "consists of multiple tasks and responsibilities that rely on their own learning and experience," which is not a small undertaking and involves reconfiguring social and kinship relations within their patients' families.

Similarly, other studies reveal the level of identity negotiations that caregivers perform in order to make meaning of their work (Solari 2006; Stacey 2005). For example, in Solari's (2006, 319) study, she revealed the ways in which immigrant home-care workers from the former Soviet Union enact and deploy two different personas—as professionals or saints—as part of their "tool kit" for performing care work. Finally, other scholars highlight the level of "body work" (Twigg 2000) or the kind of emotional labor entailed in performing what home-care workers perceive as "dirty work" (Stacey 2005). Yet despite such narratives, the public perceives caregiving or care work as "unskilled," and this perception also governs the way the caregivers I studied perceive their work.

However, they are performing a form of skilled work that involves emotional, physical, and intellectual tasks for which they are not necessarily remunerated. Many of the Filipino caregivers I interviewed are highly skilled by virtue of their educational training and prior work experiences, yet they do not necessarily perceive caregiving work as a form of skilled work, even though they have a slight advantage in the labor market. They possess a kind of pragmatic and survival care-work consciousness that is a form of skilled work, whether or not they believe that to be the case. This consciousness is a kind of internal drive and determination that they embody as care workers and that comes from a combination of their education, formal caregiving training, common sense, and cultural values, ultimately materializing in the delivery and performance of a unique kind of emotional and physical labor that allows them to perform care work in these intimate relations.

More specifically, this consciousness materializes in their efforts to draw from their breadth of work and personal experiences to seek and build knowledge that allows them to manage their patients' needs and to cultivate a sense of purpose in work that is challenging emotionally and physically. This consciousness also provides a counternarrative that responds to the public perception of care work as "dirty work," unskilled work, and/or women's work, and therefore not deserving of high pay. Therefore, while they take pride in their work, they also begin to internalize this public discourse and find difficulties in imagining themselves as skilled workers. Nevertheless, this counternarrative of care work as skilled work that requires a kind of calculated effort on the part of caregivers is evident in the way that they draw from a variety of skills and knowledge to do this work, the kind of relationships they cultivate with their wards, and the perspective they embody to survive the challenges inherent in this work. This is particularly important as they navigate the uncertainties and insecurities of their job, their downward occupational mobility, and their position as deskilled workers. This is the kind of consciousness that the PWC also upholds and attempts to formalize both in its advocacy and in its COURAGE campaign.

Binubuhay ang Pasyente (Keeping the Patient Alive)

Typical descriptions of caregiving work often encompass the fact that they provide assistance ranging from personal care and grooming maintenance to homemaking services to mobility and activity assistance. This description is characterized by Sheila Cuneta, a thirty-eight-year-old caregiver who had done this work for about three months at the time of the interview in December 2008. Cuneta holds a degree in mass communication from the Philippines, where she worked in the advertising/production industry. In her current position of caring for a ninety-year-old diabetic woman with slight dementia, she described her daily routine:

> On a daily basis, you need to give care. You yourself have to be a caring person. Number 1, I make sure that my patient is well taken care of—give her medication on time, check her vital signs to see if her blood pressure or sugar is high. She is in a wheelchair, so I am also responsible for the domestic chores—light housekeeping, preparing meals. Mobility is important, so there is lifting involved when transferring her from one place to the next. I need to remind her about her medication. I have to shoot her insulin. I have to keep a medical record. I have to go to her medical appointments, and I have to show the records to the doctor to see if there has been some improvement. And of course you have to provide love and companionship. At that age, people are very needy for attention. And since her child only visits rarely, you need to provide emotional support. And of course you do the laundry. And since she cannot walk, you have to wash her. It is a dirty job! You will smell things that you don't want to smell. . . . You have to clean her. You have to make sure she doesn't get any skin irritations or she doesn't have rashes or bed sores. You change her diaper. You comb her hair. If she watches TV, I am there next to her.

Cuneta's experience characterizes what is commonly known in the caregiver community as being an "all-around" caregiver; her description also highlights the range of work that caregivers can assume. Cuneta and the other caregivers interviewed may not necessarily describe themselves as "skilled" workers, because they have not received professional training to do the work. In addition, the official occupational classification as personal attendants or home-care aides reifies the public perception that caregiving work requires minimal training or education. In Cuneta's words, as a caregiver, "you are an unskilled worker." She sees caregiving as akin to doing mostly domestic work. Although she had not received formal training in administering insulin, she is a diabetic and is thus familiar with the procedure. However, her extensive explanation of her work and the routinized and meticulous way she conducts it seem to contradict this perception, which fails to do justice to the quality of the work that she and other caregivers perform. That is, all-around caregiving requires skill, but perhaps not in the traditional way that skill is viewed.

Similarly, Marie Atienza also challenges the notion that caregivers are unskilled workers. Atienza is a fifty-seven-year-old caregiver with a bachelor's degree in customs administration from the Philippines; she has been doing care work since 2000. For Atienza, caregiving not only involves providing services pertaining to the personal hygiene and appearance of her patient but also involves taking the initiative to do additional research about her medical care instead of simply following orders:

> As a caregiver, you should know the effects of the medications on the patient. What kind of medicine is it? Is it for the head or the stomach? What is their effect when the patient takes this medicine? As a caregiver, we should know if there is improvement on the patient and the effectiveness of the medicine. . . . Like, for example, I also read the prescription coming from the pharmacy and some write-ups about the medicine. I keep them. Then I relate them to my patients. . . . That is why if things happen, I know and I can explain to the members of the family. If they go to the doctor, they can relay to them [the patient's] reaction to a certain medication. Or if there is a need, we can call the doctor and tell the doctor the side effects of the medicine. It is not that I am trying to outwit them, but I am just taking note of the pharmaceutical information provided with each medication.

Atienza wants to pursue nursing, which may help explain her level of initiative in doing what may seem to be outside of the expected duties of a caregiver. Her patients are the primary beneficiaries of her professional aspirations, receiving high-quality care at no additional cost, a benefit that probably goes unrecognized by the patients' families. Like Cuneta, Atienza may not consider herself a skilled worker, but she nevertheless performs work that requires a certain amount of knowledge and education.

In other cases, caregivers with health-care backgrounds automatically provide this type of skilled care as a consequence of their training. Two of the women in our sample are trained as nurses. Thus, while caregiving represents significant downward occupational mobility in terms of wages and occupational prestige, it is also easier and requires only minimal, if any, additional training. These two nurses became resources for other caregivers, who looked to these women for assistance. Sonia Cordoba draws from the skills she acquired as a CNA to gain some power and autonomy with regard to her work, eliminating the need for detailed instructions from or supervision by her patients' families. The sixty-six-year-old Cordoba takes pride in her medical knowledge, and during our interview, she pulled out one of her many medical reference books. She has chosen to work as a caregiver rather than a CNA primarily because caregivers earn slightly higher wages.

Other caregivers also explain various techniques they use to keep patients healthy, a goal that involves not only tending to their physical needs but also keeping their minds active. Caregivers regularly encourage their patients to reminisce about their lives, to talk about their children and grandchildren, and in some cases to engage in entertaining activities. Myra Cordero, a forty-four-year-old caregiver, shared numerous photographs taken of a very frail female patient of whom Cordero spoke with great fondness. One photograph showed the patient wearing scrubs, and Cordero explained that she would dress her patient in different outfits for fun. The beaming smile on the woman's face showed the value of this activity for her while testifying to the dedication and imagination that Cordero and other caregivers use to keep their patients emotionally fulfilled.

"If You Are Not Able to Adjust to Her, Then You End Up Fighting"

These examples point to the requirement that caregivers have a certain amount of skill in studying not only patients' needs but also their sensibilities. Caregivers explain that one of the hardest parts of their job is figuring out their patients' moods, temperaments, and emotional needs. When caregivers have done so, they construct the relationships that will lead to amicable arrangements. For example, fifty-eight-year-old Nora Santiago serves as a live-in caregiver to a seventy-six-year-old woman five days a week. The patient is fairly mobile, so Santiago considers the work light and characterizes it as a form of companionship. However, when asked about the most difficult aspect of being a caregiver, she unhesitatingly answered, "Knowing the patient's moods and her sensibilities." She added, "Housework is something that you already know what to do. What is hard is adjusting to her. If you are not able to adjust to her, then you end up fighting." Santiago recounted the case of a friend who found herself in such a situation.

Santiago ensures that she follows her patient's requests to the letter. Santiago makes sure that the woman's breakfast does not get cold and keeps her company while she watches television. When the older woman naps, Santiago attends to the rest of the house, so the older woman has Santiago's undivided attention when she is awake. At night, the woman likes to have her door ajar so that she can feel comforted by knowing that Santiago is near. Santiago also anticipates her patient's needs, handing her glasses to her when she gets out of her bedroom. Santiago knows that the woman enjoys talking about her life and her family, and they engage in these sorts of conversations every day. Because the patient does not like the smell of garlic, Santiago does not cook her own food in the woman's house, instead bringing precooked food with her when she arrives. We interviewed Santiago at her patient's house, and she had us enter through the side door, in keeping with her patient's preferences regarding the maintenance of her privacy. Consequently, the patient seemed to welcome our presence in the house and made it a point to wish us an enjoyable visit as she went to take a nap. Santiago and her patient seemed mutually to respect each other, a consequence of the ways that Santiago has skillfully orchestrated their interaction. Other interviewees saw such careful study of a patient's sensibilities as the key to being a good caregiver who provides high-quality care, which, in turn, is important for job security.

While caregivers such as Santiago may characterize this work as unskilled or as coming "naturally" to or being a distinctive trait of Filipinos, they also believe that caregivers ought to be valued for this work. Diane Williams, a fifty-five-year-old woman with a bachelor's degree in business administration, explained, "Caregivers are very important. We are the ones who make the elderly happy. We are the ones who extend the lives of the elderly. In fact, we should be the highest paid because we are the ones who give inspiration to the elderly. If we don't take care of the elderly, what will happen to them? That is why our salary should be high. We are the ones who do things for the elderly when they cannot do it."

Williams and other caregivers know and express that while the general public perception is that they perform work that may not necessarily involve skills that need to be learned, they nevertheless provide high-value work. Many caregivers perceive that their wards' families consider the patients a burden, so the caregivers are providing attention and inspiration that may prolong people's lives and allow them to live with dignity. This perception underlies their study, understanding, adjustment to, and production of a stable working environment.

"You Have to Be Inspired"

While caregiving may seem like an easy employment niche to enter as a result of the nature of this work and the prevailing demands for such services, caregivers' experiences also reveal how this work comes at the expense of their social and familial lives as well as their physical and mental health. Isolation, boredom, and loss of sleep are three of the most-cited problems with this work, especially for live-in caregivers, who often go for days interacting solely with their patients.

As Cuneta reasoned, "This kind of work causes burnout because sometimes you work five days straight without seeing anybody except your patient. Your whole world revolves in this one person. Sometimes you tend to forget yourself. You have needs, too." Some caregivers prefer to work as relievers so that they are not confined to one setting or patient. Others make sure that they have various items at their disposal when they are on duty—cell phones, laptops, books, crossword puzzles, and even bicycles—that can help minimize their loneliness and boredom. Most of the caregivers we interviewed have experienced extreme loss of sleep and fatigue at one point or another in their jobs. This can happen if a patient needs twenty-four-hour monitoring and wakes up more than once at night to use the bathroom. It can also happen if the patient decides to stay awake past bedtime, thereby shortening caregivers' sleeping hours.

Caregivers also commonly shared their aversion to dealing with their patients' urine and bowel movements and generally the intimacy of the body labor (Kang 2003) they must sometimes learn to accept as a critical aspect of their job. Caregivers who were not previously nurses have particular difficulty with these sorts of tasks. According to Roxas, "I am really good at managing finances. That is my line of work, and I enjoy that work. But the work I'm doing now is so far from what I used to do. Before, I had my own secretary. I had someone who was doing my errands." She was shocked by the kind of body labor demanded by caregiving: "You will get frustrated with the smell! My God! The first time I did this, I told myself not to think about the smell. [She told herself,], 'Every time you wipe someone's butt, that action is worth a dollar! Wipe the butt, that's a dollar. You are not used to doing this work. But you don't have a choice. What will you eat?' So you think of this job in terms of dollars." Another caregiver, Bing Fernandez, age twenty-five, similarly told us, "You have to be inspired" to succeed at this job. A strong motivation is necessary to survive this work. For Fernandez, part of her discomfort stemmed from guilt that she was providing intimate services to a stranger instead of to a member of her family.

The work of caregiving can also be dangerous to workers' health and expose them to patients with contagious diseases or those with violent tendencies that caregivers are ill prepared to handle. In one instance, Atienza was once assigned to a patient who was described only as having Alzheimer's disease and was told only to wear a long-sleeved shirt and long pants. The patient, however, was physically violent and was strong enough to hurt Atienza. In another case, fifty-four-year-old Vilma Reyes learned that she was handling a patient with hepatitis. Uncertain about the patient's contagiousness, Reyes refused the assignment but then found herself blacklisted within the home-care agency community. Given the amount of lifting that is often required of the work, back-related pain and injuries are also common health problems when caregivers have not received proper training.

But caregiving also has costs to workers' families. Many of the caregivers we interviewed pursue this employment specifically as a means of financially sustaining their families in the Philippines, who count on regular remittances to pay for housing, food, and tuition fees. However, many of these women now must manage transnational families and have been separated from their children for periods as long as ten years. Therefore, the pragmatic consciousness that enables them to perform skilled work also involves negotiating the meaning of this work for themselves and the material and familial realities of their lives.

PWC and the COURAGE Campaign

Cultivating this pragmatic and survival consciousness among Filipino caregivers is central to the work of the PWC, a grassroots organization that has been at the forefront of understanding the plight of Filipino caregivers and providing them with the tools needed to navigate this industry. The PWC was officially established on May 1, 1997, based on the idea that all individuals have the right to a healthy quality of life, including safe working conditions, living wages, access to health care, and human dignity. PWC is a low-wage, worker-based, grassroots social justice organization that primarily serves Los Angeles's low-income Filipino community. The PWC's mission is to provide services and resources that help meet urgent needs of Filipino workers and their families in the short term and to organize them collectively to address workers' needs and issues both in the community and in the workplace for long-term change. Over the years, as Ghandnoosh (2010) described, PWC's ethnic-focused (Filipino-identity) organizing has evolved to include addressing issues that Filipinos face in various industries and occupations as a way of establishing multi-ethnic coalitions.

On September 15, 2001, the PWC created a multi-industry membership organization, the Association of Filipino Workers (AFW), with more than one hundred members. The AFW created a space where workers could develop their leadership skills and collectively advocate for their issues. Membership has subsequently topped six hundred, most of them female caregivers. In 2004, the PWC organized a campaign, Caregivers Organizing for Unity, Respect, and Genuine Empowerment (COURAGE) to address the many needs of the Filipino caregivers.

The COURAGE campaign has four major features:

- Educating caregivers about their rights and about their legal options through various methods such as the creation of employee handbooks, pamphlets, and workshops
- Distributing an employer handbook that informs employers about their responsibilities under existing U.S. labor laws

- Helping caregivers file claims for back wages with the Division of Labor Standards Enforcement
- Partnering with the Philippine Nurses Association to offer a caregiver training program that teaches skills such as lifting without injury, personal care, and first aid / CPR

Through these efforts, the COURAGE campaign has helped caregivers win approximately three hundred thousand dollars in back wages, and more than fifty people have graduated from COURAGE programs to develop professional and leadership skills. In 2007, the PWC also became one of the founding members of the California Household Worker Coalition, teaming up with Assemblywoman Cindy Montanez to educate legislators about the plight of household workers and to create more equality in the labor laws. Montanez then proposed the Household Worker Equity Bill, which formally includes caregivers in the category of household workers. (Under current labor law, caregivers are classified as personal attendants, like nannies, and therefore are not entitled to overtime and holiday pay.) The bill passed the California General Assembly but was vetoed by Governor Arnold Schwarzenegger. The coalition is currently laying the foundation for another campaign aimed at improving the laws that protect the rights of household workers. The PWC has been gaining media exposure for caregivers' issues, which the general population and various institutions such as universities and local governments are now recognizing.

Formalizing the Informal through COURAGE

As part of the COURAGE Campaign, the PWC seeks to transform the private home-care industry so that it upholds the dignity of both workers and their patients by raising wages and improving working conditions for caregivers and elevating the standards of quality care. The best way to achieve these goals is to empower workers and build institutions where wages and working conditions are improved and where the voices of both workers and patients are heard. The PWC envisions the creation of a self-sustaining institution, the COURAGE Co-Op, that demonstrates these principles in practice.

The Homecare Workers Cooperative (the COURAGE Co-Op) would offer its employees (primarily low-income Filipino immigrant caregivers) living wages and health benefits. It would also improve working conditions by upholding the Caregivers' Bill of Rights, bring the home-care workers out of isolation, and connect home-care workers to a larger community. The co-op would replace the third-party agencies that take a substantial portion of the fees that patients pay for their home caregivers. Workers would be transformed into worker/owners, and those fees would go toward raising wages and benefits for the caregivers. The co-op would also place workers in jobs and offer leadership development training. The co-op would help to create scheduling and work arrangements that would allow workers to come together, reduce isolation, and provide a culturally welcoming community of support for the worker members. Based on the example provided by the Cooperative Home Care Association, a Bronx, New York, co-op, the COURAGE Co-Op would provide a more comprehensive and in-depth training for the caregivers and would incorporate the voices of patients themselves and senior and disability rights advocates.

Thus, the PWC is using the COURAGE campaign to make visible the quality and scope of work that caregivers are fulfilling, including both their emotional and physical labor. In addition, by cultivating a space where caregivers can share resources, knowledge, expertise, and skills, COURAGE helps workers develop their human capital while simultaneously building leadership from within. PWC organizers recognize that caregivers possess a range of skills, and that in a majority of cases they are already acting as resources for one another; thus, it makes sense to harness and cultivate these resources in ways that can benefit the group as a whole. Such benefits may come in terms of medical knowledge from those trained as nurses; interpersonal, management, or organizational skills from those who have worked in administrative positions; and even technical skills from those who have worked as engineers. However, as the narratives of the caregivers also indicate, formalizing the kind of informal knowledge building that is taking place with regard to caregiving is also challenging, given the ways that the public views this work and the aversion caregivers have to various aspects of it. Ultimately, however, the PWC seeks to manage these contradictory messages and cultivate and reify the dignity in this work through continued advocacy and through the establishment of a cooperative that would work to significantly improve working conditions.

Conclusion

Many of the caregivers interviewed stated something like, "I am *only* a caregiver." They thus acknowledge the low status and prestige that accompany a type of work that is perceived as requiring little skill. However, the experiences of the caregivers outlined here challenge the way we think about what is defined as skill or skilled work. How they manage to keep their wards alive suggests that this is not a type of work that just anyone can do. How caregivers negotiate the day-to-day interactions in ways that prevent conflict and tension requires skill. How they envision and embody the meaning of their work for themselves and their families influences the quality of work they deliver and what they are willing to withstand. The creativity, patience, and determination that caregivers exhibit and how these characteristics are transferred to care work ought to count as skill. In other words, might we imagine the performativity of doing caregiving work— whether in terms of the routinized, meticulous, and compassionate care work that caregivers provide or in terms of their embodiment of a sense of survival and pragmatic consciousness—a kind of skilled work? This consciousness—a kind of internal drive and determination—comes from a combination of their education, formal caregiving training, common sense, and cultural values, and ultimately it materializes in the delivery and performance of a unique kind of emotional and physical labor. And the PWC, through its COURAGE campaign, seeks to harness and formalize precisely this framework as a way to create a more just system in which caregivers can provide this invaluable labor and thrive as individuals, workers, parents, and community members.

Notes

1. All of the names used in this paper are pseudonyms selected by the participants.

2. We use the term *patient* because this is the way that many of the caregivers refer to the individuals for whom they care. The other term they use is *alaga*, which translates to *ward* or *dependent*.

3. By *gray market*, we refer to caregivers who are paid through their clients' personal funds or long-term care insurance and find employment through nonmedical home-care agencies or through caregivers' social networks.

4. These settings include clients' homes, nursing homes and assisted living facilities, board and care facilities, and retirement homes.

5. The Community Care Licensing Division of California defines "residential care" to include facilities that have anywhere from six to one hundred beds and provide care, supervision, and assistance with such daily life activities as bathing and grooming. This definition includes assisted living facilities, retirement homes, and board and care homes (see their website at http://www.ccld.ca.gov).

6. See the Migration Information Source website at http://www.migrationinformation .org.

References

Aronson, Jane, and Sheila Neysmith. 1996. "'You're Not Just in There to Do the Work': Depersonalizing Policies and the Exploitation of Home Care Workers' Labor." *Gender and Society* 10:59–77.

California Department of Aging. 2005. *California State Plan on Aging: 2005–2009.* http:// www.aging.ca.gov/. Accessed December 3, 2007.

Choy, Catherine Ceniza. 2003. *Empire of Care: Nursing and Migration in Filipino American History.* Durham: Duke University Press.

Collins, Jane. 2002. "Mapping a Global Labor Market: Gender and Skill in the Globalizing Garment Industry." *Gender and Society* 16:921–40.

Ghandnoosh, Nazgol. 2010. "Organizing Workers along Ethnic Lines: The Pilipino Workers' Center." In *Working for Justice: The L.A. Model of Organizing and Advocacy*, ed. R. Milkman, J. Bloom, and V. Narro, 49–70. Ithaca: Cornell University Press.

Guevarra, Anna Romina. 2003. "Manufacturing the 'Ideal' Workforce: The Transnational Labor Brokering of Nurses and Domestic Workers from the Philippines." PhD diss., University of California, San Francisco.

———. 2010. *Marketing Dreams, Manufacturing Heroes: The Transnational Labor Brokering of Filipino Workers*. New Brunswick, N.J.: Rutgers University Press.

Ibarra, Maria de la Luz. 2003. "The Tender Trap: Mexican Immigrant Women and the Ethics of Elder Care Work." *Aztlan* 28:87–113.

Kang, Miliann. 2003. "The Managed Hand: The Commercialization of Bodies and Emotions in Korean Immigrant-Owned Nail Salons." *Gender and Society* 17:820–39.

Neysmith, Sheila, and Jane Aronson. 1996. "Home Care Workers Discuss Their Work: The Skills Required to 'Use Your Common Sense.'" *Journal of Aging Studies* 10:1–14.

Paraprofessional Healthcare Institute. 2008. *Occupational Projections for Direct Care Workers: 2006–2016*. http://phinational.org/sites/phinational.org/files/clearinghouse/BLSfactSheet4-10-08.pdf. Accessed December 26, 2012.

Solari, Cinzia. 2006. "Professionals and Saints: How Immigrant Careworkers Negotiate Gender Identities at Work." *Gender and Society* 20:301–31.

Stacey, Clare L. 2005. "Finding Dignity in Dirty Work: The Constraints and Rewards of Low-Wage Home Care Labour." *Sociology of Health and Illness* 27:831–54.

Steinberg, Ronnie J. 1990. "Social Construction of Skill: Gender, Power, and Comparable Worth." *Work and Occupations* 17:449–82.

Tung, Charlene. 1999. "The Social Reproductive Labor of Filipina Transmigrant Workers in Southern California: Caring for Those Who Provide Elderly Care." PhD diss., University of California, Irvine.

———. 2003. "Caring across Borders: Motherhood, Marriage, and Filipina Domestic Workers in California." In *Asian/Pacific Islander American Women: A Historical Anthology*, ed. Shirley Hune and Gail M. Nomura, 301–15. New York: New York University Press.

Twigg, Julia. 2000. "Carework as a Form of Bodywork." *Aging and Society* 20:389–411.

14 FLOResiste

Transnational Labor, Motherhood, and Activism

NILDA FLORES-GONZÁLEZ

AND RUTH GOMBERG-MUÑOZ

> It is important to understand that the way the system is structured forces us to forsake our words, our feelings, our upbringing, our dignity, and what we consider as our principles as human beings. . . . From my perspective and my experiences as a displaced indigenous mother, I consider that the cruelest thing about denying our humanity is that this system accepts us as workers without the right to raise and live with our children. Family unity and integration is the basis of our continuation as a people.
>
> *Flor Crisóstomo*

FLOResiste is the name of a blog created by Flor Crisóstomo, an immigrant worker and mother turned activist, to denounce neoliberal policies that have led to the migration of women and indigenous people and resulted in the separation of families. In her own words:

> This blog is inspired in resistance to the actual economic policies (NAFTA) in Mexico and Latin America that have been imposed by the North American government that cause us to be displaced to the United States. The current repressive immigration laws in this country have caused Flor to flourish in these dark times. And this is the story of my resistance inspired by the same situation in which 12 million immigrants live on a daily basis in this country. And this is why Flor Resists!!! We expect you to do the same!!! (Crisóstomo 2012)

Crisóstomo's story begins like countless other immigrant stories. In May 2000, Crisóstomo, a single mother of three, left her children under the care of her mother in her native Mexico and migrated to the United States to work. Crisóstomo's story initially was typical for a transnational working mother—she endured oppressive work conditions and long periods of separation from her children. But her life took an abrupt turn when she was apprehended in a worksite immigration raid six years later. Rather than sending Crisóstomo back to her family in Mexico, the raid was transformative in a wholly different way. Crisóstomo's arrest catapulted her to the front ranks of Chicago's immigrant rights movement. Within this movement, she developed a political vision as a transnational worker and a transnational mother, ultimately resisting deportation and denouncing a system that relies on immigrant female workers at the expense of family unity.

In this chapter, we show what Hondagneu-Sotelo and Ávila (1997) call a "gender transformative odyssey" through an exploration of Crisóstomo's life as a transnational worker, mother, and activist. We focus on the nexus of gender, class, race, migration, work, and political activism to examine her marginalization as a worker and mother, her politicization, and her redefinition of motherhood in a transnational context. We begin the chapter by situating Crisóstomo's story within theoretical understandings of transnational motherhood.[1] We then explore the circumstances that led her to migrate to the United States and expand on her experiences as a transnational worker until the raid. Finally we trace her politicization through the immigrant rights movement, her defiance of a deportation order, and her activism, and examine how these events have transformed her perceptions and practices regarding parenting and situate those ideas in a transnational and neoliberal context.

Transnational Motherhood

Crisóstomo is among an increasing number of women who, unable to find employment that pays livable wages in their countries of origin, migrate to postindustrial nations to work (Guevarra 2009; Hondagneu-Sotelo and Ávila 1997; Parreñas 2001). These women are drawn to countries such as the United States because of the demand for low-wage migrant workers in the expanding service sector (Glenn 2002; Guevarra 2009; Hondagneu-Sotelo and Ávila 1997; Parreñas 2001; Romero 2002). In particular, the high demand for low-wage domestic workers translates into increasing work opportunities for immigrant women.

When mothers migrate, they often leave their children at home, entrusting their care to family members, preferably the maternal grandmother (Boehm 2008). These "other mothers" can also be aunts or godmothers and are sometimes professional child-care providers (Hondagneu-Sotelo and Ávila 1997). Most mothers believe that the separation from their children will not last long and that they will return as soon as they have saved enough money to buy a home or open a business. Many end up enduring years of separation because they are unable to travel back home as a consequence of their undocumented status or lack of money. The costs and dangers of crossing without documentation, lack of affordable child care in the United States, and safety concerns discourage these women from sending for their children (Dreby 2006; Parreñas 2001).

For transnational mothers, migrating *is* a mothering strategy: a way to provide financially for their children. Single mothers such as Crisóstomo often migrate because they lack child support and face bleak employment opportunities; migration is their best means to sustain a family. For most women, transmigrant work is necessary to provide their children with necessities such as clothing, shoes, and school supplies. For others, it allows them to provide their children with a "middle-class lifestyle" (Parreñas 2001). In addition to meeting their basic material needs, these mothers seek to provide extras, such as private school, in hopes that better education will enable their children to have better employment opportunities as adults.

Leaving their children behind is a heart-wrenching decision that causes emotional distress to mothers and children. For mothers, separation is often accompanied by feelings of guilt and can lead to depression (Parreñas 2001). These emotions are aggravated by the stigma surrounding transnational mothers, who are criticized for violating gender norms that dictate that the mother is responsible for the daily emotional care of the children (Hondagneu-Sotelo and Avila 1997). Regardless of the mother's ability to provide financially for her children, she is still judged by her (in)ability to provide emotionally for them in their everyday lives (Dreby 2006). As Dreby (2006, 55) states, "What matters is the expression of care, rather than the actual material goods."

According to Parreñas (2001, 387), these "traditional notions of mothering haunt migrant women transnationally." Despite the emotional costs, transnational mothers believe that the financial benefits of separation far outweigh the hardships.[2] As a result, transnational mothers may try to lessen the impact of separation by overcompensating with material goods, denying or downplaying the emotional impact of separation, and rationalizing the need to be separated (Parreñas 2001). Nicholson (2006) adds that reliance on a "solid extended family network" lessens the impact of separation on children who are left under the care of trusted caregivers such as grandparents. Children often are familiar with their caregivers because they are part of an extended household (Nicholson 2006). Leaving the children with supportive caregivers eases the children's emotional adjustment to the mother's absence (Schmalzbauer 2004). Seeking to forestall the loss of intimacy that results from separation, transnational mothers attempt to preserve close emotional bonds by keeping in regular contact with their children (Dreby 2006). Frequent calls home keep mothers up to date on their children's daily lives.

By breaking with rigid notions of motherhood, transnational mothers are constructing new definitions of the "good mother" (Hondagneu-Sotelo and Avila 1997; Parreñas 2001): "They challenge prevailing notions that dictate that children should be raised by their mothers and that the mother's physical absence equates to emotional abandonment" (Hondagneu-Sotelo and Avila 1997). To sustain this view, women use culturally accepted ideas of motherhood that call for sacrifice for the well-being of their children. Unlike middle-class notions that give primacy to emotional over economic responsibilities to children, Segura (2007) found that working-class Mexican women subscribe to the notion of "family economy," whereby all members of the household are expected to contribute to the family's economic survival. Motherhood, thus, includes the fulfillment of economic and emotional responsibilities for the well-being of children. As Dreby (2006, 54) states, "Mexican mothers' morality is tied to how well they care for their children. For single mothers, migrating is a moral way of fulfilling familial duties: In the absence of an economic provider, a good mother should sacrifice herself for her children via migration." Morality is upheld when women subscribe to a "household model of decision making" by which the decision to migrate was not individual but was reached by family consensus and made possible through family support (Nicholson 2006).

In this chapter, we show how Crisóstomo restores her dignity and morality by redefining motherhood. She is a "good mother" because she sacrificed for her children by migrating: She suffers physical and emotional hardships to fulfill her financial and emotional responsibilities to her children. Yet Crisóstomo expands the definition of "good mother" beyond the provision of material and emotional care through sacrifice. Our conversations with Crisóstomo indicate that reconfigured conceptions of motherhood can include helping children develop social awareness and political consciousness through transnational activism. She believes that understanding the neoliberal forces that shape their separation, and seeing themselves and their families as part of something larger, will lessen the impact of separation and transform them into agents for social change.

Migrating So That Her Children Can Have a Childhood

Crisóstomo's decision to migrate without her children stemmed from her determination to provide them with the childhood that she had been denied. At age seven, Crisóstomo's parents separated and her mother moved with her four children from the Zapotec community in Oaxaca to rural Guerrero. Lack of financial support from their father and her mother's inability to make ends meet meant that Crisóstomo had to help her mother at work and at home. At age nine, Crisóstomo woke up at dawn to help her mother at the restaurant where she worked; Crisóstomo also took care of her siblings before and after school and returned to the restaurant in the evenings to help clean. She explained, "Every day I had to wake them up, get to my mother's workplace, sweep, mop, move the chairs, dust, clean the bathrooms so that at 7:30, I could make coffee, which we would have for breakfast with cookies. We would get our school things and go together to school. . . . Back from school it was the same thing. I could not study or pay attention to my grades. Instead, I had to feed my siblings, change them from their [school] uniforms, check their homework, and keep working . . . keep working because if people came to the restaurant I had to serve as a waitress at nine years old. . . . I was doing this for years. Since my mom got so involved with work, there came a moment that I became my siblings' mother. . . . Now that they are [grown] men, [my brothers] see me differently. I am not their sister. I am like their mother."

Crisóstomo became pregnant at age fifteen. Her child's father, a teenager himself, did not assume responsibility for her or the baby, and his family treated her like a servant. Crisóstomo briefly returned to her mother's house before moving to live with a man twenty years her senior. Over the next few years, she bore him two children and lived as his common-law wife. He physically abused Crisóstomo and would not allow her to further her education beyond high school. When he lost his truck-driving job because of stricter licensing requirements brought about by the North American Free Trade Agreement (NAFTA), he abandoned her. Crisóstomo and her three young children returned to live with her mother, who had been operating a small family restaurant that catered to truckers and provided enough income to support the family. As Mexico entered headlong into the neoliberal era, workers like Crisóstomo's mother did not share in the prosperity. Crisóstomo recalled, "In 1993, a company called ICA Construction came to town; they were working on some alternate routes from the town, on the other side. . . . When we heard about the big inauguration, that was when our business started to decline. . . . From when the Sun Highway went up, it was one tragedy after another. It left behind a ghost town. We didn't realize what the government had done to our livelihoods."

Her mother's restaurant closed as the truckers—the heart of their business— were rerouted along the newly constructed highway. With the loss of the family business, Crisóstomo's brothers dropped out of school and began to work. But jobs were scarce, and those that existed paid very low wages. When Crisóstomo and her three children returned to the household, her brothers' incomes were not enough to support the larger family, and they decided to migrate to the United States. Having no education beyond a high school diploma and no marketable skills, Crisóstomo was unable to find work that paid a living wage in Guerrero, and her brothers' remittances were not enough to support the family. Determined to get her children an education and with her mother's support, Crisóstomo decided to leave her children in her mother's care and follow her brothers up north. Crisóstomo cried as she recalled the day she left her children: "When I was going to get on the bus my children hugged me, and I kissed them. I tried not to look at them, not to hold them too long. My oldest grabbed my leg, and my younger son cried with a lot of anger—a little boy of four and a half years old—kept looking at me with lots of anger. It was very difficult. When the bus left and I turned to look back at the bus station, my children were still [crying] uncontrollably." Crisóstomo was just twenty-one years old, and her children were six, four, and two.

Gendered Labor

After Crisóstomo reached the United States, her status as an undocumented worker and single mother rendered her especially vulnerable to various abuses and exploitation. Driven by a dual role in which they are the primary providers for children back home, Crisóstomo and many other immigrant working mothers endure low pay, brutal work schedules, poor living conditions, and exploitative working situations, often in an unregulated informal sector (Guevarra 2009; Hondagneu-Sotelo 2007; Romero 2002). Immediately after arriving in the United States, Crisóstomo joined her brothers in California and began doing piecework in a garment shop. Her low salary forced her to balance competing needs: "I didn't even make twenty dollars a day sometimes, and I thought, 'What am I going to do with this money? I need to pay my coyote [the smuggler who helped her cross the U.S. border], I need to send money to my kids, I have to buy clothes'—because I came with no clothing—'I need to be able to eat here.'" Crisóstomo's need to provision her family eventually pushed her to move to Chicago, where relatives offered to help her find employment. She first found work taking care of horses at a racetrack before moving to the assembly line at a canning factory. She eventually landed a better-paying job at a factory making pallets (used in packaging and transportation), supplementing her income with a night-shift janitorial job at a department store. She says, "My life went by with work, work, and more work." Crisóstomo often slept on the bathroom floor at the factory for an hour. Although the pay at the factory was better than in other places, her job cutting wood for the pallets was dangerous. Furthermore, Crisóstomo and her lone female coworker were subjected to repeated sexual harassment and assault by a foreman, who threatened to fire her if she reported him to his supervisors. When she finally got the courage to speak up, the foreman was moved to a different section of the plant, but he continued to verbally harass her. Crisóstomo tolerated his harassment because she could not afford to lose a "good paying" job.

Crisóstomo was making preliminary arrangements to bring her children to live with her when she was apprehended as part of a string of worksite raids in 2006. Crisóstomo was one of two women among the twenty-six workers arrested at the Chicago factory on April 2006. While in custody of the Immigration and Customs Enforcement (ICE) agents, Crisóstomo and her female coworker were subjected to further sexual harassment as male ICE officers conducted body searches in full view of their detained male coworkers and other male prisoners. As her female coworker began sobbing, ICE agents sneered: "She [the coworker] said, 'This is the worst humiliation I've ever had.' That is when I felt rage against the system. That is when I said, 'I can't take it any more. If they are going to deport me, then deport me. If they are going to put me in prison, then imprison me. . . . If you are going to give me [twenty years in prison] then do so, but do not keep touching me that way.'"

In 2006 the United States deported 196,000 people (U.S. Immigration and Customs Enforcement 2009). That year marked a steep increase in the number of worksite raids, like the ones at the factory where Crisóstomo worked, where large numbers of undocumented workers could be arrested at one time. Like Crisóstomo, most of those arrested and deported were working parents with no criminal records, since undocumented status is a civil offense. With no legal way to fight their deportation, most detainees (both legal and undocumented) are quickly and quietly deported. Crisóstomo, however, was different. Although she lacked any legal basis for fighting her deportation, she delayed it by appealing her case in court; when she lost, she sought sanctuary in a church.

The Politicization of a Transnational Working Mother

Defying deportation was only possible for Crisóstomo because of the timing and location of her apprehension. Her arrest happened in the spring of 2006, at the same time that massive immigrant rights mobilizations swept across the United States. Chicago saw the largest mobilizations in the city's history and among the largest in the nation, with more than one hundred thousand people marching on March 10 and more than five times that many marching on May 1 (see Pallares and Flores-González 2010).

When Crisóstomo was released from the detention center, she walked into a large protest organized by immigrant rights activists denouncing the detention of the factory workers. The Centro Sin Fronteras, a longtime immigrant rights organization, offered legal aid to Crisóstomo and her coworkers and ultimately became a vehicle for her political education, helping her develop the political consciousness that would shape her strategy toward mothering her children. Until her arrest, Crisóstomo had no experience as a political organizer and had given little thought to political issues. Up to that point, she was simply a single working mother struggling to provide for her children back home. With Centro Sin Fronteras's support, however, Crisóstomo immediately assumed a leadership role among the factory workers. She explains, "I took the baton and pushed the workers to go to Washington, to organize, to distribute flyers with our story to the community to get support. I was always the one that pushed them by calling them on the telephone, being present wherever it was necessary, in meetings or mobilizations in the city." Just one month after her arrest, Crisóstomo joined activist Elvira Arellano on a twenty-two-day hunger strike (see Toro-Morn, this volume). Arellano, the single mother of a U.S. citizen, was fighting deportation after being arrested in post–September 11 security sweeps at O'Hare International Airport, where she worked as a cleaner. Arellano was the head and face of Familia Latina Unida (see Pallares 2010), an organization of families facing separation through deportation formed by Centro Sin Fronteras. During the hunger strike, Crisóstomo traveled with Arellano and a delegation of more than fifty people to Washington, D.C., to lobby for a moratorium on immigration raids and deportations. There they met with Illinois representative Luis Gutiérrez and then Illinois senator Barack Obama as well as other members of the U.S. Congress.

As her political participation with Centro Sin Fronteras intensified, Crisóstomo began to feel at odds with the Familia Latina Unida campaign: "I thought, maybe I'm not the appropriate person, because I felt like I couldn't advocate as a mother. My children are in Mexico—they were born in Mexico, and they continue in Mexico." She felt that others had little sympathy for the struggle of single mothers, especially those who had left behind their children. Comparisons with Arellano were inevitable, and they disadvantaged Crisóstomo. As Arellano was fighting deportation to avoid separation from her U.S.-born son, Crisóstomo was fighting deportation to remain in the United States and thus be separated from her children. Facing stigmatization as a "bad mother" and unable to financially provide for her children, Crisóstomo questioned her rationale for being apart from them. She discussed the possibility of returning to Mexico with her family. But the limited job opportunities in Mexico would not allow her to support her children. Crisóstomo and her family collaboratively decided that returning was not a viable option: "When I spoke with my mother, she told me to stay here, that with the little money I was sending since my arrest, they had just enough to live on and that in Mexico there was no future for me. [She said] that if I thought that I could support my children with thirty-five dollars [a week] working in a maquiladora then I should return but that if I had the option to fight and to be able to fix my status in this country, that I better stay. [She told me] that my children are well, that I should not worry, and that as long as she was alive and young, she would continue to help me."

Although Crisóstomo's resolve to remain in the United States was based on a family decision, her politicization provided her with a moral claim to legalization.

This claim was based on the effect of U.S. neoliberal policies on Mexican families, making it impossible for parents like her to provide for their children in their home country. According to Crisóstomo, "I began my own political development, my own vision, I began analyzing a lot of things. I was doing what I had never done in my life—I began to study. I never had time [before]. All the time I worked for a company that does not give you any time for yourself. I started to learn more about what is happening in Mexico, why we are here. I began to analyze my children's lives, my brothers' [lives], of rural Mexico." Surrounded by activists, Crisóstomo "started putting it all together and [began] to talk politically about the American economic projects in Latin America" that push people like her to migrate. With this new understanding, Crisóstomo took to other issues. Early on, she focused on the violation of human rights at detention centers, an issue she had experienced firsthand: "That's when my political vision developed, in reference to what I had lived, and I started to meet a lot of people and receive a lot of support. . . . Elvira was talking about the issue of family separation. . . . My point was to talk about the issue of the violation of human rights in the detention centers—how the immigration agents treat us, how the women are mistreated—from the point of view of the [undocumented] worker in the United States." But she soon turned her attention to the effects of NAFTA on the Mexican people and particularly on transnational mothers and indigenous people like her.

As she began taking a more prominent role in the immigrant rights movement, she developed new networks that furthered her politicization. She became involved with the Mexican Solidarity Network,[3] which sent her on a nationwide speaking tour in October 2006 and October 2007. In January 2007, Crisóstomo launched a campaign, America Abre Los Ojos (To Make America See), that sought to educate the American public about the role played by U.S. policies—especially NAFTA—in undocumented immigration.

Through the Centro Sin Fronteras, Crisóstomo became involved in several local projects that helped her develop her organizing skills. She began conducting workshops on cervical cancer prevention among immigrant women. When a nearby city debated signing up for Section 287g,[4] Crisóstomo risked arrest by joining local activists in organizing efforts against the measure, including a boycott of local businesses that supported it.

In November 2007, Crisóstomo started another hunger strike in front of former Illinois representative Rahm Emanuel's district office, demanding that he push Congress for immigration reform. She also traveled with Centro Sin Fronteras to Texas, New Jersey, and New York, speaking at public events. In New York City, she confronted conservative commentator Lou Dobbs as he exited a building, blocking his path and telling him, "I pay taxes. I am not a criminal."

As her deportation date neared, Crisóstomo decided to seek sanctuary at the Adalberto United Methodist Church, the same church that had provided refuge to Elvira and Saúl Arellano. Entering sanctuary was not an easy decision for Crisóstomo and her family. Her confinement would mean that she could no longer work odd jobs and earn money to send to her family. Although she simply could have moved elsewhere in the United States to start over in the hope that immigration reform would eventually enable her to legalize her status, her politicization made her resolve to seek sanctuary.

Activism within the Confines of Sanctuary

Sanctuary marked a new stage in Crisóstomo's life both as an activist and as a mother. Secluded in a second-floor apartment with lots of free time, she began social organizing using a computer and a telephone instead of a bullhorn. Unable to take part in outside actions, Crisóstomo began to set her sights on the future she envisioned for herself and her family. She began to conceive of motherhood as a responsibility that involved a commitment to social justice as a means to effectively change the conditions that limited her children's future. That is, she began to conceptualize her activism as a more holistic form of mothering.

This conceptualization of motherhood grew deeper as Crisóstomo reestablished regular contact with her Zapotec aunts in Oaxaca, Mexico. Reconnecting with her extended family opened new avenues for her to think about her activism. After talking with her aunts, Crisóstomo learned that her indigenous community had been losing young women to migration and was at risk of losing some traditional crafts because too few young people remained to learn and continue the traditional trades: "[My aunts] are so worried that they told me 'Our traditions are being lost because we now have only two *peineros* [weaving comb makers] since now girls do not want to weave. They want to go to the United States when they turn fifteen years old.' . . . They say that 'now our youth turn sixteen, seventeen years old, and the next step after finishing high school is to leave for the United States, and who are we going to pass on our teachings to if they are leaving us?'"

Crisóstomo's aunts had started a weaving cooperative in an attempt to provide an alternative livelihood that would encourage young women to remain in the community. The cooperative would also help the community retain its Zapotec traditions.[5] Having been uprooted from the Zapotec community as a child, and having experienced migration as a young woman, Crisóstomo felt compelled to help her aunts prevent other young Zapotec women from leaving the community. Understanding that the cooperative faced a saturated local market, Crisóstomo pushed her aunts to capitalize on the global North's cravings for organic and indigenous products. Obtaining a sample of their textiles, and using contacts she had made through her activism, Crisóstomo soon found specialty stores interested in carrying the textiles. Confined to the sanctuary, there was not much more she could do for the cooperative beyond making these initial contacts.

Mothering from Sanctuary

Before she sought sanctuary, Crisóstomo's involvement in her children's daily life was restricted by her long work schedule. She recalled, "Mother's Day, Christmas—all those times are times when you realize that those times cannot be recovered because a year goes by and your children are there with your gift on the table and another year goes by and again you are not with them. Their birthdays go by, and sometimes you even forget to call them because you are working. There are a lot of things that you accumulate over the time you live that practically make you open the eyes of your heart, not the eyes you have in your head, but the ones in your heart. And now that my son is growing, he tells me, 'I do not know you. I cannot remember you.'"

Sanctuary afforded Crisóstomo time to deepen her connection with her children, to get to know them, and to become more involved in their day-to-day lives. She began calling daily and was able to look after their physical and emotional health by reaching out to other adults in their lives: "I call the school principal to see about their grades, their conduct. I speak with the social workers, with their doctors. With people around our little family . . . the town's women . . . the children's godmothers. [I ask them about] how they are and how are they behaving." Her daily calls mean that she keeps abreast of what is going on in her children's lives and is able to guide them through life. These conversations are not easy, as her children sometimes lash out in anger and frustration over her long absence. She listens to them and cries with them, providing emotional support during these hard times and letting them know that she is also suffering because they are apart: "With my children, I can get to their level and speak to them in words that they understand. But when we have to talk seriously, we speak seriously. When I have to reprimand them, I do. And with all the pain in my heart, when my son feels lonely, feels sad, I cry with him. When he breaks up with his girlfriend, I cry with him. When he feels changes in his body, I talk to him as if I were his father." Mothering her children by being involved and available to them in their daily lives would not have been possible if Crisóstomo had continued working long hours. But the most profound change in Crisóstomo's view on mothering is the shift from an individual to a social perspective on motherhood based on social justice.

FLOResiste: On Transnational Motherhood, Work, and Activism

Crisóstomo's experiences as a transnational mother, worker, and activist ultimately have drastically changed the way she conceives of parenting. She initially migrated as a survival strategy, with little understanding of the structural forces that drive mothers to migrate without their children. Her role as the sole bread-winner for her children back home rendered her more vulnerable to low pay and sexual harassment at work. Her involvement in the immigrant rights move-ment opened her eyes, helping her realize that political and economic forces tear families apart. In her words, "As a family, we have been denied the fundamental *privilege* to stay together as mother and children. Historically, our governments have pushed us to live in a system of family disintegration. We know well that this is part of a system of oppression and physical, mental, and spiritual exploi-tation where the only beneficiaries are our governments, the big corporations, and a small number of people." With this new understanding, Crisóstomo be-gan to break with gender schemas that labeled women like her "bad mothers" for leaving their children. In a scalding critique, Crisóstomo declared that "a 'good mother' is considered by colonized minds a woman that stays with her oppressor so that her children can grow up with the idea of a perfect family. A 'good mother' is one that prefers looking at the hunger, thirst, and illness in her children's faces instead of putting a knee on the door and pushing it to get out of that pain. A 'good mother' is the one that wants to live off her children while her children are dying to live. A 'good mother' is one that hides behind her children and denies them the right to be children, to be young, and to develop their own life experiences."

Crisóstomo's past experiences of lost childhood, poverty, and physical and emo-tional abuse can be read between these lines. In telling us that her mother never hugged her, made her work as a child, and mistreated her, but was always pres-ent in her life, clearly places her in this "good mother" category. Yet her mother has made up for the pain she inflicted by supporting Crisóstomo and caring for her children. To Crisóstomo's children, she is a loving and doting grandmother. Her change of heart may have resulted from her experiences as an abused and abandoned single mother who sees herself reflected in her daughter's eyes, or from her economic dependence on Crisóstomo as the household breadwinner.

In contrast to a hegemonic concept of a "good mother," Crisóstomo conceives an alternative model of motherhood that redeems "bad mothers." She calls this form of motherhood *madre-paternal* (mom-dad): "I can say that I am a mom-dad who, in spite of the distance and the years of separation, has had the fortune of having succeeded at what many so-called good parents who live with their children in the same house, sit down to eat at the same table, and seem to be the realization of a perfect family have not been able to do. With a lot of effort, I have been able to win my children's love, understanding, tolerance, trust, and above all their respect. For this, I have simply used the most valuable weapon that the Creator gave us as human beings: communication and showing them how you struggle for your family and dignity. Being a mom-dad from a distance is the hardest challenge faced daily by millions of women who are regarded by society as bad mothers, bad women neglecting our responsibilities."

Crisóstomo believes that distance has nothing to do with being a good mother. She argues that "good mothers" may be physically present in their children's day-to-day lives but are emotionally unavailable. Crisóstomo's worth as a mother is based on her emotional presence in her children's life. She sees herself as a successful mother who despite the distance is caring for her children's physical and emotional development. She is indeed a mom-dad who takes on both the breadwinning and emotional responsibilities of parenting.

Crisóstomo's approach to motherhood goes beyond physical and emotional care. It is based on sacrifice for social change that can transform her children's lives. And by sacrificing, she is teaching her children a valuable lesson in respect, dignity, and justice. She explained,

> Defying deportation from the U.S. was not only pushed out of concern for the economic subsistence that has succeeded in keeping my family stable and together in their country of origin. My conscience as a mother and as a human being made me realize that apart from the education that I have been able to give my children from a distance, I had to let them participate in my personal decisions that involve my political actions . . . since they are the most affected by the actions of our governments. Personally, I believe it contributes to their vision, analysis, and political formation about both countries. Furthermore, I think that keeping them abreast of the situation and making them the main factor driving my decisions in the different actions I have taken contributes to their spiritual growth, to finding their real identity and developing a conscience as sons and daughters, as men and women, and above all as human beings of the new generations they represent.

And although remaining separated from her family is painful, she ultimately believes that it is the most responsible parenting decision and the best thing for her children.

Conclusion

As ever-increasing global flows and transnational connections cause scholars and activists to reconceptualize categories such as "citizen" and "nation," so too do gendered experiences of migration encourage a reconceptualization of motherhood, particularly among single working mothers. Transmigrant women, an ever-greater proportion of the global workforce, learn to provide for themselves and their families and in so doing find innovative ways to parent their children—often from thousands of miles away. Flor Crisóstomo's story exemplifies this neoliberal paradox.

Crisóstomo's experiences with domestic violence, abandonment, migration, detention, and threat of deportation have cost her a great deal. Yet Crisóstomo is not a mere victim. Her experiences, good and bad, have led her to build knowledge, skills, and social connections that continue to improve her life and the lives of others. Within severe gendered and legal constraints, she has emerged as a new transnational working mother. Crisóstomo's strong will to survive for her children ultimately drives her commitment to social justice and economic viability for indigenous communities and single migrant mothers. In her words, "With my actions, I do not see myself as the heroine of the story. I do not justify the mistakes that I have made as a mother. But neither could I live waiting for someone to get me out of the hole. My children are my strength and the foundation that sustain my struggle, and I hope that tomorrow they do not feel that their mother did not try her best."

As Crisóstomo emphasizes parenting in a context of social activism, she expands the definition of a "good mother" from one who is merely present in the lives of her children to one who teaches her children about social and political consciousness by involving them in struggle, even at great personal cost. Her activism has centered on debunking the misconception that mothers who leave their children behind are selfish and uncaring. Crisóstomo ultimately made her decision to remain in the United States and apart from her children. Her transmigrant experience has ceased to be solely a vehicle for financial provisioning and has become also a tool for political awakening. And she believes that this political awakening is critical for her development and for that of her children.

Notes

1. This chapter is based on more than twelve hours of interviews with Crisóstomo as well as on ethnographic observations and publicly available documents.

2. For children, the financial benefits of separation do not outweigh its emotional costs. For more on the impact of separation on children, see Dreby (2006) and Parreñas (2001).

3. The Mexico Solidarity Network denounces neoliberal policies that have created political, social, and economic turmoil in Mexico—particularly in indigenous communities. Its activities include speaking tours, study abroad programs, and an alternative economy program to promote fair trade.

4. Section 287g is the part of the Illegal Immigration Reform and Immigrant Responsibility Act of 1996 that allows local and state law enforcement agencies to forge partnerships with federal immigration authorities to enforce federal immigration laws.

5. Stephen (2005) states that in the 1980s, Zapotec women began forming weaving cooperatives to ensure fair pay for their work. They initially supplied the local market, but Mexico's economic decline forced them to look for new markets abroad. While many

sell their products to exporters, members of the community who have migrated to the United States often serve as middlemen by finding a market for their textiles.

References

Boehm, Deborah. 2008. "'For My Children': Constructing Family and Navigating the State in the U.S.-Mexico Transnation." *Anthropological Quarterly* 81:777–802.

Crisóstomo, Flor. 2012. FLOResiste. http://floresiste.wordpress.com. Accessed on May 14, 2012.

Dreby, Joanna. 2006. "Honor and Virtue: Mexican Parenting in the Transnational Context." *Gender and Society* 20:32–59.

Glenn, Evelyn Nakano. 2002. *Unequal Freedom: How Race and Gender Shaped American Citizenship and Labor.* Cambridge, Mass.: Harvard University Press.

Guevarra, Anna R. 2009. *Marketing Dreams, Manufacturing Heroes: The Transnational Labor Brokering of Filipino Workers.* New Brunswick, N.J.: Rutgers University Press.

Hondagneu-Sotelo, Pierrette. 2007. *Domestica: Immigrant Workers Cleaning and Caring in the Shadows of Affluence.* Berkeley: University of California Press.

Hondagneu-Sotelo, Pierrette, and Ernestine Avila. 1997. "'I'm Here, but I'm There': The Meanings of Latina Transnational Motherhood." *Gender and Society* 11:548–71.

Nicholson, Melanie. 2006. "Without Their Children: Rethinking Motherhood among Transnational Migrant Women." *Social Text* 24:13–33.

Pallares, Amalia. 2010. "Representing la Familia: Family Separation and Immigrant Activism. In *¡Marcha!: Latino Chicago and the Immigrant Rights Movement*, ed. A. Pallares and N. Flores-González, 215–36. Urbana: University of Illinois Press.

Pallares, Amalia, and Nilda Flores-González, eds. 2010. *¡Marcha!: Latino Chicago and the Immigrant Rights Movement.* Urbana: University of Illinois Press.

Parreñas, Rhacel Salazar. 2001. "Mothering from a Distance: Emotions, Gender, and Intergenerational Relations in Filipino Transnational Families." *Feminist Studies* 27:361–90.

Romero, Mary. 2002. *Maid in the U.S.A.* New York: Routledge.

Schmalzbauer, Leah. 2004. "Searching for Wages and Mothering from Afar: The Case of Honduran Transnational Families." *Journal of Marriage and the Family* 66:1317–31.

Segura, Denise. 2007. "Working at Motherhood: Chicana and Mexican Immigrant Mothers and Employment." In *Women and Migration in the U.S.-Mexico Borderlands*, ed. D. Segura and P. Zavella, 368–87. Durham: Duke University Press.

Stephen, Lynn. 2005. *Zapotec Women: Gender, Class, and Ethnicity in Globalized Oaxaca.* Durham: Duke University Press.

U.S. Immigration and Customs Enforcement. 2009. "Worksite Enforcement Overview." http://www.ice.gov/pi/news/factsheets/worksite.htm. Accessed May 13, 2009.

Afterword

HÉCTOR R. CORDERO-GUZMÁN

The essays included in this volume make a unique contribution to our understanding of the current condition and position of immigrant women in the U.S. economy. The volume makes a number of significant contributions that set it apart from other works in the fields of gender, migration, and low-wage work.

Essays in this volume seek to explain and situate the current status of immigrant women and work in larger global forces, state structures, and institutional mechanisms that set the context within which low-wage women operate and that constrain their access to better employment opportunities. The volume focuses on the specific experiences of women of color and sheds light on the relationship (or intersectionality) between gender, social class, and racial/ethnic/national origin dynamics. The essays focus on a number of case studies—including personal narratives, examinations of racial/ethnic/national origin based experiences, and organization-level analysis—to help us better understand the lived experiences of low-wage women. The material presented allows us to navigate from the macro-structures through meso-level institutions and organizations to individual experiences and outcomes. The volume argues that neoliberal globalization, flexibilization, and informality have transformed global production and the way labor is used and procured globally and locally. This has had a particular impact on working-class and low-wage immigrant women who need to continuously navigate through labor markets, jobs, and a range of earning opportunities in order to find support for their families. Production opportunities are increasingly mobile and diversified, and low-wage female labor has been central to the movement of production, to the diversified provision of goods and services, and to the provision of support for middle-class and more affluent families.

As Toro-Morn, Guevarra, and Flores-González articulate in the introduction, the book covers a vast terrain: from the context and structure of work and how work happens and is experienced; the emerging sectors of the informal economy and their increasingly intricate connection to the formal economy and the personal services sector; and the changing nature, character, and role of evolving ethnic enclaves in both providing opportunities for low-wage women but creating contests where exploitation, marginalization, and abuse become rampant and intolerable for the workers. The detailed case studies on street vending, home care, elder care, domestic work, and related low-wage sectors help us better understand labor situations, contexts, and experiences shared by large segments of the population but where the largely female labor is on the one hand essential and central to the lives of consumers but where the wages, working conditions, and benefits of these workers are ignored and their demands delegitimized and marginalized.

Community-based organizations and nongovernmental organization–based strategies play a prominent role in the analysis of low-wage women and work. The volume covers a number of important examples where nonprofit groups, organizations, and service providers have developed a range of initiatives, campaigns, and programs aimed at addressing the challenges and conditions faced by low-wage and marginalized women in the U.S. labor market. Through leadership development, organizing, and public education campaigns, these organizations are able to bring together workers and advocates, articulate the needs and challenges of the workers, and develop forms of representation and resistance that build public support and improve conditions in the labor market for women workers.

The volume has a number of concrete implications for research on and policies regarding low-wage women and work. Organizations and programs that incorporate grassroots female leadership are better able to understand concrete situations and women's marginalization, and to develop effective program and advocacy strategies. Research on low-wage women and work needs to continue to focus on developing more case studies that add to the understudied areas in the fields of gender, immigration, labor markets and the economy, urban studies, and human rights. Funders and philanthropic organizations interested in improving the working and living conditions of low-wage women need to have research and information as they develop effective funding strategies and should continue to build networks between academics, practitioners, community-based organizations, and policy makers.

Contributors

PALLAVI BANERJEE is a postdoctoral fellow in the Department of Sociology at Vanderbilt University. Her research interests are situated at the intersection of sociology of immigration, gender, transnational labor, and minority families; globalization; and feminist theory. Her dissertation, entitled "Constructing Dependence: Visa Regimes and Gendered Migration in Families of Migrant Indian Workers," explores how certain immigration policies and visa regimes of United States affect families of migrant Indian professional workers in the United States. Her current project explores how transnational and global corporations influence state policies that foster a gendered and racialized labor migration from the global South to the North.

GRACE CHANG is an associate professor of Feminist Studies at the University of California Santa Barbara, where she teaches research methods and ethics; globalization and resistance; and grassroots, transnational feminist movements for social justice. She is the author of *Disposable Domestics: Immigrant Women Workers in the Global Economy* (South End Press, 2000) and is now completing her new book, *Trafficking by Any Other Name: Transnational Feminist, Immigrant and Sex Worker Rights Responses*, to be published by the New Press. She serves on the research advisory board for a project with the National Domestic Workers Alliance, supported by the Ford Foundation, to conduct a national survey on domestic workers and employers.

MARGARET M. CHIN is an associate professor of Sociology at Hunter College and the Graduate Center at the City University of New York (CUNY). Her research interests include family, immigration, the working poor, ethnic communities, and Asian Americans. She is the author of *Sewing Women: Immigrants and the New York City Garment Industry* (Columbia University Press, 2005). Her current project focuses on Asian Americans who lost their jobs during the Great Recession of 2008.

JENNIFER JIHYE CHUN is an associate professor in the Department of Sociology at the University of Toronto Scarborough. Her areas of specialization include comparative labor organizing; culture, power, and politics; race, gender, and migration; and transnational mobility. She is the author of *Organizing at the Margins: The Symbolic Politics of Labor in South Korea and the United States* (Cornell University Press, 2009). Her second book project is an in-depth case study of Asian Immigrant Women Advocates in the San Francisco Bay Area.

HÉCTOR R. CORDERO-GUZMÁN is a professor at the School of Public Affairs at Baruch College (CUNY) and in the PhD programs in Sociology and in Urban Education at the City University of New York (CUNY). Over his career, Cordero-Guzmán has collaborated with many government, research, philanthropic, and community-based organizations, and his research, publications, and policy work have focused on issues related to education, employment, labor markets, poverty, race/ethnicity and inequality, nonprofit organizations, international migration, transnational processes, social movements, economic development, and social welfare policy. He worked as a program officer in the Economic Development and Quality Employment Units at the Ford Foundation where he developed and managed a portfolio supporting organizations that focused on providing services and expanding opportunities for low-wage workers.

EMIR ESTRADA is an adjunct professor at the University of Southern California. Sparked by her own immigration experiences, her research focuses on immigrants from Mexico and Central America who work in the informal sector of unregulated or semiregulated jobs. More specifically, she examines children's involvement in the informal sector and their role in the family's economic survival.

LUCY T. FISHER is assistant adjunct professor in the School of Nursing, University of California, San Francisco. Her research interests include gerontology and long-term care, chronic mental illness, and immigrant women in the health-care profession. Much of her work focuses on nursing homes and the interprofessional training of health-care providers. Fisher was the director of the Transitions to Adulthood Plans Study, an ethnographic study of families of youth with concomitant developmental and physical disabilities and the adolescents' transition to adulthood. She is a member on the California Commission on Aging. Currently, she is part of a team collaborating with a community-based nonprofit translating TAPS findings into an intervention study for families with a disabled youth.

NILDA FLORES-GONZÁLEZ is an associate professor with a joint appointment in Sociology and Latin American and Latino Studies at the University of Illinois at Chicago. Her work focuses on race and ethnicity, identity, immigration, and education among Latino youth. She is the author of *School Kids, Street Kids: Identity Development in Latino Students* (Teachers College Press, 2002) and coeditor of *¡Marcha!: Latino Chicago in the Immigrant Rights Movement* (University of Illinois Press, 2010). She has published several articles on various topics such as Puerto Rican high achieving students, extracurricular participation and retention, youth and social justice, race and Latino identity, and the Puerto Rican community of Chicago. Currently, she is working on a book examining the development of ethnic, racial, and political identities among Latino youth.

RUTH GOMBERG-MUÑOZ is an assistant professor of Anthropology at Loyola University–Chicago. Her research interests include unauthorized migration and the connection between immigration policies and inequality in a "postracial" United States. She is the author of *Labor and Legality: An Ethnography of a Mexican Immigrant Network* (Oxford University Press, 2011). Gomberg-Muñoz is currently conducting an ethnographic study of immigrants in the Chicago area who are undertaking the process of immigration status adjustment.

ANNA ROMINA GUEVARRA is an associate professor of Asian American Studies and affiliated faculty of Gender and Women's Studies and Sociology. Her scholarly, creative, teaching, and activist work focus on immigrant and transnational labor, the Filipino labor diaspora, transnational feminist solidarities, and feminist ethnographic methods. She is the author of the award-winning book *Marketing Dreams, Manufacturing Heroes: The Transnational Labor Brokering of Filipino Workers* (Rutgers University Press, 2010). She is working on multiple projects that explore questions around critical pedagogies, transnational feminist politics/practice and movement building, community engagement, and the politics of racialized/gendered skilled labor.

SHOBHA HAMAL GURUNG is an assistant professor of Sociology at Southern Utah University, and the core faculty member of Women and Gender Studies Minor Program. Her areas of teaching and research include gender and work; globalization, immigration, migration, and transnational issues; human trafficking and the sex trade; comparative family and community; and International and South Asian studies. Her current research focuses on the narratives and lives of Nepali female migrants and immigrants who work in the informal economic or service sectors in Boston, New York, and Los Angeles. Using intersectional and transnational frameworks, she examines women's work conditions, labor relations, and work experiences in relations to their race, class, gender, nationality, and immigration and citizenship status.

PIERRETTE HONDAGNEU-SOTELO is a professor in the Department of Sociology at the University of Southern California. Her research focuses on gender and immigration, informal sector work, and religious-based activism for immigrant rights. She is the author or editor of eight books, the most recent of which are *God's Heart Has No Borders: How Religious Activists Are Working for Immigrant Rights* (University of California Press, 2008) and *Nation and Migration, Past and Future*, coedited with David Gutierrez (Johns Hopkins University Press, 2009).

MARÍA DE LA LUZ IBARRA is an associate professor of Chicana and Chicano Studies at San Diego State University. Her areas of research are globalization and social reproduction, immigration and paid domestic labor, landscape and memory, aging, and ethics of care. Her research focuses on the intersection of migration, gender, and paid domestic labor. She is writing a book on transnational elder care.

MILIANN KANG is an associate professor in Women, Gender, Sexuality Studies at the University of Massachusetts, Amherst. Her book *The Managed Hand: Race, Gender and the Body in Beauty Service Work* (University of California Press, 2010) addresses immigrant women's work in Asian-owned nail salons and has won book awards from the National Women's Studies Association and the American Sociological Association. She is currently researching work–family issues for Asian American women, particularly the intersections of gender and race in shaping motherhood and career paths.

GEORGE LIPSITZ is a professor of Black Studies and Sociology at the University of California, Santa Barbara. His most recent book is *How Racism Takes Place* (Temple University Press, 2011). Lipsitz edits the Critical American Studies series at the University of Minnesota Press and is coeditor of the American Crossroads series at the University of California Press. He chairs the board of directors of the African American Policy Forum and is a member of the board of directors of the National Fair Housing Alliance.

LOLITA ANDRADA LLEDO is a long-time activist who actively participated in the anti-Marcos dictatorship struggle in the Philippines in the 1970s until the dictator was ousted in the People Power Revolt in 1986. She graduated from the University of the Philippines with an AB Sociology degree and a Diploma in Labor Studies. After migrating to the United States in 1997, she helped organize the Pilipino Workers Center (PWC) based in Los Angeles, California. PWC focuses on organizing and empowering low-wage immigrant Filipino workers, the majority of whom are women and caregivers. Currently, she serves as PWC's associate director.

LORENA MUÑOZ is an assistant professor in the Department of Geography at the University of Minnesota. She is an urban/cultural geographer whose research focuses on the intersections of place, space, gender, sexuality, and race. Her current work examines the production of Latina/o informal economic landscapes in transborder spaces. Her current project examines how queer Latina immigrant women working in the low-wage service sector negotiate and perform their gendered and queer identities differently across supposedly heteronormative, male-dominated spaces of low-wage labor in Los Angeles. Her other research interests focus on minority students' access to STEM education, work that has been funded by the National Institute of Health.

BANDANA PURKAYASTHA is a professor of Sociology and Asian American Studies at the University of Connecticut. She has published books, peer-reviewed journal articles and chapters on race/gender/class, transnationalism, peace, and human rights. She has won several awards for teaching and leadership and has been recognized by the Connecticut legislature for her work with immigrants. She is a member of the editorial board of the Journal of South Asian Diasporas, and served as the deputy editor of Gender and Society, from 2005 to 2011; she was recently elected to serve as president of Sociologists for Women in Society (in 2013–2014).

M. VICTORIA QUIROZ-BECERRA is a research associate at the Low-Wage Workers and Communities policy area at MDRC. She has conducted research on forms of political engagement among marginalized groups. For her dissertation, Victoria conducted ethnographic work among undocumented Mexican migrants in New York City to understand how marginalized groups experience citizenship. She tries to combine her academic work with community organizing. She co-directs a grassroots organization based in Sunset Park, Brooklyn.

MARY ROMERO is a professor and faculty head of Justice Studies and Social Inquiry at Arizona State University. Her areas of research are gender and racial justice; gender, race, and work; critical race studies; ethnography; narrative and qualitative methods; and Latina/o and Chicana/o studies. She is the author of

Maid in the U.S.A. (Routledge, 1992, Tenth Anniversary, Edition 2002) and *The Maid's Daughter: Living Inside and Outside the American Dream* (New York University Press, 2011).

YOUNG SHIN obtained a law degree from Hastings College of Law in 1983. She is a cofounder and the current executive director of Asian Immigrant Women Advocates (AIWA), a community-based organization that offers training and develops leadership among Chinese, Filipina, Korean, and Vietnamese women working in the hotel, garment, restaurant, electronics, and nursing home industries. As executive director, Shin oversees the administration and coordination of the Workplace Literacy Project, Leadership Training Program, Civic Engagement Project, and the Youth Build Immigrant Power project. In 1985 she participated in the United Nations' Women's Forum in Nairobi as a scholarship recipient of the Ford Foundation. She has been recognized many times for her commitment to economic justice for women, including the Gloria Steinem award in 1991; awards from the Institute of Policy Studies and Catholic Campaign for Human Development in 1996; Women Warrior Award, Pacific Asian American Women Bay Area Coalition in 1998; KQED Local Hero of the Year; Asian Pacific American Heritage Month Award in 1999; and the Robert Wood Johnson Community Health Leadership Program in 2002.

MICHELLE TÉLLEZ is an assistant professor in the Division of Humanities, Arts, and Cultural Studies and in the Social Justice and Human Rights Program at the New College of Interdisciplinary Arts and Sciences, Arizona State University. Her research focuses on transnational community formation along the U.S./Mexico border, cross-border labor organizing, migration, and identity. Currently, she is writing a book, "Gender, Citizenship, Land and the State: The Struggle for Autonomy at the U.S. Mexico Border," examining the border as a transformative space where women come together to reimagine and redefine gendered, class-based, and racialized social structures. Téllez is a member of the board for the Arizona Interfaith Alliance for Worker Justice based in downtown Phoenix, serves on the board of the National Association of Chicana/o Studies, is a founding member of Arizona Scholars in Support of Ethnic Studies in Schools, and sits on the editorial review board for *Chicana/Latina Studies: The Journal of Mujeres Activas en Letras y Cambio Social.*

MAURA TORO-MORN is the Director of the Latin American and Latino Studies Program and Professor of Sociology at Illinois State University in Normal. Her first book, *Migration and Immigration: A Global View* (coedited with Marixsa

Alicea), was published by Greenwood Press in 2004. Through both her research and teaching, she is devoted to investigating, educating, and working toward equality for people on issues of ethnicity, race, gender, and social class. She is the author of numerous articles on the intersection of race, class, and gender in the migration of Puerto Ricans; gender issues during the Special Period in Cuba; and gender in the Latino experience. Her current project addresses the gendered dimensions of global migrations.

Index

The University of Illinois Press
is a founding member of the
Association of American University Presses.

Composed in 10.5/13 Adobe Minion Pro
with Frutiger display
by Lisa Connery
at the University of Illinois Press
Manufactured by Sheridan Books, Inc.

University of Illinois Press
1325 South Oak Street
Champaign, IL 61820-6903
www.press.uillinois.edu